Father William Doyle

Biography of the Irish Priest and Chaplain Renowned for His Spiritual Wisdom and Personal Bravery

By Alfred O'Rahilly

Published by Pantianos Classics

ISBN-13: 978-1-78987-125-8

First published in 1922

Contents

Preface to First Edition v
Preface to Second Edition vi
Preface to New Impression vi
Chapter One - Childhood and Youth (1873-1891) 7
Chapter Two - From Noviceship to Priesthood (1891-1907) 12
Chapter Three - Tertianship (1907-1908) 26
Chapter Four - Diary of Long Retreat 33
Chapter Five - Apostolate 49
Chapter Six - Inner Life 65
Chapter Seven - Mortification and Suffering 89
Chapter Eight - Spiritual Direction 123
Chapter Nine - Military Chaplain (1916) 153
Chapter Ten - Military Chaplain 195
Appendix - Some Further Letters of Father Doyle 238
Afterword - An Apology for Saints 253

Father William Doyle, S.J.
Born March 3rd 1873.
Died August 16th 1917.

Preface to First Edition

AFTER the death of Father Doyle, who was not only my friend but the guide and helper of several who are near and dear to me, I undertook, at my sister's suggestion, to write a brief memoir of his life. This task, lightly undertaken as a personal tribute, has now grown into unforeseen dimensions. Neither I nor anyone else then suspected the existence of a series of spiritual journals and personal records which Fr. Doyle had written for his own exclusive use and guidance. Had he died after an ordinary illness in his own room, he would undoubtedly have completely destroyed these intimate papers. It was the chance, the providential chance, of his death as a martyr of charity on a far-off Flemish battlefield which rescued these notes from the fate that he had destined for them. They were found among his few belongings in his room in Rathfarnham Castle, accompanied by explicit instructions directing that in the event of his death they should be burnt unopened. Fortunately his Superior, Fr. J. Brennan, S.J., and his brother, Fr. C. Doyle, S.J., decided that this injunction would be best observed by formally violating a request which had been inspired by motives that had ceased to count. These papers were accordingly handed over to me; and it is from these intimate self-revelations, which were never intended for any eye save the writer's own, that the greater, or at least the more valuable, portion of the present book has been compiled. Had I anticipated that this mass of material existed, I would have left this biography to more competent hands, especially as I could devote to it only some of the scanty leisure of a busy life.

But having once undertaken it, I felt that I could not act as a mere transcriber or editor. Without in any way obtruding my own views, which in such matters are of no account, I have attempted to give a study as well as a record. I have sought not only to chronicle the thoughts and experiences of Father Doyle, but also in some measure to give them their true perspective by inserting them in the rich and inclusive tradition of Catholic spirituality. With this object in view I have drawn, more extensively than is usual in a mere biography, on other spiritual writers, especially on those who were Fr. Doyle's favourite authors. I have tried, in particular, to lay stress on the spiritual ideals of S. Ignatius, as revealed in his Letters and in the Spiritual Exercises, and to distinguish carefully between these general ideals and their individual adaptations or special developments. On this point I may have been excessively careful and irritatingly insistent. But my intention, however defective its execution, has been to make this book not merely a sketch of the life of Fr. Doyle, but also, as I am convinced he himself would have wished, the prolongation of his life-work.

The latter portion of this memoir recounts Fr. Doyle's experiences as Military Chaplain. It has been compiled almost entirely from the letters or budgets which he used to send home to be perused by his relatives and intimate friends, without the slightest ulterior thought of publication. In including these interesting letters from the Front, it has not been my intention, any more than it was the writer's, to make another addition to 'war literature.' This book claims to be simply the record of an apostolic life and the study of a very remarkable spiritual personality. His experiences at the Front are of biographical and spiritual interest and help to correct what might otherwise be a partial or misleading impression.

In obedience to the decree of Pope Urban VIII. I protest that all that is written in this life of Fr. Doyle has no other force or credit than such as is grounded on human authority. Hence no expression or statement is intended to assume the approbation or anticipate the decision of the Church.

Were it not for the continual assistance and encouragement of Father Charles Doyle, S.J., this memoir would never have been undertaken or written. Father F. Browne, S.J., readily supplied me with information on many points connected with the last two chapters. I have to thank my sister, Sister M. Anthony, for much help in transcription. The map was kindly drawn for me by Mr. D. R. Kennedy, B.E. I am much obliged to the printers, Messrs. Purcell and Co., Cork, for their interest, attention and efficiency.

Cork, February, 1920.

Preface to Second Edition

ONLY a few minor changes have been made in this edition. I have added in an Appendix some further letters of Fr. Doyle which have subsequently come to light. In an Afterword I have attempted, by some general considerations on Catholic hagiography, to reply to the very few unfavourable criticisms which have reached me. The publication of Fr. Doyle's Life has been amply justified by the unexpectedly rapid sale of the first edition.

Cork, July, 1920.

Preface to New Impression

The second edition was sold out immediately on publication. I set about preparing a final and complete edition, but circumstances over which I had no control interfered with my work. I am therefore compelled to re-issue the second edition in order to satisfy the insistent demand. I have added a photograph of Fr. Doyle at the age of fifteen; and in the light of further information I have modified the notes.

Military Prison in Field,
Bere Island, June, 1921.

Chapter One - Childhood and Youth (1873-1891)

IT is chiefly in the light of a man's subsequent development that the incidents of childhood become interesting and significant, for the child is father of the man. It is often in the artless sayings and doings of the child, and in the impulsive spontaneity of the youth, that we can best discern that groundwork of natural character which in the man is generally concealed by conventionality or self-control. Unfortunately in the case of the present biography the records are scanty, but by collecting some scattered anecdotes and reminiscences, it has been possible to trace in the boyhood of the future Jesuit and Apostle some of those human and lovable characteristics which remained to the end.

William Joseph Gabriel Doyle was born at Melrose, Dalkey, Co. Dublin, on 3rd March, 1873. His father is Mr. Hugh Doyle, an official of the High Court of Justice in Ireland, who is still alive and active though in his eighty-eighth year; his mother was Christina Mary Doyle, *née* Byrne. [1] Willie was the youngest of seven children, four boys and three girls. The eldest and youngest of the girls married; the second became a Sister of Mercy. The eldest boy after a short stay in the Jesuit Novitiate entered Holy Cross College, Clonliffe, whence he passed to the College of the Propaganda, Rome. Ten days before his ordination he caught fever and died in 1887 in the twenty-eighth year of his age. The second son entered the legal profession and is the present Recorder of Galway. Willie's third brother, a few years older than himself, and the inseparable companion of his boyhood, became a Jesuit.

Willie was a frail and delicate child, though like most highly strung children, he had great reserves of energy. All through life, indeed, ill-health was one of his great trials, and for some years before his death he suffered acutely from an internal complaint. But, curiously enough, his nearest approach to death was due, not to sickness, but to an accident. When he was quite a little fellow, his nurse one night placed a lighted candle on his little cot, probably to enable herself to read or sew. The nurse fell asleep, and the candle overturned and set the bed clothes on fire. Fortunately his father, who was sleeping in the next room, was awakened by the smoke and rushed into the nursery. He found the cot on fire, and little Willie fast asleep with his legs curled up, as though he felt the fire creeping towards him. In an instant the child was lifted out of bed, and the mattress and bed clothes thrown out through the window. As a military chaplain Father Willie once laughingly alluded to this escape as his first experience under fire.

For all his future holiness, Willie was by no means a stilted or unnatural child. He played games and he played pranks; and though he cannot be said to have been naughty, he was also far from being irritatingly or obtrusively pious. It is consoling to find that, like most of us, he played at being a soldier. He was seven years old when it was decided that he should emerge from the stage of velvet suit and long curls. On his return from the fateful visit to the hairdresser's, his mother seemed sad on seeing Willie with his shorn locks. But the little fellow himself was delighted, and sturdily insisted that soldiers did not wear curls, at least not nowadays. His mother had to make a soldier's suit for him, with red stripes down the sides; and when he won a great battle, a couple of stripes had to be added to one sleeve! This is how his old nurse describes his youthful exploits:

"His love to be a soldier even from his babyhood was wonderful to fight for Ireland. He would arrange his soldiers and have them all ready for battle. The nursery was turned upside down, to have plenty of room for fighting, building castles, putting up tents, all for his soldiers. Poor nurse looked on, but was too fond of him to say anything. He and a brother with some other little boys were having a great battle one day. He was fighting for Ireland; his brother was fighting for England, as he said his grandmother was English. There was a flag put up to see who was able to get it; the battle went on for some time, then in a moment, Master Willie dashed in and had the flag in his hand, though they were all guarding it. They could not tell how he got it; he was the youngest and smallest of the lot."

How curiously and prophetically appropriate is this characteristic of him, who was to be enrolled in the Company of Jesus and to die on the battlefield as a soldier of Christ!

There are many indications that Willie's youthful militarism was prompted by something deeper than a primitive instinct of pugnacity. Just as in after years he loved to aim at the Ignatian ideal of "distinguishing oneself in the service of one's Eternal King," so, even as a youngster, he felt the call to be foremost in energy and service. Long before he read of the saint of Manresa, he had a natural affinity with the soldier of Pamplona. And it was not always the mimic battle of the nursery; even at this early age he started real warfare, he began a life-long struggle against himself. At the beginning of Lent, when he was quite a little boy, an old Aunt, chancing to go into his Mother's bedroom, found him gesticulating and talking in front of the mirror. "You villain, you wretch," he kept saying to his reflection, "I'll starve you, I'll murder you! Not a sweet will you get, not a bit of cake will you get!"

This is one of the few glimpses we obtain of Willie's interior life during his boyhood. Even of his maturer soul-struggles we should know little or nothing were it not for the chance preservation of his notes and diaries. There is a danger lest these revelations of penance and mortification should mislead a reader, who was not personally acquainted with Fr. Doyle, into fancying that he was exteriorly repellent or gloomily ascetic. Throughout his life he retained a fund of humour and kindliness; no one would suspect his slow struggle for self-mastery and perfection. That even in boyhood he sought self-conquest and recollection, and experienced the working of God's grace, we can have no doubt. There is no record, however, save in the archives of

Him who seeth in secret, where even the sparrow's fall is registered and the hairs of our heads are numbered. But neither in youth nor in after life was his virtue fugitive and cloistered; his light so shone before men that they saw his good works, his thoughtful kindness and self-sacrificing charity.

No man, it is said, is a hero to his valet; at any rate, domestic servants are apt to be severe critics. Willie, however, was deservedly a favourite. He always tried to shield the maids when anything went astray or was neglected. He was ever on the look out for an opportunity of some act of thoughtfulness. Thus sometimes after a big dinner at Melrose, the cook would come down next morning and find the fire lighting and the dinner things washed. Willie had been playing the fairy! Again, whenever a maid was looking ill, he used to volunteer privately to do her work. A servant of the family, who gave many years of faithful service, still remembers her first arrival at Dalkey. As she was timorously proceeding to Melrose, she met the two brothers walking on stilts along the road. "How are you, Anne?" said Willie, divining that this was the new maid. He alighted and insisted on taking whatever she was carrying. Before she had her things off, he had tea ready for her.

"I know I was really awkward after leaving the rough country," writes Anne. "I had got orders to have the boots cleaned that evening. But the good saint took them out to the coach-house and brought them in shining. No one knew only Kate (the parlourmaid) he did it so quietly. To put it off he made the remark, 'I dare say you have no such thing in the country as blacking.' Not understanding the coal fire, and while I was learning, he would run downstairs and have the fire lighting and the kettle on by the time I would arrive. Then when breakfast was ready, he would come to the kitchen and ask how did I get on with the fire that morning?"

For the poor people on Dalkey Hill Willie constituted himself into a Conference of St. Vincent de Paul. He raised funds by saving up his pocket-money, by numberless acts of economy and self-denial; he begged for his poor, he got the cook to make soup, he pleaded for delicacies to carry to the sick. Once he went to the family apothecary and ordered several large bottles of cod-liver oil for a poor consumptive woman, and then presented the bill to his father! He bought a store of tea with which under many pledges of secrecy he entrusted the parlour maid. On this he used to draw when in the course of his wanderings he happened to come across some poor creature without the means of providing herself with the cup that cheers. He by no means confined himself merely to the bringing of relief. He worked for his poor, he served them, he sat down and talked familiarly with them, he read books for the sick, he helped to tidy the house, he provided snuff and tobacco for the aged. One of Willie's cases if such an impersonal word may be used was a desolate old woman whose children were far away. One day noticing that the house was dirty and neglected, he went off and purchased some lime and a brush, and then returned and whitewashed the whole house from top to bottom. He then went down on his knees and scrubbed the floors, amid the poor woman's ejaculations of protest and gratitude. No one knew of this but the cook and parlourmaid who lent him their aprons to save his clothes and kept dinner hot for him until he returned late in the evening. While thus aiding his poor friends temporally, he did not forget their souls. He contrived skilfully to remind them of their prayers and the sacraments; he also strongly advocated temperance. There was one old fellow on the Hill whom Willie had often unsuccessfully tried to reform. After years of hard drinking he lay dying, and could not be induced to see a priest. For eight hours Willie stayed praying by the bedside of the half-conscious dying sinner. Shortly before the end he came to himself, asked for the priest and made his peace with God. Only when he had breathed his last, did Willie return to Melrose. His first missionary victory!

When we hear of these acts of charity and zeal exercised at an age which is often associated with selfish thoughtlessness, we may be inclined to imagine that Willie Doyle was a prim, stilted, 'goody-goody' sort of boy. Nothing of the kind. He had a wonderful freshness and spontaneity. One never could feel that his kindness was artificially produced or that his goodness was forced. His virtue, like his laugh, had the genuine ring in it. One of his most endearing characteristics throughout life was his sense of humour. "Don't take yourself too seriously," he once said to a rather lugubrious would-be-saint; "a sense of humour is one of the greatest aids to sanctity." As a boy he was full of humour, even when he was doing good. He once brought to one of his poor people a carefully wrapped parcel which was joyfully acclaimed as a pound of butter; but when extricated it proved to be a stone! Next day, however, the real article, with much more besides, was brought to console the good woman. Sometimes Willie was able to combine kindness and fun. Thus, in order to shield the maids, he used to rake and settle the cinders on top of the ashes, and he would then wait for his grandmother who had a little weakness for insisting that the cinders were sifted and always enjoyed her remark, "Oh, how nicely cook has the cinders riddled!" With his brother Charlie he loved to engage in fun and frolic. As schoolboys they used to amuse themselves by dressing up as "nigger minstrels," blackening their faces and hands. For this purpose Willie saved up and bought a banjo. All the household, including the maids, used to be assembled for these entertainments. Some of us who feel alas! that we have too little in common with Fr. William Doyle, can thus at least claim human kinship with Willie Doyle!

Between Willie and his brother, Charlie, there was a close bond of attachment from early days of childhood. As they were only a few years apart in age, they were naturally more closely united with one another than with their elder brothers and sisters. Together they learnt their first letters, together they fished and bathed, and built themselves a wonderful house in the branches of a mighty elm, together they knelt and prayed. Their prayers and catechism and all things religious were lovingly superintended by the future nun of the family, whom her young brothers, with boys' quick instinct for hitting off a character with a name, dubbed "the missionary," thereby also recording a tribute to their sister's religious influence. Willie's devotion to his elder brother was remarkable even in a household where all the members of the family were so united and affectionate. Nothing was too good for Charlie, everything was shared with him sweets, secrets, sorrows. Wherever he went, Willie followed, ready to run, to fetch and carry at a word from his brother; and when bed-time came the last goodnight, conveyed in a mysterious formula, was always to Charlie. And these two who as boys played and studied together, fought their mimic battles together, and shared their little joys and sorrows, were destined not to be divided in life. For in ways mysterious they both joined the Society of Jesus.

In September, 1884, at the age of eleven, Willie went to Ratcliffe College, Leicestershire, conducted by the Fathers of the Institute of Charity, where his elder brother had already spent a year. Here in the cloisters and classrooms of Pugin's beautiful college six pleasant and profitable years were passed. A good place was consistently secured at the various examinations, and every year saw one or more prizes brought back to delight the dear ones at home. Willie excelled at sports; he was for several years a member of the cricket eleven and of the football team. This proficiency at games stood him in good stead years afterwards when he became one of the Prefects at Clongowes. He was a general favourite among his school-fellows, and his brotherin-law, at whose house in Sheffield he usually spent the Christmas vacation, declared in a letter that Willie was "the nicest schoolboy he had ever met." Each summer found the two brothers home in Ireland. Vacation time passed in boyish games and amusements; yet, as the years went on, the more serious side began to show itself in Willie's character. It was then that he developed more and more his love for the poor and helpless. At times he would slip away from the cricket and tennis and seek out his poor on Dalkey Hill, where "Master Willie" was a welcome visitor. There was one family of his own name, with many ramifications on the Hill, which was the object of his special predilection. By a curious coincidence one of the first men he met on joining his regiment after his appointment as military chaplain was a William Doyle, a grandson of his. old friend on Dalkey Hill.

In the summer of 1890 Willie left Ratcliffe. During his last year at college his health had given cause for anxiety. It was therefore decided that he should remain quietly at home, in order to build up his strength and reflect on his future. What this future would be, those who knew him never doubted. It had long been an open secret in the family that Willie would be a priest. He himself had never any doubt or hesitation. Beneath all his boyish fun and lightheartedness there lay, discernible to a careful observer, a life of deep purposive faith. This was shown not only in his pure upright character, his generous unselfishness, and his love of Christ's poor, but also in his childlike piety. Long before the decree of Pope Pius X. which restored frequent and daily Communion, Willie was a weekly communicant. His devotion to our Blessed Lady was also noticeable; he always went to her altar when he paid a visit to the church. The priesthood seemed but the logical development of a life thus begun.

In July, 1890, Willie paid a few days' visit to St. Stanislaus' College, Tullamore, the Novitiate of the Irish Province of the Society of Jesus, where his brother, Charlie, had entered ten months previously. One day during the visit the subject of Willie's vocation came up for discussion. Charlie knew that Willie was going to be a priest. But was it a secular priest or a religious? "I hope soon to enter Clonliffe," said Willie. "Did you ever think of the religious life?" asked his brother. "Never!" was the emphatic reply. "I have always wanted to fill the gap left by Fred's death, and to become a secular priest." "But do you know anything about the religious state?" persisted the zealous novice. "No, nothing," said Willie; "but in any case I would never come to this hole of a place!" This led to an animated discussion concerning religious Orders in general and the Society of Jesus in particular. Willie was so far shaken as to accept a copy of St. Alphonsus Liguori's work on the Religious State, [2] with a promise to read it and to think over it. The sequel can be told in Willie's own words:

"On Christmas Day I was alone in the drawing-room when Father came in and asked me if I had yet made up my mind as to my future career. I answered 'Yes' that I intended to become a Jesuit. I remember how I played my joy and happiness into the piano after thus giving myself openly to Jesus."

On 31st March, 1891, Willie entered the Jesuit Novitiate of Tullabeg, near Tullamore, King's Co.

[1] She died at 7 a.m. on 19th March, 1915, at the age of 83. Willie had just returned from a Mission in Glasgow and so was able to be with her at the end and to say Mass immediately for her. Next year, in a letter from the Front 17th March, 1916) he writes to his Father: "I shall not forget the anniversary on Sunday, though I doubt if she needs our prayers."

[2] *Instructions and Considerations on the Religious State.* Eng. trans, (no date) published by the Art and Book Co.

Chapter Two - From Noviceship to Priesthood (1891-1907)

(1.) TULLABEG, (1891-1893.)

WHEN half way through his second year's novitiate Willie's health began to give anxiety to his superiors, and a complete nervous breakdown following a fire at the College led to his being sent to his home in Dalkey for some months. In fact there was question at this time of his having to leave the novitiate for good owing to his health. Several doctors declared he was quite unfit for the strain of religious life, while superiors were almost unanimous in their opinion that he should not be kept. But Willie clung to his vocation, which he felt was from God; and the Provincial, Fr. Timothy Kenny, who from the first had formed a high idea of the young novice, declaring him to be "as good as gold," supported him warmly. A few months of his native air and among his beloved poor on the Hill, who joyfully welcomed back "Master Willie" and saw very much of him now, restored strength and steadiness of nerve, and after making good in the novitiate the time he had spent at home, Willie had the happiness of taking the three vows of religion on the 15th August, 1893.

Only a few stray sheets survive to give us all too meagre information concerning the inner life of the novice. Fortunately one precious little document remains to attest his astonishing fervour.

A.M.D.G. ac B.V.M.
My Martyrdom for Mary's Sake.

"Darling Mother Mary, in preparation for the glorious martyrdom which I feel assured thou art going to obtain for me, I, thy most unworthy child, on this the first day of thy month, solemnly commence my life of slow martyrdom by earnest hard work and constant self-denial. *With my blood I promise thee to keep this resolution, do thou, sweet Mother, assist me and obtain for me the one favour I wish and long for: To die a Jesuit Martyr.*

May 1st, 1893.

May God's will, not mine, be done! Amen."

The words here italicised are in the original written with the writer's own blood for ink; and on each side of the word "martyr" is a smudge of blood, as if thus to seal his compact with our Lady. [1] "One feels that it is a sacred privilege to gaze after the lapse of twenty-six years on this touching contract between the Jesuit novice and his heavenly Mother, chivalrously sealed with his blood. Think of the twenty-four years of life which remained to the novice! Right well did he keep his compact; his was a "life of slow martyrdom by earnest hard work and constant self-denial." And the compact was kept in heaven also. As on earth of yore, "Mary kept all these words, pondering them in her heart." Our Blessed Lady obtained for him the one favour he wished and longed for. William Doyle died a Jesuit Martyr. [2]

Some reflections and resolutions which he recorded during the triduum of preparation for his vows, have also happily survived and may here be set down.

"It depends entirely on myself whether I become a saint or not. If I *wish* and *will* to be one, half the battle is over. Certainly God's help is secured. Every fresh effort to become holy gets fresh grace, and grace is what makes the soul holy and pleasing to God.

"God has a work for each one to do; the devil also. For each one can be an influence for good or evil to those around. No one goes to heaven or hell alone. Unless I am holy, I may do the devil's work. The closer I try to imitate the Sacred Heart, the holier shall I become. How can I get nearer that Divine Heart than by receiving Holy Communion often and fervently? The Sacred Heart will "then be next my own and will teach me quickest and best how to be a saint.

"Can I refuse to become holy when God Himself entreats me to be holy? 'Walk before Me and be perfect.' 'Be perfect as your heavenly Father is perfect.' Another great motive for becoming a saint the wish, the command of God! I have been -called by God to be a member of the Society of His Son. To be a true Jesuit I must be a close imitator of Jesus Christ, an 'alter Christus.' The Society was instituted to glorify the Name of Jesus by its learning, by its zeal, but above all by its holiness. I must, therefore, strain after three things: to become learned, an authority on all subjects, not for self or the glory of self, but for God and the glory of God; to become a lover of souls; to become holy, this first and foremost, because the Jesuit without sanctity is no true son of Ignatius.

"O loving Saviour, forgive me the past, accept me repentant, help me, for I am going to become with Thy assistance A Thorough Jesuit and a Great Saint."

(2.) CLONGOWES, (1894-1898.)

Soon after taking the vows of religion Willie's health again broke down. So once more he was sent to recuperate in his native air and as before with good results. By the following August he was able to take up his new duties in Clongowes Wood College to which he was now assigned. Willie was stationed in Clongowes during two periods, from 1894 to 1898, and again from 1901 to 1903. His first year there was spent in teaching, the other five as prefect. He showed considerable ability as a teacher, but other qualities which he possessed decided his superiors to entrust him with the difficult work of prefecting. As prefect he won remarkable success and popularity. He was a good organiser, excelled in all outdoor sports, while he threw himself with characteristic energy into the interests and activities of the little world around him. With the boys he was a favourite. He was very kind and very just, two qualities that appeal to boys and win their respect and esteem. Yet there was a certain awe mingled with their affection, for, as they used to say, they could never quite make him out. This was the result of his imperturbability and evenness of temper, joined to a strong will and virile character. He was never angry with the boys, yet he always had his way; they simply had to do what he wanted them to do.

One who was under him as a boy writes: "I first met Fr. Doyle when I was a small boy at Clongowes. He was then Third Line Prefect, and had under his care some seventy or eighty boys ranging from ten to fifteen years of age. This particular set were rowdy and quarrelsome, and during my first year in the Line there were two periods, at least, of acute disturbance. Not that the trouble circled round Fr. Doyle or was directed against him, nor was it caused by any act on his part, but arose out of feuds among the boys themselves. The manner in which Fr. Doyle dealt with this difficult situation impressed me even at the time, and I have been more deeply impressed again and again in retrospection. Hot tempered by nature, I believe, he never allowed himself to be carried into arbitrary action by the intemperate or unreasonable conduct of those in his charge. He was firm, but never unjust; indeed, if he erred at all, it was on the side of leniency. But apart from his self-control, the quality that struck me most was his optimism, his breezy cheerfulness in the midst of difficulties. He never lost his good spirits; he never seemed to be depressed; he never appeared to consider for a moment how trouble in his department affected himself; he was intent always on setting others on the right track.

"I recall one memorable scene. It is a common occurrence in Clongowes for one cricket club to challenge another. The consequences for the loser are serious, since the beaten side is liable to confiscation of its bats, pads, in fact all its good gear, and to get in exchange the battered property of its rival. This is the material aspect of the result, but there is a more important element at stake, the loss or gain, namely, of prestige. In the instance to which I refer, the game was keenly contested and feeling ran high. The junior club won eventually by a narrow margin. Whereupon the beaten side declared that the victors had 'doctored' the score. Immediately there was uproar, and quiet was restored only when someone proposed that Fr. Doyle should be called in to arbitrate. He gave the case against the defeated eleven. This verdict so exasperated one of the boys that he called Fr. Doyle a 'd--- cheat!' This outburst cleared the atmosphere and produced a sudden calm, as nobody knew what would follow this amazing piece of impudence. But Fr. Doyle did nothing. Two or three days passed, and the culprit, who was prepared to take a flogging and hate his Prefect to the end of his days, began to grow sorry for his conduct when he saw that no move was being made against him. At last he apologised, offering to accept punishment, but Fr. Doyle only laughed good humouredly, and gave him biscuits and lemonade and a few pieces of sound advice. Fr. Doyle won a fast friend and a most loyal supporter, but his self-control under the circumstances needed character.

"Fr. Doyle's example worked good. His cheerfulness, his energy, his enthusiasm were infectious and inspiring. His whole conduct was marked by gentleness and a kindly thoughtfulness that gained him loyalty and affection. In the playing fields he was a tower of strength. I can still recall the admiration with which I watched him play fullback, or stump a batsman who had his toe barely off the ground. But above all he gave the impression to us boys of one who lived much in the presence of God. I know one boy, at least, who entered the Society of Jesus, partly, at any rate, because Fr. Doyle was such a splendid man and splendid Jesuit."

Another who lived and worked with Willie in his early days in the Society and at Clongowes writes: "Thinking of Fr. Willie Doyle, I recall especially his gay, light-hearted ways, the cheery laugh and snatch of song with which he enlivened recreation hours or holiday excursions. Into the latter he threw himself with zest and was an excellent companion. He could not resist the temptation of indulging from time to time in a practical joke. Practical jokes are not welcomed by everyone, but he carried them through with such good humour and playfulness that the victim was soon tempted to relax and join in the laugh. Indeed his love of a joke never wholly deserted him. He grew graver as he had more and more to do with the burdens and cares of life and how many were the persons whose burdens he helped to carry! but even to the end he retained in a large measure his gaiety of heart and his cheery outlook. Nothing seemed able to depress him for any length of time.

"One did not have to live long with him to see that his gaiety of disposition, an essential part of his nature though it was, was still only the sparkle on the surface, and that below it ran the current of a downright earnest religious life a current that deepened and gained in strength as he advanced in life. Not that he made any ostentation of piety or asceticism there was not the slightest sign of this about him. On the contrary, he was ever reserved about himself and guarded closely the secrets of his spiritual life. But many little acts of self-restraint, self-denial and self-sacrifice, made me feel that he was trying seriously and steadily to acquire the solid virtues which befit a man who would give himself wholly to God.

"After the novitiate and juniorate Fr. Doyle and I were together for some years in Clongowes Wood College. In the life there, with its larger liberty of action, new phases in his character showed themselves. He began to display a more than common spirit of initiative and enterprise, an energy and resourcefulness in carrying out what he had undertaken, and a marked tenacity of purpose. His production of *The Mikado* may be instanced. For some considerable time elaborate plays had not been attempted at Clongowes, owing to the heavy demands on time and attention made by the Intermediate examinations. When Mr. Doyle obtained permission to try his hand at producing this opera, he seemed to be attempting the impossible. Few good singers and actors were known to be among the boys. Everything was wanting, scenery, costumes, and the money to buy them; and above all time to practise, for the studies could in no way be allowed to suffer. There appeared to be a sufficiency of one thing only cold water; and that was freely poured on the scheme. Mr. Doyle kept his own counsel and set to work quietly and determinedly. He unearthed talent, trained his actors and singers assiduously, enlisted help, and by his tact, energy and perseverance, he overcame every obstacle, and in the end *The Mikado* was a triumphant success and proved to be one of the most brilliant performances ever witnessed on the stage of Clongowes.

"As another instance of his spirit of initiative I may mention the starting of the college magazine, *The Clongownian,* of which he was the Founder and the first Editor. Here again there were the usual difficulties and opposition to a new venture, but these were put aside with unfailing courage and perseverance, and the first number of *The Clongownian* appeared during the Christmas of 1895.

"Though not a Clongownian Mr. Doyle had much to do with the founding of the Clongowes Union which was proposed and worked up in *The Clongownian* for a considerable time before it actually came into being.

"Viewing his character as a whole, it seems to me that the fundamental quality in it was courage; courage of a fine and generous type. When confronted with difficulties, with danger or labour or pain, instead of hesitating or weakly compromising, he was rather braced to a new and more intense resolve to see the matter out. Give in, he would not. It was this courage, supported, no doubt, by a natural liveliness of disposition, that enabled him to preserve through life his gaiety of heart and to face his troubles as they came with a smiling countenance; it was this courage, too, that steeled him to hold fast to his purpose no matter what difficulties or obstacles might arise."

We have here the testimony of one who for many years lived and worked with Fr., or, as he was then, Mr. Doyle. It is the more valuable as the writer could only guess at the inner life of him whom he pictured as remarkably courageous and encouragingly cheerful. Unfortunately, no intimate jottings of this period could be found; so we can only dimly conjecture the deep undercurrent of faith and grace which made Willie Doyle so wholehearted and efficient in carrying out the duties which obedience had assigned.

There seems to the outward glance an enormous difference between the claustral seclusion and silence of Tullabeg and the busy bustling life of Clongowes. We find it curious that the demure introspective novice should rather suddenly develop into a distracted college prefect immersed in games and plays. That is because we miss the inner key, the Ignatian ideal of God in everything. The point is worth emphasising if we would rightly understand the life of a Jesuit, such as this biography. In 1551 St. Ignatius wrote to the Rector of Coimbra that "he desired to see all the members of the Society animated with such a spirit that they do not find less devotion in works of charity and obedience than in prayer and meditation, since they ought to do everything for the love and service of God our Lord." [3] Ignatius consistently refused to increase the time allotted to scholastics' daily prayer beyond one hour. He once said to Fr. Nadal that "no one would ever make him change his opinion that one hour was sufficient for those engaged in study, provided they have mortification and self-denial; for thus they will easily fit more prayer into a quarter of an hour than others who are unmortified into two hours" [4] "During their works and studies," he wrote, [5] "they can lift their hearts to God; and if they direct everything to the divine service, everything becomes a prayer."

It is this apostolic fusion of work and prayer which a Jesuit noviceship is designed to produce. The semi-monastic quietness and solitude is not an end in itself; it is merely the stillness of the power-house where unseen, but energy laden currents are generated. When Brother Doyle resolved as a novice to begin a "life of slow martyrdom by earnest hard work and constant self-denial," he was not only a true child of St. Ignatius but he was making a resolution destined to be immediately realisable. He who erstwhile had his heart set on the priesthood had to turn aside and devote the fresh energy of his youth to minding thoughtless and unruly youngsters, settling their little squabbles, entering into their petty interests, mending cricket gear, and rehearsing theatricals. Earnest hard work was done in full measure, and has received its human tribute. God's angels alone can estimate the constant self-denial involved. How little can the world's coarse thumb and finger plumb the inner depths of what outwardly is serenity, pleasantness, and ready service! In this period of Willie Doyle's life we can see only the outer expression, later on we shall be privileged to read the record of his soul. It is well to realise now that seemingly natural activities and humdrum duties are based on an inner struggle and a life of faith. It will be well to remember afterwards that an interior life of slow martyrdom does not imply an unnatural or morose exterior.

(3.) PHILOSOPHY, (1898-1901.)

In the ordinary course of events the young Jesuit Scholastic, [6] on emerging from the two years' noviceship, spends one or two years in the "juniorate" completing his college studies; or, more usually nowadays, he studies for a university degree. After this he pursues a course of philosophy for three years, and only then is he sent to some college to act as master or prefect for some years before he begins his theological studies. In the case of Willie Doyle considerations of health led to a deviation from the usual course. His juniorate had to be interrupted by a long visit to his home in Dalkey, and when sufficiently recovered, he was sent to Clongowes. After he had worked four years there, it was decided that he was sufficiently strong to resume his studies. In 1898 he was sent to Belgium to study philosophy. He joined the exiled French Jesuits of the Champagne Province, who had a house of studies at Enghien, near Brussels. But continental life told severely on a constitution that was still delicate, and he suffered much. Through it all, however, he was just the same cheerful, light-hearted comrade as before, repressing any sign of pain or discouragement he may have felt, and breaking out every now and then into some audacious prank that made him the wonder and despair of the good French fathers. After a year of ill-health he was transferred to Saint Mary's Hall, Stonyhurst, where he pursued his philosophical studies for two years more. Even here bad health continued and made work very hard, but he persevered unflinchingly. Though suffering very much from digestive trouble, he never complained and was always bright and cheerful. His extraordinary good spirits were most remarkable, indeed quite infectious. It was difficult to be out of sorts in the company of one who was known to be suffering, but who nevertheless was full of fun and gaiety. Yet he could be very determined and earnest; and when he took anything in hand, he saw it through to the end, cost what it might.

Among the philosophers at Stonyhurst, Willie was a universal favourite; his simple, unassuming character, his high spirits, above all his readiness to "sacrifice himself for others, endeared him to everybody. He was at Stonyhurst during the Boer War when feeling naturally ran high among the different nationalities which formed the community, but though he took a different view from the majority with whom he lived, he never lost the respect and esteem of any, even of those from whom he most differed. Thanks to his playful vivacity he could venture to joke and chaff about matters that touched differences of national sentiment, and by so doing he helped to prevent any sense of strain from creeping into the situation. His love of fun was inexhaustible and led to many amusing incidents. One of the winters he spent at Stonyhurst was very severe and there was much tobogganing. Willie was very anxious to possess a sledge that would be a credit to the Old Country he was always thoroughly Irish. Accordingly he approached the Father Minister of the house for permission to get the carpenter to finish a toboggan for him. It turned out that the "finishing" meant the making it, Willie's part being to furnish the wood and the idea. When "finished," the "Irish Mail" was the envy of all!

No records survive to tell us of Willie's inner life at this period. Just one letter has been found. It was written to his parents from Stonyhurst on 3ist March, 1901, and was evidently treasured up as a precious keepsake consoling to the heart of a Catholic father.

"Ten years ago, to-day, I went to Tullabeg and entered on my career as a novice of the Society. Looking back on it all now, it seems hard to realize that ten long years have gone by since that eventful day on which I took a step which has meant so much for me, and which, thank God, during all this time I have never for a moment regretted. Our Lord was very good to me at that time, smoothing away many difficulties and making that day, which, to human nature at least, was full of sorrow, one of the happiest of all my life.

"I remember well my arrival at Tullabeg and the way I astonished the Father Socius (as he told me afterwards) by running up to the hall door three steps at a time. He was not accustomed, he said, to see novices coming in such a merry mood, evidently enjoying the whole thing; and, though I did not know it then, it was the best of signs of a real vocation.

"Since then I have gone on from day to day and year to year, with the same cheerful spirits, making the best of difficulties and always trying to look at the bright side of things. True, from time to time, there have been trials and hard things to face even a Jesuit's life is not all roses but through it all I can honestly say, I have never lost that deep interior peace and contentment which sweetens the bitter things and makes rough paths smooth.

"I think this will be a consolation to you, dearest Father and Mother, for I have often pictured you to myself as wondering if I were really happy and content. I could not be more so, and were I to look upon religious life from the sole aspect of what makes for the greatest happiness, I would not exchange it for all the pleasures the world could offer. Thank God for all His goodness, and after Him, many grateful thanks to you both, dearest Father and Mother, for that good example and loving care to which we all owe so much."

No records survive to tell us of Willie's inner life at this period. Just one letter has been found. It was written to his parents from Stonyhurst on 31st March, 1901, and was evidently treasured up as a precious keepsake consoling to the heart of a Catholic father.

"Ten years ago, to-day, I went to Tullabeg and entered on my career as a novice of the Society. Looking back on it all now, it seems hard to realize that ten long years have gone by since that eventful day on which I took a step which has meant so much for me, and which, thank God, during all this time I have never for a moment regretted. Our Lord was very good to me at that time, smoothing away many difficulties and making that day, which, to human nature at least, was full of sorrow, one of the happiest of all my life.

"I remember well my arrival at Tullabeg and the way I astonished the Father Socius (as he told me afterwards) by running up to the hall door three steps at a time. He was not accustomed, he said, to see novices coming in such a merry mood, evidently enjoying the whole thing; and, though I did not know it then, it was the best of signs of a real vocation.

"Since then I have gone on from day to day and year to year, with the same cheerful spirits, making the best of difficulties and always trying to look at the bright side of things. True, from time to time, there have been trials and hard things to face even a Jesuit's life is not all roses but through it all I can honestly say, I have never lost that deep interior peace and contentment which sweetens the bitter things and makes rough paths smooth.

"I think this will be a consolation to you, dearest Father and Mother, for I have often pictured you to myself as wondering if I were really happy and content. I could not be more so. and were I to look upon religious life from the sole aspect of what makes for the greatest happiness, I would not exchange it for all the pleasures the world could offer. Thank God for all His goodness, and after Him, many grateful thanks to you both, dearest Father and Mother, for that good example and loving care to which we all owe so much."

(4.) CLONGOWES AND BELVEDERE, (1901-1904.)

Having completed his course of philosophy, Willie returned to Clongowes in 1901 for another period of prefecting. Here he remained for two years, and he was then transferred to the teaching staff of Belvedere College, Dublin, where he spent a fruitful year of labour. For, as the immediate preparation for the priesthood drew near, zeal for souls that was afterwards to become so strong and ardent, began now to show itself more markedly in his life. He did much good work for the Apostleship of Prayer and for temperance among the boys in Belvedere, with whom he was even more popular than among those he had left behind in Clongowes. The stirring little talks he gave occasionally to his class made an impression which some of his pupils still recall. Especially was he insistent on the spirit of self-sacrifice and on Holy Communion. His attractive character and kindness led many of the boys to give him their confidence and seek help and counsel in their difficulties and doubts; and more than one vocation was discussed and decided at these interviews.

A fellow religious who lived with him during his last years in the colleges, and who was in America at the time of his death, wrote: "I can safely say he was a perfect Jesuit and often reminded me of St. John Berchmans. His was a combination of real solid piety with a truly human character. Bright and joyous himself, he always made others happy and was evidently happy to be able to do so. To those who knew his self-sacrificing devotedness there could be no doubt as to the identity of the heroic Irish Padre the first despatches recording his death spoke of. So certain was I, that I told my friends here that the hero was Fr. Willie. Only three weeks later did I receive corroboration from the Irish papers." Yet later on Willie was to reproach himself for his want of zeal and general tepidity during his years as prefect and master. "I only wish you could see," he once wrote to a dear friend, "how heartily ashamed of myself God makes me by each fresh grace. Perhaps you will realize this better when I tell you that at one period of my religious life, before I was a priest, I led a very careless spiritual existence. It began by overwork of my own making so that often I was not in bed until three in the morning, with the usual results. I felt at last I was walking near the edge of the precipice, while all the time, though it may sound incredible, God was tugging at my heart for a life of perfection, and I was writing down at each triduum and retreat my determination to become with His grace a saint! Can you understand now why I am so eloquent on the tepid religious? This could not go on. I was driven half mad by the thought of the abuse of grace and the gentle pleading day and night of Jesus. Then in the midst of all this tepidity, when I was praying little, when there was hardly a deliberate act of self-denial in the day, there came an extraordinary grace one I felt I could not resist to make the Holy Hour each week. I actually began to do so, though at the time it must have been torture to me, I think. I would not do what God wanted me to do, so He made me. I fought against Him like a tiger, but His mercy and patient gentleness won; and I should be a strange ungrateful creature if I did not long now with all my soul to love Him passionately."

We gather from this touching letter of self-revelation that, strenuously active and efficient as he was at his college duties, he felt that "God was tugging at his heart for a life of perfection" and grace was urging him to more than ordinary holiness. Now, too, he began a practice which for the remainder of his life he regarded as a fruitful source of grace and strength: the Holy Hour. Looking back indeed on these years in the light of his maturer experience and spiritual progress as a priest, he bewailed them as years of careless abuse of grace. God grant that many of us may reach even such "tepidity "!

(5.) THEOLOGY, (1904-1907.)

In September, 1904, Willie Doyle went to Milltown Park, Dublin, to begin the study of theology. He now felt the handicap of the deficient course of philosophy which his ill-health had necessitated. But he worked hard and courageously, not so much to become a brilliant theologian as to obtain a solid knowledge of all subjects useful to the sacred ministry. While he diligently studied Latin manuals which he must have often found dull and difficult, he was not unmindful of Father de la Colombière's advice to a young theologian: "For myself, had I the opportunity of going through my theological studies again, I would, I can assure you, give to meditation double the time devoted to reading. It is only by meditation that one can gain any insight into things spiritual or form any stable opinion upon matters controversial." [7] The officially prescribed theological lectures and textbooks are, after all, only the skeleton; it is left to the student himself, or rather with God's grace, to add substance and life. Willie Doyle strove not only to advance in personal holiness, but also carefully devoted himself to conscientiously preparing himself for his future work of retreats and missions. The numerous manuscript books which at this time he filled with extracts, spiritual considerations and sermon-plans, serve to show us that it was by diligent drudgery and faithful cooperation that he merited God's blessing on his fruitful subsequent ministry.

He seems at this time to have kept a private spiritual diary, but of this only a few detached leaves remain. One of these is dated 25th November, 1906, and bears the title, "The Practice of Humility ":

"I will strive to get a great contempt for myself, to think little of and despise myself, and to pray and desire that others may do the same. I have nothing which God has not given me; I can do nothing without God's grace and help. In a few, very few, years my name will be forgotten. What would people think of me if they knew me as I know myself? My pride and desire for praise; my mean uncharitable thoughts about others; my fear of humiliation; the imperfect way I have lived in the Society; the sins I have committed, the scandal given, the terrible harm done to others by making them tepid, breaking rules etc.; my resolutions broken in an hour; the many faults not corrected after sixteen years of religious life. In spite of all this I deceive myself that I am pleasing God..."

Another undated sheet is headed: "What must I do to become a saint?"

"(1) Excite in myself an ardent desire and determination to become one, cost what it may.

(2) Beg and pray without ceasing for this grace and the desire of holiness.

(3) Take each action and duty as if it were the last and the only one of my life, and perform it with extraordinary fervour.

(4) Have a fixed duty for each moment and not depart from it; never waste a moment.

(5) The spirit of constant prayer.

(6) Relentless war against my will and inclination; agere contra at every moment in all things.

(7) The faithful practice of little mortifications."

On 7th June, 1907, he noted down the following resolution: "While making the Holy Hour to-day, the Feast of the Sacred Heart, I felt inspired to make this resolution: Sweet Jesus, as a first step towards my becoming a Saint, which You desire so much, I will try to do each duty, each little action, as perfectly and fervently as I possibly can. St. John Berchmans, help me."

A letter which he wrote to his sister a month before his ordination will serve to show how hard he found his life as a theologian and how eagerly yet tremulously he looked forward to the great consummation:

"I can scarcely believe I have all the long years of study, which I used to dread so much, really over. You know I was never intended by Almighty God to keep my nose buried in books all day. Climbing up chimneys or walking on my head across the roof of a house is more in my line! When I came here, three years ago, my health was anything but good, and kind friends said I would not spend six weeks at theology. But after the first Christmas things began to improve and, thank God, have gone on improving steadily ever since, so that now in spite of the hard work and it has been hard and trying I am in far better health and able to do more than when I came here. I look upon this as a great grace from God, and I only hope I shall not prove ungrateful to Him for all He has done.

"As you may imagine, all my thoughts at present are centred on the Great Day, July 28th. The various events of the year have helped to keep it before my mind, learning to say Mass, the Divine Office etc.; but now that such a short time remains, I find it hard to realise that I shall be a priest so very soon. Were it not for all the good prayers, especially yours, sister mine, which are being offered up daily for me, I should almost feel in despair, because these long years of waiting (nearly seventeen now) have only brought home to me how unworthy I am of such an honour and such dignity."

Willie Doyle was ordained priest on 28th July, 1907. Next day he celebrated his first Mass. Of his inner feelings we have just one little private record: "My loving Jesus, on this the morning of my Ordination to the Priesthood, I wish to place in Your Sacred Heart, in gratitude for all You have done for me, the resolution from this day forward to *go straight for Holiness.* My earnest wish and firm resolve is to strive with might and main to become a Saint."

(6.) SOME NOTES WRITTEN DURING THEOLOGY.

Among the notes which Fr. Doyle recorded during his theology, there are many which have a personal touch and embody his own ideals and aspirations. Some of them will be here quoted in order to help us to understand his ideas of holiness. He who was soon to be perhaps imprudent himself, at least made no mistake as to what constituted true sanctity.

"How many deceive themselves," he wrote, "in thinking sanctity consists in the 'holy follies' of the saints! How many look upon holiness as something beyond their reach or capability, and think that it is to be found only in the performance of extraordinary actions. Satisfied that they have not the strength for great austerities, the time for much prayer, or the courage for painful humiliations, they silence their conscience with the thought that great sanctity is not for them, that they have not been called to be saints. With their eyes fixed on the heroic deeds of the few, they miss the daily little sacrifices God asks them to make; and while waiting for something great to prove their love, they lose the countless little opportunities of sanctification each day bears with it in its bosom." (Sept. 1905.)

Again he writes to the same effect.

"What is it to be a saint? Does it mean that we must macerate this flesh of ours with cruel austerities, such as we read of in the life-story of some of God's great heroes? Does it mean the bloody scourge, the painful vigil and sleepless night, that crucifying of the flesh in even its most innocent enjoyment? 'No, no, the hand of God does not lead us all by that stern path of awful heroism to our reward above. He does not ask from all of us the holy thirst for suffering, in its highest form, of a Teresa or a Catherine of Siena. But sweetly and gently would He lead us along the way of holiness by our constant unswerving faithfulness to our duty, duty accepted, duty done for His dear sake. How many alas! who might be saints are now leading lives of indifferent virtue, because they have deluded themselves with the thought that they have no strength to bear the 'holy follies' of the saints. How many a fair flower of innocence, which God had destined to bloom in dazzling holiness, has faded and withered beneath the chill blast of a fear of suffering never asked from it." (April, 1905.)

Words such as these, coming from the pen of one who was not unfamiliar with scourge and vigil and fast, are helpful and consoling. Not that they picture the path of holiness as other than the royal road of the cross. Fr. Doyle wished rather to remove the mirage of an unreal and impossible cross from the way of those of us whose true holiness is to be found in meeting the daily and hourly little crosses, humanly inglorious perhaps, but divinely destined for our sanctification. In the lives of canonised saints, and of him whose life we are recording, there are doubtless 'holy follies' and grace-inspired imprudences. But these are not the essence of sanctity; they are its bloom, whereas its stem is self-conquest. Without these there can be great holiness - no terrifying penances marked the life of St. John Berchmans or of that winsome fragile nun who is known as the Little Flower. But without the slow secret mortification of doing ordinary and mostly trivial duties well, there can be no spiritual advance. Heroism is not a sudden romantic achievement; it is the fruit of years of humdrum faithfulness. This is not only the lesson of Fr. Doyle's heroic life and death, it is the idea which here at the outset of his apostolic career he clearly fixed for himself. His favourite motto was St. Ignatius's phrase, *agere contra:* Act against yourself. Into these two words there is condensed the essence of practical and delusion-proof holiness. Act, not merely think or feel; not against outer or imaginary enemies but against our lower selves. "How much is comprised in the little words *agere contra!* Therein is the real secret of sanctity, the hidden source from which the saints have drunk deep of the love of God and reached that height of glory they now enjoy." (Oct., 1905.)

Again he records his view of heroism, which always had an attraction for his chivalrous, impulsive, generous nature.

"Heroism," he says, "is a virtue which has an attraction for every heart. It seems to lift us out of our petty selves and make us for a moment forget our own selfish interests It appeals irresistibly to the noble-minded; to the cowardly even, it is a powerful stimulus. Thus it is that in all times the saints have ever had such an attraction for men they are heroes! In their secret hidden lives of prayer and penance men saw a heroism which was not the one sharp pang of a fearless deed, leaving their names to history as a nation's pride, but a nobler heroism of a life of countless noble deeds, unknown perhaps to man; by God alone were their secret victories seen." (Nov., 1905.)

A few months later he wrote out a short sermon on Heroism, taking as his text *St. John* x. n.: "The good shepherd giveth his life for his sheep."

"And you, (he cries), wives and bread-winners, have you no task within the fold, no little flock to tend and guard? Has not God committed to your care the innocent lambs, the little ones of your household? Within the pasture of your own family are you the good shepherd, or the thief and the hireling? ...Jesus does not ask from His shepherds now the shedding of their life-blood But He does ask from them a death more hard, more lingering, a life-long death of sacrifice for His flock, ...the daily crucifying of every evil passion, the stamping out of sloth, of anger, of drunkenness, the constant striving after the holiness of your state of life... Look upon the great Christ, the Good Shepherd, hanging on the Cross. He is our model, our hero. Gaze well upon His bleeding wounds, His mangled limbs, that sad agony-stricken face. Look well, and pray with generous heart that he may make you in word and deed heroes in His service." (April, 1906.)

The final phase of Fr. Doyle's life has been so often described as heroic by those who were well fitted to estimate heroic service in a human cause, that these few thoughts on heroism written many years before, must have for us not only a biographical interest, but an earnest impressiveness. They were not only written, they were lived.

A similar personal interest attaches to this little sketch of St. Francis Xavier's death.

"Xavier's hour has come, the hour of his eternal reward and never-ending bliss. In a little hut, open on all sides to the biting blast, the great Apostle lies dying. Far from home and all that makes this life pleasant, far from the quiet of his own religious house, alone upon this barren isle, our Saint will yield his soul to God. What joy fills his heart now at the thought of the sacrifices he has made, the honours he has despised, the pleasures left behind. Happy sufferings! Happy penances! He thinks of what his life might have been, the life of a gay worldling, and in gratitude he lifts his eyes to thank his God for the graces given him What matter now the hardships he has endured? All, all, are past, for now the sweet reward of heaven is inviting him to his eternal rest." (3 Dec., 1905.)

As we read of this death-scene of the great Jesuit apostle, unsheltered and unhelped, in his wind-swept hut on San-Cian, our thoughts inevitably pass to another Jesuit missioner's death-bed on the shell-swept ridge of Frezenberg Thus, too, he faced his eternal rest.

[1] Compare Bl. Margaret Mary's resolution written in her blood. - *Life* (Visitation Library, Roselands, Walmer, Kent, 1912), p. 42.
[2] Even as a boy he longed to be a martyr.
[3] *Epistolae* iii. 502. (*Monumenta Historica S.J.*)
[4] *Scripta de S. Ignatio* i. 278. As a matter of fact a Jesuit Scholastic nowadays has at least two and a-half hours of daily prayer.
[5] *Epistolae* vi. 91.
[6] A Jesuit is a "scholastic" during the whole formative period from his first to his final vows.
[7] E. Sequin, *Life of the Ven. Fr. Claude de la Colombière,* 1883, p. 33. The Curé of Ars, let us not forget, failed at his examination in theology. - *Life* by A. Monnin, Eng. trans. (Burns & Gates, n.d.), p. 35.

Chapter Three - Tertianship (1907-1908)

TWO years in the novitiate, seven years in the colleges, three years at philosophy, three years at theology it is a long professional course. But it is not yet completed. St. Ignatius did not consider the Jesuit fully formed until, in addition to the two years' noviceship, he has undergone a third year of probation, or a tertianship, as it is called. The long years of study and teaching have left their impress on the religious, especially if pursued with that thoroughness which the Founder inculcates. "Let them anxiously and constantly apply their minds to their studies; let them in their prayers frequently ask for the grace to advance in learning." So speak the Rules for Scholastics. And assuming this programme to have been carried out, St. Ignatius considered that his men needed a year in "the school of the heart" before they were fit to work in Christ's vineyard. The tertianship is the noviceship over again; once more the spiritual exercises are undertaken for an entire month. Yet there is a difference, for after years of study and discipline, the raw schoolboy has developed into a mature religious and has been ordained priest. The tertianship is the last training-period of a Jesuit, often it is his last chance of quiet leisure and spiritual reflection. Hence for many it is a turning-point in life; it sheds a new light on the past hurried years seen now in critical retrospect, it creates energy and reawakens ideals which permanently influence the future. So, at least, it was for Willie Doyle.

In October, 1907, he went to Tronchiennes, near Ghent, to make his tertianship. For business reasons his route to Belgium was through Pai is. This gave him the opportunity of making several excursions of devotion, some details of which survive in an account which he sent home. A kind friend had provided him with his fare second class to Paray-le-Monial, the home of Saint Margaret Mary. By travelling third class he was able to go to Lyons and thus visit Ars, to whose saintly Curé, Blessed John Vianney, he had a special devotion. At Paray the Jesuit Fathers were living Scattered in twos or threes about the town. He found his way to a poor little house where he was welcomed by an old, almost blind, French Jesuit who was just sitting down to supper when he arrived. "A lay brother put before me," he wrote, "what I thought was a rather large bowl of soup for one; but nothing daunted I was starting to demolish the lot when the brother whispered in alarm: Oh, mon père, c'est pour tous!" [1] Here at Paray Fr. Doyle had the happiness of saying Mass at the very altar where our Lord appeared so often to Saint Margaret Mary. In spite of missing a train, and after an adventurous journey on a very primitive steam-tram, he found himself in the spot hallowed by the Cure of Ars. Fr. Doyle insisted on seeing everything the room in which the saint died, the half-burnt curtains said to have been damaged by the devil, the little pan in which the holy man cooked the flour-lumps which he called cakes. He was allowed as a special privilege to sit in the Cure's confessional, and above all he was able to say Mass at his shrine, using the saint's chalice. Just above the altar reposed the Cure's body in a case of glass and gold. "It gave one a strange feeling," wrote Fr. Doyle, "to see the holy old man lying before one during Mass, calm and peaceful, with a heavenly smile on his face, just as he died fifty years ago." "I shall never forget my visit to Ars," he concluded; "I knew all about the Blessed Curé's life, so that each spot had an interest and charm for me."

After this Fr. Doyle spent two days in Lyons, saying Mass twice at the shrine of our Lady of Fourvières. Then back to Paris where during an interval of business he paid a visit to what was once the Jesuit house in the Rue de Sevres. "All the Fathers are gone," he wrote, "and now in each room of the huge house a family is living, for it has been let by the Government as a tenement house, whilst the beautiful church has been turned into a cinema hall. In another street where we had a large college, a stage has been erected on the very altar; and where people once heard Mass, they now listen to music-hall songs. A stirring contrast to this is the perpetual adoration at Montmartre bands of women pray all day and men watch at night." Fr. Doyle's little trip was soon over and he arrived in Tronchiennes a few days before the opening of the Long Retreat (the Spiritual Exercises for thirty days), which, with three "repose days" lasted from loth October till I3th November. Writing in December, Fr. Doyle thus refers to the retreat and the tertianship:

"I shall not try to describe the Long Retreat, as we call our thirty days' retreat. It is a wonderful time and leaves an impression on me such as no number of eight days' retreats could do. There is no doubt that it is a trying time, though I found it much easier than I expected. But the thought that this is the Great Retreat, the harvest time of graces helps one wonderfully. The thirty days' retreat is indeed a great privilege, yet the year we are given here is even a greater favour. St. Ignatius intended that, after devoting fifteen or sixteen years to acquiring all the knowledge possible, this year of tertianship should be devoted wholly to the study of perfection; hence practically the entire day is given to spiritual things. Are we not fortunate in having such an opportunity of doing something for our souls and acquiring a store of grace for the battle which is to come?"

Father Doyle was much helped by the Spiritual Father, Pere Adolphus Petit, (author of the well-known book, *Sacerdos rite instructus*), and he thus describes him in a letter:

"There is a wonderful little old priest here, named Fr. Petit, small in name and small in size he is about three feet high. He is eighty-five, but as active as a man of thirty, being constantly away giving retreats. I have tried several times to get down to the chapel at four o'clock in the morning before him, but he is always there when I come in. He is a dear saintly old man with wonderful faith and simplicity. In the middle of an exhortation in the chapel, he will turn round to the Tabernacle and say: 'Is not that true, my Jesus?' He is giving a retreat here this moment to a hundred and ten gentlemen."

It is from his tertianship to his death that Fr. Doyle's spiritual notes are most copious. He had evidently destroyed all his earlier manuscripts. Even those which now survive were destined for the flames. The writer left strict instructions that all his personal notes should be destroyed. It is only by disobeying the author's pious wishes an act which, now that he is beyond the temptations of earth, he will surety forgive that these self-revelations have been reverently rifled, in the hope that thus his good work for souls may be prolonged, and that though dead he may yet speak to us. Only let us remember that these intimate outpourings were written solely for God and himself. We are not reading an autobiography or a *journal intime* written for publication. We are privileged to see the real inner development of a saint, a hero in the making.

According to these notes the tertianship was a landmark in Fr Doyle's life. He went apart into a desert place to commune with his Master; his sojourn was to him a rebirth; he emerged reinvigorated and recreated; henceforth to him to live was Christ and to die was gain. It was especially in the Long Retreat his, notes on which will be presently given that the call to heroic perfection came to him clear and strong, concentrating into its intensity all the past yearnings of a lifetime. But indeed during the year (July 1907 to July 1908) he had altogether fifty-two days of retreat - eight days before ordination, thirty days in the long retreat, two triduums, and eight days more at the close of the tertianship. In January, 1908, he also gave a retreat (his first) to some fifty girls in a convent at Hamont, near Antwerp; and during the Lent of that year he gave missions in Aberdeen and Yarmouth. Altogether it was for him a wonderful year of grace and fervour.

This is how he reviewed the year during his retreat in July, 1908:

'I have finished the tertianship. Looking back on the past year, I see now in how many ways I could have spent this time more profitably, been more faithful to order of time, more exact, etc. At the same time I thank God from my heart that this year has been fruitful in grace, and, I feel, has worked a wonderful change in me. I feel a greater desire to do all I can to please God and to become holy; a greater attraction for prayer, more desire for mortification and increased facility in performing acts of self-denial. I know the work of my sanctification is only begun, the hard work and the real work remains to be done.

"This closing retreat of the tertianship has confirmed the resolution made during the Long Retreat to refuse God nothing, to strive might and main to make up for the past wasted years of my religious life by all the fervour arid earnestness I am capable of.

"The desire to be a saint has been growing in my heart all during this year, especially the last couple of months. God has given me this desire; He will not refuse the grace, if only I am faithful in the future. How good you have been to me, O my God, waiting so patiently for me to return to You! Help me now generously to do all You want me to do. Amen."

He then recorded a solemn resolution to shape the remainder of his life according to two great principles: (1) *Vince teipsum - Age contra* (Conquer thyself - Act against) (2) *Communia non communiter* (Common things uncommonly well.) These are indeed the leading ideas of that type of spirituality which we may call the Ignatian, so much has it been impressed on the Catholic world through the instrumentality of the Spiritual Exercises of the Spanish soldier-saint. He does not seek to prescribe with mechanical precision the free flight of the soul to God or the workings of the gratis-given graces of the Holy Spirit. Rather does he show how to conquer oneself and regulate one's life and to avoid coming to a determination through any inordinate affection." His object is to remove obstacles and, so to speak, to give God a chance. This he does by leading men to perform spiritual *exercises,* to become soul-athletes and soldiers of Christ, to undergo a sort of drill and discipline. St. Ignatius is intensely earnest and practical, he applies conscious determination to every detail. In his meditations such phrases as *id quod volo,* (what I wish), and *ut fructum aliquem capiam,* (that I may reap some fruit), are typical of his practical view of prayer as a consciously designed means to self-conquest. *"Vince teipsum,"* wrote Fr. Doyle in some notes of a retreat for, priests. "This is the secret of the Exercises. 'I learnt no other lesson from my master Ignatius,' said St. Francis Xavier, referring to his first retreat at Paris. Here we all fail good men, zealous men, holy men. Prayer is easy, works of zeal attractive; but going against self, till grace and perseverance give facility, is cruel work, a hard battle."

St. Ignatius, with the true instinct of a general, wishes us not merely to defend ourselves against sensuality and deordination, but to take the offensive (*agere contra*), if we wish to be distinguished (*insignes*) in the service of Christ. And once more with soldier-like precision, Ignatius plans the campaign. He will have no vague enthusiasm, no emotional generalities; he is always relentlessly methodical and detailed. *Vince teipsum* is not enough, he also adopts the policy of *divide et impera.* [2] He did not invent the Particular Examen, [3] which attacks sins or faults one by one or essays the conquest of virtues in single file; but he helped to make it a widespread practice of the spiritual life. St. Ignatius merely laid down the general rule of attempting one thing at a time and concentrating one's energy on an immediate objective. It is for each, under proper guidanca, to apply this maxim of spiritual tactics to his own character and circumstances. Intensified into a process of spiritual statistics such as Fr, Doyle adopted for his aspirations the Particular Examen would certainly be unsuitable to many souls. In all such delicate matters of spiritual psychology there are no rigid general rules.

Fr. Doyle's second maxim "common things not commonly" is adopted from St. John Berchmans, and is thoroughly characteristic of St. Ignatius's realism, and what may be called his idea of intensive culture rather than mere extension. "I will strive ever to perform each action as perfectly as possible," continues Fr. Doyle, "paying special attention to small duties, *e.g.,* saying grace, odd Hail Marys etc. It seems to me that God is asking this particularly from me, and by this means I am to find the chief road to sanctity." In appearance this resolution of minute fidelity is modest and easy; but in reality it constitutes a slow heroism of self-conquest, a martyrdom, whose pain is drawn out into a life-long succession of pin-pricks. Thus testified Père de la Colombière who made a similar resolution in his tertianship retreat: [4]

"It seems as if it would be easy to spend any other kind of life holily; and the more austere, solitary and obscure it might be and separated from all intercourse, the more pleasing it would appear to me to be. As to what usually terrifies nature, such as prisons, constant sickness and even death, all this seems easy compared with this everlasting war with self, this vigilance against the attacks of the world and of self-love, this living death in the midst of the world. When I think of this, I foresee that life will seem to be of prodigious length, and that death will never come soon enough."

This grim earnestness of minute and painstaking perfection, this concentration of enthusiasm into the narrow mould of daily duties and rules, is characteristic of the Jesuit type of holiness. Doubtless, in holiness, as in art or literature, there are types, and within those types there is scope for individuality. In our Father's house there are many mansions, and so too in the Church Militant there are diverse and even divergent, though not contradictory, types and schools of sanctity, coextensive with the myriad richness of the human mind. The catalogue of the saints includes King Louis, the Crusader, as well as Simeon Stylites, repeating litanies on his pillar, Joan of Arc, the warrior-maiden, the mystic Teresa of Jesus, the verminous beggar Benedict Joseph Labre. Is it not one of the marks of the Church that within the unity of the faith she not only tolerates but fosters variety and diversity? There are many religious orders each with its own speciality and characteristic, many rites and ceremonies, a richness of liturgy, a multitude of devotions; there is room for everyone with tolerance and charity. It has, however, been sometimes said that the spirituality of St. Ignatius is a cast-iron system, repressive of emotions and cramping individuality. But this is merely a second-hand perversion, a criticism based on texts rather than on living men. The Spiritual Exercises, which have been aptly termed a soldier's pocket-book, cannot be understood apart from the living voice of the master and the spiritual experience of the exercitant. In his preliminary annotations St. Ignatius instructs the director to "allow the Creator to act immediately with the creature and the creature with its Creator and Lord"; and again, he insists that the exercises "ought to be suited to the disposition of those who wish to make them." Within the ambit of certain general principles, each soul must pursue its own individual path.

There is a saying attributed to St. Ignatius which ought not to be forgotten: "It is very dangerous to try to force all to reach perfection by the same road; such a one does not understand how manifold are the gifts of the Holy Spirit." [5] It is not due to St. Ignatius, but to some of his interpreters, that the flexibility of the Exercises, for instance in the modes of meditation and prayer, has not always been realised. Sometimes, too, those who write for the beginners in the art of prayer think it necessary to enter into a rather disconcerting apparatus of rules and details. In the last analysis these expedients are all means to the end, which is converse with God. The Directory of the Exercises, com" posed by order of Fr. Claudius Aquaviva, after explaining the methods proposed by St. Ignatius, adds: [6]

"It must not be thought that thereby are excluded other methods which the Holy Spirit teaches and which men, exercised in the spiritual life, adopt according to experience, reason and sound doctrine, or which each one discovers by practice to be useful for his spiritual progress. This also applies to Ours, always with the approval or consent of the superior or spiritual director, to whom each one should manifest his method of prayer, all the more so if in any way it departs from the ordinary."

Such reasonable liberty is perfectly compatible with the general utility of certain helps, expedients, and devices for helping weak human nature in the spiritual combat. We must neither slavishly imitate each practice or particularity of every or any saint; nor yet must we be so deluded with a sense of our own self-sufficiency, as to reject summarily those methods and practices which have been adopted and recommended by many masters of the spiritual life.

These considerations will not be irrelevant when we come to read Fr. Doyle's diary and retreat-notes. As we begin with his Long Retreat, it may be useful to add here by way of preface a few general ideas about the scope of the Exercises. According to St. Ignatius, "the name of spiritual exercises is applied to any method of preparing and disposing the soul to free itself from all inordinate affections, and after it has freed itself from them, to seek and find the will of God concerning the ordering of life for the salvation of one's soul." [7] Thus a retreat is designed for earnest souls only in a very attenuated form can the Exercises be adapted to a mission for sinners; and it has a definite object to find God's will. At the beginning St. Ignatius lays down the "first principle and foundation" which must be admitted at the outset. It is the basis of all valuation of life: Man was made for God, all other things for man to bring him to God. Thus the exercitant accepts in advance and in general the practical consequences which logically follow from this acceptance of the Creator's sovereign rights. Then for a whole week he must seek to eliminate all sin and disorder and to examine his soul. In the second week the exercitant is brought face to face with Jesus Christ. Will he follow the invitation and enlist in the King's service? He must count up the cost, he must study Christ's standard, he must at least aspire to the highest and noblest service. Then comes the great choice, which St. Ignatius calls "the election," and which is the culminating point of the Exercises.

In ordinary retreats, of course, there is no great decisive choice to be made, [8] but there is always some "reformation of life," some re-ordering of one's life in the light of the great spiritual truths and scenes which have been marshalled before the soul. God's will is known and accepted. One more week is spent in meditating on the Passion, and a fourth and last is devoted to the contemplation of the Risen Master, in order to habituate the soul to pure love and to strengthen the resolutions taken. Such, in brief essentials, are the Exercises through which in then: entirety each Jesuit passes twice in his life, once as a novice at the outset of his spiritual life, and finally as a priest at the outset of his ministry. The following chapter contains the diary which for his own guidance Fr. Doyle kept during his second and last Long Retreat.

[1] "Oh, Father, that's for *all* of you!"
[2] Divide and conquer.
[3] Even the pagan Sextius practised a daily examination of conscience (Seneca, *De ira* iii. 36, i). Cassian (*Collationes* v. 14) advocated the Particular Examen. (The word 'examen' is hardly English, but it has become so customary in Catholic devotional literature that it would be pedantic to avoid it.) Benjamin Franklin (who presumably never read the Spiritual Exercises) practised this method and kept a graphical record of particular faults. - *Autobiography* ch. 6, ed. Hutchinson & Co., 1903, p. 97.
[4] *Lights in Prayer* (Quarterly Series), p. 140.

[5] *Selectae S. Patris nostri Ignatii Sententiae,* 8. So also St. Francis Borgia P. Suau, *Histoire de S. F. de Borgia,* p. 393.
[6] *Directorium* 37. 13.
[7] *Annotations,* S. i. Reference will in future be made to the convenient English' translation of *The Text of the Spiritual Exercises of St. Ignatius,* London, Burns & Dates, 1913. See also *The Spiritual Exercises of St. Ignatius Loyola, Spanish and English, with a continuous Commentary,* by Joseph Rickaby, S.J., 1915.
[8] In his Long Retreat Fr. Doyle made his election to volunteer for the toreign mission. See p. 53.

Chapter Four - Diary of Long Retreat

[1]
Tronchiennes, 10th October, 1907.

I BEGIN the Long Retreat this evening with very varied feelings. I feel a great desire and determination to make this retreat as I have never made one before, for I know this is the turning point in my life I can never be the same again. I want to be generous with God and to refuse Him nothing. I do not want to say, "I will go just so far and no farther." Hence I feel my cowardly and weak nature dreading this retreat, for I feel our Lord is going to ask some big sacrifice from me, that He expects much from me. He has been tugging at my heart for so many years, urging me in so many ways to give myself wholly to Him, to give all and refuse Him nothing. I dread lest now I shall again refuse Him perhaps it is the last time He will ask me to do what He wants. My loving Jesus, I will, I will be generous with You now at last. But You must aid me, it must be Your work, I am so cowardly. Make me see clearly Your holy will. *Domine, quid me vis facere?* [2]

[THE FOUNDATION.]

[3]
God had some special end in creating me, some particular part in His great plan. I was not created as it were one of a great number who came into the world on the same day; but God had a particular object in giving me life. Why did He create me?

How miserable has been my service of God since I entered religion! A bit fervent one day, the next dissipated and careless, even since my ordination. I have fallen away from the fervent way in which I had resolved to live henceforth. I feel inclined to despond; but with God's help I will go on, trying now at last to make some little progress in serving Him worthily. My true service of God consists in performing the ordinary actions of the day as perfectly and as fervently as I can, with a pure intention for love of my Jesus. It is a mistake to think that I can only serve Him by preaching, saving souls, etc. What would have become of me if I had treated an earthly master as I have served God?

To be indifferent does not mean to desire things which are hard to nature, but a readiness and determination to embrace them when once the will of

God is known. In this sense I think I am indifferent about going to the Congo. But I must force myself to be willing to accept the way of life which God seems to be leading me to and wants me to adopt. My God, I dread it but "not my will but Thine."

God has a perfect right to ask from me what He wills; I am His servant. How then can I be free to do or not whatever He may ask?

I close the *Fundamentum* with feelings of humility and sorrow at the thought of my past service of God. How little reverence! Thank God, I have still time to make up for it. One thing alone can repair the lost years a life of great fervour.

FIRST WEEK.

[SIN.]

I can say with all truth that only for the great mercy of God I should now have been in hell. I deserved it for my years of tepidity in Clongowes. Never did the good God show His goodness to me more than in saving me from grievous sin. I have here a second motive of gratitude to urge me to do all He wants.

The meditation on the barren fig-tree (*S. Luke* 13.) recalled to my mind this gospel which I read in the Mass at Paray-e-Monial. For sixteen years has Jesus been seeking fruit from my soul, and especially in these last three years of preparation for the priesthood. I have no excuse for He has told me how to produce that fruit, especially by the exact discharge of each little duty of the moment. "Spare it for this year," Never shall I have this opportunity again of becoming holy; and if now I do not "dig round" this unfruitful tree so that it bear much fruit, Jesus will surely "cut it down" by withdrawing His graces and *loving invitations.*

Truly I have ever been in the community "a running sore" of harm and evil example. My Jesus, can I ever make amends for all the harm I have done? Help me from this instant to try and do so by my fervent earnest life. Help me to become thoroughly changed and to do all You want of me.

This thought came to me. If Jesus wants me to go to the Congo. I shall do more for souls there than by remaining at home. Besides, my sacrifice will obtain grace for others to do more good than I ever could.

"Because you have sinned, cursed be the earth in your work." (*Genesis* 3. 17.) I see here the reason why my work for, souls must be unfruitful God will never bless it while I have an affection for sin or lead a careless life.

[HELL.]

I can imagine I am a soul in hell, and God in His mercy is saying to me, "Return to the world for this year and on your manner of life during the year will depend your returning to hell or not." What a life I should lead! How little I should think of suffering, of mortification! How I would rejoice in suffering!

How perfectly each moment would be spent! If God treated me as I deserved, I should be in hell now. Shall I ever again have cause for grumbling or complaining, no matter what may happen? My habit of constantly speaking uncharitably of others, and, in general, faults of the tongue, seem to me the chief reason why I derive so little fruit from my Mass and spiritual duties. Nothing dries up the fountains of grace so much as an affection for sin.

[DEATH.]

Death is the end of all things here, the end of time, of merit, of pain and mortification, of a hard life. It is the commencement of an eternal life of happiness and joy. "God will wipe away all tears from their eyes." (*Apoc.* 21, 4.) In this light, life is short indeed and penance sweet. I thought if I knew I had only one year to live, how fervently I would spend it, how each moment would be utilised. Yet I know well I may not live a week more - do I really believe this?

[JUDGEMENT.]

Oct. 16th. Meditating on the Particular Judgement, God gave me great light. I realised that I should have to give an exact account of every action of my life and for every instant of time. To take only my seventeen years of religious life, what account could I give of the 6,000 hours of meditation, 7,000 Masses, 12,000 examinations of conscience, etc.? Then my time - how have I spent every moment? I resolved not to let a day more pass without seriously trying to reform my life in the manner in which I perform my ordinary daily duties. For years I have been "going to begin," and from time to time made some slight efforts at improvement. But now, dear Jesus, let this change be the work of Thy right hand.

To perform each action well I will try and do them: (*a*) with a pure intention often renewed, (*b*) *attente* earnestly, punctually exactly, (*c*) *devote* with great fervour.

How little I think of committing venial sin, and how soon I forget I have done so! Yet God hates nothing more than even the shadow of sin, nothing does more harm to my spiritual progress and hinders any real advance in holiness. My God, give me an intense hatred and dread and horror of the smallest sin. I want to please You and love You and serve You as I have never done before. Let me begin by stamping out all sin in my soul.

We could not take pleasure in living in the company of one whose body is one running, festering sore; neither can God draw us close to Himself, caress and love us, if our souls are covered with venial sin, more loathsome and horrible in His eyes than the most foul disease. To avoid mortal 3in I must carefully guard against deliberate venial sin, so to avoid venial sin I must fly from the shadow of imperfection in my actions. How often in the past have I done things when I did not know if they were sins or only deliberate imperfections and how little I cared, my God!

[THE PRODIGAL SON.]

[4]

One of the obstacles to my leading a fervent life is the thought of what others may think. I would often wish to do some act of mortification, but I am prevented because I know others will see it. Again, I desire to keep certain rules which I have often broken (*e.g.* Latin conversation), but a false shame, a fear of what others may say, stops me. [5] I know this is a foolish, mean and small spirit; but it is alas! too true in my case. I must pray to overcome it and make some generous acts against this false shame and pride.

For fifteen years has Jesus been waiting for me to return to Him, to return to the fervour of my first year of religious life. During that time how many pressing and loving invitations has He not given me? What lights and inspirations, remorse of conscience, and how many good resolves which were never carried into effect. O my God, I feel now as if I cannot resist You longer. Your infinite patience and desire to bring me to You has broken the ice of my cold heart "I will arise and go" to You, humbled and sorrowful, and for the rest of my life give You of my very best. Help me, sweet Jesus, by Your grace, for I am weak and cowardly.

FRUIT OF FIRST WEEK.

I realise in a way I never did before that God created me for His service, that He has a strict right that I should serve Him perfectly, and that every moment of my life is His and given to me for the one end of praising and serving Him. I recalled with horror how often I have wandered from this my end, what an appalling amount of time I have wasted, and how few of my actions were done for God, or worthy of being offered to Him. I see what I should have been and what I am. But the thought of Jesus waiting and eagerly looking out for me, the prodigal, during fifteen years, has filled me with hope and confidence and new resolve to turn to my dearest Jesus and give Him all He asks.

I have begun to try to perform each little action with great fervour and exactness, having as my aim to get back the fervour of my first year's novi010ate.

Domine, quid me vis facere? [6] I am ready to do Your will, no matter how hard it may seem to me.

17 October, 1907. Amen.

SECOND WEEK.

18 Oct., 1907.

[ON THE KINGDOM OF CHRIST.]

I seemed at prayer to hear Jesus asking me if I were willing to do all He would ask of me. I feel much less fear than in the first week, of what this may be, and greater courage and desire even for sacrifices.

This thought came to me: I am not to take the lives of others in the house as the standard of my own, what may be lawful for them is not for me; their life is most pleasing to God, such a life for me would not be so; God wants something higher, nobler, 'more generous from me, and for this will offer me special graces.

Meditating on the Kingdom of Christ, the thought suddenly came to me to make this offering: *O aeterne Domine...dummodo sit maius servitium Tuum et laus Tua...et si Maiestas Tua sanctissima voluerit me eligere ac recipere ad talem vitam et statum, me Tibi offero pro Missione Congolensi. Fiat voluntas Tua. Amen.* [7]

I feel that I could go through fire and water to serve such a man as Napoleon, that no sacrifice he could ask would be too hard. What would the army think of me if Napoleon said, "I want you to do so and so," and I replied, "But, your Majesty, I am very sensitive to cold, I want to have a sleep in the afternoon, to rest when I am tired, and I really could not do without plenty of good things to eat!" would I not deserve to have my uniform torn from me and be driven from the army, not even allowed to serve in the ranks? How do I serve Jesus my King? What kind of service? generous or making conditions? in easy things but not in hard ones? What have I done for Jesus? What .am I doing for Jesus? What shall I do for Jesus?

[THE NATIVITY.]

What impressed me most in the meditation on the Nativity was the thought that Jesus could have been born in wealth and luxury, or at least with the ordinary comforts of life, but He chose all that was hard, unpleasant and uncomfortable. This He did for me, to show me the life I must lead for Him, If I want to be with Christ, I must lead the life of Christ, and in that life there was little of what was pleasing to nature. I think I have been following Christ, yet how pleasant and comfortable my life has always been ever avoiding cold, hunger, hard work, disagreeable things, humiliations, etc. My Jesus, You are speaking to my heart now. I cannot mistake Your voice or hide from myself what You want from me and what my future life should be. Help me for I am weak and cowardly.

By entering religion and taking my vows I have given myself over absolutely to God and His service. He, therefore, has a right to be served in the way He wishes. If then He asks me to enter on a hard, mortified life and spend myself working for Him, how can I resist His will and desire? "Oh my God, make me a saint, and I consent to surfer all You ask for the rest of my life." What is God asking' from me now? Shall I go back on that offering?

[THE FLIGHT INTO EGYPT.]

Great as was the poverty of Jesus in the cave at Bethlehem, it was nothing compared to His destitution during the Flight into Egypt. Again this was voluntary and chosen and borne *propter me* (for my sake).

I contrast the obedience of St. Joseph with my obedience. His so prompt, unquestioning, uncomplaining, perfect; mine given so grudgingly, perhaps exterior, but not interior conformity with the will of the Superior. I realise my faults in this matter, and for the future will try to practise the most perfect obedience, even and especially in little things. "The obedient man will speak of victory." (*Proverbs* 21, 28.)

[THE HIDDEN LIFE.]

During the reflection on the Hidden Life I got a light that here was something in which I could easily imitate our Lord and make my life resemble His. I felt a strong impulse to resolve to take up as one of the chief objects of my life the exact and thorough performance of each duty, trying to do it as Jesus would have done, with the same pure intention, exquisite exactness and fervour. To copy in all my actions walking, eating, praying Jesus, my model in the little house of Nazareth. This light was sudden, clear and strong. To do this perfectly will require constant, unflagging fervour. Will not this be part of my "hard life"?

I should examine all my actions, taking Jesus as my model and example. What a vast difference between my prayer and His; between my use of time, my way of speaking, walking, dealing with others, etc., and that of the child Jesus! If I could only keep Him before my eyes always, my life would be far different from what it has been.

Each fresh meditation on the life of our Lord impresses on me more and more the necessity of conforming my life to His in every detail, if I wish to please Him and become holy. To do something great and heroic may never come, but I can make my life heroic by faithfully and daily putting my best effort into each duty as it comes round. It seems to. me I have failed to keep my resolutions because I have not acted from the motive of the love of God. Mortification, prayer, hard work, become sweet when done for the love of Jesus.

[THE TWO STANDARDS.]

My victory over myself, my inclinations, is a victory won for the cause of Jesus. I have been a deserter to the camp of Satan, a traitor; but now my King has pardoned me and received me back. How am I going to show my gratitude and make up for the past which I cannot recall the time lost, duties omitted or done without love or fervour, little sacrifices refused, my many, many sins? Shall I not be busy at every hour, fighting for my King, gaming victory after victory over the enemy, over myself? My Jesus, help me now to work for You, to slave for You, to fight for You and then *to die* for You!

[THE THREE CLASSES OF MEN.]

It is easy for me to test my love for Jesus. Do I love what He loved and came down from heaven to find suffering, humiliation, contempt, want of all things, inconveniences, hunger, weariness, cold? The more I seek for and embrace these things, the nearer am I drawing to Jesus and the deeper is my love for Him. While praying for light to know what God wants from me in the matter of mortifying my appetite, a voice seemed to say: "There are other things besides food in which you can be generous with Me, other *hard things* which I want you to do." I thought of all the secret self-denial contained in constant hard work, not giving up when a bit tired, not yielding to desire for sleep, not running off to bed if a bit unwell, bearing little sufferings without relief, cold and heat without complaint, and, above all, the constant never-ending mortification to do each action *perfectly.* This light has given me a good deal of consolation, for I see I can do much for Jesus that is hard without being singular or departing from common life.

It seems to me that Jesus is asking from me a life in which I am to make war upon "comfortableness" as far as possible, a life without comfort, even that which is allowed by the rule.

The example of men of the Third Class in the world should shame me. What determination, what prolonged effort, what deadly earnestness, in the man who has determined to succeed in his profession! No sacrifice is too great for him, he wants to succeed, he will succeed. My desire, so far, to be a saint is only the desire of the man of the First Class. It gratifies my pride, but I make no real progress in perfection I do not really *will* it.

The love of Jesus makes the impossible easy and sweet.

[THE THREE DEGREES OF HUMILITY.]

I have now reached the great meditation, the crucial point of the retreat. God has been very good to me in enlightening my mind to see His will and in filling my heart with a most ardent desire to do it cost what it may. Jesus, dear Jesus, I want to please You, to do exactly what You want of me, to give all generously this time without any reserve, and never to go back on my resolution. In this spirit I made the midnight meditation on October 25th, the Feast of B. Margaret Mary. I saw clearly what I knew years ago but would not admit: that God is asking from me the practice of the Third Degree [8] in all its perfection as far as I am capable. I cannot deny it or shut my eyes to this truth any longer. Should I not be grateful to the good God for choosing me for such a life, since it will be all the work of His grace and not my own doing? God wants me to put perfection - sanctity - before me and to "go straight" for that, for holiness. He wants me not to be content with the ordinary good life of the average religious, but to aim at something higher, nobler, more worthy of Him. He wants me to make ceaseless war on myself, my passions, inclinations, habits; to smash and break down my own will, to mortify it in all things so that it may be free for His grace to act upon; in a word, to aim at the perfection of the Third Degree and all that that means, not for one day or month or a year, but for the rest of my life, faithfully, unceasingly, constantly, *without rest* or *intermission*. To do this I must strive to cut away all comfort in my life, choose that which is "hard," go against my natural inclination, and give up the easy self-indulgent life I have hitherto led. The motive for this is the immense, deep, real love of the Heart of Jesus for *me*, His example which He wants me to follow, for He chose want of all things, suffering and a hard comfortless life, and by doing the same I imitate Him and become more and more like to Him. Can I do this for five, ten, twenty years lead a crucified life so long? Jesus does not ask that, but only that I do so for *this day* so quickly passed and with it the recollection of the little suffering and mortifications endured once over, all is over, but the eternal reward remains.

My Jesus, I feel that at last You have conquered, Your love has conquered; and last night, kneeling before the image of Your Sacred Heart, I promised You to begin this new life, to begin at last to serve You as You urged me to do during the past sixteen years. I made my promise, knowing well my weakness, but trusting in Your all-powerful grace to do what seems almost impossible to my cowardly nature. *Ego dixi: nunc coepi.* [9] I promise You, sweet Jesus, to serve You perfectly with all the fervour of my soul, aiming at the Third Degree in its perfection. I make this offering through the hands of B. Margaret Mary. Amen.

Tronchiennes, Oct. 25th, 1907.
Feast of B. Margaret Mary.

What account shall I give of this resolution when I stand before my God for judgement?

PRACTICE OF THE THIRD DEGREE.

I. *Accepto.* I will receive with joy all unpleasant things which I must bear: (*a*) pain, sickness, heat, cold, food; (*b*) house, employment, rules, customs; (*c*) trials of religious life, companions; (*d*) reprimands, humiliations; (*e*) anything which is a cross.

II. *Volo et Desidero.* I will wish and desire that these things may happen to me, that so I may resemble my Jesus more.

III. *Eligo.* With all my might I will strive every day *agere contra in omnibus* [10] (*a*) against my faults; (*b*) against my own will; (*c*) against my ease and comfort; (*d*) against the desires of the body; (*e*) against my habit and inclination of performing my duties negligently and without fervour.

Finis

The reformation of one's life must be the work of every day. I should take each rule and duty, think how Jesus acted, or would have done, and contrast my conduct with His.

I think it better not to make any definite resolutions about mortification, such as "I will never do so-and-so." I know how such resolutions have fared But I am determined to keep up a constant war against myself, now in one matter and now in another, varying the kinds of mortification as much as possible, but trying to do ten little acts each day.

We have a strict right to the love of God, because our vocation is to follow Him; we cannot do this unless we love Him. Jesus will assuredly give me a sensible love of Him, if I only *ask.* I must ask, seek, and knock daily and hourly.

Fr. Petit told me that the spirit of the Third Degree is not so much the practice of austerities as the denial of one's will and judgement and perfect abnegation of self and humility. This is the spirit of our rules which are simply the Third Degree.

Have I a real hunger and thirst for the love and the service of Jesus? Is it growing?

If I do not begin to serve God as I ought now, when shall I do so? shall I ever? This retreat is a time of special grace, and if my cooperation is wanting, Jesus may pass by and not return. The devil has made me put off my thorough conversion to God for seventeen years, making me content myself with the resolution of "later on really beginning in earnest and becoming a saint." What might not have been done in that time!

The reason, said Fr Petit, why we find our life so hard, mortification difficult, and why we are inclined to avoid all that we dislike, is because we have *no real love for Jesus.*

The Gospel says, *Erat autem diebus docens in Templo.* [11] How often, and for how long, am I in the chapel? Is the chapel the place where people know I am to be found? What a difference it would make in my visits, if only I realised the real corporal presence of Jesus in the Tabernacle. This is a grace I must earnesly ask for.

Erat pernoctans in oratione Dei. [12] I say I am anxious to imitate the life of Jesus, here is something in which I can do so, Would it not be possible (afterwards) to spend an hour at night in the chapel after examen?

FRUIT OF THE SECOND WEEK.

A great desire to know our Lord better, His attractive character, His personal love for me, the resolve to read the life of Christ and study the Gospels.

I feel also a longing to love Jesus passionately, to try my very best to please Him, and to do all I think will please Him. I see nothing will be dearer to Him than my sanctification, chiefly attained by the perfection with which I perform even the smallest action. "All for love of Jesus."

1 Nov., 1907.

THE ELECTION

REASONS AGAINST

(1) I am not certain of the will of God.
(2) I should like to remain for some years in Ireland and work for souls.

(3) Should I not do more good by remaining in Ireland instead of burying myself among a few blacks whose language I do not know?

(4) I may have a long useful life at home; on the mission probably a very short one.

REASONS FOR.

(1) The almost certain conviction that I have a real vocation for the foreign mission.

(2) This thought has been in my mind for over twenty years and the thought of it has given me great pleasure and consolation.

(3) My desire, even as a boy, to be a martyr.

(4) The letter I wrote as a novice. [13]

(5) The feeling that, if I do not offer myself, I certainly shall not please God.

(6) The attraction I feel for a life of real privation and suffering.

(7) This is much stronger since the retreat, in order to be more like Jesus.

(8) In the spirit of the Third Degree I should make this sacrifice.

. (9) The hardship of the life, a great help to holiness.

(10) The attraction the life of St. Peter Claver has always had for me, my desire to imitate him.

(n) The souls I shall be able to save, and who otherwise would never see heaven.

(12) As an English-speaking priest I may be of help to the missionaries.

(13) I feel quite content that I was doing God's will when I resolved two years ago to offer myself for the foreign mission.

A. M. D. G.
MY ELECTION.

To-day the First Friday of November, the Feast of All Saints, I made my election about offering myself for the Congo Mission. During the retreat I have been praying and thinking over this, asking for light to know God's holy will which alone I seek. The reasons for offering myself are overwhelming, but one thought troubled and upset me I see in this that it came from the evil one. "By remaining in Ireland and working zealously for many years could I not do far more for God's glory than by going on the mission where almost certainly I shall not live long?"

(1) I got light to see that this was only a delusion of self-love, seeking, under pretext of good, a life gratifying to human nature and my pride.

(2) Would this life be pleasing to God, if He wanted me to work for Him among the negroes?

(3) God is able to open up a vast field for my zeal if He wishes it, no matter where I may be.

(4) What I lose by rejecting the glorious opportunity of the foreign mission to become like to Jesus, the help to sanctity, the *possibility of martyrdom*.

(5) Lastly I simply felt I was powerless to refuse Jesus this sacrifice which He has been asking for over twenty years. I could not refuse and live and die in peace. How after such clear lights and inspirations could I face Jesus at my judgement, knowing I did not do what He wanted?

During Benediction I resolved to confirm the resolution already made at Milltown: to offer my life for the Congo mission. In doing so I choose nothing myself but place myself without reserve in the hands of my Superiors that they may declare God's holy will to me. An interior voice seemed to say, "You will never regret this resolution and offering."

I offered my resolution to the Most Sacred Heart of Jesus, praying Him to accept me for this life. Since then my soul has been filled with joy and consolation. I am quite happy and content, for I feel God has given me grace to do *what He wants.*

Feast of All Saints, 1907

THIRD WEEK.

2 Nov., 1907.

I was greatly struck and helped yesterday by these words of the "Imitation": *Fili, sine me tecum agere quod volo ego scio quid expediat tibi.* [14] They gave me courage to place myself without reserve in God's hands. How happy I feel now that I have done so and made my sacrifice.

[THE PASSION.]

All my life my study has been to avoid suffering as much as possible, to make my life a comfortable one. How unlike my Jesus I have been, who sought to suffer on every occasion for me, for me. I should be glad when pain comes and welcome it, because it makes me more like Jesus.

During His Passion our Lord was bound and dragged from place to place. I have hourly opportunities of imitating Him by going cheerfully to the duty of the moment recreation when I want to be quiet, a walk when I would rather stay in my room, some unpleasant duty I did not expect, a call of charity which means great inconvenience for myself.

My denial of Jesus has been baser than that of Peter, for I have refused to listen to His voice calling me back for fifteen years. But Jesus has won my heart in this retreat by His patient look of love. God grant my repentance may in some degree be like St. Peter's. I could indeed weep bitterly for the wasted sinful past in the Society, the time I have squandered, the little good done, and the awful amount of harm by my bad example in every house in which I have been. What might I not have done for Jesus! What a saint I might have been now! Dear Jesus, You forgave St. Peter, forgive me also for I *will* serve You now.

At the community Mass this morning *I again felt an overpowering desire to become a saint.* It came suddenly filling my soul with consolation. Surely God has an object in inspiring me so often with this desire and has great graces for me if I will only cooperate with Him.

Reflecting on this inspiration afterwards, I saw more clearly that the chief thing God wants from me at present is an extraordinary and exquisite perfection in every little thing I do, even the odd Hail Marys of the day; that each day there must be some improvement in the fervour, the purity of intention, the exactness with which I do things, that in this will chiefly lie my sanctification as it sanctified St. John Berchmans. I see here a vast field for work and an endless service of mortification. To keep faithfully to this resolve will require heroism, so that day after day I may not flag in the fervour of my service of the good God.

The fruit of the Third Week, says Fr. Petit, is great compassion and increase of fortitude. To "suffer with" Jesus, to long for sufferings, must be my aim and prayer. Since my "Promise" I have been doing ten acts of self-denial why not try to make it thirty a day? I have so much to atone for, so much time wasted in the past, so little of life left. Ceaseless war on your comfort, no rest now, eternity is long enough.

[THE SCOURGING.]

During all these long years Jesus has been standing bound at the pillar, while I have cruelly scourged Him by my ingratitude and neglect of my vocation. Each action carelessly done, the hours spent in sleep, each moment wasted, have been so many stripes on my Saviour's bleeding body. He has been bearing all this to save me from His Father's just anger. And all the while I have heard His gentle voice, "My child, will you not love Me? I want your heart. I want you to strive and become a saint, to be generous with Me and refuse Me nothing." *Can* I now turn away again as before and refuse to listen?

With Jesus naked and shivering with bitter cold at the pillar, I will try joyfully to bear the effects of cold. With Jesus covered with wounds, I, too, will try to endure little sufferings without relief.

[CALVARY.]

The greatest thirst of Jesus on the Cross was his thirst for souls. He saw then the graces and inspirations He would give me to save souls for Him. In what way shall I correspond and console my Saviour?

The thought has been very much in my mind during this week that Jesus asks from me the sacrifice of all the pleasures of the world - such as villa, [15] plays, concerts, football-matches, cinematograph, etc.; that I am to seek my recreation and find my pleasure in Him alone. Life is indeed too short now for me to waste a moment in such things. May God give me a great disgust for all these things in which formerly I took such delight!

This morning I had a great struggle not to sleep. Then God rewarded me with much light and generous resolve. I was meditating on my desire to die a martyr's death for Jesus, and then asked myself if I was really in earnest, why did I not begin to die to myself, to die to my own will, the inclinations and desires of my lower nature. I wish to die a martyr's death but am I willing to live a martyr's life? To live a crucified life 'seeking in all things my constant mortification'? [16]

A COMPACT WITH JESUS

"My God, I promise You, kneeling before the image of Your Sacred Heart, that I will do my best to lead a martyr's life by constantly denying my will and doing all that I think will please You, if You in return will grant me the grace of martyrdom."

A life of martyrdom is to be the price of a martyr's crown

FRUIT OF THE THIRD WEEK.

The thought that Jesus has suffered so much for me to atone for my sins and past careless life in religion, has filled me with a great desire to love Him in return with all my heart, I feel, too, a growing hunger and thirst for suffering and mortification, because it makes me more like to my suffering Jesus, suffering all with joy for me.

Every day has deepened my shame, sorrow and hatred for my negligent tepid life since I entered the Society, and strengthened my resolve and desire to make amends by a life of great fervour. I feel my past sinful life will be a spur for me to aim at great holiness.

FOURTH WEEK.

10 Nov., 1907.

The reason I find it so hard to love God, why I have so little affection for Him, is because of my attachment to venial sin and my constant deliberate imperfections. I have, as it were, been trying to run with an immense weight round my feet; I have tried to reach the unitive way without passing through the purgative, to jump to the top of the ladder without climbing up the steps; so that after all these years I am still as barren of real love of God as when first I entered religion. No, I must work earnestly now to remove the very shadow of sin from my life, then to imitate the humble suffering life of Jesus and thus win His love.

I look upon it as a great grace that in spite of my tepid life Jesus has given me an ardent desire to love Him. I long eagerly to love my Jesus passionately, with an intense ardent love such as the saints had; and yet I remain cold and indifferent with little zeal for His glory.

[EMMAUS.]

From the Tabernacle Jesus seems to say, "Stay with Me for it is towards evening and the day is now far spent" [17] This should urge me to come to visit Him often.

If my resurrection is a real one and is to produce fruit, it must be external, so that all may see I am not the same man, that my life is changed in Christ.

[APPARITION BY THE LAKESIDE.]

Lord, You know I love You less than any others, but I long and desire to love You more than all the rest. Take my heart, dear Lord, and hide it in Your own, that so I may only love what You love and desire what You desire. May

I find no pleasure in the things of this world, its pleasures and amusement; but may my one delight be in thinking of You, working for You, loving You, and staying in Your sweet presence before the Tabernacle. Why do You want my love, dear Jesus, and why have You left me no rest all these years till I gave You at last my poor heart to love You, and You alone? This ceaseless pleading for my love fills me with hope and confidence that, sinful as my life has been in the past, You have forgiven and forgotten it all. Thanks a million times, dearest Jesus, for all Your goodness. I *will* love and serve You now till death,

13 Nov., 1907. [18] Amen.

REFLECTIONS ON THE RETREAT.

At the close of the retreat my soul is full of many emotions. God has been more than good to me, has given me great lights and wonderful graces. During the whole month my eyes have been opening more and more to the disorder of my past life. I have been simply amazed and astounded how I could possibly have lived the life I did, especially my years in college, such abuse of grace, such awful waste of time, neglect of opportunities of learning, of becoming holy, and above all the harm this careless tepid life has done others. I have realised how little I thought about committing sin and; far less, of deliberate breaches of rule. Now, through God's great mercy, I feel an intense hatred of such a life, and as if it would be impossible ever again to live so. I feel that indeed the retreat has worked a marvellous change in me. I feel I am not the same in my views, sentiments, and way of looking at things, that I am a different man. I have never felt as I do now after any other retreat before. God must indeed have poured His grace abundantly into my soul, for it seems to me that a deep lasting impression has been made, which I trust will ever remain. My soul is in great peace. I feel as if at last I have given God all He wanted from me during so many years by making the resolutions which I have made; that I could now die content, for at last I have really begun to try and serve the good God with all my heart. I feel also a great longing to love Jesus very, very much, to draw very close to His Sacred Heart, and to be ever united to Him, always thinking of Him and praying. I long ardently to do something now to make up for my neglect in the past to give myself heart and soul to the service of God, to toil for Him, to wear myself out for Him. I wish to be able never to seek rest or amusement outside of what obedience imposes, so that every moment may be spent for Jesus. I have not a moment to lose, I cannot afford to refuse Him a single sacrifice if I wish to do anything for Jesus and become a saint before I die. If I go to the Congo, I certainly shall not live long. In any case can I promise myself even one day more? *Finis venit.* [19] I must try to look upon this day as my last on earth and do all I can and suffer all I can for these few hours. It is not a question of keeping up full steam for years, but only for to-day.

If I am faithful to the resolution of "doing all things perfectly," I shall effectually cut away the numerous faults in all my actions. By working hard at the Third Degree I shall best correct those things to which my attention has been drawn. I know all this is going to cost me much, that I shall have a fierce battle to fight with the devil and myself. But I begin with great hope and confidence, for since Jesus has inspired me to make these resolutions and urged me on till I did so, His grace will not be wanting to aid me at every step.

In the name of God, then, I enter upon the Narrow Path which leads to sanctity, walking bravely on in imitation of my Jesus Who is by my side carrying His cross. To imitate Him and make my life resemble His in some small degree, will be my life's work, that so I may be worthy to die for Him.

Thank You, O my God, for all the graces of this retreat, above all for bringing me at last to Your sacred feet. Grant me grace to keep these resolutions and never to forget my determination to strive might and main to become *a saint.*

13 Nov., 1907.

Hoc unusquisque persuasum habeat: tantum se in studiis spiritualibus promoturum esse, quantum ab amove sui ipsius et proprii commodi affectione sese abstraxerit. - St. Ignatius. [20]

A. M. D. G.
RESOLUTIONS OF LONG RETREAT, 1907.

1. I must remember that I have offered myself for the Congo. I may be sent now at any moment, and then I shall have only a very short time to live.
2. Is my life all that the life of a future missioner, and perhaps martyr, should be?
3. My ideal: the Third Degree of Humility in all its perfection.
4. My great devotion: the Sacred Heart in the Blessed Eucharist.
5. I will say as much of my Office as I can in the chapel,
6. Each day, 'if possible, 1,000 ejaculations, but never less than 500.
7. Each day 30 little acts of mortification, if I can, but always never less than 15.
8. The object of my life to be close union with and intense love of God. To acquire this I will (*a*) fly from the shadow of sin, never deliberately break a

rule, custom or regulation; (b) do each little action purely for the love of Jesus, with exquisite exactness, fervour and devotedness; (c) beg constantly and earnestly for a great increase of love.

9. I will try and bear little sufferings without seeking relief.
10. Never to give way to sleep during the day.
11. Great attention to the Rules of Modesty, especially custody of the eyes.
12. To read these resolutions once a week.

Motto: *"Agere contra"* all for the love of Jesus and to win His love.

Feast of St. Stanislaus, 1907.

[1] The retreat-journal is reproduced just as it stands. A few headings [in square brackets] have been inserted and some explanatory footnotes added. Reference should, of course, be made throughout to the text of the Spiritual Exercises.

[2] Lord, what wilt Thou have me to do? - *Acts,* 9, 6.

[3] St. Ignatius calls this preliminary consideration on the end of man "the principle and foundation" (*principium et fundamentum*).

[4] A meditation on God's mercy is usually added at the end of the First Week of the Exercises.

[5] "Let all...speak Latin." (*Rules of Scholastics,* 10.)

[6] Lord, what wilt Thou have me to do? - *Acts* 9, 6.

[7] "O eternal Lord...provided it be for Thy greater service and praise...and if Thy most Holy Majesty be pleased to choose and receive me for such a life and state," (these words are taken, from St. Ignatius's meditation on the Kingdom of Christ), I offer myself to Thee for the Congo Mission. Thy will be done. Amen.

[8] "The third degree is the most perfect humility; when...the better to imitate Christ our Lord and to become actually more like to Him, I desire and choose poverty with Christ poor rather than riches, contempt with Christ contemned rather than honours..." - Spiritual Exercises, p. 53.

[9] I said: Now have I begun. - *Psalm* 76, 11.

[10] To act against (myself) in all things.

[11] In the daytime He was teaching in the Temple. - *S. Luke* 21, 37.

[12] He passed the whole night in the prayer of God. - *S. Luke* 6, 12.

[13] Presumably he volunteered for the foreign mission.

[14] "My child, let Me do with you what I will; I know what is good for you." - *Imitation of Christ* iii. 17, 1. A favourite quotation of Fr. Doyle's.

[15] Summer vacation.

[16] *Summarium Constitutionum S.J.,* 12.

[17] Luke 24. 29.

[18] There is here inserted a table with two numbers (each about 500) corresponding to the morning and evening of each day of retreat. This evidently records the number of aspirations made.

[19] The end is come. - *Ezech.* 7. 2.

[20] "Let each be convinced that he will make progress in all spiritual matters in proportion as he has divested himself of his own self-love, his own will and self-interest." - *Spiritual Exercises* (end of second week) p, 60. Compare the *Imitation of Christ* (i. 25, 10): *Tantum proficies quantum tibi ipsi vim intuleris.*

Chapter Five - Apostolate

(1.) MISSIONS AND RETREATS.

AT the end of his tertianship Fr. Doyle was once more placed on the teaching staff of Belvedere College. Next year (1909) he was appointed Minister at Belvedere. In 1910 he was transferred to the mission staff of which he remained an active member until November, 1915. These were years of incessant work which resulted in an abundant harvest of souls. Altogether (from 1908 to 1915) Fr Doyle gave 152 missions and retreats. He had many of the natural gifts which go to make a successful missioner: an impressive appearance, a clear vibrant voice, considerable fluency, great earnestness, painstaking preparation and indomitable energy. Outside the pulpit he was even more successful. His breadth of view and his patient sympathy made him an ideal confessor, and during missions his confessional was always besieged. As a "slummer" and beater-up of hard cases he had few equals. None could withstand his winning and persuasive ways; his childlike directness and self-sacrificing kindness were irresistible. Grace seemed to go out from him. He once wrote in a confidential letter:

"I have not met a single refusal to come to the mission or to confession so far during my missionary career. Why should there be one because Jesus for some mysterious reason seems to delight in using perhaps the most wretched of all His priests as the channel of His grace? When I go to see a hard hopeless case, I cannot describe what happens exactly, but I seem to be able to lift up my heart like a cup and pour grace and the love of God upon that poor soul. I can *see* the result instantly, almost like the melting of snow."

It would almost seem as if the exerting of spiritual influence were a sensible phenomenon to the writer. He had plenty of experience, for he loved to hunt out the most hardened and neglected sinners and to bring them back with him to the church for confession. In one city he used during his mission to go down to the quays at midnight to meet ships due to arrive, and to induce the crews to promise attendance or even to go to confession at once. And next morning he was out before six o'clock on the same apostolic errand, waylaying factory girls and mill-hands going to work.

A consuming zeal for souls was the source of this untiring energy and the secret of his influence. "My intense desire and longing," he once wrote, "is to make others love Jesus and to draw them to His Sacred Heart. Recently at Mass I have found myself at the *Dominus Vobiscum* opening my arms wide with the intention of embracing every soul present and drawing them in spite of themselves into that Heart which longs for their love. 'Compel them to come in,' Jesus said. Yes, compel them to dive into that abyss of love. Sometimes, I might say nearly always, when speaking to people I am seized with an extraordinary desire to draw their hearts to God. I could go down on my knees before them and beg them to be pure and holy, so strong do I feel the longing of Jesus for sanctity in everyone, and since I may not do this, I try to do what I find hard to describe in words to pour out of my heart any grace or love of God there may be in it, and then with all the force of my will to draw their hearts into that of Jesus."

In his mission-work he relied greatly on prayers, for which he was constantly appealing to convents and schools. "Ammunition for the Missions" he called such spiritual help. "Pray for a hard case here," "A little prayer for a big fish of forty years whom I hope to land to-morrow," "Get all the prayers you can, even an aspiration may save a soul" these and suchlike requests occur constantly in his letters. "I am going to say a special Mass in future," he wrote (30th April, 1911), "on the first Sunday of each month for all those who pray for my missions and retreats, I shall be grateful if you would kindly make this known." [1]

And again on the Feast of Corpus Christi, 1913 he had been hearing confessions on the day before from half-past five in the morning until eleven at night: "I wish nuns could know the miracles their prayers work during missions in the hearts of poor sinners years away from God; it would make them do so much more." "I think," he once said, "there are too many *workers* in most religious houses, but not half enough *toilers on their knees.*" [2]

He did not confine himself to asking the prayers of others, he also toiled on his own knees. During a mission or retreat he sought to increase and intensify his own prayer instead of curtailing it. "The more I have to do," he once wrote, "the greater I feel the need of prayer, so that between the two the poor sleep has a bad time." After an arduous day's work in pulpit and confessional he would often spend a good part of the night before the Tabernacle, cutting his sleep down to three or four hours. Thus during a mission in Drogheda, the curate observed that Fr. Doyle on emerging from his confessional at eleven o'clock at night used to retire to the little oratory and remain on his knees before the Blessed Sacrament until the clock struck two; yet he was always up and out of the house before any one else was astir. And in addition to all this, there was continuous and severe penance. Few have believed so literally that the devil is cast out only by prayer and fasting. Here is one precious revelation of his nocturnal rest; it was after a hard day's work during a mission in Glasgow, and in addition he was suffering from a cold:

"I made the Holy Hour prostrate on the marble flags, and by moving from time to time I continued to get the full benefit of the cold. Then for two hours I made the Stations of the Cross, standing, kneeling, and prostrate, taking fourteen strokes of the discipline at each Station. For the rest of the night I remained kneeling before the Tabernacle, at intervals with arms outstretched, till I could bear the agony of this no longer."

The man who acted thus was no sickly or morbid solitary. He was a healthy, good-humoured, broad-minded, hard-working missioner, "with no d nonsense about him," as one penitent expressed it. But in his soul there were chords attuned to finer spiritual symphonies than our dull wits can discern.

He knew, not by theoretic reasoning but by intuition and experience, that there is a mysterious law governing the movements of spiritual energy, a divine economy in the operations of grace. Souls are won by prayer and suffering; God wishes the deficit of sin to be filled up with the overflow of chosen souls. Men sometimes reason about this and call it learned names. Fr. Doyle *lived* it. He gave to his missions not only lip-service, but the devotion of his whole being. Like his divine Master he could say, "For them do I sanctify myself." (S. *John* 17. 19.) He strove to help others out of the spontaneous redundancy of his own spiritual life. Whatever he said to others passed first through his own heart and therein it gained something deeper and more soul-stirring than any natural fluency or learning could impart.

Testimonies to his success as a missioner are numerous. "The results of your mission," wrote a Parish Priest, "have exceeded my anticipations and all previous experiences. Indeed, the people speak of it with awe, as of a miraculous manifestation and veritable outpouring of grace" "Your retreat here has been a wonderful success," says another letter, "It has completely changed many. People are still talking about it, and better still, living up to its lessons." "I can't tell you," wrote a Parish Priest after his death, "how we all loved him in D---. The people could never get enough of him, and asked to have him back again and again. I wanted him here when I came, but he was just starting for the Front." "Father," said a man at the end of a mission, "it was the holiest mission we ever had." From time to time Willie himself speaks in his letters of his mission work and how blessed it was by God.

"My success here," he writes "has far surpassed anything I looked for. But it is, of course, the work of God's grace. I do not think I could possibly find food for vainglory in anything I have done no more than an organ-grinder prides himself on the beautiful music he produces by turning a handle. God knows I only wish and seek His greater glory, and to make others love Him, if I cannot love Him myself All along I felt it was all His doing, and that I was just a mere instrument in His hands, and a wretched one at that. All through I had the feeling that I was like an old bucket full of holes, which broke the poor Lord's Heart as He tried to carry His precious grace into the hearts of His children."

"I think Jesus was pleased with our work here. He certainly showed it on Sunday when I asked Him to give me in honour of His Blessed Mother all the souls I intended to visit that day They all gave in to His grace, including several who had not been to the sacraments for very many years. People say it is hard to love God. I only wish they could realize how much He loves them and wishes their salvation and happiness."

"I have come back from the missions with feelings of joy and gratitude, for these last three missions have been blessed in a wonderful way. God seems to take a special delight in seconding my efforts, just because I have hurt Him so much in the past and have been so really ungrateful. It is one of the big humiliations of my life and makes me thoroughly ashamed of myself that our Blessed Lord for His own wise ends conceals my shortcomings from others and allows me to do a little good. But He does not hide the wretched state of my soul from myself, I am not speaking in a false humble strain, but serious truth. If you, or anyone else, could only see the way I have acted towards Jesus all my life, you would turn away from me in disgust."

"I have had much consolation in my work recently. The last mission was the hardest I have given, yet it seems to have been singularly blessed. All this love and goodness on the part of Jesus only fills me with a deep sorrow that I can do so little for Him. I am getting afraid of Him, just because He is so generous to me and blesses all I do. I feel ashamed when people praise me for my work, the sort of shame a piano might feel if someone complimented it on the beautiful melody that came from its keys. I am realizing more and more that all success is entirely God's work, and that self does not count at all. I have this strange feeling that when I get to heaven I shall have little merit for anything I have done for God's glory, since all has been the work of His Hands."

Though he accomplished so much on the general missions, he found more congenial work in giving retreats, especially to religious communities During his first two years on the mission staff he was chiefly engaged in giving retreats to sodalities and religious communities. Here was fruitful soil for the self-denial and penance, the love of God and of perfection, which were his constant themes, and for whose easy attainment he had many plans and holy devices. His zeal and enthusiasm for God and the things of God joined to attractive qualities of person and character made an impression wherever he went, and soon he was much sought after. During one summer he received more than forty invitations from religious communities to give them their annual retreat. From the very many testimonies to the good he effected a few typical sentences may be quoted.

"No retreat ever made a deeper impression on the community, or raised the tone of the house to such a "high level of spirituality, as that conducted by Fr. Doyle."

"A saintly old lay sister wept the whole retreat tears of joy, saying she had never in her whole forty-five years in religion felt and seen so visibly the effects of grace in herself and others."

"Many said they never realized before what religious life meant, but that now they were going to give God everything."

"Rev. Mother told the Bishop that no retreat for the past forty years had made such an impression."

It is curious to note that in spite of the signal success which crowned his ministry, he was at times subject to intense depression and discouragement. "Such fear, dread and hatred of the coming mission came over me," he writes to a friend, "that I was on the point of writing to ask not to be sent, and at the last moment I very nearly telegraphed to say I couldn't possibly travel."

"I went to M--- in the lowest depths of fear and misery. For some time before I had been very ungenerous with God and must have pained Him much. On this account I felt I had no right to count on His help. But Jesus took His revenge by helping me more than ever. Such loving forgiveness of injury makes me feel oh! so ashamed of my meanness."

"You would hardly believe the fierceness of the temptation the old one before beginning this mission, the temptation to ask to get off it, in fact to give up the mission life altogether as something almost unbearable. When the work starts the storm subsides somewhat, but honestly I am afraid of myself, that in my weakness I may some day ruin God's work in souls by giving in to what I see in calmer moments to be a temptation."

"For three-quarters of an hour I preached in agony, with the perspiration rolling from every pore. I was not afraid of. breaking down before the congregation that would have been a relief - but the physical effort to utter each word was torture, and the longing, time after time more intense, to come down from the pulpit was almost irresistible. They told me I preached well that night, yet I was quite unnerved, and only God knows what I went through."

Once he even wrote: "I am ending this retreat with the resolution of never giving another." Fortunately it was one of the few resolutions he never kept. Such attacks of dejection are quite intelligible in one of Fr. Doyle's emotional temperament. Even from the purely natural point of view, his exertion of personal influence on others was an exhausting experience; in all such efforts something, as it were, seems to pass out of one and to enter into one's hearers. It was probably some subconscious perception of this which made him so often in anticipation shrink from the ordeal. But he never gave way to this discouragement and repugnance. He worked till the end as a valiant soldier of Christ, laying aside all thoughts of personal predilection and considerations of ease. He crowded his mission years with unremitting toil, as if in premonition of an early death. *Consummatus in brevi, explevit tempora multa.* [3]

(2.) RETREATS FOR THE WORKERS.

It is a tribute to Fr. Doyle's broadminded character and manysided interests that he not only devoted himself to giving retreats to religious and priests, but was also a warm advocate indeed, as far as Ireland is concerned, a pioneer propagandist of retreats for working men and women. He had seen for himself the great good effected by such retreats in France and Belgium and also, since 1908, in England. He became convinced that in Ireland, too, such a work was of great social and religious urgency. Though in his lifetime he failed to overcome the forces of conservative inaction and apathy, the seed which he sowed will surely in the near future germinate into a fruitful apostolate. The question is by no means, as many at the time fancied, a mere fad or an unnecessary spiritual luxury. The provision of workers' retreats might conceivably have been a matter of argument a few years ago; to-day it is clearly an immediately imperative step, if the Church is to acquire or to retain its influence over democracy, restive, newly awakened and determined. [4] There are already in Ireland several religious houses where middle-class lay men and women can make a retreat either singly or in groups. Will it be said that it is the purely material difficulty which is allowed to debar Irish workers from similar facilities? If we admit that an annual retreat is necessary for priests and religious, and that occasional or periodical retreats are extremely advantageous to Catholic layfolk, why should any economic or social differentiation exist? The mission or public retreat, during which people live their ordinary life and pursue their usual work while attending some extra sermons, is an altogether different matter. What is here in question is strictly and literally a retreat; a withdrawal, however brief, from the scenes and cares and routine of daily life; an opportunity, were it only for a weekend, of realising Christ's message and ideal in prayerful silence and with full leisure of soul. The Spiritual Exercises are a serious and a sacred task demanding wholehearted attention and devotion; they are deprived of their efficacy and influence if they are reduced to mere interludes before and after a day filled with toil and trouble and talk St. Ignatius is insistent on the observance of the "Additions," some of which may seem rather minute to us such as the exclusion of light during the serious sombre meditations of the First Week but which altogether constitute a very necessary spiritual environment. It is indeed the lesson of our Lord Himself: the soil must be prepared for the seed. How often does the seed fall amid brambles! Many is the one "that heareth the word, and the cares of this world and the deceitfulness of riches choketh up the word, and he becometh fruitless." (*S. Matthew* 13, 22.) Preparation for seed-sowing is as necessary in soul-culture as it is in agriculture.

There is ample evidence that a retreat, filling a man's whole life for a few days amid pleasant and spiritually refreshing surroundings, makes a far deeper and more lasting impression than a public mission during which a man lives and works as usual, perhaps in the midst of squalor, noise and misery.

"Only those who have witnessed the retreats (says Fr. Plater) [5] can have any idea of the wonderful miracles of grace which they normally effect. The men plain workmen for the most part enter on the retreat with some bewilderment and even apprehension. Some are merely awkward, others almost defiant. Ringleaders of infidelity have been known to come out of curiosity, the only condition required of them being that they should keep the rules of the house. But on the second day a change is seen on the faces of all. They are very much in earnest hopeful and courageous, and for the most part as simple and docile as children It is touching to hear their expressions of gratitude for the benefits which they have received from their retreat, which all are sorry to quit at the end of three days."

"There is a vast difference," remarks Fr. Doyle in his own little pamphlet, [6] "between the methods employed and the fruit resulting from a mission and a retreat. The one makes its influence felt only at certain hours in the evening, the other 'at every hour; the first uses a few well-known means of moving the heart, the other employs every act of the day, all directed towards one definite end; in the mission it is the preacher who does the work, in a retreat the exercitant himself... The efficacy of a retreat consists in personal reflection, favoured by the absence of all distracting occupations and the logical sequence of subjects treated. Solitude, silence and serious reflection, united to fervent prayer, act powerfully upon the soul and cause it to experience sentiments hitherto unknown...It appeals not to the indifferent crowd, the careless liver, but to the elite, to those who by their intelligence or influence are capable of leading others by their example. It seeks first for the upright and virtuous, the men of character and zeal, and not content with making them better Christians, more solicitous about their own salvation, strives to mould them into lay apostles."

Fr. Doyle did not profess to be an expert social reformer, he had no panacea to advocate for curing the ills of society. But he made a contribution which sprang from the depths of his own inner experience. He realized that the social problem cannot be stated as a duel between profits and wages, that democracy cannot be built merely on increased comfort and amusement. And so he uttered his plea, unfortunately premature, that the ideals of the workers should be raised and purified and strengthened by contact with Christ, the divine Workman of Nazareth. He knew that every toiler is a person, not a mere 'hand' or chattel, an immortal soul for whom Christ died. Having himself tasted the Saviour's banquet, he proposed to "go out quickly into the streets and lanes of the city and bring hither the poor and the feeble and the blind and the lame." "When thou makest a dinner or a supper," said our Lord and are not His words as applicable to a spiritual as to a material feast? - "call not thy friends nor thy brethren nor thy kinsmen nor thy neighbours who are rich... But call the poor, the maimed, the lame and the blind." It is these, after all, who have most need of spiritual experience and help, these who, even in Catholic Ireland, live with stunted souls and impoverished bodies in hovels and tenements and garrets. Surely, for Fr. Doyle's outspoken invitation, we may say that 'recompense shall be made him at the resurrection of the just.' [7] (S. Luke 14. 12-21.)

His efforts, however, were destined to have no immediate success, in spite of the fact that he had a warm supporter in his Provincial (Fr. William Delany) who, in the autumn of 1912, sent him to the Continent to investigate. Fr. Doyle inspected many retreat-houses for workingmen in France, Belgium and Holland, and thus gained valuable information and experience. Besides the pamphlet already mentioned there survives one letter written at this time, which may be quoted more for its personal interest than for its relevancy to the question of retreats.

"I have picked up an immense amount of useful information about Workingmen's Retreats since I came here. Everybody has been kindness itself and helped me in every way. Indeed this trip has been, and will be, of great service to me and God's work. More than once the Hand of God was plainly visible in little incidents which may eventually lead to big things, the missing of a train bringing about the chance meeting of one who gave me great help, and so in other ways. When leaving Ireland I did not think my journey was to mean so much for myself spiritually. At Lourdes, at Tours, at Angers, and other places, our dearest Lord seemed to have had His message prepared and waiting for me. I had a feeling all along that my visit to Lisieux would do much for me, and I was not mistaken; so that I am coming home like a bee laden with the honey of God, which I pray Him not to allow me to squander or misuse. I saw many interesting places and things during my weeks of travel. But over all hung a big cloud of sadness, for I realised as I never did before how utterly the world has forgotten Jesus except to hate and outrage Him, the fearful, heart-rending amount of sin visible on all sides, and the vast work for souls that lies before us priests. My feelings at times are more than I can describe. The longing to make up to our dear Lord for all He is suffering is overwhelming, and I ask Him, since somehow my own heart seems indifferent to His pleading, to give me the power to do much and very much to console Him."

In spite of the information thus acquired and the subsequent propaganda in which he engaged, funds remained inadequate and public opinion seemed unmoved. Once, indeed, he was very near success. He was sent for by the Provincial who told him that a suitable residence and grounds had been offered and that he was to take charge of the first 'Retreat House for Workers in Ireland. A few days later the house destined for retreats was burnt down by suffragettes! And thus the project fell through.

In spite of this failure Fr. Doyle had the happiness of putting his views to one practical test. After many delays and difficulties it was arranged that he should give a three days' retreat to the employees of the Providence Woollen Mills, Foxford, Co. Mayo. Holy Saturday (3rd April, 1915) was selected as the opening day, so that the triduum could include the Monday Bank Holiday, on which day alone the School would be closed and the schoolrooms available. The men did not at all appreciate the idea beforehand, they were nervous and uneasy at the novel proposal, and kept wondering 'what they were in for.' The general tone was, 'Really this is too much of a good thing, hadn't we a (public) retreat in the parish a few months ago?' Only the mill-workers (and also a few outsiders, Pioneers) were invited; and. of course, they were left perfectly free to come or not as they pleased. Naturally there was some anxiety about the attendance, but to the relief of the good Sisters of Charity, a large number turned up for the first lecture. [8] Each man got a typed copy of the order of time. The day was well-filled, only small intervals being left free. Mass was at eight o'clock, there were four instructions, two or three visits to the Blessed Sacrament, the Stations of the Cross, a couple of rosaries, and some spiritual reading. The Senior School which is bright and spacious made a very devotional oratory, the lower rooms being free for reading or smoking. The convent garden was placed at the exercitants' disposal, and it was edifying to see them walking about singly or in silent groups. The rosary was said out of doors and was very impressive, the men walking in procession followed by Fr. Doyle, who recited the prayers aloud. The. brass instruments of the Mill Band accompanied the Benediction Service and Hymns, in singing which the whole congregation joined.

Almost from the very start the men gave evident signs that they had lost all their awkwardness or suspiciousness, they quickly entered into the peace and calm of this unwonted spiritual atmosphere. "No man ever made such an impression," writes one of the exercitants. "Fr. Doyle's saintly appearance and attractive manner at once captured our attention, and time passed so quickly while he spoke that each lecture, though invariably half an hour, seemed but a moment. His words were simple and clear, and delivered in so kindly and gentle a fashion that they were just what he liked to call them 'little chats.' We had been accustomed to fiery threatening sermons at missions, where God's justice is painted with so much eloquence, making one tremble at the uncertainty of salvation. But here the words of the saintly preacher sent us away with the impression: 'How easy it is after all for me to save my soul! God is good, He loves me, and what He asks is very small.'" One lecture on Reparation to the Sacred Heart made an abiding impression on the hearers. The outrages and insults heaped on Christ throughout the world were vividly depicted by one who had seen them nigh, and were consolingly contrasted with the religious mission of Ireland, whereof every Irish Catholic worker ought to be the watchful custodian.

At the close of the retreat, on Easter Tuesday morning, all the men went to Mass and Holy Communion, listened to a farewell lecture, assisted at Benediction and received the Papal Blessing. Fr. Doyle then shook hands with each man as he left the room, and by this simple friendly act captured the last corner of every heart. The typical comment was, 'It was entirely too short; if only we had another day!' Those best entitled to judge state that the retreat will never be forgotten, and are confident that the good then accomplished will not be undone. [9]

The success of this retreat shows clearly the deep spiritual influence which a House of Retreats in or near Dublin could exert on our Catholic workers, who at present often find! anti-Catholic influences far more accessible. But from this Foxford experiment we may draw another, and perhaps even more practical, inference. That is, the possibility of having, throughout the country, retreats for working men and women, without the necessity of providing special retreat houses at all. Just as the Sisters at Foxford provided facilities for their workers in their school and convent, just as the clergy themselves make their annual retreat in some diocesan college or vacant seminary, so, we begin to realise, could schools while idle in vacation time, or similar institutions with available space, be utilised for providing occasional retreats for our less fortunate brothers and sisters who toil in fields and factories and live in hovels and slums. [10] We have provided for our friends, our brethren, our kinsmen, and our neighbours who are rich. "And the Lord said: Go out into the highways and hedges and compel them to come in that My house may be filled." (S. Luke 14. 23.)

The following lines were written by Fr. Charles Plater, S.J., to whom more than anyone else the introduction of workers' retreats into England is due. [11] They constitute at once a sincere tribute from an intimate fellow-worker and a straight appeal to Catholic Ireland.

"I lived for some years with big-hearted Willie Doyle and loved him. We were seminarians together and I saw much of him. He was always bubbling over with mirth and generally at the bottom of any harmless mischief that might be afoot, but only the shallow-minded could have mistaken his gaiety for thoughtlessness. Underneath his mercurial behaviour were steadily glowing ideals and enthusiasm. He had a deep and simple piety and a burning love for Ireland.

"After he left Stonyhurst, and again still later when we were both priests, we corresponded much on the subject of workers' retreats. His quick imagination pictured the immense good which might be effected by their introduction into Ireland. With his whole soul he threw himself into the work of promoting them. His letters are just himself. ardent, enthusiastic, full of piety and love of country, He would, I am convinced, gladly have given his life to see the retreats established in Ireland. He was acutely distressed because others could not see what he saw so plainly:

"I did not write because I had nothing but disappointment, opposition, cold shower-baths and crosses to chronicle, the last and biggest cross being the sudden death of my truest supporter, Fr. X---. Your news about the success in England is glorious, and yet I am assured that mine will come in Dublin if ever a house is opened. ... I am confident the real difficulty will be to keep the men out I never realised till I got on the mission staff the immense amount of faith and love for holy things there is everywhere still in Ireland. ... It has been a four years' Calvary, but yesterday the Resurrection, I hope, began, for I heard that Rathfarnham Castle with 53 acres has been purchased at last, and I have the Provincial's promise (when that took place) to allow me to make a start *in the stables.* Ye Gods! Fancy the mighty Doyle preaching in a stable! Very like the Master is it not?' (May 20th, 1913).

"He found it hard to be patient with those who urged expense as an insuperable obstacle, for he knew that once a start was made the money would come. The Island of Saints would not allow a School for Saints to suffer through lack of funds. Again, it was objected that Ireland had not a large class of well-paid artisans, who, it was supposed, must form the bulk of the retreatants; and here, too, Willie Doyle saw that the objection was groundless as the history of popular retreats had shown. 'Why not in Ireland?' was the sub-title of his excellent pamphlet on Retreats for Workers, and his challenging question was really unanswerable.

"There is only one possible memorial to Fr. William Doyle, and that is a house of retreats for workers in Ireland. That he would have asked for; indeed, we may be sure that he *does* ask for it. Those to whom his life of smiles and tears and his glorious death have been an inspiration will surely help him to get it."

(3.) THE HOLY CHILDHOOD.

From the notes of his Long Retreat it is already clear that Fr. Doyle more than once volunteered for the foreign mission. [12] His wish was never gratified, unless perhaps we can regard as a foreign mission that last ministry fulfilled amid scenes of savagery mingled with heroism. But he remained to the end intensely interested in the field whither the Lord did not call him to harvest. Often in his retreats [13] did he ask his hearers to think of the great army of pagans which would take thirty-one and a half years to pass, one per second, in single file. Often did he kindle his zeal and increase his reparation at the thought of the sins of so-called Christians and the ignorance of them that sit in darkness. Furthermore, his interest in the foreign missions took a very practical shape, namely, that of helping the Association of the Holy Childhood. This Association, founded in 1843 by Mgr. de Forbin Janson, Bishop of Nancy, has for its object the rescue of children in Africa and Asia, who have been abandoned and left to die by their parents. By its means more than eighteen million little babies have been saved and baptised; most of these neglected mites did not long survive baptism. The members help the work of the Association by their prayers and offerings. Fr. Doyle was able to collect considerable sums by his zealous and ingenious methods. He had attractive cards printed each with a picture of a rescued babe and an invitation to buy a black baby for half-a-crown, the purchaser having the right to select the baptismal name! "I do not know," he wrote from the Front on 3ist July, 1916, "if I told you that the Black Baby Crusade, though now partly suspended, proved a great success. I got well over a thousand half-crowns; and as in some places a poor child can be bought for sixpence, there should be a goodly army of woolly black souls now before the throne of God. [14] In addition, two priests, one in Scotland, the other in Australia, have taken up my card scheme and are working it well. The idea of buying a little godchild from the slavery of the devil and packing it off safe to heaven, appeals to many." Like every other available method of saving souls, it appealed to Fr. Doyle; and he brought to it his characteristic humour and energy.

(4.) VOCATIONS.

Fr. Doyle was naturally interested in helping, encouraging and advising those who desired to work for Christ as priests or religious. This interest he showed by personal direction and correspondence and also by the publication of two simple little pamphlets which have had a phenomenal success. *Vocations*, issued in August 1913, is now in its tenth edition 100th thousand); *Shall I be a Priest?*, first issued in March 1915, has reached its seventh edition (40th thousand); both are published by the Irish Messenger Office, Dublin. In the second last letter he ever wrote, sent to his father from the Front, on 25th July, 1917, he gives an interesting account of how he came to write the brochure on Vocations. The letter itself is headed "bits and scraps for an old man's breakfast," it was hastily written in the open air and expressed in good-humored homely language for a father whom he tenderly loved and who, he knew, was interested in every detail of what he did.

"You will be glad to know, as I was, that the ninth edition (90,000 copies) of my little book *Vocations* is rapidly being exhausted. After my ordination, when I began to be consulted on this important subject, I was struck by the fact that there was nothing one could put into the hands of boys and girls to help them to a decision, except ponderous volumes, which they would scarcely read. Even the little treatise by St. Liguori which Fr. Charles gave me during my first visit to Tullabeg, and which changed the whole current of my thoughts, was out of print. I realized the want for some time; but one evening as I walked back to the train after dining with you, the thought of the absolute necessity for such a book seized me so strongly, (I could almost point out the exact spot on the road), that there and then I made up my mind to *persuade someone to write it,* for I never dreamt of even attempting the task myself.

"I soon found out that the shortest way to get a thing done is to do it yourself, or rather God in His goodness had determined to make use of me, because I was lacking in the necessary qualifications, to get His work done, for I am firmly convinced that both in *Vocations* and *Shall I be a Priest?* my part consisted in the correction of the proof sheets and in the clawing in of the shower of 'bawbees.'

"I remember well when the MSS. - which does *not* stand for 'Mrs' as Brother Frank Hegarty read out once in Clongowes: 'St. Jerome went off to Palestine carrying his Missus' - had passed the censors to my great surprise, the venerable manager of the Messenger Office began shaking his head over the prospect of its selling, for as he said with truth, 'It is a subject which appeals to a limited few.' He decided to print 5,000, and hinted I might buy them all myself!

"Then when the pamphlet began to sell and orders to come in fast, I began to entertain the wild hope that by the time I reached the stage of two crutches and a long white beard, I might possibly see the 100,000 mark reached. We are nearly at that now without any pushing or advertising, and I hope the crutches and flowing beard are still a long way off. God is good, is He not? As the second edition came out only in the beginning of 1914 the sale has been extraordinarily rapid.

"It is consoling from time to time to receive letters from convents or religious houses, saying that some novice had come to them chiefly through reading *Vocations;* for undoubtedly there are many splendid soldiers lost to Christ's army for the want of a little help and encouragement... A welcome gift from a benefactor, not a benefactress this time, has just reached me in the shape of a donation of £3 to distribute a thousand free copies of *Vocations.* The donor believes that if one cannot oneself volunteer for the war, the next best thing is to try to get someone else to do so. One never can tell into what generous heart the good seed may fall, or the number of souls that possibly may be saved by this distribution. May God bless him and send along a thousand more imitators, for 'the harvest is great and the labourers few' said our Blessed Lord, and He ought to know!"

The success of this unpretentious little pamphlet, written without any affectation of style or erudition, demonstrated very clearly the untold good that can be done by instructive and devotional literature. Fr. Doyle never intended to become an author, and modestly felt that he was not equipped for literary or theological expositions. But as abler men seemed unable to write for ordinary souls or preferred to criticise the ventures of others, he felt it his duty to put down in clear simple language the thoughts and ideals for which he himself lived and worked. And he was more than justified by the spiritual harvest he reaped thereby. Besides the letter just quoted there are in his correspondence many other references to the results of his pamphlet. Thus he writes on one occasion: "I have just had a visit from a 'rich young lady,' a perfect stranger to me, whose eyes have been opened by reading Vocations. I have had two or three cases like this recently; which is ample reward for the trouble the book cost me." "My little book on Vocations," he says in another letter, "has brought me a good deal of consolation lately. The Superior of X told me they had at least two novices whose thoughts had been first directed to religious life by reading the pamphlet and that another, whose vocation was due in great measure to the book, was expected in a few days from Australia. Yesterday I had a letter from the Fathers in London telling me several of their young men had been led to take the final step by the same means. Some time ago a Lutheran, recently received into the Church, wrote from New York saying that the pamphlet had appealed to him so much that he was now studying for the priesthood. This is encouraging and proves what I have always held, that there are vocations in abundance if only they were helped a little."

The unexpected success of *Vocations* led Fr. Doyle to write another pamphlet to which he gave the title *Shall I be a Priest?* It was written with simple direct fervour and would serve equally as a consideration for priests on the dignity of the sacerdotal office or as a help to a diffident aspirant. The frontispiece represents a little child knocking at the tabernacle-door and saying, 'Jesus, I want to be a holy priest.' The appropriateness of all this will be understood from the following letter. "It is not mine but Jesus' alone." he wrote, "for every word seemed to come from the Tabernacle before which I wrote it, the greater part on the altar itself. [15] Nominally it is written for boys, but in reality I have tried to give a message to my fellow-priests, and at the same time to stir up greater love and reverence in the hearts of all who may read it. Its defects are many, because such a subject would require the pen of an archangel. But I feel Jesus will bless the tiny book and make it do His work."

While Fr. Doyle was working with superhuman energy as military chaplain, he kept planning some further pamphlets. Except the titles - Union with God, Letters to One who is Hesitating, Spiritual Communion, An Explanation of the Priest's Actions at Mass - he committed nothing to writing except the following few jottings, hastily scribbled while crouching in some dug-out. As they refer to the subject of vocations, they may be here inserted.

"Vocation Letters."

"1. Escape from world. Christ said 'I pray not for the world.' Eagerness to get away from plague, infected places.

2 Every action, step done for God. Three things in prayer: merit, satisfaction, and impetration.

3 Fear of unhappiness. Bernadette: 'I do not promise to make you happy in this world.' 'Ought not Christ to have suffered?'

4 Joy of sacrifice; when made, great joy after fear.

5 End. 'Well done, good servant.' Real life is to come.

6 'Could do more good in world.' Many Masses, fast, works of zeal, sacrifice of will greater than all.

7 Cutting on Pagan Religious Orders; no vocation, yet perseverance; penitents to help.

8 Don Bosco refused 300 foundations for want of subjects (nuns), also Angers,

9 A good religious experiences more pleasure and consolation from a single pious exercise such as Mass, visit to the Blessed Sacrament, than people of the world take... (Ven. Fr. Champagnat.)"

Fr. Doyle's interest in vocations was not confined merely to literary advocacy. He was always generously ready with personal advice and assistance. He helped a very large number of girls to enter religious houses and a not inconsiderable number of boys to enter religion or to prepare for the priesthood. Many a visit did he pay to convents, many were the letters he wrote in his efforts to 'place' vocations. When Ireland failed, he tried England, and even America, Australia, and South Africa. Once he was satisfied that a true vocation existed, he could not be disheartened by any temporal disabilities. [16] An interesting and ingenious scheme which he started, while on leave from the Front, may be best indicated in his own words (in a letter to his father dated 25 July, 1917):

"I do not know if I have told you of a scheme which I have in my mind to help poor boys who are anxious to be priests. Before the war I came in contact with a number of very respectable lads and young men, whose one desire was to work for God and the salvation of souls, but who, for want of means, were not able to pursue their studies. I was able to help some of them and get them free places in America or England, with a couple at Mungret, but the number of applicants was far in excess of the resources.

"One day having successfully negotiated or missed a couple of shells, I was struck instead by a happy idea. I was coming home on leave and made up my mind to make an experiment with my new idea, which was this. I gave a little talk to the Sodality of the Children of Mary in a certain convent in Dublin on the need for priests at the present time, and what a glorious work it was to help even a single lad to become one of the 'Lord's Anointed.' I told them how many were longing for this honour, and suggested that they should adopt some poor boy and pay for his education until he was ordained. Two hundred girls subscribing 5/- a year would provide £50. more than enough for the purpose. I suggested that this money ought to be the result of some personal sacrifice, working overtime, making a hat or dress last longer, etc., but as a last resource they might collect the 5/- or some of it.

"The idea was taken up most warmly: nearly all the money for this year is paid in, though the girls are nearly all factory hands, and the lucky boy will begin his college course in September. I am hoping 'when the cruel war is o'er' to get the other convents to follow suit; for the scheme is simple and no great burden on any one, and is a ready solution of the financial difficulty and should bring joy to many a boy's heart. Certain difficulties naturally suggest themselves, but I think we may safely count a little at least on our Blessed Lord's help, since the work is being done for Him, and go on with confidence."

Father Doyle at the Age of Fifteen

How dear this scheme was to Fr. Doyle may be gathered from this entry in his diary: "May 24th (1917). Feast of Notre Dame Auxiliatrice, who helped Don Bosco so much in his work for young priests. I formally to-day made Mary the Protectress of the work which I am beginning for her young priests."

It will be convenient to mention here Fr. Doyle's translation of the Life of Père Ginhac by A. Calvet, S.J. "Printer after printer refused to have anything to do with the book," he wrote, "though I staked Fr. Ginhac's reputation that it would prove a financial success." Finally Messrs. R. and T. Washbourne undertook to produce the work, and it appeared in 1914 as *A Man after God's Own Heart: Life of Father Paul Ginhac, S.J.* When Fr. Doyle heard that the price was fixed at 8/6 net, he thought that the sale was killed for "not many people would care to invest such a sum in the life of a man no one had ever heard of." But to his astonishment 900 copies went through in the first year, and up to December 1916 altogether 1,244 copies had been sold. "Père Ginhac," he wrote to his father, "has certainly worked this miracle if he never did anything else; and I am beginning to think he is not a bad sort of an old chap, even though he looked so desperately in need of a square meal!" Fr. Ginhac's portrait certainly represents him as cadaverous and grim-visaged, a contrast with his admirer and translator, whose mortified life was never allowed to interfere with his buoyant naturalness and irrepressible spirit of fun. The book seems to have impressed and helped many readers, for Fr. Doyle continues: "I have had a pile of letters from all parts of the world Alaska, Ceylon, South Africa, etc. asking for relics and mentioning many favours received through the holy father's intercession; so that the labour of getting out the volume (and it was not light) has brought its own reward." Thus wrote Fr. Doyle a month before his death. Little did he dream that his own life would be written, and that his influence would be mingled with that of his fellow-religious whom he helped to make known to others.

[1] During a mission in Cork he offered prizes in a school to the children who prayed most, and gave them to the little ones himself at the close of the mission.

[2] Compare the saying of the Little Flower in her Autobiography: "O Mother, how beautiful is our vocation! It is for us on Carmel to preserve the salt of the earth. We offer our prayers and our sacrifices for the Lord's apostles; we must ourselves be their apostles, while by their words and their examples they are evangelising the souls of our brothers." *Soeur Thérèse...Histoire d' une âme,* p. 95; Eng. trans. (*The Little Flower*) p. 96. Also Soeur GertrudeMarie (Legueu, *Une mystique de nos jours,* 1910, p. 348 - a favourite book of Fr. Doyle's): "Once more Jesus made me change my day's intentions: 'To-day you will pray for all the souls who will go to confession and prepare for their Easter duty to-morrow [Palm Sunday, 1907]. You will also pray for the confessors.'"

[3] "Being made perfect in a short space, he fulfilled a long time." - *Wisdom* 4, 13.

[4] On the social results of retreats see Fr. Plater's *Retreats for the People* (1912), ch. 13.

[5] In his pamphlet *Retreats for Workers* (C.T.S. London) p. 13. See also the vivid account of Gilbert Cloquet's retreat at Fayt-Manage in René Bazin's *Rising Corn,* ch. 13.

[6] *Retreats for Workingmen: Why not in Ireland?* (Dublin, Irish Messenger Office, July, 1909) pp. Sf. It is worth observing that this plea for *retreats* was penned by a successful *missioner.*

[7] We can gauge his intense interest in the project from this entry in his diary (20 Dec., 1914): "During a visit to Church I felt urged to promise our Blessed Lady to try and give up meat on Saturdays in her honour, if she in return will bring about the starting of the Workmen's Retreats this-' summer (1915)."

[8] Of the 62 men then employed in the Mills 60 made the retreat; these were joined by five others who petitioned the favour.

[9] Fr. Doyle had originally proposed that the Sisters should provide board and lodging for the exercitants, but on becoming acquainted with the local circumstance he agreed that this was unnecessary. The men live close by. with very little in their surroundings to distract them; and they are accustomed to the bell summoning them to and from their meals. The full work-time lost on the retreat was 1¼ days (Monday and portion of Tuesday). The men were paid for this time, though they were not told this beforehand; the loss of wages was also made up to the women who were necessarily idle while the Mill was closed.

[10] During the summer vacation (Christmas) 1918, a successful retreat was made by 96 workers in Kew College, Melbourne.

[11] In his *Retreats for the People: A Sketch of a Great Revival,* 1912, p. 134, Fr. Plater says: "Before regular retreat-houses were established in England it was by no means uncommon for Irishmen living in this country to go over to

Ireland for the purpose of making a retreat in a Franciscan friary or some other religious establishment."

[12] He was so confident that he would be sent to the Congo, that he procured a catechism in the native language and interleaved it with an English translation. This little souvenir still survives as a proof of his practical and resolute zeal.

[13] See also p. 22 of his pamphlet *Shall I be a Priest?*

[14] According to the *Annals of the Holy Childhood* (Irish Branch), Nov., 1917, 90. Fr. Doyle "collected in a comparatively short time, before leaving Ireland as C.F. at the Front, the large sum of nearly £200 'to buy black babies' for God."

[15] Compare *The Priest of the Eucharist* [Père Eymard], Eng. tr. 1881, p. 22.

[16] He got one girl with a wooden leg and another with a paralysed left hand into American convents. Both are now professed and are doing good work.

Chapter Six - Inner Life

(1.) INTRODUCTION.

IT is not as a successful missioner nor as a zealous director JL that Fr. Doyle chiefly merits our attention and study. The main interest of this biography is within, in the inner life of the soul. Exteriorly there was little remarkable in his career. Many another missionary has reaped a more abundant harvest, many other directors have been far more skilled in moral and mystical theology. Doubtless, too, there are in our midst many unrecognised saints whose hidden interior life is precious in the sight of God and would be deemed glorious by men if they but knew it. But it is our good fortune that we can in the case of Fr. Doyle read, at least partially, the record of his true life; we can view his career not only as men saw it, but also as it appeared to God and to himself. And to appreciate his life at its real value we must forget altogether that adventitious halo "of earthly glory which lit up its last phase. It is most important for us to avoid placing his war-experience in false perspective or attributing to it an exaggerated importance. Whatever the world may think, his life would have been just as glorious and heroic had he never volunteered to do Christ's work on the battlefield. His life was a spiritual combat, an unseen war against all that is ignoble and evil; it needs not the fame that is won on fields of carnage. His service as a military chaplain did but serve to bring out his latent heroism, it showed to men the virtue which had already been acquired in the quiet of a religious house. Thus Fr. Doyle's life at the Front may well serve to disarm the prejudice of those who otherwise might be tempted to despise the little ups and downs, the prayers and penances, the resolutions and aspirations, which in this case are seen to be the inner facet of what is outwardly admirable. His work for the soldiers was, of course, wonderfully fruitful; his zealous ministry ended as it began, in Belgium. And one can hardly help feeling that his death was God's answer to his lifelong prayer for martyrdom. Nevertheless, the centre of Fr. Doyle's life is within, and its significance for us is quite independent of its chance relation to human warfare. One great benefit indeed we owe to his military chaplaincy: the fact that he had not an opportunity of destroying his spiritual notes. It is from these precious relics and from a few very intimate letters that we can piece together some of the special characteristics and methods of his spiritual life.

The predominant impression which is left after perusal of these papers is that Fr. Doyle is wonderfully true to type he is of the race of Jesuit heroes. He has his own particularities, of course, even peculiarities; but he is unmistakably similar to his spiritual forbears. For instance, the Jesuit pioneer missionaries of North America were men whose great achievements are written in the annals of civilisation, discovery, and ethnology. They were heroes, who for Christ left the fair land of France and buried themselves in the woods with savage Algonquins and Hurons, eating their coarse sagamite or oftener starving with them, shouldering the same burdens, living in the filth and vermin of their tepees, travelling over snow and ice, meeting not seldom with blasphemy and obscenity. Slow calculated heroism such as this is not a sudden inspiration or a wild access of emotion; it is the outcome of deep purposive thought and painful methodic effort co-operating with grace. The End of Man, the Kingdom of Christ, the Two Standards, slowly step by step does Ignatius train Christ's captains; and slowly, day by day, in humdrum routine and endless trivialities of self-mastery, do his sons develop the souls of heroes. John de Brebeuf, gloriously martyred on 16th March, 1649, used as a novice to declare: "I will be ground to powder rather than break a rule." Only to those who miss the inner key will this seem a curious preparation for foreign mission and martyrdom. Père Enémond Massé (1646), another pioneer missionary, to prepare himself for his apostolate in Canada, "whose conversion can be undertaken only by those who have on them the stigmata of the cross," made some resolutions which were found among his papers after death. As they help to reveal the spiritual affinities of Fr. Doyle, they will be here recorded:

"1. Never to sleep except on bare ground, without sheets or mattress which however must be kept in the room so that no one may know what is being done.

2. Not to wear linen except round the neck.

3. Never to say Mass without a hair-shirt, in order to make me think of the sufferings of my Master, of which the Holy Sacrifice is the great memorial.

4. To take the discipline daily.

5. Never to take dinner unless I have first made my examen, and if prevented to eat only a dessert.

6. Never to gratify my taste.

7. To fast three times a week, but so that no one will know it." [1]

Exactly similar detailed resolutions are to be found in nearly every page of Fr. Doyle's notes. His aspirations for holiness were never vague or unpractical.' During his 1909 Retreat he wrote: "It seems to me the best and most practical resolution I can make in this retreat is to determine to perform each action with the greatest perfection. This will mean a constant 'going against self' ever *agendo contra,* at every moment and every single day. I have a vast field to cover in my ordinary daily actions, *e.g.* to say the Angelus always with the utmost attention and fervour. I feel, too, that Jesus asks this from me, as without it there can be no real holiness."

There follows, at the end of these retreat-notes, a huge sheaf of resolutions. Unfortunately, some of the pages having been torn out or lost, the first thirty resolutions cannot be ascertained. Those we know are formidable enough.

[RESOLUTIONS.]

"31. God wants the sacrifice of never going to plays, concerts, cinematographs, football matches, or any sight for pure gratification.

32. With the boys absolute meekness, gentleness, and patience.

33. Never speak about your worries, troubles, amount of work.

34. Do not let an unkind, angry or uncharitable word pass your lips.

35. Don't complain of others or of anything else.

36. Always be most punctual.

37. Great fidelity to your own order of time, doing everything at the hour fixed.

38. If possible say all the Office on your knees before the Blessed Sacrament.

39. Never give yourself relief in small sufferings.

40. When in pain or unwell, try and not let others know it. Hence never say you have a headache, etc.

41. Wear hair-shirt for (erasure).

42. You have promised never deliberately to waste a moment of time.

43. Legs or feet not to be crossed.

44. Do not read letters for some time after receiving them.

45. Be very observant about the rule of silence.

46. The constant mortification of intense fervour at each little duty.

In general: (*a*) never do anything you would like; (*b*) deny yourself every gratification; (*c*) deny yourself every pleasure; (*d*) do the thing *because* it is hard; (*e*) in all things *agere contra.*

Vince Teipsum.
February 2nd, 1909.

Other Mortifications:-

1. 1,000 ejaculations morning and night.
2. Do not look at pictures, advertisements on hoardings.
3. Do not look into shop windows."

This is rather an elaborate programme. With increasing spiritual strategy, Fr. Doyle never again attempted fifty resolutions at once. Gradually he directed all his efforts to prayer and penance, and concentration on the passing act. Thus he records during his 1910 Retreat:

"What is my special end, for which God made me? More and more each retreat I see what this is, always the same thought, always the same desire and longing for *holiness.* God wants sanctity from me. This is to be acquired chiefly by three means: (1) constant little acts of mortification; (2) constant aspirations; (3) perfection of each action, even the odd Hail Marys."

We have here in three lines the chief characteristics or methods of Fr. Doyle's spirituality for the remaining years of his life. There is henceforth perceptible a remarkable consistency in his inner life. Clearly he had, with God's help, found those particular devices or modes of spiritual activity which suited his mind and character. Prayer, mortification and concentration are more or less incumbent: on all of us. It does not follow that the special forms in which these ideals took shape in Fr. Doyle's life are suitable to all. "There are diversities of graces but the same Spirit...and there are diversities of operations but the same God worketh all in all." (*I. Corinth.* 12. 4.) Each of us has his own individuality, just as each has his own particular mission; through the gates of life and death we all pass one by one. Even the members of the same family or community will differ considerably in aptitude for prayer, in visualising faculty, in spiritual gifts, in devotional attractions, in physical powers. God calls each of us individually, not as it were anonymously and in a crowd. "He calleth His own sheep by name." (*S. John* 10. 3.)

(2.) INTERIOR UNION.

Fr. Doyle had an extraordinarily vivid realisation of the spiritual world. In his life there is no trace of any doubts against faith. God was intensely real to him and prayer seemed to be an actual colloquy. Holiness appeared 'natural' to him, not in the sense that he found or made it easy, but inasmuch as it alone satisfied his yearnings and ideals. Thus he writes during his 1909 Retreat in preparation for his Final Vows:

"I feel within me a constant desire or craving for holiness, a longing for prayer and a great attraction for mortification. Even walking along the streets I feel God tugging at my heart and, in a sweet loving way, urging, urging, urging me to give myself up absolutely to Him and His service. Over and over again I say, 'My God, I *will* become a saint since You ask it.' But there is no progress, no real effort. The truth is, I am afraid of the sacrifice, afraid of doing what God wants; and I delude myself into thinking I am doing God's will and satisfying Him by an empty promise. What an abuse of grace! This cannot go on. I feel there must be a change now in this retreat, an absolute surrender to all God wants."

It was especially during his retreats that he found God's voice clear and insistent in his soul. "I am beginning my own retreat to-morrow," he wrote in

1914. "I long for this time all the year until it comes, and then dread it. I am afraid of Jesus! It is a tremendous thing to be alone with Him for eight whole days, listening to His voice, drinking in His love and then to think I may not go and do His bidding!" Just after this retreat he wrote to an intimate correspondent: "My own retreat was a happy time. It is the one little oasis in my wandering life, when I can really be alone with Jesus. The chief feature of it was a feeling as if He were giving me great strength to face His work and an increase of courage and confidence. In former retreats I used to suffer from a strange fear of our dear Lord, a fear that He might really make me see what He wanted; in my cowardice I dreaded that. In this last retreat this dread was absent in great measure, and help has come from the thought that everything will be His doing, not mine."

Even outside retreat-time he often records for his own use inspirations received in prayer, especially before the Blessed Sacrament. For instance, on 16th June, 1912, he writes: "I felt the presence of Jesus very near to me while praying in the chapel at Ramsgrange. He seemed to want me to write down what He said: 'I want you, my child, to abandon every gratification, generously, absolutely, for the love of Me. Each time you give in to yourself you suffer an enormous loss. Do not deceive yourself by thinking that certain relaxations are necessary or will help your work. My grace is sufficient for *you.* Give Me *all* at all times; never come down from the cross to which I have nailed you. Be generous, go on blindly, accepting all, denying yourself all. Trust in Me, I will sustain you, but only if you are really generous. Begin this moment and mortify every look, action, desire. No gratification, no relaxation, no yielding to self. Surrender yourself to Me as My victim and let Me make you a saint.'" Certainly not the kind of message one's imagination would take pleasure in conjuring up!

Of such messages from our Lord we have only the bare record, written for God's eye and the writer's. Whether they were vivid lights in prayer or whether they took the form of mystical locutions, we cannot tell. At any rate, they were a powerful incitement to holiness. In accordance with Fr. Doyle's impulsively generous nature, these inspirations came at times very suddenly. Thus the next entry in his diary (10th July, 1912) is as follows: "I awoke in the middle of the night with the feeling that Jesus, wanted me. I resisted, but at last got out of bed. At the foot of the altar I was thinking of something else, when suddenly He seemed to remind me of my prayer, 'Jesus come and dwell within my heart as in a tabernacle.' I felt Him urging me to this close union and He seemed to promise me that He would remain with me 'from Communion to Communion [2] if only I was recollected, but that I would easily drive Him away by unfaithfulness especially in want of guard over my eyes."

Often, too, Fr. Doyle would write down, as he knelt before the Tabernacle, a detailed message which he felt Christ was speaking to his soul. [3] This entry in his diary, made on 1st April, 1914, gives us an idea of the heroic urgings which he experienced in prayer:

"I begin to-day my twenty-fourth year in the Society, with a heart full to overflowing with gratitude for my vocation. I write this before my Jesus in the Tabernacle and I have asked Him to make me note down what He wants from me.

"Jesus says: (1) I want you to trust Me more: you are too much afraid of injuring your health by doing what I ask of you *e.g.* rising at night, sleeping on boards, taking no butter, etc. I would not urge these things so much if I did not want them from you. Trust Me more, My child. Have I not helped you to do many things you thought impossible and have you suffered for it? (2) I want you also to be My 'Suffering Love' never content unless you are making some sacrifice. You have not given Me all yet, though you know I want it, and until you do so, I cannot give you the marvellous graces I have destined for your soul. Be brave, be generous, but do not delay. There is joy in crucifixion. (3) I want this year to be one of profound recollection and intense union with Me. I have promised to dwell *physically* in you as in a tabernacle, from Communion to Communion, if you do what I have asked you guard your eyes. (4) Your faults of the tongue must cease from this day, they are working you much harm, (5) You must work for Me as you have never done before, especially by prayer and aspirations, boldly urging souls to heroic sanctity, not minding what people may say of you. Human respect is one of your faults still.'

"Before leaving the chapel Jesus said: 'In future let your *heart* speak; you are afraid of letting people know that you love Me tenderly.'"

Apparently without regarding them as directly supernatural, Fr. Doyle felt convinced that in these experiences he was listening to the voice of his Master. This explains what would otherwise seem mere impulsiveness and impetuosity. He often waited for some interior inspiration before acting, and when it came, he obeyed instantly. [4] "The resolution I feel impelled to make to-day," he wrote on the eve of his Last Vows (1909) "is to consult the Holy Ghost about everything, and to do what He suggests, to listen to His inspirations and to refuse Him nothing. I believe this would sanctify me quickly."

And again he writes on 12th Sept. 1913:

"I have felt strongly urged again to give myself entirely to the guidance of the Holy Spirit and to follow His inspirations. For example, I sometimes feel urged to take the discipline during the day, and when I have been able to overcome the repugnance to the trouble of it, my soul has been filled with joy. Many other thoughts of this kind come into my mind to rise when I wake, not to do this or that I am certain they are from the Holy Spirit, but I resist His voice, and hence feel unhappy. In future I will say a little prayer for light and then do what I am impelled to. Just now I was sitting in an armchair fearfully tired. It cost me a big effort to undress and take the discipline, and put on chain round waist. But the result was a most marvellous increase of bodily vigour."

It need scarcely be said that such a method, in the case of one untrained in theology or less mature in spirituality would be fraught with great danger. It was to St. Joseph, not to our Lady, that the angelic messages were given; and the converted Paul was sent for direction to Ananias. God wishes to help us through the medium of those whom He has appointed for the guidance of souls. So also in Fr. Doyle's own case this promptness to carry out the inspirations of grace by no means implied that he dispensed himself from the general guidance of superior, director or confessor, or, in special cases, from detailed permission. This submission to external rule and guidance is the universal characteristic of Catholic holiness. "I was once thinking," says St. Teresa, [5] "of the great penance practised by Dona Catalina de Cardona, and how I might have done more, considering the desires which our Lord had always given me, if it had not been for my obedience to my confessors. I asked myself whether it would not be well for the future to disobey them in this matter. 'No, my daughter,' said our Lord to me. 'You are on the safe and certain road. Do you observe all her penance? I think more of your obedience.'" Similarly S. Margaret Mary [6] records that our Lord said to her: "I will adjust My graces to the spirit of thy rule, to the will of thy superioress and to thy weakness; so that thou must regard as suspicious everything that might withdraw thee from the exact observance of thy rule, to which I will that thou shouldst give the preference."

It is but natural, of course, that a fully formed Jesuit is not in need of the same minute detailed direction which is necessary for weaker untrained souls. S. Ignatius supposes that the finished member of his Society is expert in the discernment of spirits, quick to detect evil influences and self-deception, alert to recognise the promptings of grace. One so steeped in the spirit of the Exercises, one so watchful in continual self-conquest, as Fr. Doyle, was well fitted to guide himself and others in the imitation of Christ. He had the direction of many gifted souls and he accepted this task only with a serious sense of responsibility. He was by no means uncritical and he was always severely practical. He had no love for that theorising about mysticism which is so common. "I would strongly advise you," he once wrote, "not to read books treating of the mystical life unless you can get a good guide. You might be imagining yourself in a certain state when you are a thousand miles away from it. ... Go on quietly, loving God and seeking to please Him, without trying to find out in what exact state of perfection your soul is." Very sound advice for any beginner who is inclined to confuse the acquisition of a mystical vocabulary and an abnormal habit of self-dissection with the actual experiences and privileges of the saints. Fr. Doyle, of course, was not always merely negative and repressive. To several holy souls he gave help and guidance in regions ordinarily inaccessible. In one or two cases, perhaps three altogether, he ultimately gave his approval to the genuineness of mystical phenomena such as locutions. Many times he records in his diary a message which one of these few spiritual children sent to him as coming from Christ. This is an instance: "Tell him I desire this union with My whole Heart; I want to teach him how to deal with My disciples." But as these messages are by no means as clear and practical as his own lights, and as we have no means of examining their authenticity, nothing would be gained by reproducing them here. Besides, it is not at all clear that occasionally Fr. Doyle's trustful sincerity was not influenced to the detriment of a more severely critical judgement which a riper experience would have created.

In Fr. Doyle's own case these celestial messages and inspirations merged by insensible gradations into more homely experiences. Like St. Ignatius tossing the reins on his mule's neck as he rode towards Montserrat, Fr. Doyle loved to see an intimation of God's will in what men usually call chance. He would 'cut' a favourite book - say, the Life of Gemma Galgani, the Life of Père Ginhac, or even the New Testament itself - in order to find some helpful text; an act to which, by the way, we owe S. Augustine's conversion. Indeed, wherever he was and whatever he saw, he was always ready to see God's hand and to hear His voice. Thus he records in his diary on 21st Dec., 1913: "At the end of the performance of *Quo Vadis?* the words of our Lord seemed to go through my soul, 'I am going to Rome to be crucified for thee.' Jesus must have given me a big grace, for I walked home stunned, with these words ringing in my ears, 'crucified for thee.' Oh! Jesus, Jesus, why cannot I be crucified for You? I long for it with all my heart, and yet I remain a coward. Thank you at least for the dear light You have given me about the life You ask from me, namely, 'to give up every comfort and gratification, to embrace lovingly every possible pain and suffering.'" A devout conclusion not always deducible from cinema shows!

Fr. Doyle's habit of interrogating everything for a spiritual message is shown in his visits to shrines. In Feb., 1911, when giving a retreat in Cork, he visited the grave of the little orphan child who is known as 'Little Nellie of Holy God.' "Kneeling there," he says, "I asked her what God wanted from me, when I heard an interior voice clearly repeating, 'Love Him, love Him.' The following day she seemed to rebuke me, when leaving the cemetery, for the careless way I performed most of my spiritual duties, and to say that God was displeased with this and wanted great fervour and perfection in them." In November, 1912, he was able to pay a visit to Lourdes. "Almost the first thing" he writes, "which caught my eye at the grotto was our Lady's words: *Pénitence, pénitence, penitence!* On leaving, I asked Jesus had He any message to give me. The same flashed suddenly into my mind and made a deep impression on me." A week later he was in Lisieux. "Kneeling at the grave of the Little Flower," he says, "I gave myself into her hands to guide and to make me a saint. I promised her to make it the rule of my whole life, every day without exception, to seek in all things my greater mortification, to give all and to refuse nothing. I have made this resolution with great confidence because I realise how utterly it is beyond my strength; but I feel the Little Flower will get me grace to keep it perfectly." While he was military chaplain in France, he was able to pay two visits to Amettes in the diocese of Boulogne, the birthplace of St. Benedict Joseph Labre. This is how he records his second visit on 1st May, 1917: "Second pilgrimage to Amettes from Locre. During the journey I felt our Lord wanted to give me some message through St. Benedict

Joseph Labre. No light came while praying in the Church or in the house; but when I went up to his little room and knelt down a voice seemed to whisper 'Read what is written on the wall.' I saw these words: *Dieu m'appelle a la me austère; il faut que je me prépare pour suivre les voies de Dieu.* [7] With these words came a sudden light to see how much one gains by every act of sacrifice, that what we give is not lost; but the enjoyment (increased a thousand fold) is only postponed. This filled me with extraordinary consolation which lasted all day."

It will thus be seen that holiness was Fr. Doyle's constant preoccupation. Though he was human and social as well as many-sided in his interests, the central realities of his life were God and his own soul. God was to him no distant Creator or far-off Judge, He was an ever-present Companion whose voice he could not mistake, to whom he always turned. Angels were to him no subtle speculation, nor were the saints merely historical examples. With childlike simplicity he spoke to them and strove to learn from them. One looks in vain among his papers for a doubt or a hint of modern scepticism. He saw things from within, and he was satisfied; he did not just read about religion, he lived it. And so he lived in our cities of to-day, those great wildernesses of stone and steel, just as if he had been dwelling in the uplands of Galilee twenty centuries ago. He passed through life with the faith of a little child, and thus out into the great Beyond, still a child, for of such is the Kingdom of Heaven.

(3.) PERSONAL ATTACHMENT TO CHRIST.

"Is it possible," asks a Protestant clergyman, no less a personage than the late Master of Balliol, [8] "is it possible to feel a personal attachment to Christ such as is prescribed by Thomas a Kempis?" "I think," he replies, "that it is impossible and contrary to human nature that we should be able to concentrate our thoughts on a person scarcely known to us, who lived eighteen hundred years ago." What a complacently uttered verdict from one who, with all his scholarship, never comprehended the inner meaning and motive-power of priest and nun, aye, and of millions of suffering toilers who in Christ alone find rest for their souls! It is precisely this intense personal attachment to Jesus that is the key to the life of a man like Fr. Doyle. It was the driving-force of that chivalrous Spanish hidalgo who, after winning earthly glory at the siege of Pamplona, hung up his sword at the shrine of our Lady of Montserrat and enlisted in the service of the King whose proclamation rang in his ears: "My will is to conquer the whole world and all enemies and thus to enter into My Father's glory. Therefore whoever desires to come with Me must labour with Me, in order that following Me in pain, he may likewise follow Me in glory." [9] Mecum (with Me) does not this little word carry in it the heart of Christianity? The sacrifices of religious life are possible because it is life with Christ. The heroism of Christian charity lives on because it is done for Christ, with Christ, to Christ. What a measureless volume of human service has been created by the presence and the ideal of Christ! What a burden of human suffering has been borne with Christ, laid beside the Passion of the Son of Man, ever since the days when Peter and the apostles went "rejoicing that they were accounted worthy to suffer reproach for the name of Jesus." (Acts 5. 41.) To-day, after twenty centuries, the name of Jesus is still as potent, and the friendship of Christ is alone able to inspire what is most sublime and heroic in humanity. Unless we grasp the ever-living reality of this companionship of Christ, we shall fail completely to understand the struggles, the ecstasies, the so-called follies of the saints and of those hidden souls innumerable of whom the world is not worthy. "The consciousness of this friendship of Jesus Christ," writes Mgr. Benson, [10] "is the very secret of the saints. Ordinary men can live ordinary lives, with little or no open defiance of God, from a hundred second-rate motives. We keep the commandments that we may enter into life; we avoid sin that we may escape hell; we fight against worldliness that we may keep the respect of the world. But no man can advance three paces on the road of perfection unless Jesus Christ walks beside him. It is this, then, that gives distinction to the way of the saint, and that gives him his apparent grotesqueness too for what is more grotesque in the eyes of the unimaginative world than the ecstasy of the lover? Commonsense never yet drove a man mad; it is commonsense that is thought to characterise sanity; and commonsense therefore has never scaled mountains, much less has it cast them into the sea. But it is the maddening joy of the conscious companionship of Jesus Christ that has produced the lovers, and therefore the giants, of history. It is the developing friendship of Jesus Christ and the Passion that; has inspired those lives, which the world in its dull moods calls unnatural and the Church in all her moods supernatural. 'This priest,' cried S. Teresa in one of her more confidential moments with her Lord, 'this priest is a very proper person to be made a friend of ours.'"

In this respect Fr. Doyle was a true member of the Company of Jesus. It scarcely needs to be proved that his whole life was pivoted on love for Christ. Without some such cardinal passion or absorbing motive, a man will not devote his life to sacrificing his natural inclinations, seeking and enduring pain, toiling in gratuitous and often unrequited service, laying down his life amid nauseating scenes of carnage. [11] Such a life can only be led with Christ, always mentally and often sacramentally present. At times Fr. Doyle felt overpowered by the intensity of this love. "Even as a child," he writes, "I longed and prayed to be a saint. But somehow it always seemed to me as if that longing could never be realised, for I felt there was some kind of a barrier like a high wall between myself and God. What it was, I cannot say even now. But recently this obstacle appears to me to have been removed, the way is open, and I feel I love Jesus now as I never did before, or even hoped to. With this comes the conviction, so strong and consoling with so much peace and happiness, that Jesus will grant my heart's desire before I die. I dare not put on paper what I feel, even if I could; but at times Jesus seems to pour all the grace of His Sacred Heart upon me until I am intoxicated almost with His love and could cry out with the pain of that sweet wounding."

"I cannot deny," he said on another occasion, "that I love Jesus, love Him passionately, love Him with every fibre of my heart. He knows it, too, since He has asked me to do many things for Him, which have cost me more than I should like to say, yet which with His grace were sweet and easy in a sense. He knows that my longing, at least, even if the strength and courage are wanting, is to do and suffer much more for Him, and that were He to-morrow to ask for the sacrifice of every living friend, I would not refuse Him. Yet with all that, with the intense longing to make Him known and loved, I have never yet been able to speak of Him to others as I want to."

And here is a precious letter in which, forgetting his usual reserve, he gives an intimate correspondent a glimpse into the inner fires of his soul. It is dated from the Presentation Convent, B---, 30th July, 1914.

"What you say is indeed true. Jesus has been 'hunting' me during these past days, trying to wound my heart with His arrows of love. He has been so gentle, so patient, tender, loving, I do not know at times where to turn, and yet I somehow feel that much of this grace is given me for others, I know it has helped souls and lifted them close to Jesus.

"I long to get back to my little room at night, to calm and quiet, and yet I dread it, for He is often so loving there. I feel He is near because I cannot go to Him in the Tabernacle. It is such a helpless feeling to be tossed about as it were on the waves of love, to feel the ardent, burning love of His Heart, to know He asks for love, and then to realise one human heart is so tiny.

"Your letter and little meditation have helped me. At times I have smiled at the folly of what you say since I realize how little you know of my real character, and then like a big wave the truth seems to burst on me, that as a fierce fire sweeps away and consumes all obstacles, so the love of God blots out the many faults and failings of my poor life and leaves me free to go to Him.

"The bands are playing in the town below, but the music in my soul is a thousand times sweeter. 'The Love of God.' I have one more lecture, some confessions and then no you may not come He wants to be alone with me for a few brief moments at least that I may pour out on Him all my love and affection and put my arms around His neck my Jesus and my All. Forgive me, child, I am foolish."

Another intimate note tells us how at times his love found vent in reverently yet affectionately embracing the image of his crucified Master. [12] "I went on to and once more had an opportunity of a quiet prayer before the life-size crucifix in the church which I love so much. I could not remain at His feet but climbed up until both my arms were around His neck. The Figure seemed almost to live, and I think I loved Him then, for it was borne in upon me how abandoned and suffering and broken-hearted He was. It seemed to console Him when I kissed His eyes and pallid cheeks and swollen lips, and as I clung to Him, I knew He had won the victory, and I gave Him all He asked." [13]

Fr. Doyle's love for Christ was thus not confined to the cold upper regions of the soul, whither many who walk in the darkness of faith must relegate it. It was something which filled his whole being and at times overflowed sensibly. "Was not our heart burning within us whilst He spoke in the way?" exclaimed the two disciples. (*S. Luke* 24. 32.) Fr. Doyle was often on the Emmaus road; Jesus seemed to speak in the way, and his heart was burning within him. His emotion then found utterance in loving transports, one of which was happily put on paper. "I know not why I am writing this," he says, "except it be to ease my straining heart, for at times I feel half mad with the love of God."

"Jesus is the most loving of lovable friends there never was a friend like Him before, there never can be one to equal Him, because there is only one Jesus in the whole wide world and the vast expanse of Heaven, and that sweet and loving friend, that true lover of the holiest and purest love is *my Jesus,* mine alone and all mine. Every fibre of His divine nature is thrilling with love for me, every beat of His gentle Heart is a throb of intense affection for me, His sacred arms are round me, He draws me to His breast, He bends down with infinite tenderness over me, His child, for He knows I am all His, and He is all mine. In His eyes the vast world, the myriads of other souls have all vanished, He has forgotten them all, for that brief moment they do not exist for even the infinite love of God Himself is not enough to pour out on the soul who is clinging so lovingly to Him.

"O Jesus, Jesus, Jesus! who would not love You, who would not give their heart's blood for You, if only once they realised the depth and the breadth and the realness of Your burning love? Why not then make every human heart a burning furnace of love for You, so that sin would become an impossibility, sacrifice a pleasure and a joy, virtue the longing of every soul, so that we should live for love, dream of love, breathe Your love, and at last die of a broken heart of love, pierced through and through with the shaft of love, the sweetest gift of God to man."

Doubtless there are stolid souls who will not appreciate these emotional outpourings, who regard such fervent language as mere sentimentalism. It is true, of course, that such utterances were never meant to be dragged from their sacred privacy into the cold light of print. But that is just the beauty of them. They well up spontaneously from the heart of a strong man, they express the pent up enthusiasm of this brave soldier of Christ, seeking an unconventional outlet. Fr. Doyle was no sickly sentimentalist or hysterical weakling. He lived what he felt, and he meant what he said. Why should we fancy that strength must be shorn of tenderness? Why should we think that only earthly love is privileged to have its delights? Paul, the man of action, was accused by some Corinthian converts of being 'beside himself.' "If we have been beside ourselves," he answers, "it was for God; if we are now in our right senses, it is for you. For the love of Christ overmasters us reflecting that as One died for all, then all were dead; and that He died for all, so that the living may no longer live to themselves but to Him who died for them and rose again... Hence if any one is in Christ, he is a new being, his old life has passed away, a new life has begun!" (II Cor. 5. 13-17.) *Charitas Christi urget nos.* Thus wrote the great Apostle of the Gentiles in a public letter. And John, "the disciple whom Jesus loved, the one who at the Supper leant back on His breast" (*S. John* 21. 20), tells us that "we know what love is through Christ's having laid down His life for us" (*I John* 3. 16.) Has not Jesus Himself set His seal on the humanness, so to speak, of our relations with Him? He will not call us servants but friends. (*S. John* 15. 15.) "You are the men who have stood by Me in My trials" (*S. Luke* 22. 28), said our Lord to His Apostles. And He had sorrowfully to add, "Even you will all be scandalized in Me to-night" (*S. Matthew* 26. 31.) Yet as a last appeal He took with Him to His agony His three favoured friends, whose slumber He then lovingly excused And as they slept, stretched there beneath the moonlit olive-trees, was He not comforted, not only by the angelic messenger, but by the countless faithful ones who would watch and pray during their 'holy hour,' who, separated in sequence of time but nigh to His eternal gaze, [14] would kneel beside Him and drink His chalice? And as His pain-racked form was raised aloft on the Hill of Golgotha, as His blood-clotted eyes looked down on a sea of mocking hardened faces, did He not feel the stream of adoring love which down the centuries was to converge on the Crucified? "And I. if I be lifted up from the earth, will draw all things to Myself." (*S. John* 12. 32.) Peter crucified head downwards, following his Master at last; Ignatius of Antioch crying "My Love is crucified"; the innumerable soi.il s whose last earthly gaze is fixed on the crucifix; and every one of us who has knelt before the image of Christ Crucified, or made the Stations of the Cross or stood in spirit on Calvary with Mary, His Mother; all are joining in reparation to the Heart of Jesus. Seen in this eternal perspective, is there not a wondrous and touching reality in Fr. Doyle's climbing up to the life-size crucifix and kissing the pallid face of the Crucified? It is just such simple, artless love which discerns the ever-present significance of the Life of Christ. [15]

As a pledge of his devotion to Christ and to bind his life to that of his Master, Fr. Doyle made a vow of consecration to the Sacred Heart of Jesus, signing his name thereto in his blood, and thus attesting his dedication of himself to the service of Him "who hath loved us and washed us from our sins in His own blood." (*Apoc.* i. 5.) It was made during one of those quiet midnight vigils which Fr. Doyle loved so well and was written by the red glimmer of the sanctuary lamp.

"Most loving Jesus, kneeling before You in the Blessed Sacrament, I solemnly consecrate myself to Your Sacred Heart by vow. I vow always to be Your faithful lover and to strive every day to grow in Your love. In imitation of the oblation which B. Margaret Mary made of herself, I now wish to give myself up absolutely and entirely, without any reserve whatever, to Your most Sacred Heart, that You may be free to do with me, to treat me, as You wish, to send me whatever suffering or humiliation You wish. I desire to put no obstacle to the action of grace upon my soul, to be a perfect instrument in

Your divine hands, to be Your victim should You so desire. I want to make this oblation and immolation of myself to Your Sacred Heart as completely as possible, and in the manner which You wish me to make it, O my Jesus. Therefore, again, by this vow, I make a complete surrender of myself and all I have to You. Do with me as You will, for from this hour I am wholly Yours

Amen.

Feast of St. Michael, Friday, Sept. 29th, 1910.
Made at Midnight. Signed W. J. DOYLE, S. J."

(4.) PRAYER.

One of Fr. Doyle's favourite devotions was that of the Holy Hour. [16] Long before he became a priest he had made it faithfully week after week and found it a fruitful source of grace. Afterwards as a hard-working priest, he contrived to increase the number of nocturnal visits. "Two years ago when at Tours," he writes on 22nd Nov., 1914, "I felt strongly urged to rise and make the Holy Hour every night. In the past twelve months I have gone down to the chapel about fifty times, though often only for a few moments; this does not include the weekly Holy Hour on Thursday. Now I feel impelled to rise each night, when at home, at least for a quarter of an hour." And in April, 1915, he resolved "to make the Holy Hour each night from ten to eleven when at home." How he made it may be best gathered from an entry in his diary under the date 1st Sept., 1911. "Last night," he writes, "while making the Holy Hour in my room, Jesus seemed to ask me to promise to make it every Thursday, even when away giving retreats, and when I cannot go to the chapel, He wants the greater part of the time to be spent prostrate on the ground, which I find very painful. I think He wants me to share in His agony during this hour, feeling a little of the sadness, desolation, and abandonment He experienced, the shame of sin, the uselessness of His sufferings to save souls. I begged Him to plunge my soul into the sea of bitterness which surrounded Him. It was an hour of pain, but I hope for more."

Fr. Doyle devoted himself to the propagation of this practice. It was long uphill work, not so much among holy souls living in the world, very many of whom adopted it enthusiastically, as among religious communities, where innovations progress slowly, even apart from the difficulty of finding room for a new devotion in an already overcrowded time-table. But the efforts were in many cases crowned with success. "Our Blessed Lord is at last blessing my efforts to establish the Holy Hour," wrote Fr. Doyle in 1914. "Up to this attempts have been more or less of a failure, but now they have taken it up warmly in all the W. convents. The Mother Provincial of the X.. nuns will push it during her visitation. Moreover the devotion has been established with full sanction of the authorities in Y., and will now spread to the other ten convents there. A letter from Z yesterday told me that they, too, after three years' wait had fallen into line." It is scarcely necessary to add that this propaganda did not always meet with approval or favour. But it deserves to be recorded that Fr. Doyle was by no means a blind enthusiast. He quite appreciated local or individual difficulties. Thus he wrote to a nun in 1911: "As regards the Holy Hour I would urge you personally not to make a practice of staying up every Thursday night. The privation of sleep tells in the end, and you are not too strong; and if you get knocked up, people will say that was the cause and may even get the Hour forbidden. God likes generosity, but we must be prudent and not expect Him to work miracles."

This practice was but one expression of his love for the Blessed Sacrament. [17] Again and again he gives vent to his eucharistic devotion. "The mad longing for His presence," he writes, "is at times overpowering. It would be hard to describe how He chains me to Him, the magnetic attraction, the more than physical force that drags me to the Tabernacle, and then the pain with which I realize at His feet how small and feeble the human heart is to give Him a love worthy of His." He spent every spare moment in church or chapel; and since spare moments grew scarcer as the years went on, he laid the hours of sleep under contribution On some feast days, such as that of Corpus Christi, he contrived to spend, at intervals, as much as seven hours before the Blessed Sacrament. But besides his want of leisure in the daytime, he had a special love for vigil before the Tabernacle. Prayer was easier in the quiet stillness of the night, he was free to express outwardly the longings of his heart, and last but not least, he liked nocturnal prayer because it was hard. To rise when one awakes, or to set one's alarum for midnight, and creep down to the chapel, even were it only for a few minutes, is no slight act of mortification. Still more heroic is the cheating oneself of the sleep earned after a hard day's work. Fr. Doyle did not ever find this easy. In his Retreat of September 1915, he records: "A greater urging to spend every available moment with Him and to try to practise nocturnal adoration oftener; 'every, night' Jesus says, but I am too cowardly and too fearful of my health. Would He not help me if I tried?" [18]

It was while he was on the mission that he most keenly felt his inability to visit our Lord at night, it was then that he realised how much a domestic chapel means. "I never knew," runs a letter of his, "how much Jesus in the Tabernacle enters our lives as religious, till I had to live for weeks in houses where He was absent. I manage to make the Holy Hour each week, though I have to wait till all are asleep before I can steal out to the chapel, sometimes a couple of miles away."

Later on when stationed in England as military chaplain he wrote: "There is one thing I cannot, (I almost wrote 'will not'), bear, the loss of our dearest Lord. It is bitterly hard to have to live day after day without His presence except for a few moments each morning during Mass, which only makes things harder still, for I am left hungering for Him for twenty-four hours. I have found a tiny chapel some miles from here, but I can seldom get there. The thought of Jesus in that lonely Tabernacle haunts me always,, and at night I seem to hear Him calling gently and sadly. Oh! how I wish I could go to Him through the mud and rain." A month later (January 1916) he writes: "We came here (Bordon Camp) in awful rain and wind, but on reaching the barracks, the first thing I saw were the words: 'R. C. Hut.' Thinking it was just the empty hut for Sunday Mass, and yet half-hoping, I opened the door to find a beautifully furnished little chapel with the red lamp that told me all. I think I now know what Mary felt when she found her Son in the temple. How I thanked Him for this gift, for His goodness in sending my regiment to camp about His dwelling! His goodness did not stop there, for without -asking him, the priest in charge gave me the key, so that I can come to Jesus at any time. I am very happy now, for I have Him, *Deus meus et omnia* [19] - all else cannot supply - His place and life seems quite changed."

Even when serving at the Front, his thoughts turned to nocturnal prayer and adoration. Here is an entry dated 25th October, 1916: "Jesus has long urged me to give Him a whole night of prayer and reparation. Last night I prayed in my dug-out at Kemmel from 9 till 5 (eight hours), most of the time on my knees. I bound myself beforehand to do so by vow in order not to let myself off. Though I had only two hours' sleep, I am not very tired or weary to-day. Jesus wants more of these nights of prayer, adoration and atonement."

Thus this true follower of the Prince of Peace pursued Ms calm inner life amid the scenes and sounds of human strife, kneeling in his dug-out and adoring his eucharistic Lord in the pyx as quietly and devotedly as if he were in the domestic chapel of Rathfarnham Castle. Two months before his death he notes (21st June, 1917): "Jesus told me to-day that the work of regeneration and sanctification is to be done by leading souls to Him in the Blessed Sacrament." And on 2nd July he records: "The conviction has been growing that nocturnal adoration will be established only if I spend much time myself before the Blessed Sacrament at night. I know well that Jesus not only wants me to sacrifice much of my sleep, but also to rise sometimes during the night to adore and console Him in the Tabernacle. The repugnance (and yet attraction) to this is extraordinary."

It will be clear from such an admission that Fr. Doyle's devotion to the Real Presence was quite compatible with dryness, drowsiness and discomfort. In advice once sent to another he gives us the secret of his own devotion to his sacramental Lord. "Real devotion to the Blessed Sacrament," he writes, "is only to be gained by hard, grinding work of dry adoration before the Hidden God. But such a treasure cannot be purchased at too great a cost, for once obtained, it makes of this life as near an approach to heaven as we can ever hope for."

Although grace worked very effectively and appreciably in his soul, it never dispensed him from 'hard, grinding work.' Even in the case of that interior union which seemed to be so spontaneously natural in Fr. Doyle, we can from his diary perceive how slow, painful and methodic were the means which he took to acquire and perfect such union. During his retreat of January 1913 he wrote: "I feel drawn still more to the life of interior union. To acquire this I must practise the following:

(1) Constant and profound recollection.
(2) To keep my thoughts always if possible centred on Jesus in my heart.
(3) To avoid worry and anxiety about future things.
(4) To avoid useless conversation.
(5) Great guard over my eyes, not reading or looking at useless things."

So, even in regions generally called mystic, he proceeded in that clear, systematic, one might say businesslike, way so characteristic of St. Ignatius. No vague yearnings after sublimities or ecstasies, no anxiety for the abnormal or singular, just a quiet persevering fidelity in small things and an unflinching determination to avail of those countless opportunities with which each day is strewn. To use an expressive phrase, St. Ignatius wishes us in our spiritual life to come to the point; he will have no pious generalities; no beating about the bush. In my meditation I am "to reflect in order to derive some fruit "; in my prayer I am "to ask of God our Lord that which I wish and desire." Above all, I must, according to St. Ignatius, specialise, I must concentrate on some special defects, needs, or devotions.

And this concentration necessarily implies an increase in self-conscious purpose, a growth in deliberate mental self-control. Thus to eradicate some special sin or fault, St. Ignatius suggests "that each time a person falls into that particular sin or defect he lays his hand on his breast, repenting that he has fallen; and he can do this even in the presence of many people without their perceiving it." Moreover he wants us to write down twice a day the number of times we have fallen; he will not have us merely enter the total number, the faults must be represented graphically by parallel rows of points, so that we can at a glance compare day with day and week with week. Such is the spiritual accountancy of the writer of the Spiritual Exercises [20] who wishes us to apply to our souls the minute care with which business men keep their ledgers. Not everyone, of course, could or should literally follow all these details on every point; but there is in them an elemental method of the human mind, which we altogether neglect only at the peril of lapsing into unpractical dreaming, vague sentimentalism, and perhaps serious self-delusion. [21]

This incisive, one might say militant, method of spirituality appealed very much to the fervent heart and chivalrous courage of Fr. Doyle. He believed in marshalling all his forces for the immediate present, in concentrating his energies on the holiness attainable here and now. In this strain he writes on the Feast of the Blessed Cure of Ars, 4th August, 1913: "Making my meditation before the picture of the Blessed, he seemed to say to me with an interior voice: The secret of my life was that *I lived for the moment.* I did not say, 'I must pray here for the next hour,' but only 'for this moment,' I did not say, 'I have a hundred confessions to hear,' but looked upon this one as the first and last. I did not say, 'I must deny myself everything and always,' but only 'just this once.' By this means I was able always to do everything perfectly, quietly and in great peace. Try and live this life of the present moment. Pray as if you had nothing else whatever to do; say your Office slowly as if for the last time;

do not look forward and think you must often repeat this act of self-denial. This will make all things much easier." Two years later we find a similar entry: "No sacrifice would be great if looked at in this way. I do not feel now the pain which has past, I have not yet to bear what is coming; hence I have only to endure the suffering of *this one moment,* which is quickly over and cannot return."

It was especially by momentary recollection and ejaculatory prayer that Fr. Doyle sought to sanctify the passing moment and to condense perfection into the immediate present. When he was tempted to break a resolution, or when he shrank from some sacrifice, he used to say five times to himself, "Will you refuse to do this for the love of Jesus?" By means of aspirations he sharpened his will into instant action and brought into play all the accumulated motive-power of the past. "This morning," he writes in his diary (Sept. 1915), "I lay awake powerless to overcome myself and to make my promised visit to the chapel. Then I felt prompted to pray; I said five aspirations and rose without difficulty. How many victories I could win by this easy and powerful weapon!" Indeed he had a wonderful idea of the value of aspirations as a source of grace and merit. "Great light at meditation," he writes, "on the value of one aspiration. If I knew I should receive £1 for each one I made, I would not waste a spare moment. And yet I get infinitely more than this, though I often fail to realise it." During the last few years of his life Fr. Doyle's conviction of the value of aspirations steadily grew; and with him to believe was to act. [22] The number of aspirations which he contrived to fit into one day advanced from 10,000 to over 100,000. This latter astounding figure was reached while he was actually engaged in the arduous duties of military chaplain at the Front. As he never revealed this to anyone and as the achievement seems rather incredible, it will be well to extract from his diaries and to give here the references and resolutions concerning aspirations. These, it should be remembered, were written solely for his own use. [23]

"I felt urged to-day to make an effort to reach 10,000 aspirations each day; if I fall short, to make up the number at another time. This would mean three and a half million acts in the year. How much grace and holiness that would mean! I have so much lost time to make up." (21st Sept., 1911.)

"During a visit to D--- I made a strong resolution, cost what it may, every day to make 10,000 ejaculations (since increased to 12,000). I have never realised before so clearly how much I was losing by not doing so." (22nd April, 1912.)

"Novena to Blessed Cure d' Ars. Resolved to bear small pains and make 20,000 aspirations." (26th July, 1913.)

"Constant urging of Jesus to make every effort to reach 20,000 aspirations daily." (18th July, 1914.)

"25,000 aspirations; if possible, 10,000 before lunch." (Resolution on New Year's Day, 1915.)

"I made a vow, in honour of Soeur Thérèse, for the rest of my life to make every day 10,000 aspirations, unless sick." (3rd March, 1915.)

"Jesus said to me: 'You must make your life a martyrdom of prayer.' This means that I must give every spare moment to aspirations etc. generously banishing idle thoughts in which I indulge so much trying to make 50,000 daily I must also increase very much the time I spend in the chapel." (1st May, 1916.)

"Feast of the Seven Dolours. Said Mass in St. Colette's home at Corbie. While visiting the chapel where she was a recluse for four years, again I felt most strongly urged to make the 50,000 aspirations the penance of my life, and to force myself, no matter at what cost, to get through them daily. I have made this resolve: that if this is impossible, I will make up the number later on." (15th Sept., 1916.)

"It seemed to me that it would please our Lord to try and make up for all the aspirations I might have made during the early years of my religious life. At the rate of 10,000 a day for 15 years this would amount to fifty-four million. I have promised Him to pay this back, counting anything over the usual 50,000 aspirations each day. It is a huge amount to face, but with His grace I shall accomplish my task, more especially as I have proved it is possible to do 100,000 daily with a little energy and courage. If He preserves my life during this war, I must work with might and main for Him in gratitude. This grace I owe to my darling Mother Mary, who has put this thought into my mind today, Saturday." (2nd Nov., 1916.)

"Again a clear interior light that God wants me to aim at the 100,000 aspirations daily. I feel a longing to take up this life of unceasing prayer and at the same time a dread and a loathing of this burden, for I must watch every spare minute of the day to perform my penance. I feel Jesus asks this in reparation for His priests. With the help of our Blessed Lady I have this day begun the big fight." (13th Dec., 1916.)

"The conviction is steadily growing stronger that I am doing what God wants specially from me by making the 100,000 aspirations. I have not experienced much trouble in doing so for the past twelve days." (1st January, 1917.)

"I find I am falling off in the 100,000 aspirations. Have bound myself for a week by vow to make the full number, (1st Feb., 1917.)

"I have made a bargain with our Lord to give me a soul for every 1,000 aspirations made over the daily 100,000." (13th Feb... 1917.)

Thus we learn from these intimate confessions that Fr. Doyle regarded this practice as the penance of his life, that he had to watch every spare minute of the day to perform this penance, that it was a burden for which he felt dread and loathing, and that nevertheless he was ultimately able "with a little energy and courage" to make a hundred thousand aspirations in the day. How he accomplished this marvellous feat must remain something of a psychological mystery, for we have no further evidence or details. It is clear that he thus utilised every spare moment; whenever he was waiting for someone, whenever he was travelling alone or even passing along the house, he occupied himself in saying his beads or in ejaculatory prayer. But even at the rate of fifty aspirations a minute it would take over thirty-three hours to make a hundred thousand ejaculations. It would seem then that by aspiration Fr. Doyle meant not so much a form of words (*e.g.* an indulgenced prayer), as a turning of the mind to God, a heartbeat of love, a lightning-flash of the soul. In this way, perhaps, he was able to turn his every movement and activity into a deliberate expression of love for Christ. [24] In a retreat to priests he pointed out that the ordinary Office contained about 12,000 words; and it is very probable that he himself regarded each word devoutly said as an aspiration. Only in this way can we explain the possibility of what he did. We must also be content with guessing at his method of counting. Probably certain duties such as Mass, Office and Rosary were reckoned at some numerical value corresponding to the average words contained. And the remaining aspirations were perhaps counted with the help of a 'watch' - a little instrument sometimes used by missioners for numbering confessions. The significance of this definite recording of the number of aspirations etc., does not lie so much in the heroic extreme to which he ultimately carried it, for this is a personal development largely inapplicable to others of a different type of mind. Its importance consists rather in the fact, which we must not leave unnoticed, that it was by this simple Ignatian device that he succeeded in initially acquiring the habit. In September 1910, during his retreat, he chronicles a failure which will be an encouraging lesson to us. "The great defect in my character," he says, "and chief reason why I make so little progress is my want of fidelity. Thus in the past eighteen months I have not marked the ejaculations and acts of self-denial over three hundred times, which means that on these days I did none." A conclusion which is surely too severe, but which at least shows us the efficacy of 'marking' our incipient efforts.

Fr. Doyle was naturally a zealous advocate of this practice for others. "There is nothing," he said in a letter, "there is nothing better than the practice of aspirations, steadily growing in number. Keep a little book and enter them once a day. ... I would like you to keep count of these little acts like the aspirations, but don't go too fast; build up and do not pull down." He realised, of course, though perhaps not sufficiently clearly in one or two cases that the systematic piling up of aspirations to reach an arithmetically denned goal might be extremely unsuitable to many minds. His views were, in fact, very prudent and tolerant. This is advice which he gave in February 1912: "As to any practice of piety there is a double danger: recommending it as infallible, or condemning it as useless. I always make a point of saying that all things are not for all people. Characters differ so much... My own experience, and that of many others, is that the beads for marking aspirations are an invaluable help; for if there is not a definite number of acts marked or counted somehow, you will very soon find that very few are done. I think you have found the benefit of counting twenty acts of self-denial; so if you like, do the same for aspirations, increasing slowly, not too many at first and no straining." "As regards counting the aspirations," he similarly wrote to another penitent in July 1914, "if you really find that it is a strain on your tired head, give up the practice."

It is indeed perfectly obvious that beyond a certain total say forty or fifty a day this arithmetical application of the Ignatian method to aspirations, or other acts of virtue, will in normal cases produce very injurious results. Any unnatural strain or tension will ruin that cheerful spontaneity and elastic freshness which is so essential to religious life. Moreover, an undue stress on the merely numerical aspect of prayer may lead to a serious depreciation of more important qualities. *How* we pray is a far more vital problem than *how much* we pray; intensity is preferable to extension. "When you are praying, speak not much as the heathens; for they think that in their much speaking they may be heard." (*S. Matthew* 6. 7.) There is a spiritual lesson for us, too, in that exquisite little scene of Jesus sitting down and watching the people putting their offerings into the temple-chests. He made no comment on the many generous donors who came; but when a poor widow came with her two farthings - surely the Master was waiting for her - He called His disciples to teach them a new principle of valuation, as applicable to the spiritual as to the material life. The widow's contribution was the highest in God's sight, because "she of her want cast in all she had, even her whole living." (*S. Mark* 12. 44.) Jesus is still sitting nigh and watching as we make our offerings. We may not be able to pray or do much, but if we in our want cast in all we have, even our whole living, if what little we give is given wholeheartedly, we need not fear the judgement of Him who cherishes the mites of the weak.

It is well to realise this qualitative aspect of prayer, because, as in the case of Fr. Doyle, the counting is purely secondary. As has already been remarked, what he meant by an aspiration was not necessarily a form of words, it was a movement of the soul. And in enumerating his aspirations he did not mean to fill his life with a series of discontinuous and separate acts, but rather to make this succession of little impulses melt into one continuous note of heaven's music. His ideal was not so much formal prayer as an uninterrupted prayerfulness. No doubt, Fr. Doyle, partly out of a desire for mortification, hammered out his enormous burden of aspirations with a degree of strenuous endurance which would have left most people limp and prostrate. Here precisely is the personal element which we must carefully avoid unthinkingly transferring into our own lives. And perhaps - for we know but little - perhaps we are really exaggerating the violence or the numerical precision of his efforts? At any rate he himself often advised his spiritual children to cultivate rather a habitual conviction of God's nearness, an effortless restful sense of companionship. These are two typical extracts from such letters:

"I think our Lord wants your whole day to be one continued act of love and union with Him *in your heart,* which has no need of words to express it. Your attitude ought to be that of the mother beside the cot of her babe, lost in love and tenderness, but saying nothing, just letting the heart speak, though the wee one cannot know it as Jesus does. There is nothing more sanctifying than this life, which few, I fear, reach to, since it means a constant effort to bring back our wandering imagination."

"By all means follow the guidance of the Holy Spirit and do not bind yourself to anything which you find a hindrance. Just let yourself 'sink into God' when in His presence. Don't try to pray in words, but love Him which, of course, is the highest prayer and then abandon yourself to His pleasure, whether that be consolation or darkness. ...In the matter of prayer always try to follow the attraction of the Holy Spirit... Try to keep our divine Lord company in your heart all day long, thinking of Him within you a union which will bring you many graces and make His presence much more real."

This advice about prayer, this emphasis on the end in view, rather than on the precise mode, will serve further to show us that Fr. Doyle's detailed calculations and daily records were simply means to the end, psychological devices suitable to his own mind and justifying themselves by their success. He kept a special series of little books, his soul's account books one might call them, wherein he noted not only aspirations but mortifications in minute detail, column after column of figures. How literally and carefully he observed the Master's precept: "Trade till I come"! (*S. Luke* 19. 13.) How ready he must have been when the great Auditor came and the account was closed! One cannot but handle with reverence these booklets with their eloquent figures summing up years of faithful service and hidden struggle. Are they not transcribed in the Book of Life wherein our lives are written? Has not every tiny act or inspiration been adjudicated upon and perpetuated into an eternal worth?

But as this spiritual book-keeping is suited to very few, it has seemed wise even to risk being irritatingly insistent in directing the reader's attention to what is permanent and universal in this method, apart from special developments adapted to individual cases. What is essential in this Ignatian method is to pin oneself down to a definite, enumerable or verifiable, achievement; to aim not at goodness in general but *this much* goodness here and now; and not only to resolve but to examine, to look back as well as forward; to record objectively the results of these experiments in the laboratory of one's own soul. These are broad principles, not so much of spirituality as of psychology; and within their amplitude there is plenty of room for individuality and initiative.

One or two further examples from Fr. Doyle's diary will help to bring out the intensely practical and definite way in which spiritual emotions and resolutions can be sharpened and applied. His Long Retreat resolutions have already been given. This is how he comments on them at a later stage (January, 1909): "Reading over my reflections and resolutions on the Third Degree during the Long Retreat, I see now they are little more than empty promises; they have produced no real change in my life. I put before myself 'always to choose the hard thing, to go against self in all things.' But have I really done so since? Has my life been more mortified from the time I made this resolution? Now, however, I am fully resolved no longer to 'beat the air,' but have drawn up a list of definite acts of self-denial by which I can test myself. If only I am faithful to these, I shall indeed have begun to lead a new and better life than formerly." And again in September 1911 he writes: "The proposed vow has been in my mind constantly as if our Lord was determined that I should not escape even if I wished to do so. I see the need of it, in order to brace my weak yielding nature. In previous retreats I have made many generous resolutions, *e.g.* to seek my constant mortification in all things. But these have never really been kept for any length of time. I must henceforth leave no loophole for escape." There speaks the true Ignatian spirit of determination to bring high ideals down to concrete definite and feasible applications, to condense generalities into accessible facts.

This refusal to take refuge in vague emotions, this persistence in reducing oneself to the test of daily and hourly achievement, is also illustrated by the book of little victories which Fr. Doyle began in 1915. In this he entered one by one the acts of self-conquest and virtue which he performed, making sure that no day would be blank. Here, for instance, are a few of the entries for April: "Morning discipline. Paper not read. Rose at night. Finished Office, very tired and sick. Slept on floor. Hour's visit to B S. Hair-shirt. No fire. Made Holy Hour. Did not take sugar. Denied eyes several times. Wore waist chain." And so on, day after day. To those who indulge in pious velleities and general resolutions, this stream of precise applications may seem like a cold douche; but it is exceedingly healthy. On I3th June he pasted in his book a little picture of our Lady of Victories, and once more began the succession of daily victories, a veritable stream of bullets with himself as target. "Slept on the floor. No relief in small sufferings. Put on chain in bad humour. Violent temptation to eat cake and resisted several times. Two hours' prayer when weary. Rose for visit at two. Unkind story kept back. Overcame desire to lie in bed." Enough has now been quoted to illustrate the severely practical and methodical way in which Fr. Doyle aimed at holiness. There is here no question of impossible arithmetic, no head-splitting efforts at enumeration. Just a grim pertinacity of daily effort at reducing to practice some of the high ideals which a less systematic person would allow to evaporate. This, whether applied to prayer or to self-denial, is characteristic of Jesuit spirituality. [25] As a matter of fact, many of the entries just cited refer more to self-denial than to prayer. In the next chapter we shall review in detail this aspect of Fr. Doyle's inner life.

[1] T. Campbell, S.J., *Pioneer Priests of North America*, vol. ii. (*Among the Hurons*), p. 59. Fr. Campbell adds: "The eighth is to punish any uncharitable word that might escape his lips. Those lips were made to pay a penalty which we prefer to omit."

[2] See also Soeur Gertrude-Marie Legueu, *Une mystique de nos jours*, 1910, pp. 193, 196.

[3] In this matter the remark of S. John of the Cross (*Ascent of Mount Carmel* ii. 29, 4) is worth remembering: "I am terrified by what passes us in these days. Any mere beginner at meditation, if he becomes conscious of locutions during his self-recollection, forthwith pronounces them to be the work of God, and hence says, God has spoken to me, or, I have had

an answer from God. But it is not true; he has simply been speaking to himself."
[4] Compare what was said of Père Ginhac: "Generally the final decision is postponed until the last moment. He waits for a sign from divine providence or the least impulse of the Holy Spirit." - *A Man after God's Own Heart*, p. 88.
[5] *Relations* iii. 12. Compare also *Foundations* 28. 18.
[6] *Life* (Paray-le-Monial), Eng. trans. 1912, p. 37.
[7] "God calls me to an austere life; I must prepare myself to follow the ways of God."
[8] Abbott and Campbell, *Life and Letters of B. Jowett*, ii. 151. Contrast S. Peter (i. i. 8): "Jesus Christ whom having not seen, you love; in whom also now, though you see Him not, you believe; and believing shall rejoice with joy unspeakable and glorified."
[9] *Spiritual Exercises*, (The Kingdom of Christ), p. 34.
[10] *The Friendship of Christ*, 1912, p. 10.
[11] Here is a note jotted down on 22nd April, 1905: "Work for Jesus! Yes, though the weary head may ache arid the tired brain refuse to act. Work on, work on; the years slip by and soon the hour of toil will cease for ever. Work for Jesus! How sweet these words! Not one effort escapes His watchful eye and He will reward you with a joy unknown for what you suffer now."
[12] This little quotation from a letter of Fr. Doyle's will help to explain his attitude still further: "The wretched spirit of Jansenism has driven our dear Lord from His rightful place in our hearts. He longs for love, and familiar love, so give him both - I need scarcely say, when others do not see you... I know a holy soul who never leaves the chapel without kissing the tabernacle door and walking backward, kissing her hand to the Prisoner of Love."
[13] Compare this from the life of S. Margaret Mary (Paray-le-Monial *Life*, Eng. trans., Visitation Library, Walmer, Kent, 1912, pp. 62, 94): "He made me repose for a long time upon His Sacred Bosom, where He discovered to me the marvels of His love." "He held me for the space of two or three hours with my lips pressed to the wound of his Sacred Heart."
[14] "Holy Father, keep them in Thy name whom Thou hast given Me... And not for them only do I pray, but for them also who through their word shall believe in Me." - S. John 17. 11, 20.
[15] Compare the second contemplation of the Second Week of the *Spiritual Exercises* (p. 39): "The first point is to see the persons; that is to say, to see our Lady and St. Joseph and the serving-maid, also the Infant Jesus after His birth, accounting: myself a poor and unworthy servant, looking at and contemplating; them and tending them in their necessities as though I were present there, with all possible homage and reverence." So S. Gertrude: "The day of Thine adorable Nativity, I took Thee from the crib, wrapped in swathingclothes. like a little infant newly born, and placed Thee in my heart." - *Life and Revelations*, London, 1865, p. 100. "Kissing the wounds of Christ" she used frequently in the day to "pour forth all her griefs into the wounds of her Lord and find therein all her consolation and all her joy" (p. 231).
[16] A brief, useful and practical account of this devotion, initiated by S. Margaret Mary Alacoque, will be found in *The Holy Hour*, by J. McDonnell, S.J. (Dublin, Irish Messenger Office). See also the quotation from S. M. Mary on p. 137. In one of his letters Mgr. d'Hulst defines devotion to the Sacred Heart as "the holy hour endlessly prolonged." - *The Way of the Heart* (Eng. trans., 1913), p. 65." The thirteenth century S. Gertrude often "kept vigil and was occupied with the remembrance of the Lord's Passion" and was "much fatigued." - *Life and Revelations*, Eng. tr. 1865, p. 227.
[17] He became a Knight of the Blessed Sacrament on 1st January, 1917, at Locre

in Belgium, where he was military chaplain.

[18] Obviously, such nocturnal prayer requires discretion and guidance. "It is incredible," says S. Francis de Sales, "how dangerous long night vigils are and how much they weaken the brain. It is not felt during youth; but it comes to be felt so much the more afterwards, and many persons have rendered themselves useless in this way." - *Letters to Persons in Religion,* Eng. trans. (Mackay), 1901, 8 p. 68 (cf. p. 43). See also the 10th Addition to the First Week of the Exercises.

[19] "My God and All" aspiration of S. Francis of Assisi. (Fioretti 2.)

[20] Particular Examen (pp. 13f.) Subsequently this same method was extended to recording positive acts of virtue, instead of merely marking defects.

[21] Père Ginhac once surprised his superior, who was confessing to him, by the unexpected query: "And what about your particular examen? Do you make it properly? What is the subject of it?" - *A Man After God's Own Heart,* p. 282.

[22] The following aspirations, jotted down in one of Fr. Doyle's notebooks, seem to have been favourites of his: (1) My Crucified Jesus, help me to crucify myself. (2) Lord, teach me how to pray and pray always. (3) Jesus, Thou Saint of saints, make me a saint. (4) Blessed be God for all thing's. (5) My loving Jesus within my heart, unite my heart to Thee. (6) Heart of Jesus, give me Your zeal for souls. (7) My God, Thou art omnipotent, make me a saint.

[23] The following typical figures, giving the number of recorded daily aspirations at different periods, are taken from the booklets wherein Fr. Doyle made such entries: 1,300, Jan. 1909; 2,000, May 1909; 3,000, Oct. 1909; 4,000, Nov. 1910; 5,000, Jan. 1911; 6,000, July 1911; 10,000, Sept. 1911; 15,000, May 1912; 20,000, Aug. 1913; 60,000, Oct. 1914; 90,000, Nov. 1914. These figures give some of the actual numbers recorded at his daily examination. That the task was not easy is shown by his many relapses and the constant resolutions he made. See his first extant resolution, made during the Long Retreat, p. 62. See reference to aspirations in letter, p. 267.

[24] Compare the advice of S. Francis de Sales: "Do all things for God, making or continuing your union by simple turning of your eyes or outflowing of your heart towards Him." - *Letters to Persons in Religion,* Eng. trans, 1901. p. 355.

[25] Compare St. Ignatius's saying: "Love ought to be found in deeds rather than words." - Contemplation for obtaining Love, *Spiritual Exercises,* p. 74.

Chapter Seven - Mortification and Suffering

(1.) SELF-CONQUEST.

"WHEN long years ago," once wrote Fr. Doyle, "I asked our Blessed Lord to make me a saint, cost what it might, I did not realise what even a small part of that cost would be. I have never regretted my compact, nor do I now, though I am half afraid God has forgotten His part of the bargain, the process of sanctification has been so slow. As time goes on, I see more clearly that God wants from me a life that consists mainly of two things, prayer and penance. Never-ceasing prayer, in spite of the natural weariness and disgust which often come, kneeling rather than in any other posture; but above all, prayer at night in imitation of His all-night prayer, and when possible, nocturnal adoration of the Blessed Sacrament. Joined to prayer must be a life of penance, interior first of all, otherwise such a life would be a delusion. But I must by no means stop short at interior penance. Jesus seems to stretch out His bleeding Hands to me, imploring for more than that, for penance almost merciless in its severity."

We have already glimpsed some of the secrets of his prayer, we must now illustrate his spirit of penance. In his Spiritual Exercises [1] St. Ignatius tells us that "exterior penances are used chiefly for three purposes: first, as a satisfaction for past sins; secondly, in order to overcome oneself, that is to say, in order that sensuality may be obedient to reason and all that is inferior be more subjected to the superior; thirdly, in order to seek and find some grace or gift which a person wishes for and desires." For ordinary cases this is an adequate explanation of exterior mortification, under which term must be included not only the voluntary infliction of pain and fasting or abstinence, but also every deliberate exterior act of self-denial, were it only the restraint of curiosity, the conquering of lassitude or perseverance in an uncongenial duty. There are many good and holy souls who have never dreamt of taking a discipline or wearing a hair-shirt; yet asceticism is not wanting to their lives. Indeed, there is always a danger lest unusual penances may be undertaken in a spirit of self-will and vanity, to the detriment of that safest and most hidden of all mortifications - the persevering perfection of common life. St. Teresa, evidently writing from personal knowledge, describes with gentle irony those religious who delight in self-imposed penance and neglect the divinely imposed penance of rules and daily duties. "It is amusing (she says) [2] to see the mortifications with which some of their own accord afflict themselves. Sometimes there seizes them a fit of immoderate and indiscreet penance, which lasts for about two days. The devil then suggests to their imagination that such mortifications injure them. So they never again do penance - not even what the rules of the order enjoin - as they have found that mortification does them harm; and they do not observe even the least injunctions of the rule, such as silence, which cannot do us any harm. And as soon as we fancy that we have a headache, we refrain from going to choir though this will hardly kill us. One day we omit going because our head aches, the next because it did ache, and three more days we keep away lest it should ache! We love to invent penances of our own."

These practical remarks remind us of what homely stuff the garment of holiness is spun. Often when we read the lives of the saints we are apt to lose the real perspective. Unconsciously singling out the special graces and extraordinary sufferings, we pay insufficient attention to the continuous background of minor physical ills, commonplace disappointments and petty annoyances, which loom so large in our seemingly ordinary lives, but which so often escape the chronicler and reader of the lives of the saints. Yet God never exempts even chosen souls therefrom, for it is precisely in this subjection to these general laws of providence that human goodness is to be attained.

"Alas, my sovereign Lord," complained Saint Margaret Mary, [3] "why dost Thou not leave me in the common way of the daughters of Holy Mary? Hast Thou brought me into Thy holy house to destroy me? Give Thy extraordinary graces to those chosen souls who will correspond with them better than I do, for I only resist Thee. All I wish for is Thy love and Thy cross; that suffices for me to become a good religious and that is all I desire." Thus these gratuitous favours are not only not sought for, but in no wise dispense the recipient from those general conditions and limitations which are so wondrously exemplified even in the life of Christ. Most of His earthly existence He spent as a village artisan; often He was footsore, weary and hungry; He was misunderstood even by those nearest to Him, He felt disappointment and, humanly speaking, failure. So too in the case of even His most faithful followers the rapturous glory of Thabor is but a transitory illumination of lives spent in obscure Nazareth-like drudgery or in a toilsome thankless mission. Saint Margaret Mary, for all her graces, had as a novice to mind the monastery donkeys; nor did God's providence prevent a windlass from hitting her in the jaw and smashing her teeth. [4] What was probably still harder, she had to suffer from the misunderstanding of holy people; her directors regarded her as a visionary, her sisters opposed what they considered a new-fangled devotion. [5]

It has ever been thus in the lives of those who have striven to follow Christ. "Whosoever does not carry his own cross and walk in My steps, can be no disciple of Mine." (S. Luke 14. 27.) This cross-carrying, however, is not a public procession, drawing tears from the onlooking daughters of Jerusalem; it is a silent drama enacted in the private theatre of the human heart. And, as a rule, the cross is not a huge visible structure, plainly recognisable and easily reminiscent of Christ; rather is it doled out to us piecemeal, in mere matches and sawdust as it were, in tiny fragments wherein only the eye of loving faith can discern the lineaments of Calvary.

This truth must not be forgotten while reading this chapter. For it is easy to chronicle what is out of the ordinary, and it is only the abnormal and artificial that is usually committed to writing; whereas the real annals of self-conquest and sufferings are garnered only by the recording angels. We shall meet, in the case of Fr. Doyle, many proofs of persevering and deliberately sought mortification, and even of heroic self-immolation. But this must not blind us to the fact that, beneath this self-imposed apparatus of suffering, there was in his life, as in ours, a continuous layer of petty troubles, pains, discomforts, annoyances, disappointments, mistakes, misunderstandings. These are God-given and have first claim on us; to shirk these and to seek out artificially constructed suffering, like those nuns gently satirised by S. Teresa, is to build the house of holiness on sand. So while we are picturing the spiritual edifice raised by Fr. Doyle, let us not forget the foundation whereon it was based. "We love to invent penances of our own," says the great Carmelite, alluding to those fervent souls whose vain ambition it is to erect castles in the air. That Fr. Doyle was not one of such, is obvious to those who knew him intimately. It would indeed be true to say that his greatest suffering in life did not consist at all in what is set down in this chapter, but rather in those limitations and disabilities, mistakes and misinterpretations, individually perhaps petty but collectively severe. This is probably true for every life as lived, though not as written; it is just as true of the saints as of ordinary folk, though not every saint, has expressed the truth with the blunt precision of S. John Berchmans: "My *greatest* mortification is common life."

At any rate, whether we invent penances or whether we confine ourselves to the acceptance of those for which God provides endless opportunities, penance we must do, if we wish to deny ourselves, to take up our cross and to follow Christ. The spirit of our time is delicate and squeamish and hypersensitive; the avoidance of pain and discomfort has become a veritable science as well as an industry. Perhaps there is even a tendency to seek anaesthetics in the spiritual life or to look for easy modes of conveyance along the royal road of the cross! But the words of Christ still ring true: "Amen, amen, I say to you, unless the grain of wheat falling into the ground die, itself remaineth alone; but if it die, it bringeth forth much fruit. He that loveth his life shall lose it; and he that hateth his life in this world, keepeth it unto life eternal." (*S. John* 12. 24.) These words not only convey a mysterious law of the spiritual world, but enunciate a truth perceptible by natural reason. Indeed, has not a great American psychologist, regarding the matter from the purely natural standpoint, written what is practically a panegyric of the Ignatian agere contra? Thus writes William James: "As a final practical maxim, relative to these habits of the will, we may, then, offer something like this: *Keep the faculty of effort alive in you by a little gratuitous exercise every day.* That is, be systematically ascetic or heroic in little unnecessary points; do every day or two something for no other reason than that you would rather not do it: so that, when the hour of dire need draws nigh, it may find you not unnerved and untrained to stand the test. Asceticism of this sort is like the insurance which a man pays on his house and goods. The tax does him no good at the time, and possibly may never bring him a return. But, if the fire does come, his having paid it will be his salvation from ruin. So with the man who has daily inured himself to habits of concentrated attention, energetic volition, and self-denial in unnecessary things. He will stand like a tower when everything rocks round him, and when his softer fellow-mortals are winnowed like chaff in the blast." [6]

As we read over these words, we realise their perfect aptness to Fr. Doyle. He was systematically ascetic or heroic in little unnecessary points; every day he did many things for no other reason than that he would rather not do them; so that, when the hour of need and big-scale heroism drew nigh, it did not find him unnerved and untrained to stand the test. [7] For most assuredly he was a man who daily inured himself to habits of concentrated attention, energetic volition, and self-denial in unnecessary things. "Other souls may travel by other roads," he once wrote, "the road of pain is mine." He developed a positive ingenuity in discovering possibilities of denying himself.

Thus he was always striving to bear little sufferings and physical discomforts were it only the irritation of a gnat without seeking relief; he tried to imagine that his hands were nailed to the cross with Jesus. He gave up having a fire in his room and even avoided warming himself at one. Every day he wore a hair-shirt and one or two chains for some time; and he inflicted severe disciplines on himself. Moreover, between sugarless tea, butterless bread and saltless meat, he converted his meals into a continuous series of mortifications.

Naturally he had, in fact, a very hearty appetite and a keen appreciation of sweets and delicacies; all of which he converted into an arena for self-denial. He began even as a young boy. When he and his brother were getting from their big sister an exhortation on kindness and unselfishness, Willie, not needing much effort to discover what *he* was very fond of, suddenly exclaimed: "Yes, May, wouldn't this be *very* selfish, if I got a pot of jam and ate it all myself without giving any of it to Charlie?" A horrible deed of gluttony of which he was never guilty! No doubt his sister's reassuring answer confirmed his good will! We can realise the wonderful continuity of his life when over thirty years later we find him pencilling this resolution on the first page of the little private notebook he kept with him at the Front: "No blackberries. Give away all chocolates. Give away box of biscuits. No jam, breakfast, lunch, dinner." Some excerpts from his diary will enable us to realise how much this struggle against taste and appetite meant to him. On 1st September, 1911, he writes: "I feel a growing thirst for self-denial; it is a pleasure not to taste the delicacies provided for me. I wish I could give up the use of meat entirely. I long even to live on bread and water. My Jesus, what marvellous graces You are giving me, who always have been so fond of eating and used to feel a small act of denial of my appetite a torture." A month later, just after giving a retreat in a Carmelite convent, he records: "I felt urged in honour of St. Teresa to give myself absolutely no comfort at meals which I could possibly avoid. I found no difficulty in doing this for the nine days. I have begged very earnestly for the grace to continue this all my life and am determined to try to do so. For example, to take no butter, no sugar in coffee, no salt, etc. The wonderful mortified lives of these holy nuns have made me ashamed of my gratification of my appetite." That he by no means found this mortification easy we have many indications. Thus on 5th Jan., 1912, he writes: "During Exposition Jesus asked me if I would give up taking second course at dinner. This would be a very great sacrifice; but I promised Him at least to try to do so and begged for grace and generosity." And again on 14th Sept., 1912: "Having again indulged my appetite, I made this resolution, that whenever I do so, no matter for what reason (health, feasts, etc.), I will enter it in the other book. I think this will be a check and a help to me to do what Jesus has asked so long - no indulgence whatever in food." "A fierce temptation during Mass and thanksgiving," he records a year later (18th Sept., 1913), "to break my resolution and indulge my appetite at breakfast. The thought of a breakfast of dry bread and tea without sugar in future seemed intolerable. Jesus urged me to pray for strength though I could scarcely bring myself to do so. But the temptation left me in the refectory, and joy filled my heart with the victory. I see now that I need never yield if only I pray for strength."

On the subject of butter there are many resolutions in the diary. Materially the subject may seem trivial, but psychologically it represents a great struggle and victory. [8] Any habit such as that of smoking may presumably be explained in purely material terms: the formation of antibodies in the system and the consequent periodical need of toxins to restore the balance. But no such type of medical explanation can alter the fundamental human fact that such a habit can be controlled or abolished by a sufficient exercise of willpower, which ordinarily cannot be accomplished without religious motives. Let us hope that old-fashioned Catholic practices for example, giving up smoking or doing without butter during Lent will not be lightly laid aside. It is in such little acts that man rises above the beast and fosters his human heritage of a rational will. So Fr. Doyle's butter-resolutions are not at all so unimportant or whimsical as they who have ever thoughtlessly eaten and drunk may be inclined to fancy. "God has been urging me strongly all during this retreat," he writes in September 1913, "to give up butter entirely. I have done so at many meals without any serious inconvenience; but "I am partly held back through human respect, fearing others may notice it. If they do, what harm? I have noticed that X takes none for lunch; that has helped me. Would not I help others if I did the same?" "One thing," he continues, "I feel Jesus asks, which I have not the courage to give Him the promise to give up butter entirely." On 20th July, 1914, we find this resolution: "For the present I will take butter on two mouthfuls of bread at breakfast but none at other meals." To this decision he seems to have adhered.

Not only did Fr. Doyle mortify himself in the quality of the food he took but he also refused to allow his appetite to be satisfied in quantity. "Towards the end of the retreat," he wrote on 3rd December, 1914, "a light came to me that, now that I have given Jesus all the sacrifices I possibly can in the matter of food, He is now going to ask retrenchment in the *quantity*. So far I have not felt that He asked this, but grace now seems to urge me to it. I dread what this means, but Jesus will give me strength to do what. He wants."

This relentless concentration of will on matters of food must not lead us to suppose that Fr. Doyle was in any way morbidly absorbed or morosely affected thereby. For oneless trained in will or less sure in spiritual perspective there might easily be danger of entanglement in minutiae and over-attention to what is secondary. All this apparatus of mortification is but a means to an end, it should not be made an end in itself. We must not be so 'busy about much serving,' we should not so burden or worry ourselves about what we eat and drink, that we are 'careful and troubled about many things' and lose sight of the 'one thing necessary' the best part chosen by Mary. (S. Luke 10. 40-42.) This persistent and systematic thwarting of appetite helped Fr. Doyle to strengthen his will and to fix it on God. He never lost himself in a maze of petty resolutions, he never became anxious or distracted. But the armour of

Goliath would hamper David. There are those whom elaborate prescriptions and detailed regulations would only strain and worry. And these best find the peace of God in a childlike thankful acceptance of His gifts, without either careless indulgence or self-conscious artificiality. "In everything God reveals His love to me," writes Soeur Gertrude-Marie. [9] "I was given a strawberry at lunch. While eating it, I said to myself: God was thinking of me when He caused this fruit to ripen. He said: It will be for My child. And I said: It will be for refreshing in me the sacred Humanity of my Saviour. Our love must be reciprocal. God gives me His good things, I wish to give them back to Him by the holy use I make of them."

As with food, so with sleep. We have already seen how Fr. Doyle often robbed himself of sleep in order to pray. Sometimes, too, he slept on the floor or put boards in his bed. "During the last three nights of the ---- retreat," he writes (20th Dec., 1914), "I slept on the floor without feeling any inconvenience after, though I woke very often on account of the pain. This is the first time I have slept this way on more than one (successive) night." On 12th July, 1915, he writes thus in his diary: "Not feeling well, I gave up the intention of sleeping on boards, but overcame self and did so. I rose this morning quite fresh and none the worse for it, proving once more how our Lord would help me if I were generous." And in September, 1915, lie made the resolution to 'put boards in his bed every night when at home.'

It is scarcely necessary to remark that all these mortifications were extremely difficult to flesh and blood. There was no such thing in Fr. Doyle as a natural pleasure or pride in, or, at least, indifference to, physical discomfort and suffering. He really loathed and detested the life which he voluntarily imposed on himself. "My God," he once wrote (22nd October, 1915), "this morning I was in despair. After some days of relaxation owing partly to sickness, I resolved to begin my life of crucifixion once more, but found I could not. I seemed to have lost all strength and courage, and simply hated the thought of the life. Then I ran to You in the Tabernacle, threw myself before You and begged You to do all since I could do nothing. In a moment all was sweet and easy. What help and grace You gave me, making me see clearly that I must never again give up this life or omit to mark my book." [10] This extract not only shows us his natural repugnance but also reveals the source of his strength. His indomitable determination to overcome himself is especially manifested in an expedient which he adopted latterly, namely, binding himself by a temporary vow to do that which he felt tempted to avoid. "Jesus taught me a simple way to-day of conquering the temptation to break resolutions. When, for example, I want to take sugar in my tea, etc., I will make a vow not to do so for that one occasion, which will compel me to do it, no matter what it may cost. I know often I shall have to force myself to take this little vow; but I realize that if only I can bring myself to say 'I vow,' then all the conflict raging in my soul about that particular thing will cease at once. This will be invaluable to me in the future." (22nd Feb., 1914.) We have several records of his using this heroic device.

"Three times to-day by making a vow I was able to force myself to do what I did not want to do. Once I had almost to shout out the vow, and then I had no trouble at all in doing what I promised to remain up till night prayers. Once the vow was followed by a fierce temptation to break it, and a great regret I had bound myself. But again I had no difficulty in doing without sugar, and much peace and strength followed the victory." (22nd Nov., 1914.)

"It came home to me to-day as it never did before, the immense help little vows would be. By this means I can force myself to do almost anything; and (such little vows) being taken for one occasion only, *e.g.* I will not read a paper to-day, are quite easy to keep. I have gained several victories by this means. I have noticed that there is often great difficulty in forcing myself to make the vow, but very little in carrying it out."

It does not appear that this rather drastic procedure ever led to anxiety or scrupulosity. Fr. Doyle had thought things out clearly; he knew exactly what he wanted and what he could do. He retained the militant enthusiasm of his boyhood. Whenever he met an obstacle in his spiritual life and found himself shying at it, he to use an expressive phrase took himself by the back of the neck and threw himself over. And, wonderful to relate, he did it all with the zest of a youth in a cross-country race. [11] His acts of self-conquest were not a cold calculated succession of deliberate inhibitions, nor was his ideal mere apathy or dehumanised perfection. In real Christian asceticism and mysticism there is always a joyous note, a paradoxical combination of gaiety and pain. "What are God's servants," asked S. Francis of Assisi, [12] "but His troubadours who seek to uplift men's hearts and to move them to spiritual joy?"

(2.) LIFE OF IMMOLATION.
A. Introduction.

We have hitherto regarded Fr. Doyle's penance somewhat after the plain matter-of-fact way in which St. Ignatius deliberately treats it in his Spiritual Exercises. Penance is designed to overcome passion and to assert the supremacy of the right will. Of course, this must not be understood in the sense of a merely naturalistic stoicism; for the supernatural motive and the action of grace have been apparent all through. No one is likely to adopt systematic self-denial just because he wants to improve the relations of soul and body. It is only religion which can inspire, vitalise, and ennoble the conquest of self. But even this admission leaves our analysis of penance exceedingly incomplete. What we have quoted from St. Ignatius would not suffice, for instance, to explain his own practice. Neither will it throw much light on Fr. Doyle's life. Beyond all these terms of will and passion, of reason and sensuality, there is something ineffably deeper and more mysterious in the economy of penance and suffering. The Christian view of sin presupposes the reality of the moral order of which sin is a violation, it implies the necessity of atonement by an inscrutable law of holiness which is of the essence of God's nature. The pagan lightly says: "Why should I be afraid of any of my errors, when I can say, See that you do it no more, now I forgive you." [13] Far different is the language of the Christian. Christ came "to give His life as a ransom for all" (*S. Matthew* 20. 28); He "died for our sins" (I Cor. I 53), "His ownself bore our sins in His body upon the tree, that we being dead to sins should live to justice." (*I Peter 2*. 24.) "Unto you," says St. Paul (*Phil.* i. 29), "it is given for Christ, not only to believe in Him but also to suffer for Him." "I fill up," he says, "those things that are wanting of the sufferings of Christ, in my flesh, for His Body which is the Church." (*Col.* i. 24.) We cannot adequately explain in words nor can we by general reasoning reach the profound and mysterious process of reconciliation with God. But the Atonement of Christ, viewed in the light of faith, enables us to perceive the inner nature of sin and redemption. "Mere repentance," says St. Athanasius, [14] "would not maintain what is reasonable with respect to God .... nor does it recover man from his (corrupt) nature; it simply means cessation from acts of sin. If sin were merely a wrongdoing and involved no consequent corruption, repentance might well suffice. But this is not the case. When once transgression had begun, man fell into the power of a corrupt nature and lost the grace of being in God's image." Our redemption was effected only when Christ "taking from our bodies one of like nature, gave it over to death in the stead of all and offered it to the Father. And this He did out of love for man. His purpose therein was twofold, (1) As we all died in Him, His death was to annul the law due to man's corruption, since its authority was fully vindicated in the Lord's body and no longer held against men of like nature. (2) As men had originally turned to corruption, He might now turn them to incorruption and quicken them from death to life, by His appropriation of a human body and by the grace of His resurrection." Thus we see from the glorious dogma of our Redemption that Christ's assumption of our humanity implies a wondrous solidarity and mystic union between us and Him. [15] As we can see in the life of Saint Margaret Mary Alacoque, it is of the very essence of the devotion to the Sacred Heart that chosen souls are specially privileged to share in this redemptive work and to fill up those things that are wanting of the sufferings of Christ. And indeed not only privileged souls but all Christians are invited by the Church to add their prayers and penances to the sufferings of our Redeemer for the conversion of sinners, to unite in loving adoration and thus atone for outrage and sin. The devotion of the Forty Hours, instituted by Clement VIII in 1592, the cult of the Sacred Heart, the founding of special religious congregations [16] and sodalities, the lives of the more recent saints and servants of God, all bear witness to the prominence of the idea of reparation in the Church to-day. If this cooperation were regarded as injuring the mediation of Christ, Luther would have been right against the Council of Trent and works would not count for justification. If the expiation of the just, quickened by our Saviour's merits, cannot be offered for the shiner, the Communion of Saints is not a reality. And it is only by thus entering into this mystic communion and as it were 'pooling' our sufferings and prayers, that we can escape from narrow individualism and depressing isolation. "For them do I sanctify myself, that they also may be sanctified in truth. And not for them only do I pray, but for them also who through their word shall believe in Me, that they all may be one; that as Thou, Father, art in Me and I in Thee, so they also may be in Us...; I in them and Thou in Me, that they be made perfect in one." (*S. John* 17. 19-23.)

This ideal of reparation and suffering, this implied mystic oneness with Christ, is, of course, intuitively felt and lived, rather than theorised and reasoned about by pious souls. Expressed in terms of our personal relation to our Lord, it at once appeals to those with living faith. "If any man will come after Me, let him deny himself and take up his cross daily and follow Me. For whosoever will save his life, shall lose it; and whosoever for My sake shall lose his life, shall save it." (S. Luke 9. 23.) This following of Christ was even incorporated by St. Ignatius into his Constitutions: [17] "Those who are advancing in spirit and seriously following Christ our Lord love and ardently desire what is altogether contrary to the things of the world, namely, to be clothed with the same garment and insignia as their Master, for His love and reverence... The better to attain to this precious degree of perfection in the spiritual life, let it be the great and earnest endeavour of each one to seek in the Lord his greater abnegation and, as far as he can, his continual mortification in all things."

In the Spiritual Exercises, too, once the First Week is passed, we find an ideal rising far above the ascetic aim of penance. S. Ignatius will have his exercitant aspire to the mystic chivalrous following of the great Leader, "in the highest degree of poverty of spirit, and not less in actual poverty if it please His divine Majesty," aye, even "in bearing reproaches and insults, the better to imitate Him in these." [18] This message, to-day so uniquely characteristic of Catholicism, is a triumphant vindication of our continuity with the early Church and of the ever-living reality of the Redemption. "Unto this you are called," says S. Peter, he who like his Master was to stretch forth his hands for another to gird him (*S. John* 21. 18), "because Christ also suffered for us, leaving you an example that you should follow His steps." (*I Peter* 2. 21.) "We suffer," says the other S. Ignatius, martyred at Rome under Trajan, [19] "we suffer that we may be found disciples of Jesus Christ our only Teacher."

In the order of time, indeed, Christ suffers no more. In His personal humanity He can no longer endure pain and humiliation. But we, His mystical Body, can. "The Church is His Body and the completing of Him who fills all in all." (*Ephes.* i. 23.) Hence it is that S. Paul could say, as already cited: "I fill up those things that are wanting of the sufferings of Christ, in my flesh, for His Body which is the Church. (*Col.* i. 24.) And this function, this association in the redemptive work of Jesus Christ, is not an ideal applicable merely to great saints and mystics; it is a function to be filled by all true Christians, each in his measure filling up the lacunae, every good life linking itself up into the wondrous unity of the moral order. Though we may not always advert to it, when we speak of the imitation of Christ and of reparation to the

Sacred Heart, we are presupposing this prolongation and extension of the Saviour's life into ours.

The first great revelation of the Heart of Jesus is contained in the seventh chapter of S. Luke's Gospel. "Dost thou see this woman?" said Christ to Simon. "I entered into thy house, *thou* gavest Me no water for My feet - but *she* with tears hath washed My feet and with her hair hath wiped them. *Thou* gavest Me no kiss - but *she*, since she came in, hath not ceased to kiss My feet. My head with oil thou didst not anoint but she with ointment hath anointed My feet... She hath loved much." This detailed antithesis, this careful balancing of neglect with service, i this sensitive juxtaposition of Simon and Magdalen in the I Heart of Christ, contains the essence of the idea of reparation. That is, if our Lord's life and mission is more than a simple historical event and is still accessible to us who live in these latter days. Many a Simon nowadays treats Christ with studied slight and scorn, and we is the role of Magdalen closed to us? Cannot Christ still address the sinner, "Thou .... but she...?" Cannot our loving much prevail and repair? And to the solitary adorer does there not still from the Tabernacle come the whisper, "The nine where are they?" (S. Luke 17. 17.)

The Gethsemane agony has passed nigh two thousand years ago. Yet here is the message to S. Margaret Mary: "Every night between Thursday and Friday I will make thee share in the mortal sadness which I was pleased to feel in the Garden of Olives. ... In order to bear Me company, . . . thou shalt rise between eleven o'clock and midnight and remain prostrate with Me for an hour, not only to appease the divine anger by begging mercy for sinners, but also to mitigate in some way the bitterness which I felt at that time on finding Myself abandoned by My apostles, which obliged Me to reproach them for not being able to watch one hour with Me." [20]

Since the day on which. "they laid the cross" on Simon of Gyrene "to carry after Jesus" (S. Luke 23. 26), many a faithful one has sprung forward to carry the Master's cross. And shall we say, Too late? Is the Cyrenaean alone to be Christ's cross-bearer? Surely, that were to deny the eternal significance and ever-present reality of Christ's Sacrifice. [21] Does not Paul himself declare "I have been crucified with Christ" (*Gal.* 2. 20)? And he added significantly: "So it is no longer I who live, but it is Christ who lives in me."

It is only in the light of these considerations that we can properly appreciate the lives of the saints. These few remarks will also help us to understand that thirst for suffering and desire of reparation which are so prominent on every page of Fr. Doyle's inner life. As S. Catherine of Siena remarks, [22] "one virtue belongs especially to one man and another to another, and yet they all remain in charity." Though Fr. Doyle's character was many-sided and eclectic, the ideal which more and more attracted him in the later years of his life was that of sacrificial self-immolation. Men have characteristic virtues just as they have predominant faults; in good as in evil we are all more or less specialists. In a very real sense every soul is unique, no two of us are exactly alike; hence there can be no question of mechanically reproducing another's life in our own. This diversity in unity is apparent even within the same religious Order. [23] Thus while many of Fr. Doyle's fellow-religious would doubtless envisage life from a different angle, to him the great message which inspired and explained his life-vocation was our Lord's saying to S. Margaret Mary: "I seek a victim to My Heart which will immolate itself as a holocaust to the accomplishment of My designs." [24] This ideal of reparation, and in particular this special offering as a victim of immolation, is thoroughly in accord with the mind of the Church. Pope Leo XIII, for example, says in one of his encyclicals: [25]

"It is most fitting that Catholics should by a great spirit of faith and holiness make reparation for the depravity of views and actions and show publicly that nothing is dearer to them than the glory of God and the religion of their fathers. Let those especially who are more strictly bound to God, those who live in religion, rouse themselves more generously to charity and strive to propitiate the divine Majesty by their humble prayers, their voluntary sacrifices and the offering of themselves."

Moreover, this ideal of a victim of reparation has in the case of several religious institutes been specially approved by Rome. [26] Indeed it is but the perfect and logical development of the devotion to the Sacred Heart which seems almost to have been reserved for this age of dwindling faith and cooling charity. [27]

B. Father Doyle's Notes.

It is only when we see this ideal of reparation carried out to a degree of heroic intensity in the life of one who has lived in our midst, that we realise its surpassing strength and beauty. And perhaps by thus witnessing this ennoblement of suffering, we shall be aided to purge our own lives of sordid repining and fretful grumbling and to see in every form of pain an ally instead of an enemy, to enlarge our souls by the sane and social mysticism of reparation. "It is quite true," writes Mgr. d'Hulst, [28] "that reparation underlies all real interior life. But you know the difference between acknowledging a truth with the intelligence and discovering it within one's heart. This discovery delayed no doubt by many infidelities, by a too external life, a life too busied with outward things I am beginning to make on my own account, after having made it more than once for other people."

It was during his 1909 retreat that the ideal of a life of absolute self-sacrifice and reparatory suffering came home to Fr. Doyle with full conviction and clearness. "I am more and more convinced," he writes, "that Jesus is asking from me the complete and absolute sacrifice of every gratification, pleasure, self-indulgence and comfort, which within the Rule and without injuring my health or work I can give Him. I have never before felt such a strong desire or such supernatural help to make and keep this resolution. Looked at in the bulk it appals me, but taken moment by moment, there is nothing which I cannot do. By the grace of God I can do all things." "I can honestly say," the journal continues, "I do not think of any sacrifice possible for me to make, which I have not written down at the end of this book,' [29] so that now for the first time in my life I have given my Jesus absolutely everything I think He asks from me. Already I taste the reward in the deep peace and happiness I experience and in the growing desire to be more and more generous in giving. This time of consolation I know will not last always, but I am ready for the storm, trusting in God's grace, for all this is His work and He will never fail me... There must be no going back now even in little things, no truce, no yielding to nature, till death." This retreat before his last vows (Feb. 1909) Fr. Doyle always called his "conversion." In his next retreat (Sept. 1910) he was able to record a distinct advance: "The past eighteen months have shown me that with the help of God's grace, sacrifices, which formerly I thought utterly impossible, were easy enough. This fills me with confidence to face others which I have been afraid of: up to this." "I must, therefore," he concluded, "eagerly welcome every little pain, suffering, small sickness, trouble, cross of any kind, as coming straight to me from the Sacred Heart. Am I not Your loving victim, my Jesus? I must, remember also my compact anything to become a saint."

At Limerick, on the Feast of the Holy Family (22nd Jan.) 1911, Fr. Doyle wrote down (or rather typed) in the form of an intimate spontaneous prayer a further elaboration of his ideal of self-immolation. It is at once pathetically human, magnificently heroic, and intensely practical:

"My dear loving Jesus what do You want from me? You never seem to leave me alone thank You ever so much for that but keep on asking, asking, asking. I have tried to do a good deal lately for You and have made many little sacrifices which have cost me a good deal, but You do not seem to be satisfied with me yet and want more.

"The same thought is ever haunting me, coming back again and again; fight as I will, I cannot get away from it or conceal from myself what it is You really want. I realise it more and more every day. But, my sweet Jesus, I am so afraid, I am so cowardly, so fond of myself and my own comfort, that I keep hesitating and refusing to give in to You and to do what You want.

"Let me tell You what I think this is. You want me to immolate myself to Your pleasure; to become Your victim by self-inflicted suffering; to crucify myself in every way I can think of; never if possible to be without some pain or discomfort; to die to myself and to my love of ease and comfort; to give myself the necessaries of life but no more (and I think these could be largely reduced without injury to my health); to crucify my body in every way I can think of, bearing heat, cold, little sufferings, without relief, constantly, if possible always, wearing some instrument of penance; to crucify my appetite by trying to take as little delicacies as possible; to crucify my eyes by a vigilant guard over them; to crucify my will by submitting it to others; to give up all comfort, all self-indulgence; to sacrifice my love of ease, love for sleep at unusual times; to work, to toil for souls, to suffer, to pray always. My Jesus, am I not right, is not this what You want from me and have asked so long?

"I feel it is. For the thought of such a life, so naturally terrifying, fills me with joy, for I know I could not do one bit of it myself but that it will all be the work of Your grace and love. I have found, too, that the more I give, the more I do, the more I suffer, the greater becomes this longing.

"Jesus, you know my longing to become a saint. You know how much I thirst to die a martyr. Help me to prove that I am really in earnest by living this life of martyrdom. O loving Jesus, help me now not to fight any longer against You. I really long to do what You want, but I know my weakness so well and my inconstancy. I have made so many generous resolutions which I have never kept that I feel it is almost a mockery to promise more. This record of my feelings and desire at this moment will be a spur to my generosity; and if I cannot live up to the perfection of what You want, at least I am now determined to do more than I have ever done before. Help me, Jesus!"

This light has come to me now:

(1) Try to live this life for one day, at least now and again; this will show you it is not impossible.

(2) Do what the Holy Ghost suggests at once - 'Make this little sacrifice,' 'Do this,' 'Don't do that,' etc."

A fortnight later (5th February, 1911), he thus records "a great grace": "To-day while praying in the Chapel, suddenly it seemed to me as if I were standing before a narrow path all choked with briars and sharp thorns. Jesus was beside me with a large cross and I heard Him ask me would I strip myself of all things, and naked as He was on Calvary, take that cross on my bare shoulders and bravely fight my way to the end of the road. I realised clearly that this would mean much suffering and that very soon my flesh would be torn and bleeding from the thorns. All the same, humbly I promised Him, that, relying on His grace, I would not shrink from what He asked, and even begged Him to drag me through these briars since I am so cowardly. This inspiration, coming so soon after the ardent desire really to crucify myself, shows me clearly what kind of life Jesus is asking from me. I felt impelled to resolve as far as possible never to be without some slight bodily suffering, *e.g.* chain on arm, etc. I have also made a vow twice (binding for one day) to refuse on that day no sacrifice which I really feel my Jesus asks from me. All this has given me great interior peace and happiness, with fresh courage and determination to become a saint." He characteristically adds, "Life is too short for a truce."

Once more (10th March, 1911), he felt an impetuous urging towards this life which, humanly speaking, was so motiveless and repellent.

"This morning (he writes) during meditation I again felt that mysterious appeal from our Blessed Lord for a life of *absolute, complete sacrifice of every comfort.* I see and feel now, without a shadow of a doubt, as certainly as if Jesus Himself appeared and spoke to me, that He wants me to give up *now* and *for ever* all self-indulgence, to look on myself as not being free in the matter. That being so how can I continue my present manner of life, of a certain amount of generosity, fervent one day and then the next day giving in to self in everything?

"When a little unwell, or when I have a slight headache. I lie down, give up work, indulge myself in the refectory. I see that I lose immensely by this, for that is the time of great merit, and Jesus sends me that pain to bear for Him.

"One thing keeps me back from a life of generosity a cowardly fear of injuring my health, persuading myself I may interfere with my work. Why not leave all this in God's hands and trust in Him? If the saints had listened to human prudence, they would never have been saints." 1

We have already seen that Fr. Doyle had once or twice made a vow binding him for that day to refuse Jesus no sacrifice. Clearly it is only one with very explicit inspirations and promptings who could make such a vow without ambiguities or scruples. Fr. Doyle proceeded cautiously step by step; and while anxious to strengthen his will, he was careful to avoid burdening himself with doubts and worries. We gather this from what he writes on the Feast of St. Mary Magdalen, 1911:

"This morning I made a vow for three days (then renewed it for two more) to refuse Jesus no sacrifice or act of selfdenial which I honestly think He asks from me. If at all doubtful, I am to consider myself not bound by the vow. For a long time I have felt impelled to do something of the kind, but only to-day got light to see how to avoid scrupulosity, by leaving myself free, unless I feel quite convinced I should make the sacrifice. I did not experience the difficulty I expected in carrying this out, but realised what an immense help it would be in bracing my weak will to generosity."

It was during his annual retreat, September, 1911, that Fr. Doyle, after these tentative experiments, resolved to make this vow daily. This he did very calmly and deliberately and after much prayer, without any sensible fervour, but rather in spite of desolation and repugnance. The following extracts contain the considerations which he jotted down as well as the terms of the vow itself: "Every meditation of this retreat seems to turn upon the vow Jesus wishes me to make. Each day more light and great graces make it clear to me that this is to be the great fruit I am to draw from these days.

(1) Meditating on St. Mary Magdalen I felt heart-broken, thinking of my sinful life in the Society. 'My Jesus, I can only offer my life in reparation take it all.' A voice seemed to reply 'I accept your offering: spend that life for Me in sacrifice and self-denial.'

(2) If I were put in a dungeon, like the martyrs, with nothing to lie on but the bare stone floor, with no protection from intense cold, bread and water once a day for food, with no home comfort whatever, I could endure all that for years and gladly for the love of Jesus, yet I am unwilling to suffer a little inconvenience now, I must have every comfort, warm clothes, fire, food as agreeable as I possibly can, etc.

(3) The devil has been exaggerating the difficulties of my proposed vow, saying human nature could not bear it. I have thought of the man in the

workhouse forty years in bed, of blind Brigid suffering for years constantly. How much we can do when we must!

(4) Sanctity is so precious, it is worth paying any price for it. I feel I shall never be a saint if I refuse to do this. God sanctifies souls in many ways, the path of daily and hourly sacrifices in *everything* and *always* is mine.

(5) Can a Jesuit, who deliberately refuses his Lord any act of self-denial, which he knows is asked from him, ever be really *insignis*? Will Jesus be content with only half measures from me? I feel He will not; He asks for all. My Jesus, with Your help I will give You all.

(6) I was greatly struck with the thought that at His birth, our Lord began a voluntary life of suffering which would never end till He died in agony on the cross. *All this for me!* I have little zeal for souls simply because I do not ask for it. 'Ask and you shall receive: hitherto you have not asked.' (*S. John* 16. 24.)

"I have gone through a great deal of desolation, discouragement, fear and dread of my proposed vow. When I make it I am quite determined now to do so it will be the result of calm conviction that I *must* do so, that God wants it from me, and not a burst of fervour. I shrink from this living death, but am quite happy in the thought that, since God has inspired me to do so, He will do all the work if once I submit my will...I was consoled by seeing Fr. de la Colombière's repugnance to making his heroic vow. He spoke of the sadness which this constant fight against nature sometimes gave him. He overcame that temptation by remembering that it is sweet and easy to do what we know will please one we really love.

A. M. D. G. et B. V. M.

MY VOW

I deliberately vow, and bind myself, under pain of mortal sin, to refuse Jesus no sacrifice, which I clearly see He is asking from me. Amen.

CONDITIONS.

(1) Until I get permission [31] to make it permanently, this will only bind from day to day, to be renewed each morning at Mass.

(2) To avoid scrupulosity, I am quite tree unless I honestly believe the sacrifice is asked.

(3) Any confessor may dispense me from the vow at any time.

Feast of St. Michael,
Tullabeg. September 29th, 1911.

Though not coming under the matter of the vow, my aim will be:

(*a*) Never to avoid suffering *e.g.* heat or cold, unpleasant people etc.

(*b*) Of two alternatives, to choose the harder *e.g.* ordinary or arm chair.

(*c*) To try and let absolutely no occasion of self-denial pass: they are too precious.

(*d*) As far as possible, not to omit my ordinary penances when a little unwell.

(*e*) My constant question to be: 'What other sacrifice can I make? What more can I give up for Jesus? How can I do this action more perfectly?'

REASONS FOR MAKING VOW.

(1) The immense help it will be to become fervent.

(2) Additional great merit from doing the acts under vow.

(3) I see now what was the strange 'want' which I have felt so often in my life. I have been urged by grace for years to take some such step, but only recently clearly saw what I should do.

(4) My sanctification depends on doing this.

(5) I wish to do my utmost to please my dear Jesus.

(6) I feel simply I must make this vow as if I had no power to refuse, which shows me that all this is the work of grace, and not my doing in the least.

(7) Since Jesus, out of pure love for me, has always lived this life, and since I have promised to imitate Him, how can I now refuse to do so?

(8) I shall gain immensely by this vow, my work for others will be blessed, more souls will be saved and greater glory given to God.

(9) What shall I lose? A little gratification which brings no real pleasure but always leaves me unhappy, for I feel I am resisting grace.

I make this vow with immense distrust of myself and my power to keep it, but place all my confidence and trust in Thee, O most loving Heart of Jesus."

At the end of his retreat he wrote down what he considered to have been its three great fruits:

"(1) The making of my vow.

(2) Resolution to get back my old love and devotion to Mary.

(3) Trying to acquire under her guidance the 'interior union.'"

Fifteen months later (January, 1913,) there occurs an entry hi his diary, which is a consoling proof that Fr. Doyle's heroic ideal was grafted on a humanity shared by us all. "During this retreat," he writes, "my eyes have been opened to this unceasing appeal of Jesus and to see how I have never really kept my resolutions. Even my vow after a short time I gave up renewing, and lately I forgot I ever made it. With God's grace I purpose to keep it every Monday, Wednesday, and Friday, and to mark each day hi the other book. On these days I will endeavour to give myself no gratification and not to avoid any little inconvenience or suffering." He was not discouraged, he started once more. And after another three months he renewed his vow, this time until the end of the year.

A. M. D. G.

SOLEMN VOW.

"After much thought and prayer, feeling myself urged strongly by grace and the ceaseless pleading of Jesus, I have resolved to lead the life of absolute crucifixion which I know He wants and which alone will please Him.

I now promise and bind myself by vow (under mortal sin) 'to give Him everything' until next Christmas Day, with the power of dispensing myself in case of necessity on any day.

Dear Jesus, I vow, with the help of Your grace, to give You all You ask for the future.

Good Friday, March 21st, 1913.
Three o'clock."

Fr. Doyle seems to have come to the conclusion that these two vows were too vague. So he made a third vow, concerning which there is the following entry in his diary under the date 21st September, 1913:

"This morning, the Feast of the Seven Dolours, I rose and made the Holy Hour from one to two. I then knelt before the Tabernacle and bound myself according to the conditions in the other book. I also made a promise to use every effort never to dispense myself from this vow, and to strive ever and always to give Jesus every sacrifice I possibly can, trying not to make any account of my health, but leaving its care to Him. I see clearly now what I must do, and my obligation under pain of mortal sin, and since I must mark each act daily I shall not forget it. This vow cancels the other two which were too vague and not realisable."

In this vow Fr. Doyle specified in detail the 'everything' which he had promised to give our Lord. The vow included certain mortifications in food (no sugar or salt, etc.) and bound him to mark daily acts on the watch and to make 15,000 aspirations during the mission. At the same time he took ample precautions to avoid scrupulosity or ambiguity. [32] The vow was to be taken during Sunday Mass and to hold for only one week; he was "free to dispense in part or in whole for any reason"; and it was "not binding when at home and if too singular on certain occasions." Concerning the renewals of this vow or any subsequent modifications in its terms we have little information. At any rate Fr. Doyle continued daily marking "the other book" with minute precision, twenty different headings being marked each day. The mind which could stand this perpetual strain was of no ordinary type. It is a marvel that his joyous spirit never felt crushed by the sheer weight of spiritual book-keeping involved. On the contrary it would seem that any relaxation only oppressed and saddened him. "During the past few days," he notes on 20th Nov., 1914, "I did not renew my vow, gave up aspirations and all penances, and indulged myself in every way. The result was great misery and unhappiness with the feeling that Jesus was very much pained, though I did not seem to care. I felt powerless to rise out of this state. This morning He came back to me during my Mass with such love and grace that I could not resist Him, and took up my former life again. Great peace and happiness since."

Is not this after all the final test? It was by means of these elaborately devised strivings and these slowly improved vows that Fr. Doyle found 'great peace and happiness.' "Everyone hath his proper gift from God," says S. Paul (*I Cor.* 7. 7), "one after this manner and another after that."

It will be convenient to collect here some of Fr. Doyle's thoughts and resolutions concerning this life of self-sacrifice and reparation. We shall thereby be enabled to realise the growing intensity with which this wonderful ideal dominated him. More and more the absorbing ambition of his life was to make himself a living holocaust, 'the victim of the Sacred Heart.' As time went on, all other motives became fused in this glowing zeal, culminating finally and appropriately in the sacrifice of life itself. "Greater love than this no man hath." (*S. John* 15. 13.)

"To-day, the Feast of all the Saints of the Society, while praying in the Chapel at Donnybrook (Poor Clares), our Lord seemed to ask me these questions:

(1) When are you going to do what I have so often urged you and begged from you a life of absolute sacrifice?

(2) You have promised Me to begin this life earnestly, why not do so at once?

(3) You have vowed to give Me any sacrifice I want, I ask this from you:

(*a*) the most absolute surrender of *all gratification,*

(*b*) to embrace every possible suffering,

(*c*) this, every day and always.

My Jesus, I shrink from such a life, but will bravely begin this moment since You wish it." (5th November, 1911.)

"For a long time past the conviction has been growing that God wants me to be His victim to be immolated on the altar of perfect sacrifice. Every act of self-indulgence, even when there was some excuse if I was not very well, has left me unhappy, for I see clearly He wants all. The thought of a life in which there would be absolutely no yielding to self, stripped of every possible comfort, has an immense attraction for me lately, even though I have not the courage or generosity to embrace it. This morning at Kilmacud Jesus again told me what He wants: 'to refuse Him no sacrifice, to bear every little pain and inconvenience without relief, to give myself absolutely no gratification at meals *even when not well or on feasts,* and to regard food only as a means of living, to increase my corporal penances.' So strong clear and persistent is this light, filling my soul with peace, that I feel absolutely convinced it is the will of God. I have begun, therefore, to mark days of 'absolute sacrifice' for Jesus." (1st January, 1912.)

"Last night I rose at two o'clock, very much against my will, and went down to the domestic chapel (Limerick). Jesus seemed to want me to come before Him as a victim of His divine anger on behalf of sinners. I knelt down in fear and dread. Acting on a strong impulse I uncovered my shoulders, bowed my head and asked Jesus to scourge me without mercy and not to spare me, cowardly as I was. Then He spoke in my soul clearly and forcibly: 'You must be your own executioner. I want you to sacrifice all, which you have never done yet though you often promised. From this hour you must never give yourself one grain of human comfort or self-indulgence even at the times you have been accustomed to do so, *e.g.* when very tired, not well, travelling, etc. I want from you *a suffering love* always, always, always. The feasts and relaxations of others are not for you. Give Me this courageously and I will grant the desires of your heart."

"Jesus seemed to ask the following: (1) perfect denial of the eyes, (2) the bearing of little pains, (3) much prayer for strength, (4) a review of each half day at examen to see if this resolution has been kept.

"My whole soul shrank from this life 'no human comfort ever.' But with His grace, for I know my own weakness too well, I promised to do all He asked, and lying on the ground, I asked Him to nail me to my cross and never again permit me to come down from it. *Fiat.*" (10th July, 1913.)

"Last night I rose at one a.m. and went down to the Church, renewing before the Crucifix my desire and promise absolutely 'to surrender all human comfort and embrace instead every possible pain and discomfort.' With my arms round the cross, I begged Jesus to give me His courage and strength to do what He asks from me. I realised that if I prayed when tempted to give in, grace would come to my help." (27th January, 1914.)

"'My way is sure.' I think I can say now without a shade of doubt or hesitation that the path by which Jesus wants me to walk is that of *absolute abandonment of all human comfort and pleasure and the embracing as far as I can of every discomfort and pain.* Every time I see a picture of the crucifixion or a cross, I feel strangely affected and drawn to the life of immolation in a strange way. The heroism of Jesus appeals to me; His 'naked crucifixion' calls to me and it gives me great consolation and peace to offer myself to Him on the cross for this perpetual living crucifixion. How often does He not seem to say to me in prayer, 'I would have you strip yourself of all things every tiny particle of self-indulgence, and this ever and always? Give Me *all* and I will make you a great saint.' This then is the price of my life-long yearning for sanctification. O Jesus, I am so weak, help me to give You all and to do it *now.*" (8th May, 1914.)

"During meditation Jesus made known to me a new life which He wants me to aim at in future, a life in which I am to seek only suffering, weariness and pain.

(1) He will send me many little bodily pains which I am to bear with joy, not to seek to get rid of them or to make them known to others.

(2) I am to inflict as much pain on myself as I can, hence I must increase corporal penance.

(3) I am to try and continue this especially when I am sick.

(4) When fatigued and weary, not to indulge myself or rest as I always do; this will be very hard, but Jesus wants it.

(5) Since constant work is so painful, I must try never to be idle one moment.

(6) In a word, because every moment of the life of Jesus was 'full of pain and suffering' I must strive ever and always to make my life resemble His." (Retreat, September, 1915.)

"Meditating on the words of our Lord to Blessed Margaret Mary: 'I seek for My Heart a victim willing to sacrifice itself for the accomplishment of My desires.' I begged Jesus to tell me the meaning of these words. This seemed to be His answer, written as I knelt before the Tabernacle:

(1) 'The victim whom I seek for must place himself in My hands that I may do absolutely what I will with him. Only in this way can My secret plans and designs be carried out. If the victim deliberately refuses to do what I want, all My plans may be spoiled.

(2) 'The victim must surrender his body for any suffering or disease I may please to send, (but not asked for). There must be no holding back in this surrender through fear of any sickness whatever. This includes the *joyful acceptance* of all little bodily pains and the not seeking remedies for them, except when absolutely necessary.

(3) 'The victim must give Me his soul that I may try it by temptation, plunge it in sadness, purify it by interior trials. In this state its prayer must be, '*Fiat,* Thy will be done.'

(4) 'Perfect abandonment to My will in every detail must be the very life of My victim, the most absolute humble submission to My pleasure his constant aim. Every little thing that happens must be recognized and welcomed as coming straight from My hand. The victim will wait till the voice of obedience speaks and then do exactly what I have made known, this promptly, earnestly, gladly because it is My will. There must be no likes or dislikes; no wishing for this thing to end or the other to begin, to be sent here or there, not to have this work to do, etc. My victim must have only one wish, one aim, one desire, to do what I want in all things; this I shall make known from moment to moment.

(5) 'The victim should strive to carry out what I seem to ask, fearless of the pain involved, regardless of the possible consequences, only trusting in My all-powerful help and protection.

In this way, using My victim as an instrument, I shall secretly accomplish my desires in souls. My child, do you accept this office with its conditions?"

Jesus, most humbly I offer myself as Thy victim. Amen." September, 1915.)

This last was written just six weeks before he received his appointment as military chaplain and two years before God accepted the final holocaust.

(3.) PRIESTLY SANCTITY AND REPARATION.

Fr. Doyle had a very high ideal of the sacerdotal vocation. This he showed not only by his efforts to procure labourers for the great harvest, but especially in his own life. His daily Mass, for instance, was celebrated with a fervour which was apparent even to strangers. Phrases, such as Kyrie Eleison, Sursum Corda, Dominus Vobiscum, which by their very iteration tend to become mechanical utterances, seemed on his lips to be always full of freshness and meaning. [33] Similarly he always strove to prevent the recitation of the Office from becoming mere routine; he regarded it as a minting of merit, every word a precious coin. He so valued the Sacrament of Penance that he resolved to go daily to Confession. This lofty priestly ideal is made abundantly evident by his growing preoccupation with the work of promoting priestly sanctity and his increasing realisation that, like the great High Priest, he should be "a propitiation for the sins of the people." (Hebr. 2. 17.) We see this idea in the following note: "*Sacerdos et victima.* [34] After the words, Accipe protestatem offere sacrificium Dei, the ordaining bishop adds, Imitamini quod tractatis.' [35] Jesus is a Victim, the priest must be one also. Christ has charged His priest to renew daily the sacrifice of the Cross; the altar is a perpetual Calvary; the matter of the sacrifice, the victim, is Himself, His own Body, and He is the sacrificer. 'Receive, O Eternal Father, this unspotted Victim.' Can a priest worthy of the name stand by and watch this tremendous act, this heroic sacrifice, without desiring to suffer and to be immolated also? 'With Christ I am nailed to the Cross.' (*Gal.* 2. 20.) ...Would that I could say 'a pure holy spotless victim.' Let Jesus take me in His hands, as I take Him in mine, to do as He wills with me." This idea is quite scriptural. "I beseech you," writes S. Paul, [36] "that you present your bodies a living sacrifice, holy, pleasing unto God." "Be you also," says S. Peter (i. 2, 5), "as living stones built up, a spiritual house, a holy priesthood, to offer up spiritual sacrifices acceptable to God by Jesus Christ." This association of priesthood and sacrifice applies also to those who are not priests, to all the faithful, who constitute "a chosen generation, a kingly priesthood, a holy nation, a purchased people." (*I Peter* 2. 9.) ft Pray, Brothers," says the priest at Mass, "that the sacrifice which is mine *and yours* may be acceptable to God the Father Almighty." And all through the Canon of the Mass the words emphasise the intimate union between celebrant and people in the great mystery which is being enacted. The assistants join not only in offering up the Divine Victim but also, as a water-drop in wine, in offering themselves as 'a living sacrifice.' [37]

Thus the Sacrifice of the Mass is the living source from which our reparation derives its efficacy and inspiration. Cooperation in the great mystery of the Redemption, says the foundress of the Congrégation de l'Adoration Réparatrice, is "the act of the Sacrifice of the Mass continued by the members of the Saviour at every moment of the day and night." [38] And this ideal of co-sacrifice with Christ leads naturally from an appreciation of the sublime function of the priesthood to the idea of a spiritual crusade, extending and supplementing the sacerdotal work and atoning for the inevitable negligences and even scandals which occur in its performance. This is the devotion which, during the last three years of his life, strongly took hold of Fr. Doyle, namely, prayer for priests to aid them in their ministry and reparation in atonement for the negligences and infidelities of those whose calling is so high. We have already seen how earnestly he besought prayers for his own work. S. Teresa exhorts her nuns to this apostolate of prayer. "Try to be such," she says, [39] "that we may be worthy to obtain these two favours from God: (1) that among the numerous learned and religious (priests) whom we have, there may be many who possess the requisite abilities...and that our Lord would improve those that are not so well prepared, since one perfect man can do more than many imperfect ones; (2) that our Lord may protect them in their great warfare, so that they may escape the many dangers of the world." She considered that her Carmelites, enjoying the seclusion and immunity of the cloister, owed this duty to the Church Militant. This ideal is still more conspicuously enshrined in some recent religious institutes, particularly in the Society of the Daughters of the Heart of Jesus. These sisters are "to ask by fervent prayers, by sufferings and even by their lives, if necessary, for the outpouring of grace on the Church, on the Catholic priesthood and on religious orders." [40] In his Brief to Mgr. van den Berghe, 14th March, 1872, Pius IX welcomed the new foundation. "It is not without consolation of heart," said the Pope, [41] "that we have heard of your plan, to arouse and spread in your country that admirable spirit of sacrifice which God apparently wishes to oppose to the ever increasing impiety of our time. We see with pleasure that a great number of persons are everywhere devoting themselves entirely to God, offering Him even their life in ardent prayer, to obtain the deliverance and happy preservation of His Vicar and the triumph of the Church, to make reparation for the outrages committed against the divine Majesty, and especially to atone for the profanations of those who, though the salt of the earth, lead a life which is not in conformity with their dignity."

The seal of the Church has therefore been set on this apostolate of prayer and reparation. There is, needless to say, no question of pride or presumption, no attempting to judge others. [42] It is merely the just principle that those who are specially shielded and privileged should aid those active religious priests, brothers and sisters who have great responsibilities and a difficult mission, and should by their faithfulness atone for the shortcomings of those who are exposed to greater temptations. "More than ever," says Cardinal Mermillod, [43] "is it necessary to console the wounded Heart of Jesus, "to pray for the priesthood, and by immolation and adoration without measure or truce to give our Saviour testimony of affection and fidelity." "There is much which needs reparation," writes Mgr. d' Hulst, [44] "even in the sanctuary and the cloisters, and indeed especially there. Our Lord expects compensation from souls who have not abused special graces." "How grievous are these scandals!" he exclaims in another letter. "Only the thought of reparation can soften the bitterness of them. To take expiation on oneself is to be like Him of whom it is said: *Vere languores nostros ipse tulit et dolores nostros ipse portavit.* [45] If this thought had thoroughly entered into us, without running after great penances, should we not give quite another reception than we usually do to sufferings, vexations, and the dulness and bitterness of our poor lives? And then the thought of reparation is so beneficial to poor souls like ours! It is a great mistake to think it is the privilege of the perfect. On the contrary, it pleases our Lord to open up these horizons to the weak, to give them courage by turning their attention away from their own wretchedness. If I am incapable of satisfying God in myself, I will try to make up to Him for others. If I cannot lament my own ingratitude sufficiently, I will learn to do so by lamenting for others." These consoling words will help to convince those whose ideal of holiness is unconsciously individualistic and self-centred, that the ideal of reparation by no means implies the possession or the delusion of perfection. Of course in all this there may creep in some spirit of censorious self-sufficiency, though indeed there is not much danger of it in the hidden humble lives of those 'victim-souls' who are devoted to the secret apostolate of prayer for God's ministers and reparation for those scandals and infidelities which occur from time to time hi the Church. It has, therefore, seemed right to show briefly here, by way of preface to Fr. Doyle's private notes, how explicitly this work of priestly sanctification and reparation has been recognised by the Church and adopted by saints and mystics. [46]

This ideal appealed greatly to Fr. Doyle. On 28th July, 1914, the anniversary of his Ordination, he wrote: "At Exposition Jesus spoke clearly in my soul, 'Do the hard thing for My sake *because* it is hard.' I also felt urged to perform all my priestly duties with great fervour to obtain grace for other priests to do the same, *e.g.* the Office, that priests may say theirs well." On the Feast of St. Teresa, October, 1914, there is this simple but eloquent record: "Last night I rose at one a m. and walked two miles barefooted in reparation for the sins of priests to the chapel at Murrough (Co. Clare), [47] where I made the Holy Hour. God made me realise the merit of each step, and I understood better how much I gain by not reading the paper; each picture, each sentence sacrificed means additional merit. I felt a greater longing for self-inflicted suffering and a determination to do more 'little things.'" During his 1914 retreat this ideal came home to him as a special mission. "The great light of this retreat, clear and persistent," he writes on 1st December, "has been that God has chosen me, in His great love and through compassion for my weakness and misery, to be a victim of reparation for the sins of priests especially; that hence my life must be different in the matter of penance, self-denial and prayer, from the lives of others not given this special grace they may meritoriously do what I cannot; that unless I constantly live up to the life of a willing victim, I shall not please our Lord nor ever become a saint it is the price of my sanctification; that Jesus asks this from me always and in every lawful thing, so that I can sum up my life 'sacrifice always in all things.'"

On the following Christmas Day (1914) Fr. Doyle records a further step. "During midnight Mass at Dalkey Convent I made the oblation of myself as a member of the League of Priestly Sanctity. During my preparation beforehand a sudden strong conviction took possession of me that by doing so, I was about to begin the 'work' which had spoken of. Our Lord gave me great graces during the Mass and urged me. more strongly than ever to throw myself into the work of my sanctification, that so I may draw many other priests to Him. He wants the greatest possible fervour and exactness in all priestly duties."

The League of Priestly Sanctity, to which reference is here made, was founded in the North of France in the year 1901, under the direction of Pere Feyerstein, S.J. (1911). Fr. Doyle became Director-General for Ireland and strove to spread the League among Irish priests. In an explanatory leaflet which he issued, it is described as "an association of priests, both secular and regular, who, in response to the desire of the Sacred Heart, strive to help each other to become holy and thus render themselves worthy of their sublime calling and raise the standard of sacerdotal sanctity." Two special objects are enumerated: "(1) The assistance of priests, and especially those of the League, in living a life worthy of their high calling. (2) The atonement for outrages to the Sacred Heart in the Sacrament of His love. This Sacrament, needless to say, is committed to priests in a special manner; and there ought to be a priestly expiation for irreverence, negligence, and particularly sacrilegious Masses, which the Divine Heart has to endure from the very ministers of His altar." [48]

Fr. Doyle had this League very much at heart and had prepared several schemes for its spread and improvement when his appointment as military chaplain interrupted the work. But while engaged in this novel sphere of activity, the ideal of a life of reparation remained uppermost in his mind and once more the special form which it took was expiation for the negligences and sins of God's anointed. He recorded this resolution on 26th July, 1916: "During a visit our Lord seemed to urge me not to wait till the end of the war, but to begin my life of reparation at once, in some things at least. I have begun to keep a book of acts done with this intention. He asked me for these sacrifices, (1) To rise at night in reparation for priests who lie in bed instead of saying Mass. (2) At all costs to make the 50,000 aspirations. (3) To give up illustrated papers. (4) To kiss floor of churches. (5) Breviary always kneeling. (6) Mass with intense devotion. The Blessed Curé d'Ars used to kneel without support while saying the Office. Could not I?"

"This is my vocation," he notes on 8th February, 1917, "reparation and penance for the sins of priests; hence the constant urging of our Lord to generosity." Appropriately enough the last entry in his diary was made on 28th July, 1917, the tenth anniversary of his ordination. Fr. Doyle's last recorded thought was about his sacrificial ideal of priestly immolation.

"The reading of *La vie Réparatrice* [49] has made me long more to take up this life in earnest. I have again offered myself to Jesus as His Victim *to do with me absolutely as He pleases.* I will try to take all that happens, no matter from whom it comes, as sent to me by Jesus and will bear suffering, heat, cold, etc., with joy as part of my immolation, in reparation for the sins of priests. From this day I shall try bravely to bear all 'little pains' in this spirit. A strong urging to this."

(4.) HOLY FOLLIES.

Neither human nor divine love expresses itself with mechanical precision and calculated nicety. The outpouring of the heart cannot be regulated as it were with a tap; the very fervour of devotion scorns all attempts at impersonal measurement. Every absorbing emotion seems tinged with foolishness or foolhardiness to one who is outside it and untouched by it. "He saved others," said the wise men on Calvary, "but Himself He cannot save." (*S. Matthew* 27. 42.) And did not Peter himself take his Master aside and rebuke Him? (*S. Matthew* 16. 22.) Only when the suffering Christ turned and looked at him, did Peter, weeping bitterly, understand the foolishness of the cross. (*S. Luke* 22. 61.) We, too, with our averaged precepts of prudence, shall often feel tempted to take God's saints aside and rebuke them. That is because we cannot catch that look divine which flashed on them; we attend more to the exterior expressions of holiness than to its interior intensity. The significance of the lives of the saints does not lie in the fact that they did foolish or even whimsical things, which they themselves (like Ignatius after Manresa) often regretted; it lies rather in the inner love and heroism of which these are the manifestations. Such acts performed under overwhelming inspiration serve, like the stigmata and trances of some ecstatica, to show forth, by their striking singularity, how high our nature can be raised and how deeply the human heart can be stirred by the reality of God's presence. It would be hard to justify by general principles many incidents in the lives of the saints; we are not called upon to do so. Such things cannot be generalised and sometimes they are certainly unwise and exaggerated. [50] In altitudes whither most of us never penetrate, even the saints are but novices and pioneers; what wonder if at times their steps are clumsy and unsure? Just as ordinary men need a confessor who will spur and stimulate them, so the saints need a director to check and restrain their impetuous ardour.

These few remarks will help to place in their proper setting some incidents in the life of Fr. Doyle, most of which, were it not for a chance-written document penned under what he believed to be God's inspiration, we should hardly suspect. It was with a firm faith in God's special providence and mission that he strove to ignore physical exhaustion and illness.' During his 1915 retreat he wrote: "I think our Lord is allowing my present state of lassitude and suffering and at the same time urging me to heroic generosity, in order to make me rely more on His strength. Humanly speaking, I ought to rest and indulge myself, I feel so run down; but Jesus does not want this. I must cast prudence to the winds, go ahead blindly, following the inspirations of grace and not counting the cost. I am convinced that my health will not suffer, as past experience has shown me that I am always better when giving Him all. Besides would it not be far better to die than to go on fighting against Him as I have done for years?" In this intimate colloquy written to reassure himself, we have his own best defence. He alone felt 'the inspirations of grace' and had the evidence of what 'Jesus wanted'; he who saved others, refused to save himself. A month later (20th October, 1915), we find him struggling hard against all prudential concessions to illness: "Feeling very unwell for the past few days, I gave way to self-indulgence in food and sleep. Jesus has made it very clear to me that this has not pleased Him: 'I have sent you this suffering that you may suffer more, not that you should try to avoid it.' He made me put on the chain again and promise Him, as long as I can hold out, not to take extra sleep etc. Great peace and contentment is the result." And, after all, was not the result his justification? God wants us to serve Him in peace and contentment; we do not all attain thereto in the same way. [51]

It was especially the night-time that Fr. Doyle chose for self-inflicted suffering. Two quotations, in addition to those already given, will show us how he thus combined prayer and penance.

"Last night I rose at twelve and knelt in the cellar for an hour to suffer from the cold. It was a hard fight to do so, but Jesus helped me. I said my rosary with arms extended. At the third mystery the pain was so great that I felt I could not possibly continue; but at each *ave* I prayed for strength and was able to finish it. This has given me great consolation by showing the many hard things I could do with the help of prayer." (22nd January, 1915.)

"Last night I rose at twelve, tied my arms in the form of a cross and remained in the chapel till three a.m. I was fiercely tempted not to do so, the devil suggesting that, as I had a cough, it was madness and would unfit me for the coming mission. Though I shivered with cold, I am none the worse this morning, in fact, the cough is better, proving that Jesus is pleased with these 'holy imprudences.' At the end of an hour I was cold and weary, I felt I could not possibly continue; but I prayed and got wonderful strength to persevere till the end of the three hours. This has shown me what I might do and how, with a little determined effort, I could overcome the greatest repugnances and seeming impossibilities. (27th September, 1915.)

It seems almost a desecration to lift the veil and to disclose aught that happened at these nocturnal interviews between Master and disciple. A citation from a very precious and intimate paper will suffice. 1 "He seems pleased when I am alone in the chapel if I kneel close to Him, uncover my breast and ask Him again to pour His grace and love into my heart. I often press my throbbing heart to the door of the Tabernacle to let Him hear its beats of love; and once, to ease the pain of love, I tried with a penknife to cut the sweet name of Jesus on my breast. It was not a success, for I suppose my courage failed; I did try a heated iron, but it caused an ugly sore."

Some other heroic acts may be instanced. [53] During one freezing winter, having previously bound himself by vow, he set his alarum for three o'clock and slipped out of the house in his nightshirt. He then stood up to his neck in a pond, praying for sinners. [54] Sometimes he turned the ordinary discipline into a horrifying scourging by using a heavy chain or even branches with long strong thorns. [55] He constantly wore the ordinary chain, and at least once he heated it, not red hot of course, and put it round his body so that the points raised blisters. Several times he undressed and rolled in furze bushes; "the pain of the thousands of little pricks," he confesses, "is intense for days afterwards." On one or two occasions he forced his way through a thorn hedge and was in consequence terribly torn and wounded. Walking barefoot on stones and nettles was a comparatively frequent achievement. Once during a retreat at Delgany in 1911, he had a severe "accident," [56] being badly stung by nettles, so much so that the doctor took a very serious view of the case. Fortunately we have the real explanation which may be best given in his own words:

"It really was not an accident. That day the love of Jesus Crucified was burning in my heart with the old longing to suffer much for Him and even give Him my life by martyrdom. This thought was in my mind when, crossing a lonely field late that evening, I came across a forest of old nettles. Here was a chance! Had not the saints suffered in this way for Him with joy and gladness of heart? I undressed and walked up and down until my whole body was one big blister, smarting and stinging. Words could never describe the sweet but horrible agony from that moment till far into the next day. Not for a moment did I close my eyes, for as the poison worked into the blood the fever mounted and the pain increased. Then began what I can only call a flogging from head to foot with red-hot needles. It started at the feet and crept up to my face and back again so regularly that I almost thought that some unseen hand was at work. More than once I knelt by my bed and offered Him my life, as I felt I could not live, and then in my weakness begged Him to have pity on me, and yet the moment after He gave me strength to murmur, 'Still more, dear Lord, a thousand times more for Your dear love.'

"Then suddenly when the pain was greatest, an extraordinary peace, happiness and joy filled my soul; and though I saw nothing with the eyes of either soul or body, I had the conviction that Jesus was standing by me the sure feeling one has when a person is in a darkened room though one cannot see him. What took place I cannot say, but it seemed to me as if He was thanking me for trying to bear the agony for Him, and then He seemed to ask me what I would have from Him in return. 'Fill my heart with Your love, dearest Lord,' I remember saying. And then I lay motionless, all suffering seemed to have ceased while Jesus I can only express it in this way took His own Heart and poured Its love into mine till It almost seemed to be empty.

"One thing more I remember saying, 'Lord, if it is really You, give me a proof of Your goodness by curing me in the morning.' When I tried to rise, my legs felt paralyzed, I staggered like a drunken man to the convent, I could only mumble the words of Mass. But the moment His Sacred Body touched my lips, I felt a change come over me, and I was actually able to give the morning lecture as usual. I suffered a good deal from the after-effects, but I believe that Jesus worked a miracle."

Such an account seems to disarm all criticism. "Here was a chance!" His love for suffering was as irrepressible as a boy's instinct for a prank. [57] To frame regulations for one so afire with the love of Christ is like reducing heroism to rule-of-thumb. A war-charger is not to be trained like a dray-horse, nor can a tiger be set mouse-catching with his weaker brother the cat. Fr. Doyle knew quite as much about the virtue of prudence as the reader of these lines. It was quite calmly and deliberately that, like many of the saints, he 'cast it to the winds.' He held that God was inspiring him to a certain course of action and helping him therein. And where is the evidence with which we can gainsay him? [58]

In order to appreciate in their true perspective these exploits of Fr. Doyle, it will be helpful to glance at some similar incidents in the life of another Jesuit. Fr. Paul Segneri (f 1694) used to walk barefooted to his missions, often traversing over eight hundred miles a year in this way. His invariable custom was to discipline himself twice or three times a day; for over thirty years he slept on bare boards, his sleep never exceeding six hours. Several times he rolled himself naked in the snow and at least once he threw himself naked among thorns; as a final refinement of cruelty, he used to cause boiling wax to drop all over his body. [59] During his missions he was not content with scourging himself publicly as was then the custom with an iron discipline," he invented another instrument yet more barbarous, which was a circular piece of cork armed with about fifty sharp points. With this he used to strike violently his naked breast during the last penitential procession, and on other occasions when he was anxious to conquer the obstinacy of such as persisted in refusing to make peace with their enemies. So much blood was by this means drawn from his veins, that in course of time the physicians, to obviate the danger of his life, found it necessary to oblige him to lay aside the practice." [60]

Exaggerated and imprudent? Perhaps. But let us not be more impatiently ready to condemn the few rare instances of indiscreet fervour than we are to denounce the widespread worship of ease and comfort. "Let not him that eateth," says S. Paul (Rom. 14. 3), "despise him that eateth not; and he that eateth not, let him not judge him that eateth." There is need for large-hearted tolerance even among those who, each in his own way, are following Christ. There are indeed dangers in all extremes; an orgy of blood-letting may be morbid and self-willed, [61] just as what is called common-sense goodness may be merely an excuse for slothful mediocrity. In one that is filled with a great ideal there is always something extreme, an impetuous enthusiasm whose expression may at times be gauche or reckless. "He that loves truly," says A Kempis, [62] "flies, runs and is always full of joy; he is free and will not be held back. He gives all for all and has all in all, because he rests in One alone... Love knows no bounds but burns with boundless fervour. Love feels no burden, counts no cost, longs to do even more than it is able for and never pleads impossibility, because everything then seems lawful and possible. Hence a lover of God is strong enough for everything and carries out many things where he that has no love fails and falls to the ground."

The instances of Fr. Segneri and Fr. Doyle show us the wise latitude with which S. Ignatius provides for different types of holiness in his Company. Not that each one may seek out his own path according to his freak or fancy, not that one's own subjective impulses and experiences are to decide the will of the Holy Spirit. S. Ignatius lays down a wise rule which may be given here by way of fitting conclusion: "The way of living, as to exterior things, ... is common; nor are there customary penances or afflictions of the body to be undergone by way of obligation. But each one may choose those which, with the superior's approval, will seem to be suitable for his greater spiritual progress, and which for the same end superiors may impose on them." [63]

[1] Notes to the Additions of the First Week, (p. 31). This is taken from S. Thomas, *Summa*, 2. 2, q 147, a i.
[2] Way of Perfection, ch. 10.
[3] *Life of Blessed Margaret Mary Alacoque*, published in French by the Monastery of the Visitation of Paray-le-Monial, Eng. trans. 1912 (Visitation Library, Roselands, Walmer, Kent), p. 60.
[4] *Ibid.* pp. 38f, 127. Compare also the "tiny little things" which Soeur Thérèse offered to our Lord: the annoyance of a bead-rattling sister, the splashing of an awkward neighbour in the laundry. *Soeur Thérèse...Histoire d'une âme,* pp. 195f; Eng. trans. (*The. Little Flower*), pp. 206-208.
[5] *Ibid.* pp. 77, 152f. Compare Mgr. d'Hulst's remarks (*Vie de la vén. Marie-Térèse du Coeur de Jésus,* 1917,16 p. 161): "At all times saints have caused suffering to saints." So the Cure of Ars was even preached against by his fellow-priests. Monnin, *Life of the B. Curé d'Ars,* (Burns & Gates, n.d.) p. 136.
[6] James, Principles of Psychology i. 126.
[7] Compare his remarks on heroism, pp. 27 f.
[8] Compare S. Margaret Mary's eight years of struggle against her repugnance to cheese. - *Life,* p. 33.
[9] *Une mystique de nos jours,* p. 454. Of this work Fr. Doyle once wrote: "I almost grudge lending you this book, I have found it so helpful." Compare *Life and Revelations of S. Gertrude,* 1865, pp. 380, 412.
[10] This he called "the book of little victories." It is consoling 1 and human to read the very next entry (5th Nov.): "Again for the past few days I have broken my resolutions and indulged myself. I see two causes of this: idleness, not overcoming my natural dislike for certain kinds of work, e.g., preparation of sermons; and above all, yielding to depression."
[11] Compare this entry in his diary (17th January, 1912): "Our Lord wants me to give Him all I can give *cheerfully,* not repining nor regretting any sacrifice; not saying, 'I wish I had not to do this or suffer this cold, pain, etc.,' but rather, 'I wish I could do more for You, Jesus, I wish it were colder.'"
[12] *Speculum Perfectionis,* c. 100.
[13] Seneca, *De ira,* iii. 36. 3.
[14] *De incarnatione,* vii. 3; viii. 4.
[15] Compare St. Thomas's teaching that there is a real physical efficiency in Christ's passion and resurrection. - *Summa,* p. 3, q 48, a 6, ad 2; q 56, a 1, ad 3.
[16] The Congregations of the *Adoration Réparatrice* and of *Marie Réparatrice,* the Society of the *Filles du Coeur Jésus*.
[17] *Summarium Constitutionum S.J.,* 1 1-12. This ideal of Christlike imitation and atonement is really distinct from the ordinary idea of asceticism or mortification. "There is in Catholic sanctity a sacrifice of the body which could not be called mortification though it resembles mortification. It is not intended as a protection to purity, as an exercise of courage, but as a holocaust to God, as an atonement for personal sin or for the sin of mankind. Such are the most adorable of all sufferings, the sufferings of Christ on the Cross. Sufferings of that kind do not come under the heading of mortification. Their explanation is more theological than psychological. There have been sufferings of that

kind in the lives of the saints, whose desire it was to resemble Christ crucified, to renew in their bodies the sufferings of Christ." - Abbot A. Vonier, *The Human Soul,* 1913, p. 129.

[18] The Two Standards - *Spiritual Exercises,* p. 47.

[19] *Ep. to Magnesians,* 9. i.

[20] *Life of Bl. Margaret Mary Alacoque* (Paray-le-Monial), Eng. trans. 1912,: p. 68.

[21] So it is said of sinners that they "are fallen away...crucifying again to themselves the Son of God and making Him a mockery." - *Heb,* 6. 6.

[22] Thorold, *The Dialogue of the Seraphic Virgin Catherine of Siena,* 1907, p. 297; cf. p. 46. S. Teresa was emphatic that "our Lord leads souls on by different roads." - *Foundations,* 18. 6.

[23] Compare, for instance, with the better known Jesuit Saints, such members of the Society as Fathers Alvarez and Surin, the Ven. Emmanuel Padtal (1725) who fell into a rapture at the mention of crib or stable, the Ven. Bernard de Hoyos (1735), a wondrous mystic and the first apostle of the Sacred Heart in Spain.

[24] *Life* p. 35. It is significant to note that S. Francis de Sales had already declared that "the daughters of the Visitation...are victims of sacrifice and living holocausts." Letters to Persons in Religion, Eng. trans. 1901 3, p. 105. Compare also *Sister Gertrude Mary* (Eng. trans, of abridged French edition, p. 24): "I appoint you My victim of reparation - the victim of My choice."

[25] *Nobilissima Gallorum Gens,* 8 Feb., 1884. - *Lettres apostoliques* i. 238. See also the special Brief (6 March, 1883) given in Mgr. d'Hulst's pamphlet *L'adoration réparatrice et nationale,* Lille, 1884.

[26] Thus the specially approved Constitutions of the Benedictines of Perpetual Adoration, "I vow and promise .... zealously to preserve the perpetual adoration and worship of the Most Holy Sacrament of the Altar, as a victim immolated to Its glory." (58, 23). On 3rd Feb. 1908, the Institute of the "Daughters or Victims of the Sacred Heart of Jesus" received formal approval.

[27] Cf. the work of Père Calage, S.J., at Marseilles (1846-66) as director of "âmes victimes" and his stimulus to the foundation of the Société des filles du Coeur de Jésus. - Laplace, *La Mère Marie de Jésus,* new ed. 1906, pp. 121 ff. See also Fr. Doyle's letters of direction pp. 193f.

[28] *The Way of the Heart: Letters of Direction,* Eng. trans. 1913, p. 56.

[29] Apparently the resolutions (only partly extant) quoted on p. 90.

[30] Compare the saying of Soeur Gertrude-Marie (*Une mystique de nos jours,* p. 593) quoted later on in Fr. Doyle's diary: "I am sure that God wishes me to go to the end without giving 1 any attention to what costs me, to what tires me, to what injures my health. I must no longer follow any rule of human prudence in what concerns my health; God has charge of it. It is strange, at the moment when I am most tired, most suffering, most exhausted, God asks me for yet more. He asks me such and such a thing: I must do it at once, without considering if it injures my health, without listening to the protests of nature. I must be crucified with Jesus. I must go as far as the extinction or self." Also the Foundress of the Society of Marie Réparatrice: "My whole being has turned into suffering; everything fatigues me, everything costs me an effort, so broken down is my nature. And nevertheless God does not wish either solace or rest for me as long as the possibility of suffering remains." *Life of Mother Mary of Jesus,* (Eng. trans, by Fr. Gallery), 1913, p. 191.

[31] This reference shows clearly that Fr. Doyle consulted his confessor and sought permission for these private vows.

[32] S. Teresa, finding her vow (to do always what was most perfect) a source of scruples, got it commuted; she renewed it in a safer form under the guidance of her confessor. See preface to Lew-

is's translation of the Foundations, 1871, p. vi.

[33] It was a similar zeal which led him to publish his little *Synopsis of the Rubrics and Ceremonies of Holy Mass,* Washbourne, 1914. One of the booklets he had projected was "An Explanation of the Priest's Actions at Mass." "How many of us," he asks, "could tell why, for example, the priest blesses the water and not the wine at the Offertory?" Cf. the Curé of Ars: "To say Mass one ought to be a seraph If we really knew what the Mass is, we should die! "Life by Abb Monnin, Eng. tr. pp. 146 f.

[34] Priest and Victim.

[35] Receive power to offer the sacrifice of God. Imitate what you handle (i.e. the instruments of sacrifice).

[36] Rom. 12. I. *Cf.* Prat, *Théologie de saint Paul,* i. 308 ff.

[37] As the ideas of Soeur Gertrude Marie were so appreciated and propagated by Fr. Doyle, we may refer here to her method of hearing Mass. - *Sister Gertrude Mary* (Eng. trans. 1915 of abridged French edition) pp. 107-111. "I ask of Jesus to place my soul, and all those whom I am recommending to Him at the Holy Sacrifice, upon the paten, and in the chalice, so that this dear Saviour may deign to offer us all to His Father. The matter of the Sacrifice is prepared. I must offer myself also to be wholly immolated ..." Compare what S. Francis de Sales says to a correspondent: "Every day I offer you on the altar with the Son of God." - *Letters to Persons in Religion,* Eng. trans. (Mackay) 1901 p. 26. Also *Imitation of Christ* (iv. 8, 1): "You also ought to offer yourself freely to Me every day in the Mass as a pure and holy offering."

[38] Mgr. d'Hulst, *Vie de la Vén. Marie-Térèse,* 1917, p. 268; Brig, trans, by Lady Herbert (*Life of Mother Mary Teresa,* 1899), p. 168.

[39] Way of Perfection, ch. 3.

[40] Abbé L. Laplace, *La Mère Marie de Jésus* (Marie Deluil-Martiny), 1894; new ed. 1906, p. 283.

[41] *Ibid.,* pp. 218f.

[42] "You should love them [priests] therefore by reason of the virtue and dignity of the Sacrament, and by reason of that very virtue and dignity you should hate the defects of those who live miserably in sin, but not on that account appoint yourselves their judges, which I forbid, because they are My Christs and you ought to love and reverence the authority which I have given them...Their sins indeed should displease you and you should hate them, and strive with love and holy prayer to reclothe them, washing away their foulness with your tears." - S. Catherine of Siena, *Dialogue,* Eng. trans. Thorold, 1907, pp. 256f.

[43] Laplace, *La Mère Marie de Jésus,* 1906, p. 288.

[44] Baudrillart, *Vie de Mgr. d' Hulst,* ii. 523; *The Way of the Heart: Letters of Direction by Mgr. d' Hulst,* Eng. trans. 1913, p. 96, (see also p. 25).

[45] "Surely He hath borne our infirmities and carried our sorrows." Isaias 53. 4.

[46] Compare the message to Gemma Galgani: "I have need of a great expiation specially for the sins and sacrileges by which ministers of the sanctuary are offending Me." - *Life* by Fr. Germanus, Eng. trans. 1913, p. 325. Also Soeur Gertrude Marie: "I wish to pray and suffer for priests. I wish that all holy souls, especially religious, had this attraction for the sanctification of priests. My God, choose souls who love and understand the importance of this apostolate! Bless and make fruitful this apostolate so dear to Your Heart!" Legueu, *Une mystique de nos jours,* Angers, 1910, p. 331. And Mere Marie de Jesus: "I think that I would willingly give my life that our Lord might find in His priests what He expects from them; I would give it that only one of them might fully realise the divine plan. Of course there are those who do, but I mean, that one more should do so my life would willingly be given." - Laplace, p. 223.

[47] He was giving a Mission here.

[48] Pius X. (Rescript of 16th Dec. 1908, and Brief of 9th July, 1909) granted a plenary indulgence once a month to priests who undertook this oblation of priestly reparation.

[49] My Canon Leroux de Bretagne (Desclée, 1909).

[50] "I make so bold as to say that a certain amount of Christian language in that matter of mortification is both metaphorical and hyperbolical. I go even further and say that, besides exaggerated language, there has been occasionally, or even frequently, exaggerated acting in individual cases. The Church is not responsible for the over-fervid behaviour of some of her best children." - Abbot A. Vonier, *The Human Soul*, 1913, p. 126.

[51] Compare the *general principles* advocated by the saints. "The poor soul must not be stifled. Let those who thus suffer realise that they are ill...Take care of the body for the love of God, because at many other times the body must serve the soul. Let recourse be had to some holy recreations such as conversation, walking in the fields, as the confessor may advise. - S. Teresa, *Life,* xi. 23-24. "If the work that you are doing is necessary to you or very useful for God's glory, I prefer you to suffer the burden of work than that of fasting-. This is the view of the Church which dispenses even from the prescribed fasting those who are doing work useful for the service of God and the neighbour." - S. Francis de Sales, *Introduction to Devout Life,* iii. 23. "The works of penance and of other corporal exercises should be observed merely as a means and not as the fundamental affection of the soul... No one should judge that he has greater perfection, because he performs great penances and gives himself in excess to the slaying of his body, than he who does less; inasmuch as neither virtue nor merit consists therein. For otherwise he would be in an evil case who from some legitimate reason was unable to do actual penance." - S. Catherine of Siena, *Dialogue,* trans. Thorold, 1907, pp. 56, 58. For S. Ignatius see pp. 165, 169, 171; S. Thomas, p. 169.

[52] This little incident from the life of the Venerable Marie-Térèse, foundress of the Sisters of Perpetual Adoration, may be quoted as showing how closely similar are the spontaneous outbursts of souls afire with love." "I was speaking aloud to our Saviour, in a transport of love more burning than fever. And as I was lovingly reproaching Him for having deceived me in my expectation in not showing me His Crown [the relic of Notre-Dame], I thought I heard these words in my heart: 'My blood flows in your heart every morning; take the blood of your heart, it is Mine, and saturate therewith this little crown' my crucifix had a very small crown of thorns. I could not have resisted, I think; I took my penknife made an incision and I marked with my blood not only the crown but all the wounds of Christ..." - *Vie* by Mgr. d'Hulst, 1917 6, p. 84; *Life of Mother Mary Teresa* (tr. by Lady Herbert, 1899). p. 56. It were surely dull-witted and materialistic to apply mechanical meticulous criticism to such dramatically heroic intensity of devotion. It is not the mere physical pain but the exteriorising of intensely realistic faith which merits attention; just as when S. Gertrude "snatched the iron nails from a crucifix which she always kept near her and replaced them by nails of sweet-smelling cloves." - *Life and Revelations,* 1865, p. 225.

[53] While on the continent where no one knew him Fr. Doyle subjected himself to a big humiliation in church: "I used to go into the church, kiss the floor before the congregation, and pray with my arms outstretched. I felt people thought I was

mad, and I nearly died of shame." Cf. p. 160.

[54] Apparently he did this on more than one occasion. Here is an entry under the date nth April, 1915: "Got into pond at two." St. Ignatius once did the same to convert a sinner.

[55] One such act seems quite indefensible as Fr. Doyle himself admitted: "Once I made a discipline with some safety razor blades. I admit this was foolish and might have been rather serious, as some blows cut to the very bone. The blood ran down my body till a small pond had formed on the floor and through prudence I ceased, but the blood flowed a long time and I suffered much from the pain of the cuts." St. Ignatius says in the Additions to the First Week (*Spiritual Exercises,* p. 31): "What seems to be most convenient and safe in the matter of penance is that the pain should be sensible to the flesh and not penetrate to the bone, so that pain and not sickness should be the result. For which purpose it seems to be more convenient to discipline oneself with small cords which cause pain exteriorly, than to do so in any other way from which may result any notable injury to the health."

[56] The nuns to whom he was giving the retreat were under the impression that he had taken internally some medicine meant for external application.

[57] Similarly we read in Lady Lovat's *Clare Vaughan* (new ed., New York, 1896, p. 26): "We happened to be passing through a stubble field, and breaking off suddenly from what she had been talking about, she cried: 'I have a splendid idea! Supposing we take off our shoes and stockings and walk barefoot through the stubble field?' It was no sooner said than done; and I can see now the calm enjoyment with which Clare walked up and down those cruel many-bristling thorns, ...till at last she was obliged to succumb and allow the poor bleeding feet to be tied up. Another day we came across a flourishing family of nettles, and she instantly seized hold of a large bunch in order to discipline herself with them at leisure on her return home."

[58] It is a curious fact that often in the case of favoured souls this holy indiscretion does not seem to produce the deleterious effects which might be expected. "In a greater degree even than the heart," remarks Père Suau, S.J., "the soul that is guided by God has reasons which human intellect is ignorant of; and when grace inspires anyone to suffer by way of reparation, that which tends to kill gives life and that which tends to heal brings on death. - *Life of Mother Mary of Jesus* (Eng. trans, by Fr. Gallery), 1913, p. 207.

[59] *The Lives of Fr. P. Segneri, Fr. P. Pinamonti, and the Ven. John de Britto,* London 1851, pp. 19, 143, 146, 149. He always entertained "a burning desire to shed his blood and give up his life in honour of Christ" and with this hope volunteered for the East Indies, (p. 16). "With regard to his mortifications, he asked and obtained general permission from his confessor to use them as far as he thought he could without considerable prejudice to his health." (p. 15).

[60] *Ibid.,* p. 27.

[61] So Fr. Doyle discouraged 'frenzy.'

[62] *Imitation of Christ* iii. 5, 4. Compare these reflections of Fr. Paul Segneri (on I. Cor., 4. 10): "There is a great difference between being wise in Christ and being a fool for Christ. Both are good; but the apostle was not satisfied with the former and preferred the latter. There is a worldly wisdom which makes a man wicked; there is a wisdom in Christ which does not prevent a man from being just; there is a foolishness for Christ which makes a man holy... Now for my conclusion. I shall never accomplish much if I measure everything by the rules of singular prudence and exact circumspection. I shall be good; but I shall never be a saint... What shall we decide to do? Why so much examination? Why so much consideration? If we do not succeed, what shall we have done?

Folly, yes; hut folly committed for Christ. That is enough for us We should therefore become foolish for Christ, which means: Let us work simply for Christ, look only at Christ, have Him for the sole end of our works, then we shall commit foolishness and we shall be saints." - "Thoughts during Prayer" in *Lights in Prayer* (Quarterly Series) pp. 305-309.

[63] *Summarium, Constitutionum* S.J., n. 4. S. Francis de Sales says similarly: "Abstinence which is practised against obedience takes away the sin from the body to put it in the heart. Let her give her attention to cutting off her own will and she will soon quit these phantoms of sanctity in which she reposes so superstitiously. She has consecrated her corporal strength to God; it is not for her to break it down unless God so order it; and she will never learn what God orders save by obedience to the creatures whom the Creator has given her for her guidance." - *Letters to Persons in Religion,* Eng. trans. (Mackay), 1901 3, p. 183. "It is advisable never to adopt bodily mortifications without the direction of our spiritual guide." - *Introduction to Devout Life,* iii. 23. Also S. Thomas: "The chastisement of the body, for example by vigils and fasts, is not acceptable to God except in so far as it is a work of virtue; i.e., in so far as it is done with due discretion, so that passion is restrained and nature not overburdened." - *Summa,* 2. 2, q 88, 3.2, ad 3.

Chapter Eight - Spiritual Direction

(1.) HIS OWN SOUL

FR. Doyle had himself so much direct spiritual experience and such great reliance on" the inspirations of the Holy Spirit, that any direction might seem in his case superfluous. Yet this would be a misinterpretation. It is obvious, of course, that a fully formed Jesuit, after years of prayer, instruction and reading, and a complete course of theology, is not in need of that minute guidance and detailed help which are usually necessary for beginners in the spiritual life and for timorous scrupulous souls. But it is a distinctive mark of Catholic spirituality, as opposed to all systems of private judgement or self-guided mysticism, that inner experience must be brought to the test of objective dogma, and also should be moulded by that comprehensive tradition of practical religion which is embodied in the wonderful structure of Catholic discipline and direction. There is nothing repressive or mechanically imposed in all this; it is only misguided individualism which is eliminated; when freakishness is obviated, liberty is increased. Within the great corporate life of Catholicism there is ample room for every individuality. [1] How marvellously diverse and manifold are the saints, and yet they have an unmistakable family likeness. They thought and spoke of God just as we do; their outward religious life was practically the same as ours; they shared the same Faith and partook of the same Sacraments. Thus we see that, apart altogether from any question of individual direction, there is in the Church an immense amount of objective guidance and help. Every one of us has to kneel at the feet of God's minister for absolution; we all gather round the same altar of sacrifice and kneel in the glad presence of our eucharistic Lord. And we thence draw not only supernatural aid, but also, by the loving economy of the Incarnation, natural help and encouragement. Without frequent confession and absolution, how could we keep our consciences pure and healthy and our souls refreshed with God's forgiveness? [2] How could religious life, naturally so irksome, bring such peace and happiness, were it not for the closeness of the Real Presence? How wonderfully are our Lord's words fulfilled: "Come to Me all you that labour and are burdened, and I will refresh you. Take My yoke upon you...and you shall find rest to your souls." (*S. Matthew* 11. 28.)

Fr. Doyle, therefore, had the sacramental helps and disciplinary guidance common to all faithful Catholics. Moreover, he had studied theology and was well read in ascetical and devotional literature. But all this did not dispense him from seeking the approval of his confessor or director. St. Ignatius says distinctly to his subjects: [3]

Fr. William Doyle, S. J. Aberdeen, 1908.

"They must not conceal any temptation, which they do not disclose to the spiritual father or confessor or superior; indeed it ought to be most agreeable to them that their whole soul should be entirely manifest to them. They must disclose not only their defects, but also their penances or mortifications and all their devotions and virtues, with a pure will desiring to be directed by them, if perchance they deviate from what is right; not wishing to be led by their own opinion unless it agrees with the judgement of those whom they have in the place of Christ our Lord."

In the intimate writings, which formed the basis of our account of Fr. Doyle's inner life, there are naturally few references to external direction. But those that do occur indicate clearly that he always submitted his plans and penances to a confessor. [4] We also know that for several years he used to go to confession to Fr. Matthew Russell, whose holiness he esteemed and with whom he liked to have spiritual talks. Once after confession Fr. Russell turned to Fr. Doyle and said, "You will go far, my child." When asked what he meant, he merely repeated, "You will go far." We may certainly conclude that Fr. Russell knew many of the secrets of his penitent. Later on, Fr. Doyle was instructed by the Provincial to submit his penances and mortifications to a certain Father. Much to Fr. Doyle's surprise, for he was expecting a drastic curtailment, this Father approved of his practices with some slight modifications and told him to follow the inspirations of the Holy Spirit who was leading him. These indications will serve to show that, while directing and guiding the souls of others, Fr. Doyle himself submitted to that divine yet human scheme whereby men are made their brothers' keepers and each can find an *alter Christus.* Not only did he seek the approval and advice of superiors and confessors, but on more than one occasion he consulted expert directors and masters of the spiritual life. [5] He thus secured that his inner life was in perfect unison with that unceasing harmony of holiness which through the ages has been one of the marks of the true Church. [6]

(2.) DIRECTOR OF OTHERS

Although Fr. Doyle laboured energetically and fruitfully as a missioner, his real gift and taste lay rather in his work as director of souls. He preferred dealing directly and personally with the individual to appealing to crowds, intensive culture of a few chosen souls rather than slight impersonal influence on many. He shrank, too, from the pain of probing into the ulcers of humanity. "The consolation of absolving sinners," he says in one of his letters (1913), "does not lessen the pain of hearing all day a litany of awful sins and outrages against the good and patient God... You have guessed rightly the longing of my heart, namely, to help others to realise the words of Scripture, 'He that is holy, let him be sanctified still.'" (*Apoc.* 22. 11.) On the other hand, his preference for work among chosen souls was absolutely removed from anything remotely approaching snobbery; his valuation was purely spiritual. He once referred to a ladies' retreat which he had to give, as "a job I do not relish it is too much of a social affair and not earnest work." He always insisted on "the real thing" in holiness, the genuine article branded with the cross; he had no patience with amateurish piety or devotional flippancy. Even by natural character he detested doing things by halves; as he said himself, he was "a wholehogger." At the outset of his ministry [7] he perhaps expected too much from weak human nature, but he soon acquired the art of gentle leading and gradual guidance. Not that he avoided all mistakes only the negative critic does that. But he went on his way, every day drawing souls closer to Christ, advocating without compromise what he knew to be Christ's ideal, modifying what he believed to be merely its outer or temporary expression, accepting as inevitable the criticism of those who prefer things as they are and deprecate the better on the plea of letting well alone.

That he was wonderfully successful as a director was shown by the void which his death created, to which many dozens of letters bear touching testimony. To this success many qualities contributed. In the first place he was unaffectedly and unobtrusively polite; a quality which, just because it is not necessarily associated with holiness, must not be undervalued. "Fr. Doyle," a nun declared with emphasis, "always treats one as a lady." Grace of manner, allied with thoughtfulness, always creates a favourable prepossession. Furthermore, Fr. Doyle was obviously painstaking and unselfish, he never shrank from trouble when the issue was the good of even a single soul, he never grumbled or complained of inroads made on his time and temper. [8] In addition to all this, he had 'a way with him,' a natural attractiveness and spontaneity, an infectious gaiety. He had nothing of prudery or stiffness about him, no depressingly impersonal smile or manner, no angularities or excrescences. [9] His emotions did not seem to move on merely celestial hinges, nor did his movements appear to be regulated by spiritual clockwork. Those whom he helped felt that he had a real personal interest in them, he did not regard them as so much undifferentiated soul-stuff. Moreover, in his retreat-talks or private conversations he did not use stilted language or conventional phraseology, he spoke with homely directness. Thus he would say: "There are three D's which you ought to avoid the Doctor, the Devil, and the Dumps. You can cheat the doctor and run from the devil, but the dumps are the *divil!*" He did not think that holiness lost by being conjoined with a sense of humour. Nor did he neglect any available helps to imagination, memory or sentiment. In giving a retreat to children and even adults he sometimes gave one of the daily instructions with the aid of lanternslides, a method of vivid presentation which always made a deep impression. [10] He also had recourse to what may be termed little dodges or stratagems. For example, one of his favourite aspirations was 'Omnipotent God make me a saint.' This he had printed on small pink leaflets which, parodying a well-known advertisement, he called (Father William's) "pink pills for pale saints" or, as he once put it, "intended to make pale souls ruddy with the love of God." He once sent a box of these to a convent with the following "directions for use": "To be taken frequently during the day, and occasionally at night, as directed by the physician; when the disease is deeply rooted and of long standing, increase the dose to every quarter of an hour; result infallible, will either cure or kill!" This may seem a rather elaborate joke, especially when put in cold print. But there are many to whom the presentation of a 'pink pill' was the first not easily forgotten introduction to the use of aspirations. Besides, this kindly humour was simply natural to the man and brought an element of humanness into relations too often regarded as formal or dismal.

Beyond and behind all these qualities and activities there was something which can only be called personal influence. It was not any gifts of mind and heart, nor was it just facility of expression, nor yet quick intuitive sympathy; it was all this and more. There was about Fr. Doyle as director that intangible indefinable thing which we term personality. It was not so much the words that moved people as the man behind the words, not so much what he said as what he was. Not that he ever spoke of himself or his own spiritual life. [11] One might perhaps guess at details of prayer and mortification. But that was not uppermost in one's mind when one came into real contact with him; one thought., not of details, but of the whole man. One seemed to feel the radiance of the love with which he was afire as distinctly as if it were a physical rise of temperature. He was so transparently earnest, the words came, as it were, charged with something more than meaning. To those who knew Fr.

Doyle by casual acquaintanceship, all this may sound exaggerated. But it is a faithful description of the impression which he made on those who sought from him guidance and help. And it enables us to realise that in such spiritual relationship there is something more than moral or ascetic theology, more than eloquence or elocution. Does not the secret lie in our Lord's own criterion of fruitfulness? "Amen, amen, I say to you, unless the grain of wheat falling into the ground die, itself remaineth alone; but if it die, it bringeth forth much fruit." (*S. John* 12. 24.) Or, to change the simile but not the reality: "As the branch cannot bear fruit of itself unless it abide in the vine, so neither can you unless you abide in Me." (*S. John* 15. 4.) [12]

Fr. Doyle did not confine himself to personal interviews, he kept up a heavy correspondence. How he managed it, in spite of his other multitudinous activities, is something of a mystery. It was to the end a heavy strain, absorbing much time and energy. Often he found it a wearisome burden and felt inclined to abandon what after reflection he always came again to consider a real apostolate. "When a man takes the pledge for life," he once wrote, "he generally asks for just one more drink. I have made a resolution this year not to grumble about letters, so I am entitled to have one last growl. The growl is only an apology for not answering your welcome letter sooner. But it reached me with twenty-four others, and ten came by the next post! No matter, since He wills it; but you will understand why at times I neglect you." [13] "Ask Jesus," he says to another correspondent, "to help me with all the letters I have to write. A big temptation came to me some time back that this letter-writing was a huge waste of time and no good was done. I could not help feeling that the answer came from our Blessed Lord Himself in the following extract: 'It may console you to know that your letter has been the means of saving me from at least one hundred mortal sins since. When these fierce temptations come upon me, I take it out and read it over, and somehow it helps me to fight the devil and say, 'No, I will not offend God again.' That has given me fresh courage." Hence Fr. Doyle threw himself into a task which was far from congenial to him and which candid critics did not hesitate to describe as a wasteful delusion. He never shirked any toil or trouble once he became convinced that it was helping the interests of his Master. "Don't be afraid of writing if I can help you," he said to a diffident religious. "But if you want to make me angry, apologise for 'giving me trouble'! How could that be called trouble which helps you to love our dearest Lord even one tiny scrap more?" To his zealous heart the question seemed unanswerable.

His voluminous correspondence was concerned exclusively with spiritual matters. For mere chat or gossip he had neither time nor inclination. "Now for a scolding!" he wrote to a well-meaning news-sender. "A good deal of your last letter consisted of 'news,' I know you meant kindly, but I only want to hear about your soul and your progress in perfection, or at least such things as bear directly on the interests of God." His letters consist, therefore, practically altogether of personal advice and spiritual direction. All this was, it is hardly necessary to say, written for particular individuals in known circumstances, and was not intended to form a general treatise on the spiritual life. One cannot always generalise individual spiritual guidance, any more than one can indiscriminately apply a doctor's prescription. But in so far as general principles are advocated, it seems useful to collect some typical passages from letters written by Fr. Doyle, especially to nuns. Some such excerpts have been already given, particularly in the account of his own inner life. A further selection, roughly classified under convenient heads, will enable us to appreciate more accurately the main outlines of his spiritual direction. This arrangement has the advantage of letting Fr. Doyle speak for himself. It is, of course, obvious that a succession of extracts from letters to different correspondents will necessarily include some repetitions, and cannot in any sense be regarded as a compact or unified treatment. At least they will form a little anthology of counsels and thoughts, among which the reader can pick and choose whatever seems appropriate or true. [14]

(3.) DISCOURAGEMENT.

Judging by the frequency with which Fr. Doyle's letters deal with it, discouragement must be the besetting sin of those who are striving towards holiness. Doubtless sometimes it shows a secret pride and over-reliance on our own unaided efforts; we are quite surprised and hurt that we did not do better; we are irritated by the discovery of our faults, especially if others share that discovery. Discouragement such as this is not dissipated by harsh sincerity nor excised by drastic spiritual surgery; it must be converted into humble childlike trustfulness in Christ who knows our weakness and our difficulties, who sees them from our side and not as human critics do. Another form of discouragement lies in that natural human shrinking from struggle and suffering, such as our Lord Himself felt in Gethsemane.

He, who chose three companions to be near Him and prayed for the passing of the bitter chalice, knows well what it is to be sorrowful, sad and fearful Surely He does not begrudge human counsel and companionship to those who begin to fear and to be heavy. "The spirit indeed is willing but the flesh is weak." (*S. Mark* 14. 38.) Hence it is that a discerning and sympathetic director can do so much for one who is faithful, but discouraged, acting as "an angel from heaven strengthening him." (*S. Luke* 22. 43.) The pith of Fr. Doyle's advice can be put in these two short sentences of his: "When you commit a fault which humbles you and for which you are really sorry, it is a gain instead of a loss." "Recognize God's graces to you, and instead of thinking of yourself and your faults, try to do all you can for God and love Him more." Here are some further excerpts from his letters.

(A). "There is one fault in religious which should not be forgiven either in this world or in the world to come, and that is *discouragement;* for it means we are playing the devil's game for him his pet walking stick, someone has called it. Thank God, we have not to judge ourselves, for, as St. Ignatius wisely remarks, no one is a judge in his own case. Let me judge you, my child, as I honestly think God judges you. My verdict must be that you have grown immensely in holiness during the past few years. To begin with, every particle of merit and there must be millions of them since you first entered religion is waiting for you in heaven, for no amount of infidelity or venial sin can ever diminish that by one iota. Then, in spite of your sufferings and weak health, you have worked on and struggled on from day to day a life which must have pleased God immensely. Don't lose heart, my dear child, the darkness you feel is not a sign of God's displeasure, for every saint has gone through it. You are 'minting money' every instant you live, you are helping to save soul after soul each hour you suffer. So you should say with St. Paul, (2 Cor. ,7. 4): 'I exceedingly abound with joy in all our tribulation.'" (July, 1913.)

(B). "You seem to have been going through a harder time than usual lately, and this evidently has come as a surprise to you. But is it not the best of signs that all is well, that God has accepted your generous offer to bear all He wishes to send you, and that the devil is furious and alarmed at the progress you have made in perfection and mad at the harm you have done to his evil cause? The storm has come upon you, and you, foolish child as you always were, have thought all is lost because you have bent a little like the reed before the wind. No, the want of courage, firmness and generosity will only serve to tumble and throw you the more confidently into the strengthening arms of our dear Lord, since it makes you see that without Him you can do nothing.

"God always seems to permit this to happen even to His saints. I read recently in the life of a holy soul who had promised to give our Lord all: "Three times to-day I *deliberately* avoided a humiliation and a little act of self-denial." Hurrah, boys! I say; if the saints act like that, there is some hope for you and me. If there has been any falling off in your generous resolution, go back humbly to the feet of Jesus now and take up bravely the cross which means so much for His glory and your happiness." (December, 1912.)

(C). "In spite of all our efforts, we fall into faults from time to time. God permits this for two reasons: (1) to keep the soul humble and to make it realise its utter powerlessness when left alone without His fostering hand, and (2) because the act of sorrow after the fault not only washes it completely away, but immensely increases our merit, and being an act of humility bringing us really heartbroken to His feet, delights Him beyond measure." (April, 1913.)

(D). "Our Lord is displeased only when He sees no attempt made to get rid of imperfections which, when deliberate, clog the soul and chain it to the earth. But He often purposely does not give the victory over them in order to increase our opportunities of meriting. Make an act of humility and sorrow after failure, and then never a thought more about it.

"He sees what a 'tiny little child' you are, and how useless even your greatest efforts are to accomplish the gigantic work of making a saint. But this longing, this stretching out of baby hands for His love, pleases Him beyond measure; and one day He will stoop down and catch you up with infinite tenderness in His divine arms and raise you to heights of sanctity you little dream of now." (May, 1913.)

(E). "You need not be uneasy to see in your soul apparent contradictions: an ardent desire to love God and to suffer for Him, and then when the opportunity comes, a shrinking from pain, and even a refusal to bear it. Fortunately we are dealing with our Lord who can read the heart and who knows our protestations of love are sincere and genuine, with One, too, who knows the weakness of our human nature and who does not expect much from us. He does not forget His own human weakness on earth. 'With desire have I desired to eat this Pasch with you before I suffer,' He said showing His longing for His Passion. And then an hour after He seems to take His offering back: 'Father, if it be possible, let this chalice pass from Me.' The very longing to love Him and bear much for His sake is dear to our Lord, even if our courage fails when tested." (June, 1913.)

(F). "Our dear Lord is certainly testing the extent of your love for Him before He takes you to Himself. But should not that make you rejoice, my dear child, since the harder and sharper the fight, the closer will be your union with Him in heaven? I have just one fault to blame you for: you have always kept your eyes fixed on your faults - I do not deny there are plenty! - and have never helped yourself by thinking on what you have done and suffered for His dear sake. If you have forgotten all this, He has not; and when you meet Him, the gratitude of His loving Heart win hide the imperfections and faults of former years. Be brave and generous to the end, my dear child, and do not take back what He asks you to give, though He knew well what it would cost you." (August, 1912.)

(G). "I think there is no harder trial in the spiritual life than the one you speak of. One feels so weary of it all, fighting and struggling against things which seem so small and mean, and where there is apparently so little merit to be gained, and then comes the longing to throw it all up and be content with just doing the bare necessary to save one's soul. You must have great patience with yourself, my dear child, and not expect to get into a region of perfect peace where there would be no trials or worries or fighting against self even the saints did not enjoy that calm. Remember, God sees the intention, which in your case is generous and unreserved. He is quite pleased with that, and only smiles when He sees us failing in our resolve and determination to be perfect. To console you, here is the confession of the great S. Teresa (*Life* 30. 15): 'The devil sends me so offensive a spirit of bad temper that at times I think I could eat people up.' She was canonised, so there is some hope of salvation for us yet." (March, 1912.)

(H). "Are you not foolish in wishing to be free from these attacks of impatience, etc.? I know how violent they can be, since they sweep down on me at all hours without any provocation. You forget the many victories they furnish you with, the hours perhaps of hard fighting, and only fix your eyes on the little tiny word of anger, or the small fault, which is gone with one 'Jesus forgive me.'" (April, 1912.)

(I). "I fear you are allowing the devil to score off you by getting so much upset over these bothersome, but harmless, temptations. You must let our Lord sanctify you in His own way. Were we to pick our own trials and modes of sanctification, we should soon make a mess of things. The net result of your temptations is a deeper humility, a sense of your own weakness and wretchedness, and is not this all gain? 'My brethren, count it all joy, when you shall fall into divers temptations,' says St. James (i. 2). All I ask you to do is to try to crush down the first movements of temptation, which perhaps can best be done by praying that others may be more favoured or esteemed than you There is a danger you may not suspect in thinking and grieving too much over temptation and faults. First of all there is oftentimes a secret pride hidden in our grief and anger with ourselves for not being as perfect as we thought or as others thought. Then this worrying over what cannot well be avoided distracts the soul from God. After all what God wants from you, my child, is love, and nothing should distract you from the grand work of love-giving. Hence when you fail, treat our Blessed Lord like a loving little child, tell Him you are sorry, kiss His feet as a token of your regret, and then forget all about your naughtiness."

(J). "I hope by the time you receive this you will have realised how foolish it is of you to bother about *anything* - no matter what it may be - in your past confessions. Generously make the sacrifice of never thinking or speaking of them again. You may do so with an easy conscience when you act under obedience. God wants to have your soul in a state of perfect peace and calm, for only then will He be able to fill it with His love and dwell there undisturbed." (May, 1912.)

(K). "Desolation is not a punishment for past infidelity, but a special grace reserved for the few. The only danger comes from the temptation of the devil, that God has abandoned you and that it would be better to chuck it all up. He will beat you in the fight at times, making you weary of this never-ending war against self and forcing you to yield to nature. But no harm is done provided you *start again*."

(L). "St. Vincent de Paul used to say: 'One of the most certain marks that God has great designs upon a soul is when He sends desolation upon desolation, suffering upon suffering.' Do you doubt for a moment that God has not great designs upon your soul? The clear and consoling proof is in the terrible trial you are going through. Do not let the assaults of the enemy disturb you. He is showing his hand by this last storm and his fierce fury that you did not yield in the direction that he wanted. Treat his suggestions with silent contempt, simply lifting your heart to God now and again, but above all not trying to drive these thoughts away, nor being fearful of giving any consent even though you may seem to do so under the violence of the attack. Keep your will firm, and do not trouble about feelings and desires.

"I do not think your 'false humility' is pleasing to God, though I do not suggest for a moment that you are putting it on. Drop self and all thought of reparation out of your life, and work now only for Him and the salvation of souls. If an aspiration, on the authority of the B. Cure d' Ars, often saved a soul, what must you not do each day you suffer so bravely! This thought certainly will help you and make the pain almost nothing, and will add to its merit, since the motive for bearing it will be all the higher." (1913.)

(M). "I noticed a tone of despondency in your letter, a yielding to that commonest of all the evil suggestions of the tempter, *Cui bono?* What is the use of all this struggling without any result, and so much prayer followed by no apparent improvement? It is a clever temptation, and a successful one with most souls, resulting in the giving up of the very things which are slowly but surely making them saints. If only one could grasp this fact: Every tiny thing (aspiration, self-denial, etc.,) makes us holier than we were. Just think of the thousand of tiny things done each day for God, *e.g.* each step we take; all is done for Him, every one of them has added to our merit, making us more pleasing in His sight, and each moment holier. No one can see this gradual spiritual growth, though sometimes when we have gained a big victory, such as the secret one you won recently over yourself, we wonder where the strength came from to do it. I have watched your steady progress in perfection with the greatest joy and gratitude for your generosity, and so I want to warn you not to listen to such a suggestion that your efforts have been in vain. Your biggest fault at present, my child, is that you have not yet completely bent your will to God's designs. I think it would please Him immensely to have no wishes of our own, apart from holy ones, so that He could bend and twist and fashion us just as He pleases, knowing well that we will not even murmur. Remember this does not mean that our *feelings* will die also." (January, 1916.)

(N). "Surely, my child, you are not surprised to find that you have broken your resolution, or rather, that the devil has gained a victory over you. I am convinced from a pretty big experience that perfection, that is sanctity, is only to be won by repeated *failures*. If you rise again after a fall, sorry for the pain given our Lord, humbled by it, since you see better your real weakness, and determined to make another start, far more is gained than if you had gone on without a stumble. Besides, to expect to keep any resolution, till repeated acts have made it solid in the soul, is like one expecting to learn skating, for example, without ever falling. The more falls, the better (that is if you do not mind bumps), for every fall means that we have begun again, have made another effort and so have made progress. I mention this because I know that you like myself [15] are given to discouragement and tempted to give up all when failure comes." (July, 1915.)

(O). "You seem to be suffering, my dear child, from a very common religious malady discouragement and want of patience with yourself, looking for and expecting to see great results from your efforts to become holier. You forget what a clog the body is on the soul, and how in spite of the most generous intentions and determination, it prevents us, time after time, from carrying out our plans. You remember St. Paul's bitter complaint that the good he wished to do he did not: 'I am delighted with the law of God, but I see another law in my members, fighting against the law of my mind and captivating me in the law of sin.' This is the experience of all who are striving to serve God well. They cannot always do what they would like and what they know He asks of them, but in the end the grace of God S. Paul's remedy will bring the victory, if only we persevere. Another consolation is that our Lord is often as much pleased (more, S. Teresa says) by our good intentions and desires than by their execution. The good desire, the longing and wish to be perfect, is strong in you, and as long as that remains you need never fear displeasing God. Besides you have a tremendous lever of sanctification in the power of love that enables us to do things, especially what costs us an effort, for our Lord's dear sake. Mind, this does not mean feeling, sensible affection, but simply a dry act of the will, intending to make the sacrifice or action an act of pure love. 'My God, I do this for the love of You, and for no one else in the world would I do it.' Try this in easy things, and occasionally make a dive at a really big sacrifice which costs, for love means sacrifice, and sacrifice leads infallibly to love." (October, 1913.)

(P). "Will it be any help to you to learn that I know many who suffer as you do? Hence I can perfectly understand what you are going through; the disgust for everything spiritual, the almost hatred of God, and the mad longing almost to leave it all behind and run away. However we know that such a step would not end the trouble or bring relief in any form, on the contrary, that would simply mean playing into the devil's hands and could only lead to one thing in the end. We know also that these trials come from God and that if one is only patient, they will pass. Hence, my dear child, you must set your teeth and hold on; spiritual life, remember, is a warfare and you will surely not run away when the real attack comes, but rather boldly face the enemy." (August, 1915.)

(O). "Surely you are not right in trying to keep our Lord away from you, or in thinking that He looks upon you with displeasure. When sin in the past is repented for, the poor soul who once strayed from Him has a strange attraction for His gentle Heart. You pain Him intensely if you think He does not love you now, nor wish for your affection. Give Him all you can, warmly and naturally, like a little child, and rest assured that the one longing of His Heart is to see you advance rapidly in holiness and perfection. You must try and cultivate great confidence and trust in our dear Lord's love and mercy, driving far from you sadness and regret of all kinds. Give it no quarter, it is all from the devil and so most harmful." (August, 1913.)

(4.) UNION AND ABANDONMENT.

With equal soundness of spirituality and accuracy of insight, Fr. Doyle counselled the elimination of anxieties, distractions and worries, not so much by direct counterattack and detailed defence as by the energizing power of a great ideal. Just as a magnet attracts and orientates a confused mass of iron filings, marshalling and linking them harmoniously, so an all-embracing ideal will influence and direct all our powers and activities. See God everywhere, he said in effect; He is behind every event, even what men miscall accidents; desolation is but the shade of His hand outstretched caressingly; gladness is the sunshine of His presence. Above all, He is within our souls, often sacramentally, always by His immanent indwelling; He thinks with us, He shares our very consciousness as no other being can. With the growing realization of this union with God within us and abandonment to God's acting on us from without, life will become easier and happier; all our piecemeal striving and individual troubles will gradually coalesce into one lifelong continuous act of conformity to God's will. "Abandon yourself completely into the hands of God and take directly from Him every event of life, agreeable or disagreeable; only then can God make you really holy." "Holiness," he wrote elsewhere, "is really nothing more than perfect conformity to God's will." "This worrying over what cannot well be avoided," he said in a letter already cited, "distracts the soul from God; after all, what God wants from you is love, and nothing should distract you from the grand work of love-giving." Distractions are to be conquered by one overmastering attraction; a strong man will be conquered and dispossessed only if a stronger than he come upon him. Thus, as Fr. Doyle advocated it, this ideal of conformity consisted in no mere negative quiescence or patient resignation; [16] it was a positive active amalgamation of the human will with God's, culminating logically in that perfect act of immolation which was the keynote of his own holiness. All this, be it noted, was no mere scheme of destructive will-crushing or punitive repression, it was designed as a constructive expansion of the will, a joyous chivalrous uplifting of the soul. [17] The heart was not to be left swept and garnished, ready for seven other spirits more wicked than the unclean spirit already driven out. True abandonment was to be consummated only by union. [18] "He that loveth Me shall be loved of My Father; and I will love him and will manifest Myself to him... And We will come to him and will make Our abode with him." (*S. John* 14. 21.)

(A). "I want you to make a greater effort to see the hand of God in *everything* that happens, and then to force or train yourself to rejoice in His holy will. For example, you want a fine day for some reason and it turns out wet. Don't say, 'Oh, hang it!', but give our Lord a loving smile and say: 'Thank You, my God, for this disappointment.' This will help you to keep down impatience, irritability, etc., when people annoy you. Then when some hard trial is past, look back on it, see how you ought to have taken it, and resolve to act that way in future." (March, 1915.)

(B). "Try to draw closer each day the bonds of union with Him, thinking often of His dwelling within your soul, and so making your heart beat in union with His; that is, seeking and wishing for only His adorable will in all things, even the smallest. This will conquer all worries, for nothing which comes from the loving hand of God can ever be a worry to us." (March, 1913.)

(C). Your difficulty is merely God's plan for your sanctification. 'My child, let Me do with you what I will.' This is hard to submit to, especially when our Lord hides Himself in the background and uses other instruments to do His work on us. Never mind, my dear child, you are making undoubted progress. Jesus may hide it from your eyes, but He does not hide it from mine. I do not trouble in the least about your little faults and failings which will vanish as you become more perfect and grow more in the love of what is hard to nature. For your consolation remember that everyone I have ever met found the struggle for perfection hard because most of the work is done in the dark. It is a question of faith and courage, going along bravely day after day, gathering up a sacrifice here and there, and although many are let slip, every one we lay at the feet of our Lord means so much solid progress."

(D). "May our dear Lord help you to bear the cross His love has sent you. Try to keep this one thought before you all through your trial: This is God's doing. Hence do not indulge in useless regrets about want of care, etc. Even if there was negligence, God permitted it to give you this golden chance of being brave and generous under the cross. What has happened will bring you much grace and even happiness, if you take it in the right way. 'Let Him act,' must be your motto. Jesus will bring all things right in the end. The more I get to know God, the more inclined I feel to let Him work out things in His own way and time, and to go on peacefully not troubling about anything. This cross is a sign of God's love for you, and the surest way of increasing your love for Him. Though you indeed try to take courageously the crosses God sends you, still there seems to be a want of that complete submission to God's wishes that He looks for and longs for in every detail of your life. Endeavour still more to give Him the desire of His Heart."

(E). "I have been praying earnestly to know what our Lord wants from you during this year, and if I mistake not, this is His message to you. He wants a very close union with Him which you will try to effect in this way. Each morning at Holy Communion invite Jesus, with all the love and fervour you can, to enter into your heart and dwell there during the day as in a tabernacle, making of your heart a living tabernacle which will be very dear to Him... This union will be impossible without complete abandonment to God's pleasure in all the little worries of your life. Do whatever you think is most for His glory ...and then calmly watch Him upset all and apparently bless your efforts with failure, and even sins on the part of others. I have long had the feeling that your over-anxiety to keep things right or prevent uncharitableness which has caused you a good deal of worry, is not pleasing to God and prevents Him from drawing you closer in His love. *Non in commotione Dominus.* [19] Labour, then, with might and main to keep your soul in peace, put an unbounded trust in His loving goodness. If you live in Jesus and Jesus in you, striving to make each little action, each morsel of food, every word of the Office, etc., an act of love to be laid at His feet as dwelling in your heart, you will certainly please Him immensely and fly to perfection." (January, 1912.)

(F). "This morning during Mass I felt strongly that Jesus was pained that you do not trust Him absolutely, that is trust Him in every detail of your life. You are wanting in that childlike confidence He desires so much from you, the taking lovingly and trustfully from His hands all that He sends you, not even wishing things to have happened otherwise. He wants you to possess your soul in peace in the midst of the many troubles, cares and difficulties of your work, looking upon everything as arranged by Him, and hence something to welcome joyfully. Jesus will not dwell in your soul as He wishes unless you are at peace. This is the first step towards that union which you desire so much but not so much as He does. Don't keep Him waiting, my child, but by earnest and constant efforts empty your heart of every care that He may abide with you for ever." (May, 1913.)

(G). "We do not mind what God does with us so long as it more or less fits in with our own wishes, but when His will clashes with ours, we begin to see the difficulty of the prayer, 'Not my will, but Thine be done.' All the same I think we can never expect really to please God till we become like wax in His hands, so that He will never have to hesitate before sending a cross or trial no matter how hard." (April, 1913.)

(H). "As regards this union with our Lord, it is really nothing more than a blending of our will with His, in such a way that we wish only what He wishes, and as far as possible only think of and interest ourselves in those things that are His.

"I would urge you to avoid worry and anxiety which always show that self is still strong and that the human will is not completely dead.

"In the matter of suffering I think you are inclined to confound the act of the will with feeling. You do not really 'draw back' when suffering comes, since you have the will to bear all things for the love of Jesus; but nature shrinks from pain and at times makes our 'will to suffer' give way.

"To-day at Exposition I asked our Lord to let me know what He wished you to correct especially during your retreat. It seems to me, my child, that most of your faults come from a want of perfect abandonment to the will of God. For example, when you get annoyed with people and speak sharply, you lose sight of God's directing hand, which prompted or allowed people to act in this way. God's will is constantly clashing with ours, and unless a soul is perfectly submissive, interior peace is disturbed or lost. True abandonment means crushing out self and welcoming with sweetness and joy all God sends."

(I). "Try to grasp the fact a very hard thing to do that in the spiritual life 'feelings' count for nothing, that they are no indication of our real state; generally speaking they are just the opposite...You are perfectly right when you say that the first thing to do is 'to give up your own will.' Why not aim at making God's will alone yours in every detail of life, so that you would never desire or wish for anything except what He willed, and look on every detail as coming from His hand, as it does? Such a one is never 'put out' by anything bad weather, unpleasant work, annoying incidents, they are all His doing and His sweet will. Try it, though it means high perfection." (October, 1916.)

(J). "Do nothing without consulting Him in the Tabernacle. But then act fearlessly, if you see it is for His honour and glory, never minding what others may think or say. Above all, "cast your care upon the Lord and He shall sustain you." (*Psalm* 54. 23.) Peace and calm in your soul, prayer ever on your lips, and a big love in your heart for Him and His interests, will carry you very far."

(K). "You know well that even the smallest cross and happening of your life is part of our Blessed Lord's plan for your sanctification. It is not easy, I know, to look at things in this light. But one can train the will to look upon the acts of others, even their sinful acts in as much as they concern ourselves, as coming from the hand of God. There is so much real holiness and so very much solid happiness and peace and contentment in this little principle, that I am very anxious you should try and acquire it, so that nothing may really ruffle the peace of your soul. Don't think this is easy, it is not; and you will fail time after time in your efforts, but with perseverance, steady progress will be made." (November, 1914.)

(L). "A quiet hidden life is not possible for you in one way, and yet perfectly so in another by building a solitude in your heart where you can ever live alone with Jesus, letting the noise and worry of life, cares and anxieties of the world, pass over your head like a storm, which will never ruffle the peace of your soul. You will enjoy perfect calm and peace of soul, the requisite condition for a life of union, by keeping Jesus ever with you as a Friend, and remembering that everything happens by His permission and is in fact His work. Let this principle soak in and it will make you a saint. Apply it to every detail of your life, and you will not be far from what you seek; in fact humiliations, slights, annoyances, worries will all disappear, since it is not X, but Jesus, who is trying you in this way." (June, 1916.)

(M). "Make this Act of Immolation to-morrow, Good Friday, at three o'clock. If you mean it and try henceforth to live up to its spirit, it will be 'a holocaust in the odour of sweetness,' a perpetual sacrifice of your own will, ever ascending before the throne of God, and will draw down upon you, I am convinced, many great and wonderful graces.

"The practice of this act is simply that you give yourself into the hands of Jesus in the most absolute manner possible, abandoning especially your own will, that He may do with you, at every moment and in every way, as He pleases; you give yourself to Him as His witting victim to be immolated to His good pleasure, and should He so please, to be sacrificed and to suffer without complaint or murmur whatsoever He may wish.

"Trials, disappointments, failure, humiliations, suffering of body and soul may crowd upon you, at least from time to time, but if you welcome them all as coming direct from His hand in answer to your generous offering, and as part of the immolation of His willing victim, you will find a sweetness and a delight in these things you never tasted before.

"This is the life I promised to point out to you which, I said, would make you a greater saint than if you were buried in a cloister. For your present life is daily full of opportunities of proving that you wish and are willing to suffer, to be immolated and sacrificed for the love of Jesus, 'the Victim of Love' who is ever offered still on our altars. Make the act in a spirit of deep humility but with immense trust and confidence in the grace of God which will not fail you. May our crucified Jesus take you now, my dear child, and nail you to the cross with Himself." (Holy Thursday, 1913.)

The following is the Act which is here referred to. [20]

Act of Immolation.

O most sweet Jesus, with all my heart, united to the dispositions of Your holy Mother upon Calvary, through her and with her, I offer myself to You and to the adorable Trinity, upon all the altars of the world, as a most pure oblation, uniting in myself every sacrifice and act of homage.

I offer Your Sacred Wounds and all the Blood You have shed, particularly the sweet Wound of Your Sacred Heart with the blood and water which flowed from It, and the precious tears of Your Mother.

I offer this most holy sacrifice in union with all the souls who love You in Heaven and on earth for all the intentions of Your Divine Heart, and especially as a victim of expiation and impetration on behalf of Your priests and of the souls whom You have consecrated to Yourself.

I offer myself to You to be Your Victim in the fullest sense of the word. I deliver to You my body, my soul, my heart, all that I have, that You may dispose of and immolate them according to Your good pleasure. Do with me as You please, without consulting my desires, my repugnances, my wishes.

I offer myself to Your Justice, to Your Sanctity, to Your Love. To Your Justice, to make reparation for my sins and those of all poor sinners. To Your Holiness, for my own sanctification and that of all souls consecrated to You, especially Your priests. To Your Love, in order that You may make of my heart a perpetual holocaust of pure love.

O Jesus! receive me now from the hands of Your most holy Mother, offer me with Yourself and immolate me along with You. I offer myself to You by her hands in order that You may unite me to Your ceaseless Immolation, and that through me and by me You may satisfy the burning desire which You have to suffer for the glory of Your Father, the salvation of souls and especially the perfection and sanctification of Your priests and Your chosen souls.

Receive and accept me, I beg of You, in spite of my great unworthiness and wretchedness. From henceforth I shall look upon all the crosses, all the sufferings, all the trials, which Your Providence has destined for me and will send me, as so many signs which will prove to me that You have accepted my humble offering. Amen.

(N). "As regards the Act of Immolation I give you full permission to make it. But do not complain to our dear Lord if He takes you at your word and makes you His victim. You need not fear whatever He may send you to bear, since His grace will come with it; but you should always try to keep in mind your offering, living up to the spirit of it. Hence endeavour to see the hand of God in everything that happens to you now; *e.g.* if you rise in the morning with a headache, thank Him for sending it, since a victim is one who must be immolated and crucified. Again, look upon all humiliations and crosses, failure and disappointment in your work, in a word, everything that is hard, as His seal upon your offering, and rouse yourself to bear all cheerfully and lovingly, remembering that you are to be His 'suffering love.'" (September, 1914.)

(5.) THE CROSS.

Thus Fr. Doyle's ideal of conformity to God's will meant a gradual development of passive patient resignation into a joyful spontaneous acceptance of everything from God's hands and a watchful promptness, not only to obey the inspirations of grace, but also to embrace what he loved to call "the hard things." "As a rule you will find," he said, "that when you do the hard thing just because it is hard, great consolation and love always follow." While he utilised every psychological expedient to help spiritual progress, he never attempted to substitute an easy short cut for the royal road of the cross; there is no detour round the hill of Calvary. When a religious asked him for a spiritual motto, he wrote, "Lord, make me a saint and do not spare me in the making." And when the latter half was objected to, he rejoined, "If you desire the accomplishment of the first part, you must be ready to accept generously and wholeheartedly the latter part no compromise!" In this stern teaching, however, he was careful to emphasise three points and to guard against errors, (1) It is not a question of feelings, but of will. Naturally we hate suffering and dread pain; were it otherwise, we should be either coarsely or morbidly insensitive. The ideal is not to suppress or eliminate emotion and feeling, that would be an inhuman aim; nor is it even to attain an unnatural state of indifference and quiescence. The Christian ideal is rather to strengthen and elevate the will, the higher self; the struggle is one of soul, not of body. (2) Nor is it necessary to conjure up possibilities of suffering and humiliation; we need only live from day to day amid the circumstances which God's providence has woven round us. The imagination should not be allowed to terrify the soul by picturing future trials which may never come. There is no need for discouragement because one feels unable to pray for suffering. "To ask for suffering," says Fr. Doyle, "is often secret pride or presumption; but you may offer yourself to our Lord to bear whatever He may wish to send you." (3) This attitude towards suffering will never be attained merely by concentrating on details, by immersing oneself in the actual trials to be borne. Our gaze should be fixed not on the Cross but on the Crucifix, not on self-crucifixion but on "Jesus Christ and Him crucified" (1 *Cor.* 2. 2.) The mistake is often made by holy souls of allowing their attention to be engrossed in the petty details of their actual sufferings or premeditated penances, occupying themselves, as it were, in pin-pricking. It is bad psychology and bad spirituality. The apostles went forth "rejoicing that they were accounted worthy to suffer reproach for the name of Jesus" (*Acts* 5. 41); their joy was not in counting the stripes but in the thought of Jesus. And so it has ever been; the men and women who have dared and done hard things have always been led by some great ideal or overmastering passion. We shall face the Cross only if we are filled with the love of the Crucified.

(A). "I have long had the feeling that, since the world is growing so rapidly worse and worse and God has lost His hold, as it were, upon the hearts of men, He is looking all the more earnestly and anxiously for big things from those who are faithful to Him still. He cannot, perhaps, gather a large army round His standard, but He wants every one in it to be a *Hero*, absolutely and lovingly devoted to Him; if only we could get inside that magic circle of generous souls, I believe there is no grace He would not give us to help on the work He has so much at heart, our personal sanctification Every day you live means an infallible growth in holiness which may be multiplied a thousand times by a little generosity. When you get the chance hammer into the 'Little Flowers' around you that holiness means three things: Love, Prayer, Sacrifice."

(B). "A want of will is the chief obstacle to our becoming saints. We are not holy because we do not really wish to become so. We would indeed gladly possess the virtues of the saints their humility and patience, their love of suffering, their penance and zeal. But we are unwilling to embrace all that goes to make a saint and to enter on the narrow path which leads to sanctity. A strong will, a resolute will, is needed; a will which is not to be broken by difficulties or turned aside by trifling obstacles; a determination to be a saint and not to faint and falter because the way seems long and hard and narrow. A big heart, a courageous heart, is needed for sanctification, to fight our worst enemy our own self-love." (20th November, 1905.)

(C). "'One thing is wanting to thee.' (S. Luke 18. 22.) How many souls there are upon whom Jesus looks with love, souls who are very dear to His Sacred Heart, for they have done much and sacrificed much for Him. Yet He asks for more, He wants that last sacrifice, the surrender of that secret clinging to some trifling attachment, that their lives may be a perfect holocaust How many souls hear this little voice, 'One thing is wanting to you that you may be perfect,' one generous effort to break away from the almost severed ties of self-love, and yet they heed it not. Liberty, home and family they have given up, the joys and pleasures of this world they have despised, for a life of easy comfort they have embraced the poverty of Christ; but still they cling to some trifling gratification, and heed not the pleadings of the Sacred Heart." (3rd November, 1905.)

(D). "Over and over again I asked myself, when reading that book, [21] was it not strange that I should come across the very ideas which had been in my mind so long: namely, the longing of our Lord for more souls who would be absolutely at His mercy, His pleasure and disposal; souls in whom He could work at will, knowing that they would never resist Him, even by praying to Him to lessen the trials He was sending; souls who were willing and longing to be sacrificed and immolated in spite of all the shrinking of weak human nature.

"Now I have long thought He wants that from you. And everything that is happening seems to point that way. If you make such a surrender of yourself absolutely into His hands, I know not what humiliations, trials and even sufferings may come upon you, though you must not ask for them. But He will send you grace in abundance to bear them, He will draw immense glory out of your loving crucifixion, and in spite of yourself He will make you a saint...This must be chiefly an act of the will, for it would be unnatural not to feel trials or humiliations; but even when the tears of pain are falling, the higher nature can rejoice. You can see this is high perfection, but it will bring great peace to your soul. Our Lord will take the work of your sanctification into His own hands, if you keep the words of the *Imitation* (iii. 17. i) ever before you: 'Child, suffer Me to do with thee whatever I will.' Do not be afraid for He would not ask this if He did not intend to find you the grace." (February, 1912.)

(E) "You must bear in mind that, if God has marked you out for very great graces and possibly a holiness of which you do not even dream, you must be ready to suffer; and the more of this comes to you, especially sufferings of soul, the happier it ought to make you. St. Francis de Sales says that 'One of the most certain marks that God has great designs upon a person is when He sends desolation upon desolation, suffering upon suffering.' Love of God is holiness, but the price of love is pain. Round the treasurehouse of His love, God has set a thorny hedge; those who would force their way through must not shrink when they feel the sharpness of the thorns piercing their very soul. But alas! how many after a step or two turn sadly back in fear, and so never reach the side of Jesus.

"You will see, therefore, that your present state is quite a natural one to expect, and instead of depressing you, should rather console and rejoice your heart. Do not be surprised if you find the life of sacrifice, constant sacrifice, a hard one. Crucifixion is ever so to human nature, even the big saints found that, and shrank from it with all their might. Poor weak human nature is ever crying, 'Come down from the Cross,' and the devils, of course, will pull us down if they can; the easier life of others, too, is a temptation to us and is naturally more attractive; all of which often plunges one into a feeling of sadness and that feeling of 'being crushed,' about which you speak."

(F). "You seem to be a little upset at not being able to *feel* more that you really love our Lord. The mere longing desire to do so is a certain proof that love, and much of it, exists in your heart. But you can test your love infallibly and find out how much you have by asking yourself this question: What am I willing to suffer for Him? It is the test of St Francis de Sales: 'Willingness to suffer is a certain proof of love.' This question I will answer for you. Though naturally you dread and shrink from pain and humiliation, I am certain there is no humiliation or suffering which you would refuse to accept if God asked you to bear it. That being so, you can say to our Lord with all the confidence of Peter who seemed to doubt his own heart: Lord, Thou knowest that I love Thee with all my heart and soul and strength, for I would gladly lay down my life for Thee." (March, 1913.)

(G). "You seem to be troubled that you cannot love God when trials come and all is darkness. But that is just the moment when you love Him most and prove your love the best. If only, when you are in desolation and dryness, you *force* yourself to utter an act of love or an oblation of yourself without a particle of feeling, you make an offering which is of surpassing value in His eyes and most pleasing to His Sacred Heart. A dry act of love is a real act of love, since it is all for Jesus and nothing for self. Therefore welcome the hard black days as real harvest time." (December, 1912.)

(H). "Don't lose sight of this principle, that true holiness is based on humility which can never be attained except by humiliations and plenty of them. Pray daily that 'the hard knocks of humiliation' may increase, for holiness will grow in proportion. Do not forget, with reference to what you have to suffer from others, that it is all part of God's plan for your sanctification. If you want to be a saint, you must suffer and in the way that pleases God, not yourself. Till you come to recognize that you are a 'football' and really deserve to be kicked by everyone, the grace of God will not produce its effect in your soul. 'He hath regarded the humility of His handmaid.'" (*S. Luke* i. 48.) (March, 1916.)

(I). "I can quite understand your difficult position and the suffering caused I can quite believe unintentionally by the Sister you speak of. ... Once get hold of the principle that all that happens comes straight from the hand of God, and you have found the secret of deep peace which nothing can disturb. You must look upon this Sister as the 'chisel' in the Almighty Worker's hand. He knows the best tool to use, and all we have to do is to let Him use it as He pleases. Don't expect that poor weak human nature will submit to the blows without a murmur. But with an effort of the will we can crush this down, until in the end what once caused us pain and tears becomes the source of great interior joy, since we have realised how these things help on our spiritual progress. Hence I would advise you without any hesitation, not to try to get a change unless it be to a house where you will have *two* disagreeable Sisters instead of one! This may sound a bit heroic, but...there is no happiness like seeking and embracing the 'hard things' for the love of Jesus." (July, 1914.)

(J). "Remember the devil is a bad spiritual director, and you may always recognise his apparently good suggestions by the disturbances they cause in the soul. Our Lord would never urge you to turn away from a path which is leading you nearer to Himself, nor frighten you with the prospect of future unbearable trials. If they do come, grace will come also and make you abound with joy in all your tribulations." (July, 1913.)

(K). "You may make the most complete and absolute offering of yourself to God to bear every pain He may wish to send. Renew this frequently and place yourself in His hands as His willing victim to be immolated on the altar of sacrifice. But it is better not to ask directly for great sufferings; few of the saints did so." [22] (April. 1912.)

(L). "I read through your diary of little victories with intense joy, until I came to the entry, 'actually felt glad at receiving a snub to-day,' when I felt my cup of happiness was full... This is what I have been longing for...To yearn for, to seek and delight in the hard thing, is not only the road to heroic sanctity, but means a life of wonderful interior joy." (February, 1916.)

(M) "God wants you to suffer *willingly.* Many rebel and fight against what God gives them; many more take their cross in a resigned 'can't be helped' spirit; but very few look upon these things as real blessings and kiss the Hand that strikes them." (1912.)

(6.) LITTLE THINGS.

Idealism, however fervent and absorbing, must never be an excuse for vague and unpractical emotion. As already pointed out, the genius of S. Ignatius consisted in his careful and methodic exploitation of religious energy Steam is of no use, rather a nuisance, until we have a cylinder and piston for it. How much spiritual fervour goes to waste, without a particular examen and definite applications! A gallon of petrol might be misused to blow a car sky-high; with care and inventiveness it can be employed to propel it to the top of a hill. These comparisons will show us that Ignatius, though a soldier, might be even more aptly described as a spiritual engineer. There is always this touch in Jesuit spirituality. Not too much of the spectator's aesthetic appreciation of a mighty spiritual cataract, rather a tendency to calculate its horse-power and to get it harnessed and guided. In the case of a naturally impulsive, emotional and perhaps wayward character like that of Fr. Doyle, the effects and advantages of this applied science of the soul are particularly obvious. Not only in his own case, but especially in directing others, he sought not to deaden energy, ; not to paralyse will-power, not to kill emotion, but to convert them all into driving forces for the mills of God. And God's mills grind exceeding slow! The just awakened energy of the novice usually seeks to expend itself in weird ventures, in sudden outbursts, in anarchic violence, in impossible outlets. Ordinary life, with its dull tasks and sluggish routine, seems unworthy of the high ideals and chivalrous emprise of one who has caught the accents of Christ. So too thought the erstwhile Don Inigo, now Christ's pilgrim, clad in the picturesque aristocracy of sheer beggary. Far otherwise did he begin to think as he toiled at Latin grammar in Barcelona, learnt logic at Alcala and studied theology at Paris. And finally this great stream of spiritual energy which started with wild turbulence in Loyola and Manresa, is conveyed sluiced and piped, as it were, to a dingy room in Rome where Ignatius dealt with administration and correspondence.

It is the lesson which Fr. Doyle loved to teach. He showed his spiritual children how to focus their idealism on the seemingly little things of life and the day's drab details. Little things why do we call them little at all? We must not measure spirituality in cubic feet, nor should we judge holiness by the acreage of our activities. "Nothing is too small to offer to God," Fr. Doyle used to say; "for what is small to men may be great in the Master's eyes. It is in little acts that heroism is acquired, it is by patient perseverance and methodic effort that sanctity is won. [23] Such is the message straight from his own life, a life whose real greatness was within.

(A). "What more insignificant than the ordinary daily duties of religious life! Each succeeding hour brings with it some allotted task, yet in the faithful performance of these trifling acts of our everyday life lies the secret of true sanctity. Too often the constant repetition of the same acts, though in themselves they be of the holiest nature, makes us go through them in a mechanical way We meditate, we assist at holy Mass, more from a sense of duty than from any affection to prayer. Our domestic duties, our hours of labour, of teaching, are faithfully discharged but what motive has animated us in their performance? Have we not worked because we *must*, or unconsciously because the bell has rung, rather than from the motive of pleasing God and doing His will?" (15th April, 1905.)

(B) "One thing I ask of you, dear child: Don't be a saint by halves, but give Him all He asks and always."

(C). "Life is only a day quickly passed and gone, but the merit of it, the glory given to God, will remain for ever. Give Him all you can generously and lovingly, do not let one little sacrifice escape you, they are dear to Him because He finds so few really generous souls who think only of Him and never of themselves."

(D). "Live for the day, as you say but let it be a generous day. Have you ever tried giving God one day in which you refused Him nothing, a day of absolute generosity?"

(E). "Try to take your days one by one as they come to you. The hard things of yesterday are past, and you are not asked to bear what to-morrow may have in store; so that the cross is really light when you take it bit by bit." (November, 1914.)

(F). "I am glad you have found profit from the particular examen You must push on with this, for remember you are no beginner in the spiritual life. From time to time increase the number of acts when you find facility coming. However it is better to keep to a fixed number steadily than to go jumping up and down, better, for example, to make twenty-five acts every day than fifty one day and ten the next. The rule to keep before you is: Look upon nothing as too small to offer to God. Big sacrifices do not come very often, and generally we are too cowardly to make them when they do. But little ones are as plentiful as blackberries in September, and stiffen the moral courage, by the constant repetition of them, to do, in the end, even heroic things. Expect, too, that at times this steady keeping up the fixed number will pall upon you; possibly you will even pitch up the examen for a day or two, but pick it up again and no harm will be done; these failures will become fewer by degrees.

Again, nothing is too small; in fact the smaller it is the better, so long as it is some denial of your will, some act you would just as soon not do." (February. 1912.)

(G). "Possibly you have been a little too generous in the time of fervour and have attempted more than you were able for, which would account in part, at least, for the feeling of 'being crushed.' However you should have been prepared to find that the generous spirit which carried you along from sacrifice to sacrifice was not intended to last, it was only meant to strengthen you for the time of trial. To serve God generously when the music of consolation is sounding in our ears is no doubt pleasing to Him, but to be equally faithful when all is black and dark is not only a thousand times more sanctifying, but is heroic virtue. Hence God in His eagerness for our perfection takes away, at times, all sensible consolation, yet is really nearer to us than before.

"The great danger to be faced is that one feels inclined to lose heart, to be discouraged 'the devil's pet walking stick' and in the end to give up all striving for perfection, aiming only at being content with that curse of every religious house Mediocrity.

"As I said before, my dear child, I fancy you tried to do too much, to be too generous. Do not try to run till you can walk well. Draw up a list of certain little sacrifices which you feel God is asking from you and which you know you will be able to give Him without very much difficulty better be cowardly than too generous. Then, come what may, be faithful to your list and shake it in the face of the tempter when he suggests that you should give it up. After some time, when greater facility has come by practice, you might add a little to what you did at first, and so on till, please God, one day you will be able to say, 'I know only Jesus Christ, and Him crucified; with Christ I am nailed to the Cross.'" (*I Cor.* 2. 2; *Galat.* 2. 19.)

(H). "I think He would like you to pay more attention to *little things,* looking on nothing as small, if connected with His service and worship. Also try to remember that nothing is too small to offer to Him that is, the tiniest act of self-conquest is of immense value in His eyes, and even, lifting one's eyes as an act of love brings great grace."

(I). "I want you to stick to two things: the aspirations and the tiny acts of self-conquest Count them and mark, them *daily.* You need nothing else to make you a saint. The weekly total, growing bigger as you persevere, will show you how fast you are growing in perfection."

(J). "It is indeed easy to condemn oneself to death, to make a generous offering of self-immolation; but to carry out the execution daily is more than most can do…Go on bravely, don't expect too much from yourself, for God often leaves one powerless in acts of self-conquest in order to make one humble and to have more recourse to Him. Remember above all that even one small victory makes up for a hundred defects."

(K). "The notebook was most helpful to me as showing the way by which Jesus is leading you to perfection if only you have the courage to face it. All these trials, snubs, unpleasantnesses, etc., do not come to you by chance. They are precious jewels from the hand of God; and, if you could only bring yourself to look upon them in the right light they would make you a really great saint."

(7.) PRAYER.

The extracts given above from Fr. Doyle's letters make it evident that the ideals which he sought to impress on others were partial transcripts from his own inner life. It will therefore be clear that his strenuous advocacy of prayer was also born in his personal experience. This indeed has already been made manifest in dealing with his belief in the apostolate of prayer and in the efficacy of aspirations. Hence it will be sufficient to collect here a few further quotations. Brief as these are, they illustrate his conviction of the importance of prayer, his idea that it ought, so to speak, be spread out thinly over one's day or one's life as well as heaped up in the early morning or during a retreat, his wonderful faith in prayer as the unseen motive-power of missionary effort. "Get more prayer into your life if you can," "Give the full time to spiritual duties," are typical pieces of advice. He never held out delusive prospects of easy contemplation. "Don't forget," he wrote once, "that prayer is the hardest corporal penance." "It is an unnatural thing," he said another time, "that is, a supernatural thing, and hence must be hard always; for prayer takes us out of our natural element. But pray on all the same." There is only one way of learning, he used to say, and that is to pray often, to fill up all the little chinks and interstices of our day with aspirations and prayers. "Keep in God's presence going through the house and try to grasp then any lights you may have got in prayer." On the other hand, he tried to make prayer as easy, unstrained and familiar as he could. He prescribed no rigid method, he made no attempt to move all along the same groove. "Follow the attraction of the Holy Spirit, for all souls are not led by the same path." was his tolerant counsel. [24] He would have agreed with St. Teresa's saying [25]: "Mental prayer is, in my opinion, nothing else but being on terms of friendship with God, frequently conversing in secret with Him who, we know, loves us."

(A). "You seem to have fallen into the common snare of Satan, namely, mistaking your work for prayer and pouring yourself out over it. Thus the soul gets dried up and the body so fatigued that a proper service of God is impossible. Give the full time to spiritual duties. Try to get a minute to yourself, and a half hour on Sundays, and walk about quietly and examine your state. Note where you have fallen off, etc., and begin again, instead of waiting for the next retreat to pull you up."

(B). "You seem lately to have had a bad attack of want of confidence in God and a feeling of despair of ever becoming a saint. Yet, my dear child, it is neither impossible or hopeless as long as God leaves it in our power to pray. You know these words of Fr. de Ravignan (leaflet enclosed). [26] I never realized how true they were until I began to go about the country and get into close touch with souls. I assert fearlessly that if only we all prayed enough, and I mean by that a constant, steady, unflagging stream of aspirations, petitions, etc., from the heart, there is not one, no matter how imperfect, careless or even sinful, who would not become a saint and a big one. I am perfectly and painfully conscious that, for my own part, I do not pray a hundredth part of what I should or what God wants."

(C). "Without constant union with our Lord there is not and cannot be any real holiness, one reason being that without recollection the inspirations of the Holy Spirit are missed and with them a host of opportunities of little sacrifices and a shower of graces. As a means of gaining greater recollection, each morning at Holy Communion invite Jesus to dwell in your heart during the day as in a tabernacle. Try all day to imagine even His bodily presence within you and often turn your thoughts inwards and adore Him as He nestles next your heart in a very real manner, quite different from His presence in all creation. This habit is not easily acquired, especially in a busy life like yours, but much may be done by constant effort. At times you will have to leave Him alone entirely, but as soon as you can, get back to His presence again." (February, 1912.)

(D). "As regards prayer, you should try to follow the attraction of the Holy Spirit, for all souls are not led by the same path. It would not be well to spend all the time in vocal prayer, there should be some meditation, thought or contemplation. Try 'basking in the sun of God's love,' that is, quietly kneeling before the Tabernacle, as you would sit enjoying the warm sunshine, not trying to do anything, except love Him, but realizing that, during all the time you are at His feet, more especially when dry and cold, grace is dropping down upon your soul and you are growing fast in holiness." (May, 1913.)

(E). "You ask how to pray well the answer is, Pray often, in season and out of season, against yourself, in spite of yourself there is no other way What a man of prayer St. James, the Apostle, (his feast is to-day) must have been since his knees became like those of a camel! When shall we religious realize the power for good that prayer, constant, unflagging prayer, puts into our hands? Were you convinced of this, you would not 'envy me my spiritual work.' Because if you liked, you could do more than any priest who is not a man of prayer, though you might not have the satisfaction of seeing the result in this world. Did it ever strike you that when our Lord pointed out the 'fields white for the harvest,' He did not urge His Apostle to go and reap it, but to *pray*?" [27] (May, 1912.)

(F). "'I have called upon Thee in the day of my trouble.' (Psalm 85. 7) Jesus is our comforter. What burden is there which He cannot lighten? What cross, He cannot make sweet? Be our troubles what they may, if only we will call on Jesus and implore His aid, we shall find our sufferings lessen and the rough ways smoothed for our bleeding feet." (8th February, 1905.)

(G). "How often have we murmured against the good God because He has refused our petitions or frustrated our plans. Can we look into the future as God can do? Can we see now and realize to the full the effect our request would have had if granted? God loves us, He loves us too dearly to leave us to the guidance of our poor judgements; and when He turns a deaf ear to our entreaties, it is as a tender Father would treat the longings of a child for what would work him harm." (24th February, 1905.)

(H). "You are bound to throw yourself heart and soul into the work God has given you to do. The devil's object is to get you so absorbed in your work, so anxious and worried about its success, that you will become, as you say, a religious only in name. However, to see his snares, as St. Ignatius calls them, is half the battle. You must go directly against what he wants. But how? First try to stir up your faith and see in everything, big and little, that happens the hand of God, remembering that He is often more glorified by our failure than by success. This will prevent irritability, and having done your best, will lessen worry, though for most of us it is impossible quite to free ourselves from that weakness. Next, a big effort, and it needs a big one at first, resolutely to give every moment to the spiritual duties and to shut out every other thought. Prayer calms the soul as nothing else can, more especially if during the day you help the grace of God by trying to keep your heart united with God, who is dwelling within your very soul. At all costs you must conquer and keep your peace of mind (after all in a few years what will it matter to any of us whether we have gained success or not?), otherwise good-bye to holiness Though little acts of penance and aspirations may seem to be done mechanically, on no account should you omit them, they are far more meritorious in your present state." (October, 1911.)

(I). "You seem to be a little troubled at finding yourself cold at prayer and as if our Lord had abandoned you. Were it otherwise I should feel uneasy; for this is one of the best signs that you are really pleasing to God, since He puts your fidelity to the test by sending desolation. There is no happiness to be compared to the sweets one tastes at times in prayer; but this, the greatest of all sacrifices, He will ask from you at times. Hence in darkness and dryness, when weariness and disgust come on you, when the thousand petty worries of every day crowd upon you, sursum corda, raise your eyes with a glad smile to the face of Jesus, for all is well arid He is sanctifying you." (October, 1912.)

(J). "Work away at the life of union, but union remember with God *within* you, not outside; so many go wrong on this point. Do not give up prayer on any account, no matter how dry or 'rotten' you feel; every moment, especially before Him in the Tabernacle, is a certain, positive gain; the effect will be there though you may not feel it. If you feel drawn 'to rest in God,' to let yourself sink down as it were into Him, do so without bothering to say anything. I think the best of all prayers is just to kneel quietly and let Jesus pour Himself into your soul." (July, 1917.)

(K) "A deadly pitfall lies hidden in the desire of some to pour themselves out in works of zeal for God's glory, to which the evil spirit not uncommonly urges those whom he sees full of zeal. It is evident even to one little versed in the way of the spiritual life that a multiplicity of external occupations, even though good and meritorious in themselves, must by their very nature hinder that calm peace of soul which is essential for interior union with God.

"For one who has advanced in the way of interior union, no life, no matter how occupied or full of distracting work, will prove much of a hindrance; such a one has learned how to ride on the waves of worldly care and not to be engulfed, by them, he refuses to put himself out or be totally absorbed in things which have only a fleeting interest; but it is not so with the beginner in the spiritual life. Overwork has broken down not a few weakly bodies but has ruined far more souls, drying up if not destroying all love for prayer and the things of God, leaving the wreck of many a 'spoiled saint' strewn on the road of life.

"A heavy responsibility rests on the shoulders of those who heap an impossible burden on the shoulders of the 'willing horse,' more anxious for the material success of their particular charitable undertaking than for the spiritual progress of those whom God has entrusted to their care." (1916.)

(8.) MORTIFICATION.

It will be useful to record here some sentences conveying Fr. Doyle's advice to many different correspondents on the subject of penance in this matter he always laid stress on mortification of the *will*, especially concerning habitual faults. At times he could put this very bluntly. Thus a religious who was rather addicted to criticism and comment asked him to recommend her some special acts of self-denial to be practised at table. "I recommend you, my dear Sister," he replied, "to put a little mustard on your tongue!" So while he firmly inculcated asceticism, he was by no means a fanatic for bodily penance. The following quotations will clearly prove his gentleness, thoughtfulness, and prudence. "He saved others, himself he cannot save." (*S. Matthew* 27. 42.) Is there not a sense in which this is true, not only of Christ, but of His saints?

(A). "I am glad you wrote to me for I, at least, can understand exactly what you are suffering; it is really a question of nerves, not of soul. You arc run down like an old fiddle string, hence you can get no sweet music out of yourself, try as you may. Now, my child, don't be troubled or uneasy, imagining God is displeased with you or that you are abusing grace. For a little while give yourself all the rest; relaxation and indulgence you can; there is to be no penance, few spiritual duties, except Mass and Communion, and you are just to do like a little child whatever your superiors tell you, read story books, etc.; rest and riot is to be your programme just now. When the old nerves get a bit settled, you will run ahead like a giant to sanctity. I am afraid you must make up your mind for fits of depression from time to time, but that, too, will pass when you become more your old self. I shall pray for you and I know you will do the same when you get good again, but not before." (May, 1912.)

(B). "It ought to encourage you to feel the desire for penance growing in your soul. After all is it not a mockery to call ourselves the spouses of a crucified Love if our lives are not to some extent *crucified* also? You need to be careful in the matter of privation of sleep more than in other things, but let there be no limit to interior mortification."

(C). "Every little victory in the matter of food is a real triumph, for this is a real test of generosity. You will find many persons given to prayer, works of zeal, penance, but most seem to fly from the denial of their appetite. 'My health, Father; the greater glory of God, etc.' St. Francis de Sales used to say, 'Unless you deny your appetite, you will never be a saint' a mighty saying!"

(D). "To stay on your feet when you have a bad headache may be even heroic and is not likely to injure you in any way. What a love the saints all had for suffering! There must be something in it."

(E). "I want you to give up *all* corporal penance and to take for your particular examen 'self-denial in little things' Make ten acts for each examen, and the more trivial they are the better, so you will do twenty a day." (January, 1912.)

(F). "I believe strongly in corporal penance as a. means to the end. But a denial of your own will often costs more than a hundred strokes of the discipline. To interior penance you need not, and must not, put any limit." [28] (February, 1912.)

(G). "If you are not yet strong enough to seek humiliations, just accept the little reverses that come. When you say or do awkward things, give them to our Lord and tell Him you are glad of them. Say: 'All these are humiliations, so they *must* be good for me.'"

(H). "The big penance must be the joyful embracing, for the love of suffering Jesus, the many little hard and painful things which come to you hourly, Take them all from His hand sweetly, trying to seek the unpleasant things and the hard disagreeable things; and keep hammering away at the tiny acts of self-denial. This is the goal to aim at: I am never to do a thing I like. Don't try to do that at present it might easily dishearten and crush you but keep it always in view."

(I). "I do not want, in fact I forbid you, to be imprudent in the matter of corporal penances. But, my dear child, if you let a whole fortnight go by without any self-inflicted pain, can you honestly look Jesus in the face and say, 'I am like to Him?'"

(J). "I must warn you against the danger of wishing to go too fast or to do too much at first. You must begin humbly and build up that is, increase your penances by degrees, otherwise you might be very generous for a short time, then get tired and give up all, As a rule do not make any penance a great burden it is better to discontinue it if it becomes such nor do anything excessive or continued very long."

(K) "Your desire for penance is an excellent sign, and this in spite of what X said. But have a fixed amount to be done each day and do not be doing it in fits and starts. Anything like what you call 'frenzy' ought to be suspected and resisted."

(L). "In urging you to be generous, I wish you at the same time to be sensible. Keep in mind these two rules, (1) If after honest trial you find anything is really injurious or hampers your work, it must be abandoned. (2) Be on your guard lest the body be too much oppressed and the spirit take harm, as says wise Ignatius. 1 Everything is not for everyone, nor must you undertake too much in the beginning." (1912.)

[1] The sense of spiritual freedom is the first feeling of converts from Protestantism. "When my conversion to the Catholic Church was accomplished, I was filled with the happy consciousness, Now at last I am free. Protestants will very probably have supposed the contrary." - Albert von Ruville, *Back to Holy Church* (1910), p. 127. "I can register one impression at once, curiously inconsistent with my preconceived notions on the subject...I have been overwhelmed with the feeling of liberty, the glorious liberty of the sons of God." - R. A. Knox, *A Spiritual Aeneid*, 1918, p. 247. See also Fr. Maturin, *Price of Unity*, 1912, p. 241; and Mgr. Benson, *Confessions of a Convert*, p. 160.

[2] "If there were nothing else known to me of the Catholic Church," writes Dom J. Chapman (*Bishop Gore and the Catholic Claims*, 1905, p. 120), "but her system of confession as I know it by experience, it would be enough alone to prove to me her divine origin." And even William James acknowledges that by confession "a man's accounts with evil are periodically squared and audited, so that he may start the clean page with no old debts inscribed; any Catholic will tell us how clean and fresh and free he feels after the purging operation." - *Varieties of Religious Experience*, 1902, p. 128. See also the testimonies of Irish Catholic soldiers later on in this book.

[3] *Summarium Constitutionum*, n. 41. Cf. n. 48: "The chastisement of the body ought not to be immoderate Hence each one should disclose to his confessor whatever he does in this matter." A similar injunction occurs in the rule of S. Benedict (ch. 49).

[4] We find the following entry in his diary: "Penances allowed, 2nd July, 1914. (1) Discipline fifteen strokes once a day; (2) arm-chair till dinner; (3) waist-chain or hair-cloth an hour daily; (4) rise for moment at night; (5) sleep on boards occasionally; (6) little butter at breakfast; (7) none at lunch; (8) no sweets, etc., at meals; (9) Holy Hour weekly. Revoked in November, 1914."

[5] During his visit to the Continent in 1912, Fr. Doyle took the opportunity of consulting Père Petit, S.J., and the Abbé S. Legueu, the director of Soeur Gertrude-Marie and editor of her autobiography (*Une mystique de nos jours*, 1910).

[6] "The real and secure teaching 1 on the subject [of locutions and inspirations] is, not to give heed to them however plausible they may be, but to be governed in all by reason and by what the Church has taught and teaches us every day." - S. John of the Cross, *Ascent of Mount Carmel* ii. 30, 5.

[7] Compare Père Ginhac: "In the beginning he did not make sufficient allowance for the frailty of human nature in his desire to advance souls to the very highest perfection Later on he became as large-hearted and indulgent in his direction as he was formerly inclined to be rigid... Towards the end of his life [he lived to over 70], gentleness became his chief characteristic." - *A Man After Gods Own Heart*, p. 63. "Fr. Ginhac at this period of his life was not quite enough on his guard against the impulses inspired in generous souls by their first fervour...Later on, taught by experience, he restrained these immoderate desires for corporal mortification." - *Ibid.*, p. 101.

[8] There are in his diary two entries bearing on this. "I felt greatly annoyed today because I was kept hearing confessions for nearly five hours without lunch, and also on arriving at X because asked to hear more confessions...I see now that it was Jesus did it all and that in future I must let nothing ruffle me since these things come straight from His hand." (26th July, 1914.) "I was very much annoyed at Y about extra work and confessions during the retreat. Our Lord reproached me for this, making me see more clearly that all this came from His hand and not from 'the thoughtlessness of others' as I told myself. I told several people about what I suffered and my pains, etc., which Jesus wanted me to keep to myself." (1st September, 1915.) Even holy people can at times be thoughtless and provoking; on such occasions Fr. Doyle was clearly not helped by any natural obtusity or placidity.

[9] Père Ginhac was thus criticised by one of his novices: "Every one of his movements is studied. If he speaks affectionately, if he smiles or is amiable, one can see that it is all regulated by the will and that he acts thus because God wishes it so. One would prefer something a little more spontaneous, something a little more from the heart." - *A Man After God's Own Heart,* p. 96.

[10] He had projected a meditation book, the chief innovation in which was to be that each meditation was accompanied by a picture representing the scene or "composition of place."

[11] Compare this, written to a nun: "I fear you have let fall from time to time little hints about God's graces to you, which people have taken in joke. You must be careful to hide the King's secret from all."

[12] Here is a quotation from a letter to Fr. Doyle (1916) to which many similar testimonies could be added: "Everyone I met seemed to hold me back instead of helping me forward, but you brought new hope [of being a saint] into my life. I have done more acts of self-conquest in the past eight months than in all the rest of the twenty years I have been in religion."

[13] One letter ends thus: "God love you i there are rows of people waiting for confession, and I shall be eaten." (April, 1912). Compare what Mgr. Baudrillart says of Mgr. d'Hulst: "Correspondence certainly added greatly to the overloading of his life; he dreaded the postman's knock." - *The Way of the Heart: Letters of Direction,* Eng. trans. 1913, p. viii.

[14] As far as possible the date is affixed to each. The few extracts dated 1905 are from the Notes referred to in Chap. One.

[15] Compare this entry in his diary (27th June, 1915) made just a month previously: "I am writing in great desolation and sadness, tempted even to abandon my vocation and plunge headlong into sin. All this is the result of having given in to myself, broken my resolutions and indulged myself in every way. Oh, my God, what am I to do? I made a fresh start with great generosity and determination, and in three days was worse than ever. I see my deadly enemy is my weak character and inconstant will, which I have made worse by years of yielding to it. My Jesus, I am humbled and crushed. Is there any use trying more? Every effort means a new failure and disappointment to You; and still I feel You urging me on to nobler things, to begin again." The very exaggeration of the language is a measure of the despondency.

[16] "This is not to be a kind of resigned, or perhaps rebellious, conformity, but a generous cheerful (though not felt) embracing of what He wills." - (October, 1916.)

[17] Fr. Doyle advocated as an important part of this conformity that docility to the inspirations of the Holy Spirit, which was so conspicuous in his own life.

[18] "The state of divine union consists in the total transformation of the will into the will of God, so that every movement of the will shall be always the movement of the will of God only." - S. John of the Cross, *Ascent of Mount Carmel*. 11, 3. So Teresa, *Foundations* 10.

[19] "The Lord is not in the earthquake." - III. *Kings* 19, 11.

[20] Some of the sentences in this Act of Immolation are taken from Soeur Gertrude-Marie - *Une mystique de nos jours*, p. 145 (abridged Eng. trans., p. 25).

[21] Probably the Life of Mère Marie de Jésus (Marie Deluil-Martiny).

[22] Compare Mgr. d'Hulst: "After offering the Holy Sacrifice for you and praying-, I tell you there is a slight change to be made in the terms of your offering. Instead of wishing for suffering, you must wish for the surrender of your whole self to all He may desire of you." - *The Way of the Heart: Letters of Direction*, Eng. trans. 1913, p. 306.

[23] Fr. Doyle was very insistent on businesslike and systematic efforts. Thus he would make his penitent note down certain failings or acts of self-denial and on his next visit he would carefully inspect the little book. See extract L.

[24] Once when a religious, a penitent of his, asked him how he 'himself prayed, he knelt down and with childlike simplicity and directness repeated some of the thoughts and prayers of his morning meditation.

[25] Life viii. 7.

[26] This leaflet contained the words: "Believe me, my dear friends, believe an experience ripened by thirty years in the sacred ministry. I do here affirm that all deceptions, all spiritual deficiencies, all miseries, all falls, all faults, and even the most serious wanderings out of the right path, all proceed from this single source a want of constancy in prayer. Live the life of prayer, learn to bring everything, to change everything into prayer pains and trials and temptations of all kinds."

[27] S. John 4. 35; 5. Matthew 9. 38.

[28] "We have nothing of our own but our will," says the Curé of Ars. "It is the only thing which God has so placed in our own power that we can make an offering of it to Him. Thus we may be assured that a single act of renunciation of the will is more pleasing to God than a fast of thirty days." A. Monnin, *Life of the B. Curé d'Ars*, p. 251. "Oh how I love those little mortifications which are seen by no one, such as to rise a quarter of an hour earlier or to rise a few moments in the night for prayer!" (ibid. p. 97).

[29] "It is not good that anyone should be so loaded with bodily work that the spirit is oppressed and the body suffers harm." - *Summarium Constitutionum*, 47.

Chapter Nine - Military Chaplain (1916)

THERE has hitherto been nothing outwardly remarkable in Fr. Doyle's life. Hence his biography has largely consisted in a study of his spiritual ideals and of those interior strivings and hidden virtues which were mostly unknown even to those with whom he lived. But now there comes a phase in his life which can be esteemed, not only by those who know the inner springs of action, but also by such as measure worth by external achievement. It is only when the life which was hidden in religious houses and expressed in the ordinary activities of a missioner, is transferred to dug-out and trench and is seen amid the reek and din of battle, that most people will appreciate greatness of soul. There is herein a further advantage. Many who read the chapters on Fr. Doyle's interior life and mortifications will be inclined to picture him as a dour austere individual in whom the sources of human feelings and genuine affection had been dried up. And, on the other hand, they who knew him only as a military chaplain, saw indeed his wonderful geniality and helpfulness, but could hardly suspect the inner drama of his soul, his mystic immolation and unceasing recollection. Now it is precisely the juxtaposition of these two aspects which is necessary in order to judge Fr. Doyle's character as a whole and to see whence heroism comes and whither holiness leads. The events of the last year and a half of his life will, therefore, be recounted more in detail. This is fortunately possible with the aid of the long letters which he regularly sent to his Father, supplemented by a few more intimate notes and jottings. This correspondence was, of course, never intended for publication; it is therefore the more interesting biographically. Its direct and homely language is far more eloquent than any attempt at studied composition. For we have not only a vivid picture of what warfare really means but also the accurate transcript of one man's actual thoughts and deeds.

(1.) THE GREAT ADVENTURE.

"I used to discuss with my brother," says S. Teresa, (*Life* i. 4.) "how we could become martyrs. We made up our minds to start together, begging our way for the love of God, to the country of the Moors, so that we might be beheaded there." The youthful crusaders were, however, ignominiously brought back to Avila by their uncle; but the spirit of this great adventure remained. Rodrigo died as a captain in the conquest of La Plata; Teresa learnt that *pati* was harder than *mori*. He whose life we are here chronicling had a double answer to his childish ambition for martyrdom, Teresa's life and Rodrigo's death. "Did I ever tell you," he asked in an intimate letter, 5th November, 1914, "did I ever tell you that even as a child I was convinced that one day God would give me the grace of martyrdom? When quite small I read and re-read every martyr's life in the twelve volumes of Butler's Lives of the Saints, and longed and prayed to be a martyr, and I have often done so ever since. As years went on, the desire grew in intensity, and even now the sufferings of the martyrs, their pictures, and everything connected with their death, have a strange fascination for me and help me much. When I was ordained I begged for the foreign missions, never doubting that my request would be granted. But it was not to be, and never can be now; and I was left wondering why God should have put that intense longing into my heart when He did not mean to gratify it. Then slowly light came. He did ask martyrdom, but not in the way I thought, a martyrdom far longer and a thousand times more painful and crucifying, a living martyrdom and a ceaseless crucifixion. So strong and clear is this light, especially recently, that I never pray now: 'Lord, what will You have me do?' but, 'Lord, help me to do what I know You wish.' Yes, Jesus is right when He says: 'I have told him over and over again what I want, but *he will not give it to Me*.' That is what is breaking my heart, as I feel it is breaking His, the pleading for a life of absolute annihilation, and at times what I can only call my powerlessness to give it; want of love, of generosity, is there, I know, but these words do not really express my state. If He does mean me to lead the life which is sketched out in my mind, then I can understand why He lets me feel my utter misery and powerlessness, so that I may see clearly that it must be all the work of His grace. Jesus is very gentle but very firm with me. For some years past He has shown me that I must not shrink from what He asks. He is ever beside me urging me in the same direction you know where His divine Face was turned so constantly during life and at its close. I am not afraid of sacrifice; He has given me an intense love of suffering and humiliation. But why, oh! why did He make me so wretchedly weak that I cannot take one step if His strong arm is not around me?"

Still he did not abandon the hope of laying down his life for Christ. Four days later he says in another letter: "What I am going to tell you now may pain you. I have volunteered for the Front as Military Chaplain, though perhaps I may never be sent. Naturally I have little attraction for the hardship and suffering the life would mean; but it is a glorious chance of making the 'ould body' bear something for Christ's dear sake. However, what decided me in the end was a thought that flashed into my mind when in the chapel: the thought that if I get killed I shall die a martyr of charity and so the longing of my heart will be gratified. This much my offering myself as chaplain has done for me: it has made me realise that my life may be very short and that I must do all I can for Jesus now."

A similar thought occurs in his private diary under next day's date, (10th November, 1914): "My offering myself as war chaplain to the Provincial has had a wonderful effect on me. I long to go and shed my blood for Jesus and, if He wills it, to die a martyr of charity. The thought that at any moment I may be called to the Front, perhaps to die, has roused a great desire to do all I can while I have life. I feel great strength to make any sacrifice and little difficulty in doing so. I may not have long now to prove my love for Jesus."

He waited a year before the sacrifice was asked of him. On 15th November, 1915, he makes this brief entry: "Received my appointment from the War Office as chaplain to the 16th Division. *Fiat voluntas tua.*" "What the future has in store I know not," he writes to a correspondent on the same day; "but I have given Jesus *all* to dispose of as He sees best. My heart is full of gratitude to Him for giving me this chance of being really generous and of leading a life that will be truly crucified." How hard he found this may be gathered from some words written a fortnight later on the eve of his starting for Whitely Camp, Surrey: "A last farewell, for I shall be far away when you receive this. My *via crucis* is nearly over; but only in heaven will you know how I have suffered all this week. It is all for Him and I do not regret it; but He filled my cup of bitterness this evening when I left my darling old Father. Thank God, at last I can say, I have given Him all; or rather He has taken all from me. May His sweet will be done." He seems to have had a premonition of death, as indeed had several who knew his fearless zeal. "I want you to know," he writes on 14th January, 1916, "what I went through by volunteering for the Front. God made me feel with absolute certainty I suppose to increase the merit of the offering that I shall be killed. The struggle was hard, for I did not want to die; not indeed that I am afraid of death, but the thought that I could never again do more for God or suffer for Him in heaven made the sacrifice too bitter for words." In the same strain he writes from Bordon Camp, Hants, a week later to a dear friend who was anxious for him: "He knows what is best for all of us. Would it not be more perfect then not to pray for my safety but rather that His designs may be carried out? ...I have only one regret now that death is such a distinct possibility that I have done so little for our Blessed Lord and His glory. But it consoles me much to remember that one can still make up by a loving generosity for a past which is beyond recall."

A few letters survive to tell us his impressions of camp life. On 15th December, 1915, he writes: "I cannot say I am quite in love with camp life, which in many respects is very repellent. But even in these disagreeable things there is a joy and secret pleasure, since it means all the more merit and, let us hope, a richer harvest of souls. My eyes have been opened still more to the awful godlessness of the world and the need, the immense need, there is for us who owe so much to our Blessed Lord to try and make up to Him for all this by greater love and generosity. It will never equal, I fear, the worldly generosity of these men. For example, this morning a regiment marched out of camp at 5 a.m. in torrents of rain merely for exercise. When they return to-night, they will dry their wet underclothing by sleeping in them!"

On New Year's Day Fr. Doyle with his regiment (8th Royal Irish Fusiliers) moved from Whitely Camp to Bordon Camp. The change was welcome to him for the reason given in the following letter four days later: "Before I thank you for your letter which was doubly welcome in my exile, I want to tell you the New Year's gift our Lord gave me. We had an awful time of storm and rain coming over here, but the first thing I saw on reaching the barrack square was a hut marked R.C. Church. I took it for granted that it was just the usual hut set apart for Sunday Mass, but on trying the door you can imagine my delight to find a small but beautifully furnished chapel with a lamp burning before the altar, which made my heart leap with joy.

"I felt as if all the hardships of my life had vanished, for I had found Him again who makes the hard things easy and the bitter things sweet. What did anything matter now since I could go and tell Him all about it and get help and consolation from Jesus. I really think that this month's privation of the Blessed Sacrament has taught me the true value of the Tabernacle. But His goodness did not stop here; the other priest who had the key gave it to me without my even suggesting it, so I can go to Him at any hour of the day or night if I want to do you think I shall? Is He not good to have put the little chapel where He did, as it might have been in any other part of the camp, miles away? I do not think there is a happier man in England than I to-day. I am writing this, sitting on a piece of wood no chairs in our quarters. There are about 1,200 Catholics in our brigade now. I get a few 'big fish' each evening."

The reference to soul-fishing will remind us that his life was by no means contemplative at this time, except in so far as he was able to be Martha by day and Mary by night. His work was very arduous and grew more so as the day of departure drew near. It was the last great chance for the soul of many an Irish lad. "There is nothing like the prospect of a German shell," wrote Fr. Doyle, "for putting the fear of God into one; and many an old rooster whom no mission ever moved has been blown out of his nest by the news of our departure." "We are having desperate work these days," he told a friend (i4th February, 1916). "The good God is simply pouring out His grace on these poor fellows and reconciling them before they die. It has to be quick work, no time for 'trimmings.' I have positively a pain in my arm giving Absolution and Communions in the morning. I was able to manage Exposition all day last Sunday, which brought in many an erring sheep. I realize that from this on my life will be a martyrdom in a way I never thought of. I have got to love my brave lads almost like my own brothers and sisters. They are so wild and reckless, and at the same time so full of faith and love of God and His Blessed Mother. Yet soon I shall have to see the majority of them blown to bits, torn and mangled out of shape. Our Brigade is leaving to-morrow for France. I am waiting till Friday night, so as to get in all the confessions I can. Do pray I may be able to say daily Mass. I shall carry everything necessary on my back, and so may manage the Holy Sacrifice in the train. Whilst here I have given Jesus two things which He often asked, but which I refused through 'prudence and a fear of interfering with important work,' a very old trick of the devil, which my eyes are open to see now. The first was sometimes to fast strictly all day once I did a hard day's work ending up with a fifteen miles' march on a cup of tea. The second was to spend the whole night in prayer. Including confessions I was able one night to pass eleven hours with Jesus telling Him every five minutes I was going after five more."

(2.) EN ROUTE.

He received unexpected orders from the General to proceed overseas on Thursday, 17th February. Half an hour before starting he wrote to his father: "I set out to face the future with a certain amount of trepidation... Strange to say, I have not the smallest anxiety about the possible dangers, of warfare, not so great for me as for others, but I do dread the horrors of the battlefield which all say no words can picture. Still it is a consolation to know what a comfort the mere presence of a priest is to both officers and men alike. They are one and all going to face their duty with the joy of heart which comes from a clean conscience; many of them had not been to confession for over twenty years." Of the crossing itself he wrote to his father a brief description which indirectly reveals some characteristic traits. One passage may be quoted: "The moon was surrounded by a magnificent halo or crown, which I promptly bagged for myself. I was fortunately able to get some tea on shore, for though they served us out with lifebelts, nothing in the shape of dinner or rations came along. There were only a few bunks which I left to the other officers, and as there was no place to sleep, except the stoke hole, which I was not having this journey, I picked a comfortable? corner on deck and prepared for a snooze, when alas! down came the rain. Providence however came to my rescue: the second engineer passing by very kindly offered me a share of his cabin, and I slept like a top on the settee. He was awfully kind to me, even offering me a share of his bunk, and this morning he had hot coffee and buns ready when I awoke; but as I was hoping to be able to celebrate Mass on shore, I had to postpone that luxury. At present there seems little prospect of either Mass or breakfast, as it is now nine and we have been lying off shore since four this morning. 11.30 a.m. Just landed. Seeing there was no chance for Mass, I rooted up a Chinaman and secured a welcome cup of tea; he brought me also a plate of cold liver and potatoes likewise cold a dish to tempt one's appetite after a channel crossing!"

After a tiresome day at Havre, the rain never for a moment ceasing, the men entrained for their base. And after twenty-one and a half hours in the train there was a march of twelve miles. "I shall not try to describe that march," writes Fr. Doyle, "but you can gather what it was, with strong, big men falling down now and then from sheer exhaustion. Under other circumstances I should not have minded the tramp, but I was near the end of my tether and was carrying a great coat, pack and water-bottle." After about two hours' plodding, an officer seeing Fr. Doyle's exhaustion induced him to get on an artillery limber. It was only when the waggons stopped at 2 a.m., that he discovered he was separated from the infantry and his regiment had gone to its unknown destination; he was lost. After three hours' sleep under a cart, he walked on for a couple of miles and found himself in a good-sized town. Though except for two sandwiches he had not tasted food for thirty-five hours, he deferred breakfast till he could say Mass. Then, finding there were no passenger trains, he boarded a slowly moving goods train and thus, sitting on uncomfortably explosive shells, he was taken a good way on his journey. Finally a Catholic officer whom he chanced to meet motored him to his destination Amettes, the birthplace of St. Benedict Joseph Labre, to whom, since his college days, he had a special devotion. Fr. Doyle had a comfortable room in the little convent. As he had a bad chill as the result of his three nights' exposure, he was lucky to have come under the kindly care of the good sisters.

On 26th February the men left their comparatively snug quarters and began moving in easy stages towards the trenches. The grim reality of war grew nearer.

(3.) CURÉ OF MAZINGARBE.

"I am suffering much in every way," wrote Fr. Doyle in a private letter on

5th March, 1916, "most of all, perhaps, from sheer fatigue. As regards food and lodging I am not badly off, but the discomforts of the life would be long to tell. However, like S. Paul I can say that I superabound with joy in all my tribulations; for I know that they come from God's hand and that they are working out some plan of His in my soul. What a joy to be able to offer oneself entirely, even life itself, each morning at Mass, and to think that perhaps before evening He may have accepted the offering!" "Though the life is perhaps the very last I would choose humanly speaking," he wrote in another letter (15th March), "I am ever so happy and contented, because I know I am doing what God wants and there is much good work to be done."

It was not long before he had an experience of real danger. On Sunday, 5th March, he said Mass for the 8th Fusiliers. After he had finished (about 9 o'clock) he mounted his bicycle in order to go to the 8th Inniskillings, of whom he also had charge, and say Mass at eleven for them. They were stationed four miles away near the ruined village of Mazingarbe. Fr. Doyle may be left to describe his adventure in his own words.

"On the way I noticed that heavy firing was going on ahead, but it was only when I reached a bend in the road that I realized the enemy were ac-

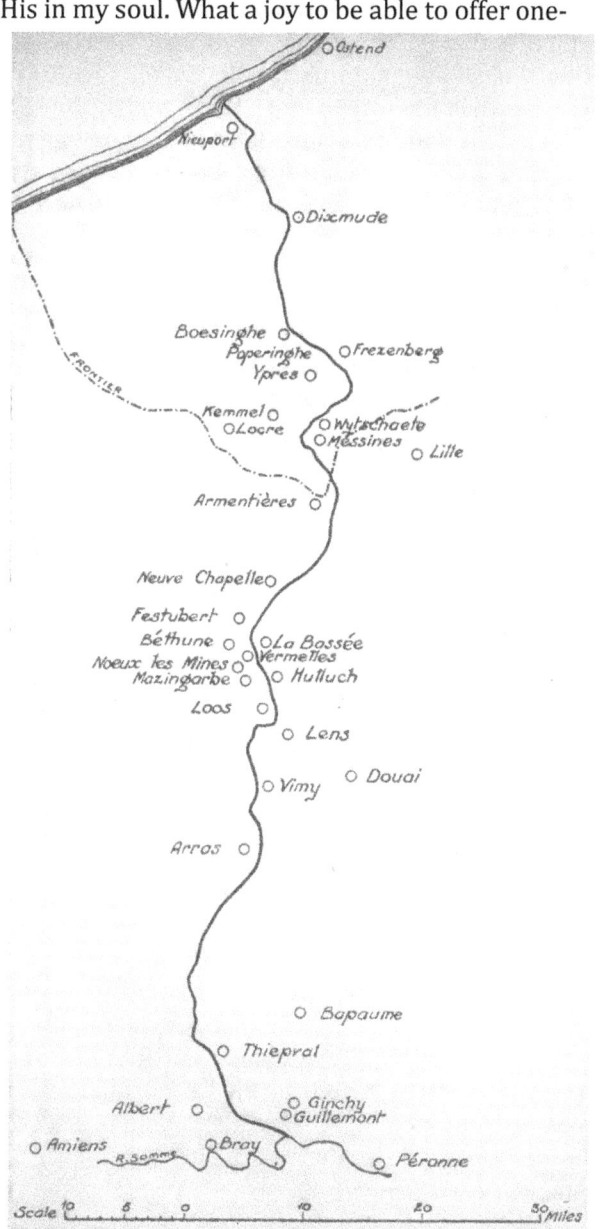

Map showing the approximate position of the Western Front from the Sea to the Somme during the first half of 1916.

tually shelling the very spot I had to pass. Some soldiers stopped me, saying it was dangerous to go on. At the moment I was wondering what had become of the side of a vacant house which had suddenly vanished in a cloud of smoke, and I was painfully aware of the proximity of high explosive shells.

"Here was a fix! I knew my regiment was waiting in the village for Mass, and also that half of them were going to the trenches that afternoon for the first time; if I did not turn up they would lose Confession and Holy Communion, but the only way to reach them was by the shell-swept road. What really decided me was the thought that I was carrying the Blessed Sacrament, and I felt that, having our Lord Himself with me, no harm could possibly come to me. I mounted the bicycle and faced the music. I don't want you to think me very brave and courageous, for I confess I felt horribly afraid; it was my baptism of fire, and one needs to grow accustomed to the sound of bursting shells. Just then I was wishing my regiment in Jericho and every German gun at the bottom of the Red Sea or any other hot place.

"Call it a miracle if you will, but the moment I turned the corner the guns ceased firing, and not a shell fell till I was safely in the village Church. My confidence in God's protection was not misplaced. Naturally I did not know this was going to happen, and it was anything but pleasant riding down the last stretch of road, listening for the scream of the coming shell. Have you ever had a nightmare in which you were pursued by ten mad bulls, while the faster you tried to run, the more your feet stuck in the mud? These were just my feelings as I pedalled down that blessed road which seemed to grow longer and longer the further I went.

"At last I turned the corner, reached the Church, and had just begun Mass when down came the hail of shells once more. One or two must have burst very close, judging by the way the walls shook, but I felt quite happy and quite ready to be blown from the altar, for I saw a fine plump Frenchwoman just behind me; she might have been killed, but I was quite safe!

"I mention this little adventure as I think it will console you, as it has consoled me, showing that all the good prayers are not in vain, and that this is a happy omen of God's loving protection from all dangers. I have just heard that one, at least, of the men to whom I gave Holy Communion that morning was killed the same night in the trenches."

The curé being away at the war, Fr. Doyle regarded himself as priest of the parish and was able to act as such on a few occasions. Thus one evening (Qth March) he heard quite by chance that an old woman was very ill; he gave her the last Sacraments and she died almost before he got home. "You see my life has many consolations," he adds; "and it is just as well, for this is a sad, sad war of which you at home have but the faintest idea; may the good God end it soon."

This is the description which Fr. Doyle gave of some of his activities on Sunday, 19th March.

"I started at seven in the morning by giving Holy Communion to the men whose Confessions I had heard the previous evening, a goodly number I am glad to say. This was followed by a number of Confessions in French for the townspeople and some French soldiers. I am quite ready to face any language at the present moment. This brought me up to nine, when my men had Mass Parade.

"By chance the whole Regiment were in the village which meant of course that the Church would not hold them, so I had arranged for Mass in the open. The spot I selected was a large courtyard in front of the school whereby hangs a tale. Armed with the Mayor's permission I approached the schoolmaster for his sanction, and I must say found him most obliging and very gracious, even helping to get things ready. It was only afterwards that I discovered that this man was a red-hot anti-clerical, anti-everything that was good in fact, quite a bad lot, so that my request was about the same as asking the Grand Master of the Orange Lodge in Belfast for permission to have Mass in his hall! He was so staggered, I suppose, by my innocent request that he could not find words to refuse. But the good folk of the town are wild with delight and immensely tickled by the idea of Mass in the porch of his school above all people; needless to say, they have rubbed it into him well.

"I had never celebrated Mass in the open before, and I think the men were as much impressed as I was. It was a glorious morning with just a sufficient spice of danger to give the necessary warlike touch to the picture by the presence of a German aeroplane scouting near at hand. I was a wee bit anxious lest a bomb might come down in the middle of the men, but I fancy our unwelcome visitor had quite enough to do, dodging the shells from our guns which kept booming all during Mass; besides I felt confident that for once our guardian angels would do their duty and protect us all till Mass was over.

"When I finished breakfast, I found a big number of men waiting for Confession. I gave them Communion as well, though they were not fasting, as they were going to the trenches that evening and being in danger of death could receive the Blessed Sacrament as Viaticum. It was the last Communion for many poor fellows who, I trust, are praying for me in Heaven now.

"Having polished off all who came to the Church, I made a raid on the men's billets, and spent a few hours in stables, barns, in fact anywhere, shriving the remainder who gladly availed themselves of the chance of settling up accounts before they started for the front. The harvest, thank God, was good and consoling. Just before they marched at six in the evening, I gave the whole regiment the Catholics, at least a General Absolution. So the men went off in the best of spirits, light of heart with the joy of a good conscience. 'Good-bye, Father,' one shouted, 'we are ready to meet the devil himself now' which I trust he did.

"I dined with the two transport officers who bring up the rations and ammunition to the soldiers, and then mounted my horse and rode up to Headquarters at the communication trenches... My work done, I mounted again and made for home. It was rather weird riding past the shattered houses in the dark, with the ping of a stray bullet to make you uncomfortable, while every few minutes a brilliant star-shell would burst overhead and the guns spat viciously at each other...I reached my billet and tumbled in just as the clock struck midnight."

This of course is the record of a specially strenuous day. But it gives us a good idea of the chaplain's wonderful energy and devotedness. He was proud of the men for whom he worked. "They are really a fine lot of fellows," he wrote on 31st March from the rest-billets," and make a good impression on the people wherever they go, more especially here in the North of France, the mining district, where most of the men are too busy washing the dirt out of themselves on Sunday to bother about much else. Hence it is an object lesson to the *parlez-vous* to see the crowds who come to Mass and Communion daily and Benediction in the evening."

(4.) LOOS.

At 6 p.m. the whole four regiments of the 49th Brigade left their quarters in Noeux-les-Mines (near Béthune - see map) and went forward to the firing line. Up to this time half remained behind and Fr. Doyle stayed with them, as practically nothing could be done in the trenches themselves, while at the rear he had his hands full, with an odd visit to his absent men to cheer them in their mud and slush. On this occasion Fr. Doyle accompanied the men. Nearly all had been to Holy Communion that morning or the morning before and they now received General Absolution. The town of Loos was held in a salient and as the road to it was commanded by the German guns, it could be entered only at night. "Single file, no smoking," came the order as the danger zone was reached. After another mile came a second order, "Men will advance by twos, twenty paces apart." Stray bullets were buzzing about, fortunately no shells. Suddenly down the line came the command, "Every man lie flat." The road was being swept by a machine gun. After the leaden hail had stopped, the men moved on again into the town where the Staff remained and then out to man the trenches. That night Fr. Doyle slept for the first time in a dug-out.

Next morning, which he notes as the twenty-sixth anniversary of his entrance into the Society, he emerged to view the havoc and ruin of what was once a town. He discovered a tiny wayside chapel of Our Lady of Consolation with the altar still standing; and here amid the inferno of shot and shell he celebrated Mass.

That afternoon he had 'the most exciting experience of his whole life.' The doctor and himself set out to visit the Field Ambulance Station at the other end of the town, where the wounded were sent at night from the Regimental Aid Post. [1] Without knowing it they walked along a road by broad daylight in full view of the German trenches and escaped only by a miracle. Fr. Doyle joined some officers in the cellar, who were having a tea party enlivened by a gramaphone. "McCormack," says Fr. Doyle, "had just finished the last bars of 'She is far from the land,' which brought back old memories, when suddenly Bertha Krupp opened her mouth in a most unladylike way, let a screech which you could hear in Dublin, and spat a huge shell right into our courtyard." For half an hour the shells kept raining all around and the inmates of the cellar expected each moment to be their last. "As we went home in the dusk of the evening," writes Fr. Doyle, "I came to the conclusion that there are worse places to live in than poor old Ireland and also that I had had quite enough thrills for one day."

It was not to be, however, for still another adventure awaited him. On returning, he found that a dead man had been brought in for burial. "The cemetery, part of a field, was outside the town in the open country, so exposed to shell and rifle fire that it could not be approached by day. As soon as it was dark we carried the poor fellow out on a stretcher, just as he had fallen, and as quietly as we could began to dig the grave. It was weird. We were standing in front of the German trenches on two sides, though a fair distance away, and every now and then a star-shell went up which we felt certain would reveal our presence to the enemy. I put my ritual in the bottom of my hat and with the aid of an electric torch read the burial service, while the men screened the light with their caps, for a single flash would have turned the machine guns on us. I cannot say if we were seen or not, but all the time bullets came whizzing by, though more than likely stray ones and not aimed at us. Once I had to get the men to lie down as things were rather warm; but somehow we felt quite safe, as if the dead soldier's guardian angel was sheltering us from all danger, till the poor dust was laid to rest. It was my first war burial though assuredly not my last. May God rest his soul and comfort those left to mourn him." [2]

The burials soon became more frequent, and Fr. Doyle had many gruesome experiences. Thus a few days later two bodies fell to bits when lifted off the stretcher and he had to shovel the remains of one poor fellow into the grave a task which taxed his endurance. On 1st April he had a further vivid experience of the horrors of war.

"Taking a short cut across country to our lines I found myself on the first battle field of Loos, the place where the French had made their attack. For some reason or other this part of the ground has not been cleared, and it remains more or less as it was the morning after the fight. I had to pick my steps, for numbers of unexploded shells, bombs and grenades lay all round. The ground was littered with broken rifles, torn uniforms, packs, etc., just as the men had flung them aside, charging the German trenches. Almost the first thing I saw was a human head torn from the trunk, though there was no sign of the body. The soldiers had been buried on the spot they fell; that is, if you can call burial, hastily throwing a few shovelfuls of clay on the corpses: there was little time, I fancy, for digging graves, and in war time there is not much thought or sentiment for the slain. As I walked along, I wondered had they made certain each man was really dead. One poor fellow had been buried, surely, before the breath had left his body, for there was every sign of a last struggle and one arm was thrust out from its shroud of clay. A large mound caught my eye. Four pairs of feet were sticking out, one a German, judging by his boots, and three Frenchmen friend and foe are sleeping their long last sleep in peace together. They were decently covered compared with the next I saw; a handful of earth covered the wasted body, but the legs and arms and head were exposed to view. He seemed quite a young lad, with fair, almost golden, hair. 'An unknown soldier' was all the rough wooden cross over him told me about him; but I thought of the sorrowing mother, far away, thinking of her boy who was 'missing,' and hoping against hope that he might one day come back. Thank God, Heaven one day will reunite them both. I found a shovel near at hand, and after a couple of hours' stiff work was able to cover the bodies decently, so that on earth at least they might rest in peace."

These few weeks in Loos were a time of great strain; but, of course, there were intermissions. After three days and nights in the front trench the men moved back again for three days to a village out of range of rifle fire, though not immune from occasional shells. After this triduum of comparative rest they moved up to the support trench, and then three days later back once more in Loos where sometimes the Fusiliers had to spend nearly a week. "It was a memorable six days for us all," writes Fr. Doyle, "living day and night literally face to face with death at every moment. When I left my dug-out to go up or down the street, which I had to do scores of times daily, I never knew if I should reach the end of it without being hit by a bullet or a piece of shell; and in the comparative safety of the cellar, at meals or in bed, there was always the pleasant prospect of being blown to bits or buried alive if the shell came in a certain direction. The life was a big strain on the nerves, for it does make one creepy as happened to myself yesterday to hear the rattle of shell splinters on the walls on either side of the road, almost to feel the thud of a nice jagged lump right behind and to see another fragment go hopping off the road a few yards in front. Why, Daniel in the lions' den had a gay time compared to a walk through the main street of Loos." The secret of his confidence can be guessed from the description of the Cross of Loos which he saw on 3rd April. "I had an opportunity, a rare one, thanks to the fog, of examining closely in daylight one of the wonders of the war, the famous Crucifix or Calvary of Loos. This is a very large cross standing on a mound in a most exposed position, the centre of fierce fighting. One of the four trees standing by it has been torn up by a shell, the branches of the others smashed to bits, a tombstone at its feet lies broken in half and the houses on either side are a heap of ruins. But neither cross nor figure has been touched. I looked closely and could not see even one bullet hole. Surely if the Almighty can protect the image of His Son, it will be no great difficulty to guard His priest also, as indeed He has done in a wonderful way."

Fr. Doyle was cure of this parish of trenches, his church being his dug-out situated in the support trench near the doctor's dressing station. [3] He also humorously included innumerable rats, insects and vermin among his parishioners! Of his men he was really proud. "Our poor lads are just grand," he says. "They curse like troopers all the day, they give the Germans hell, purgatory and heaven all combined at night, and next morning come kneeling in the mud for Mass and Holy Communion when they get a chance; and they beam all over with genuine pleasure when their Padre comes past their dug-out or meets them in the trench." It may be added that he was often in the front trench to encourage and bless the rain-sodden, mud stained, weary watchers. On Easter Sunday, 23rd April, he celebrated his first Mass in the trenches. He had quite a congregation, chiefly of officers, as the men were unable to leave their posts. "My church was a bit of a trench," he writes, "the altar a pile of sandbags. Though we had to stand deep in mud, not knowing the moment a sudden call to arms would come, many a fervent prayer went up to heaven that morning."

(5.) A GAS ATTACK.

On the evening of Wednesday, 26th April, the Germans began a slight bombardment which was the prelude to a formidable attack. It was Fr. Doyle's first experience of a battle and proved near being his last. Having met an officer who, though only slightly scratched, was badly shaken by an exploding shell, he brought him to his dug-out, tended him and made him sleep in his own bunk. Later on when he himself tried to sleep, he found he could not do so as the night was cold and he had given up his own blanket. His subsequent adventures may be best given in the words of his own vivid narrative.

"About four o'clock the thought struck me that it would be a good thing to walk back to the village to warm myself and say an early Mass for the nuns, who usually have to wait hours for some chaplain to turn up. [4] They have been very kind to me, and I was glad of this chance of doing this little service to them. The village is about two miles behind our trench, in such a position that one can leave cover with perfect safety and walk there across the fields. As I left the trench about 4.45, the sun was just rising. It was a perfect morning with a gentle breeze blowing. Now and again came the crack of a rifle, but all was unusually calm and still: little did I think of the deadly storm about to burst and hurry so many brave men into eternity. I had just reached a point half way between our trenches and the village when I heard behind me the deep boom of a German gun quickly followed by a dozen others. In a moment our gunners replied and before I could well realize what was taking place, the air was alive with shells. At first I thought it was just a bit of the usual 'good morning greeting' and that after ten minutes' artillery 'strafe' all would be quiet once more. But I soon saw this was a serious business, for gun after gun, and battery after battery, was rapidly coming into action, until at the lowest number 500 guns were roaring all round me. It was a magnificent if terrifying sight. The ground fairly shook with the roar of the guns, for the 'heavies' now had taken up the challenge, and all round the horizon I could see the clouds of smoke and dust from the bursting shells as both sides kept searching for their opponents' hidden cannon.

"There I stood in the very centre of the battle, the one man of all the thousands engaged who was absolutely safe, for I was away from the trenches, there were no guns or troops near me to draw fire, and though tens of thousands of shells went over my head, not even a splinter fell near me. I felt that the good God had quietly 'dumped' me there till all danger had passed.

"After a while seeing that this heavy shelling meant an attack of some kind, and that soon many a dying man would need my help, I turned round and made my way towards the ambulance station. As I approached the trenches I noticed the smoke from the bursting shells, which was hanging thickly over them and was being driven towards me across the fields. For once, I said to myself, I am going to smell the smoke of a real battle, and I stepped out quite gaily the next moment I had turned and was running back for my life - the Germans had started a poison gas attack which I had mistaken for shell smoke, and I had walked straight into it!

"After about 20 yards I stopped to see what was to be done, for I knew it was useless to try and escape by running. I saw (assuredly again providentially) that I had struck the extreme edge of the gas and also that the wind was blowing it away to my left. A hundred yards in the opposite direction, and I was safe.

"I must confess for a moment I got a shock, as a gas attack was the very last thing I was thinking about - in fact we thought the Germans had given it up. Fortunately too I had not forgotten the old days of the chemistry room at Ratcliffe College nor Brother Thompson and his 'stink bottles,' so I knew at the first whiff it was chlorine gas and time for this child to make tracks.

"But I was not yet out of the wood. Even as I was congratulating myself on my good fortune, I saw both right and left of where I stood the green wave of a second gas attack rolling towards me like some huge spectre stretching out its ghostly arms. As I saw it coming, my heart went out to God in one fervent act of gratitude for His goodness to me. As probably you know we all carry 'smoke helmets,' slung over our shoulders in a case, to be used against a gas attack. That morning as I was leaving my dugout I threw my helmet aside. I had a fairly long walk before me, the helmet is a bit heavy on a hot day, and as I said, German gas was most unlikely. So I made up my mind to leave it behind. In view of what happened, it may appear imagination now, but a voice seemed to whisper loudly in my ear: 'Take your helmet with you; don't leave without it.' [5] I turned back and slung it over my shoulder. Surely it was the warning voice of my guardian angel, for if I had not done so, you would never have had this letter.

"I wonder can you picture my feelings at this moment? Here was death in its most awful form sweeping down towards me; thank God I had the one thing which could save me, but with a carelessness for which I ought to be scourged, I had never tried the helmet on and did not know if it were in working order. In theory, with the helmet on I was absolutely safe, but it was an anxious moment waiting for the scorching test, and to make things more horrible, I was absolutely alone. But I had the companionship of One Who sustained me in the hour of trial, and kneeling down I took the Pyx from my pocket and received the Blessed Eucharist as Viaticum. I had not a moment to spare, and had my helmet just fixed when I was buried in a thick green fog of poison gas. In a few moments my confidence returned for the helmet worked perfectly and I found I was able to breathe without any ill effects from the gas.

"By the time I got down to the dressing station the guns had ceased fire, the gas blown away, and the sun was shining in a cloudless sky. Already a stream of wounded was coming in and I soon had my hands full, when an urgent message reached me from the front trench. A poor fellow had been desperately wounded, a bullet had cut him like a knife across the stomach, with results you can best imagine. He was told he had only a few minutes to live, and asked if they could do anything for him. 'I have only one wish before I die,' he answered, 'could you possibly get me Fr. Doyle? I'll go happy then.' It was hard work to reach him, as parts of the communication trench were knee deep in water and thick mud. Then I was misdirected and sent in the wrong direction, but I kept on praying I might be in time, and at last found the dying man still breathing and conscious. The look of joy, which lit up his face when I knelt beside him, was reward enough for the effort I had made. I gave him Absolution and anointed him before he died, but occupied as I was I did not notice that a third gas attack had begun. Before I could get my helmet out and on, I had swallowed a couple of mouthfuls, which did me no serious harm beyond making me feel rather sick and weak.

'As I made my way slowly up the trench, feeling altogether 'a poor thing,' I stumbled across a young officer who had been badly gassed. He had got his helmet on, but was coughing and choking in a terrible way. 'For God's sake,' he cried, 'help me to tear off this helmet I can't breathe. I'm dying.' I saw if I left him the end would not be far; so catching hold of him, I half carried, half dragged him up the trench to the medical aid post. I shall never forget that ten minutes, it seemed hours. I seemed to have lost all my strength: struggling with him to prevent him killing himself by tearing off his helmet made me forget almost how to breathe through mine. I was almost stifled, though safe from gas, while the perspiration simply poured from my forehead. I could do nothing but pray for help and set my teeth, for if I once let go, he was a dead man. Thank God, we both at last got to the aid post, and I had the happiness of seeing him in the evening out of danger, though naturally still weak.

"Fortunately this last attack was short and light, so that I was able to take off my helmet and after a cup of tea was all right. The best proof I can give you of this, lies in the fact that I have since put in three of the hardest days' work of my life which I could not possibly have done had I been really gassed, as its first effect is to leave one as helpless as a child."

This last remark was made in order to relieve his father's anxiety. But it was, to say the least, a meagre summary of his heroic work and almost miraculous escape. A year later he lifted the veil somewhat. "I have never told you," he then confessed, "the whole story of that memorable April morning or the repetition of it the following day, or how when I was lying on the stretcher going to 'peg out,' as the doctor believed, God gave me back my strength and energy in a way which was nothing short of a miracle, to help many a poor fellow to die in peace and perhaps to open the gates, of heaven to not a few.

"I had come through the three attacks without ill results, though having been unexpectedly caught by the last one, as I was anointing a dying man and did not see the poisonous fumes coming, I had swallowed some of the gas before I could get my helmet on. It was nothing very serious, but left me rather weak and washy. There was little time to think of that, for wounded and dying were lying all along the trenches, and I was the only priest on that section at the time.

"The fumes had quite blown away, but a good deal of the gas, being of a heavy nature, had sunk down to the bottom of the trench and gathered under the duck-boards or wooden flooring. It was impossible to do one's work with the gas helmet on, and so as I knelt down to absolve or anoint man after man for the greater part of that day, I had to inhale the chlorine fumes till I had nearly enough gas in my poor inside to inflate a German sausage balloon.

"I did not then know that when a man is gassed his only chance (and a poor one at that) is to lie perfectly still to give the heart a chance of fighting its foe. In happy ignorance of my real state, I covered mile after mile of those trenches until at last in the evening, when the work was done, I was able to rejoin my battalion in a village close to the Line.

"It was only then I began to realise that I felt 'rotten bad' as schoolboys say. I remember the doctor, who was a great friend of mine, feeling my pulse and shaking his head as he put me lying in a corner of the shattered house, and then he sat beside me for hours with a kindness I can never forget. He told me afterwards he was sure I was a 'gone coon,' but at the moment I did not care much. Then I fell asleep only to be rudely awakened at four next morning by the crash of guns and the dreaded bugle call 'gas alarm, gas alarm.' The Germans had launched a second attack, fiercer than the first. It did not take long to make up my mind what to do who would hesitate at such a moment, when the Reaper Death was busy? and before I reached the trenches I had anointed a number of poor fellows who had struggled back after being gassed and had fallen dying by the roadside.

"The harvest that day was a big one, for there had been bloody fighting all along the Front. Many a man died happy in the thought that the priest's hand had been raised in absolution over his head and the Holy Oils' anointing had given pardon to those senses which he had used to offend the Almighty. It was a long, hard day, a day of heartrending sights, with the consolation of good work done in spite of the deadly fumes, and I reached my billet wet and muddy, pretty nearly worn out, but *perfectly well*, with not the slightest ill effect from what I had gone through, nor have I felt any since. Surely God has been good to me. That was not the first of His many favours, nor has it been the last."

This was written a year later. In his first letter, while concealing the extreme risks he had incurred, he gave his father a brief consoling account of his two days' work amid the ghastly battlefield.

"On paper every man with a helmet was as safe as I was from gas poisoning. But now it is evident many of the men despised the 'old German gas,' some did not bother putting on their helmets, others had torn theirs, and others like myself had thrown them aside or lost them. From early morning till late at night I worked my way from trench to trench single handed the first day, with three regiments to look after, and could get no help. Many men died before I could reach them; others seemed just to live till I anointed them, and were gone before I passed back. There they lay, scores of them (we lost 800, nearly all from gas) in the bottom of the trench, in every conceivable posture of human agony: the clothes torn off their bodies in a vain effort to> breathe; while from end to end of that valley of death came one low unceasing moan from the lips of brave men fighting and struggling for life.

"I don't think you will blame me when I tell you that more than once the words of Absolution stuck in my throat, and the tears splashed down on the patient suffering faces of my poor boys as I leant down to anoint them. One young soldier seized my two hands and covered them with kisses; another looked up and said: 'Oh! Father I can die happy now, sure I'm not afraid of death or anything else since I have seen you.' Don't you think, dear father, that the little sacrifice made in coming out here has already been more than repaid, and if you have suffered a little anxiety on my account, you have at least the consolation of knowing that I have, through God's goodness, been able to comfort many a poor fellow and perhaps to open the gates, of Heaven for them."

After this terrible experience Fr. Doyle was glad to have a few days' rest at the rear. For the first time in a fortnight he was able to remove his clothes and he slept for thirteen continuous hours in a real bed. He had, as he himself said, 'nearly reached the end of his tether' For his conduct on the occasion he was mentioned in dispatches. [6] On which he remarks: "I hope that the angels have done their work as well and that I shall get a little corner in their report to Head Quarters above." Fortunately, there is no doubt about the latter point! Not angels only but human souls speeded heavenwards bore tribute to the self-sacrificing zeal of the soldier of Christ.

During the comparative lull which succeeded this attack Fr. Doyle was kept busy by the men, "scraping their Kettles," as they expressed it. "I wish mine were half as clean as some of theirs," he adds. Thus on Sunday, 14th May, between 600 and 700 men went to Holy Communion. Once more he eulogizes his little flock. "One cannot help feeling proud of our Irish lads," he writes. "Everyone loves them the French girls, naturally that goes without saying; the shopkeepers love them for their simplicity in paying about five times the real .value of the goods they buy. Monsieur le Cure would hug them each and everyone if he could, for he has been simply raking in the coin these days, many a one putting three and five franc notes in the plate, to make up, I suppose, for the trouser buttons of the knowing ones; and surely our Blessed Lord loves them best of all for their simple, unaffected piety which brings crowds of them at all hours of the day to visit Him in the Tabernacle. Need I add that the Padre himself has a warm corner in his heart for his boys, as I think they have for him, judging by their anxiety when the report spread that I had got knocked out in the gas attack. They are as proud as punch to have the chaplain with them in the trenches. It is quite amusing to hear them point out my dug-out to strangers as they go by: 'That's our priest,' with a special stress on the our." For which assuredly the Fusiliers had good reason.

What did he himself think of it all? The following little description of another Crucifix will help to show us where his thoughts lay.

"I paid a visit recently to another wonder of the war, the Church of Vermelles. Little remains of it now, for the town has been held in succession by the Germans, French, and ourselves, and every yard of ground was lost and won a dozen times. The church is just a heap of ruins: the roof has been burnt, the tower shot away, while the statues, Stations, etc., are smashed to dust, but hanging still on one of the broken, walls is a large crucifix absolutely untouched. The figure is a beautiful one, a work of art, and the face of our Lord has an expression of sadness such as I have never seen before. The eyes are open, gazing as it were upon the scene of desolation, and though the wall upon which the crucifix hangs is riddled with bullet holes and shell splinters, the image is untouched save for one round bullet hole just through the heart. The whole thing may be only chance, but it is a striking sight, and cannot fail to impress one and bring home the fact that if God is scourging the world as it well deserves, He is not indifferent to the sorrows and sufferings of His children."

A few intimate letters written at this time give us a precious glimpse of his inner life. We are thus enabled to see a little of that inward soul-world, so calm and undisturbed, so perfectly hidden beneath the multifarious activities and cheerful vigour of a military chaplain. He felt that his present life, so repellent to his natural self, was at once the fulfilment and the test of all his previous aspirations for the foreign mission and martyrdom. His experience seemed to him a purifying preparation for some great task, the consummation of all his striving and sacrifice. "Life out here," he writes, "has had one strange effect on me. I feel as if I had been crushed under some great weight, and that the crushing had somehow got rid of much that was bad in me and brought me closer to Jesus. If it should be God's holy will to bring me safe out of this war, life will be too short to thank Him for all the graces He has given me here. I am already dreaming dreams of the big things I shall try to do for Him, but I fancy He wants to crush me still more before I get out of this. I read a passage recently in the letters of Père Liberman [7] which is consoling. He says that he found from long experience that God never filled a soul with an ardent and lasting desire for anything, *e.g.*, love, holiness, etc., without in the end gratifying it. Has He not in the lesser things acted thus with me? You know my desire for the foreign missions because I realized that the privation and hardships of such a life, the separation from all naturally dear to me, would be an immense help to holiness. And here I am a real missioner, if not in the Congo, at least with many of the wants and sufferings and even greater dangers than I should have found there. The longing for martyrdom God has gratified times without number, for I have had to go into what seemed certain death, gladly making the offering of my poor life, but He did not accept it, so that the 'daily martyrdom' might be repeated. How I thank Him for this keenest of all sufferings, the prospect of death when life is bounding within one, since it makes me a little more like the Saviour shrinking from death in the Garden! Even my anxiety to have more time for prayer has been gratified, because while waiting for one thing or another or going on my rounds, I have many opportunities for a little talk with Him."

What he especially valued was the privilege of being a living Tabernacle, of always carrying the Blessed Sacrament around with him. This was to Fr. Doyle not only "a constant source of consolation but also enabled him to overcome his natural loathing for the scenes of strife and slaughter around him, and to manifest an amazingly imperturbable courage which he was really far from feeling. "I have been living in the front trenches for the last week," he says in another letter, "in a sea of mud, drenched to the skin with rain and mercilessly peppered with all sorts and conditions of shells. Yet I realize that some strange purifying process is going on in my soul, and that this life is doing much for my sanctification. This much I can say: I hunger and thirst for holiness, and for humiliations and sufferings, which are the short-cut to holiness; though when these things do come, I often pull a long face and try to avoid them. Yet lately I have come to understand as never before that it is only 'through many tribulations' we can hope to enter the Promised Land of sanctity. I think when this war is over (about twenty years hence), I shall become a hermit! I never felt so utterly sick of the world and worldlings. All this bustle and movement has wearied my soul beyond measure. I am longing for solitude, to be alone with Jesus, for He seems to fill every want in my life. All the same as the days go by I thank our Blessed Lord more and more for the grace of getting out here. Not exactly because of the consolation of helping so many poor fellows or because of the merit the hard life must bring with it, but because I feel this experience has influenced my whole future, which I cannot further explain except by saying that God has given me *the* grace of my life since I came.

"Then in addition there is the great privilege and joy of carrying our dear Lord next my heart day and night. Long ago when reading that Pius IX carried the Pyx around his neck, I felt a foolish desire, as it seemed to me, for the same privilege. Little did I think then that the God of holiness would stoop so low as to make me His resting-place. Why this favour alone would be worth going through twenty wars for! I feel ashamed at times that I do not profit more by His nearness, but I know that He makes allowances for weak inconstant nature, and that even when I do not directly think of Him, He is silently working in my soul. Do you not think that Jesus must have done very much for Mary during the nine months she bore Him within her? I feel that He will do much, very much, for me too whilst I carry Him about with me."

Writing on 7th May he lets an intimate correspondent see clearly the source of all his strength and courage. "Sometimes God seems to leave me to my weakness and I tremble with fear," he confesses. "At other times I have so much trust and confidence in His loving protection that I could almost sit down on a bursting shell feeling I could come to no harm. You would laugh, or perhaps cry, if you saw me at this moment sitting on a pile of bricks and rubbish. Shells are bursting some little distance away on three sides and occasionally a piece comes down with an unpleasantly close thud. But what does it matter? Jesus is resting on my heart, and whenever I like I can fold my arms over Him and press Him to that heart which, as He knows, beats with love of Him." [8] With what wonderful literalness does this attitude reproduce the message of our Lord Himself: "I say to you, My friends, Be not afraid of them who kill the body and after that have no more that they can do. ... Are not five sparrows sold for two farthings and not one of them is forgotten before God? Yea, the very hairs of your head are all numbered. Fear not, therefore; you are of more value than many sparrows." (*S. Luke* 12. 4.) To which we may surely add the next verse: "Whosoever shall confess Me before men, him shall the Son of man also confess before the angels of God." A guarantee that not one of the unrecorded deeds of Christian heroism 'is forgotten before God,' and that Fr. Doyle, flitting like an angel of mercy over the gas-stricken field of Loos, got what he calls his little corner in the report to Head Quarters above.

(6.) ANOTHER SPELL AT THE FRONT.

On 2nd June, Fr. Doyle secured a much needed leave of absence. "I do not think," he says, "I ever looked forward to a holiday with such keenness in my life before." The nerve-racking, ear-splitting, ceaseless warfare; the constant stream of soldiers to be helped, shriven, anointed or buried; the physical discomforts, the rats and the vermin, the intense cold and knee-deep slush succeeded now by the aching glare of the chalk trenches; the poison-gas working on his body, and the nauseating scenes of bloodshed working on his mind; all this, quite apart from his self-imposed martyrdom of prayer and penance, had told severely on Fr. Doyle, though outwardly he was as joyous and gay as ever. His all too short holiday of ten days was soon over, however; and once more he was back in the trenches.

He was hardly back when a new adventure befell him. "It seems right," he tells his Father, "that I should not keep from you this last mark of the good God's wonderful protection which has been so manifest during the past four months."

"I was standing in a trench, quite a long distance from the firing line, a spot almost as safe as Dalkey itself, talking to some of my men, when we heard in the distance the scream of a shell. It was evidently one of those random shots, which Brother Fritz sends along from time to time, as no other came after it. We very soon became painfully aware that our visitor was heading for us, and that if he did not explode in front of our trench, his career would certainly come to an end close behind us. I did not feel uneasy, for I knew we were practically safe from flying fragments which would pass over our heads, but none of us had calculated that this gentleman had made up his mind to drop into the trench itself, a couple of paces from where I stood.

"What really took place in the next ten seconds I cannot say. I was conscious of a terrific explosion and the thud of falling stones and debris. I thought the drums of my ears were split by the crash, and I believe I was knocked down by the concussion, but when I jumped to my feet I found that the two men who had been standing at my left hand, the side the shell fell, were stretched on the ground dead, though I think I had time to give them absolution and anoint them. The poor fellow on my right was lying badly wounded in the head; but I myself, though a bit stunned and dazed by the suddenness of the whole thing, was absolutely untouched, though covered with dirt and blood.

"My escape was nothing short of a miracle, for a moment before I was standing on the very spot the shell fell and had just moved away a couple of paces. I did not think it was possible for one to be so near a high explosive and not be killed, and even now I cannot account for my marvellous escape. In saying this I am not quite truthful, for I have not a doubt where the saving protection came from. I had made up my mind to consecrate some small hosts at my Mass the following morning and put them in my Pyx as usual, but as I walked through the little village on my way to the trenches, the thought came to me that with so much danger about, it would be well to have our Blessed Lord's company and protection. I went into the church, opened the Tabernacle, and with the Sacred Host resting on my heart set out confidently to face whatever lay before me; little did I think I was to be so near death or how much depended on that simple action. That is the explanation of the whole affair; I trusted Him and I believe He just allowed this to happen on the very first day I got back to make me trust Him all the more and have greater confidence in His loving protection." [9]

Even the week's rest in billets, though a change from life in the trenches, meant no cessation of work or risk. It was a busy time for the chaplain, as the men availed of the opportunity for Confession and Holy Communion. Even here, well behind the firing line, danger was not absent, for the German long range guns often sent unwelcome visitors. "One shell hit this house," he complained, "came slick through the brick wall into my poor bedroom of all places, very shabby I call it, missed my bed by just an inch, took a dive through the floor into the room below, and having amused itself with the furniture, coolly walked out through the opposite wall without condescending to burst, in indignation, I suppose, because I was not there. No one was hurt and not much harm done. I have put the head of my bed in the hole in the wall, for it is a point of honour among shells not to come twice through the same spot, and in consequence I sleep securely." "With all these prayers going on," he added to reassure those at home, "a fellow has no chance of getting hit; it's not fair, I think!"

At any rate, it was not Fr. Doyle's fault that he was not hit, for when there was question of ministering to his men, he was absolutely heedless of danger. Further proof of this is unnecessary, but one or two more instances occurring at this time (July, 1916) may be recorded. He wanted to go quickly to a certain village which his men were holding. The journey by 'the underground,' otherwise 'trench street,' would take a couple of hours, whereas a quarter of an hour's cycle ride over the high road would bring him to the village.

The road, however, was in full view of the German trenches which were quite near, and no one ever ventured along it in daylight. Fr. Doyle was the exception. He cycled the whole way without one bullet being fired. Moreover he had to slacken speed several times in order to avoid the shell holes with which the road was pitted, and he had to dismount once to pick up his bicycle pump which had been jerked off. "Judging by some remarks which have reached me since," he concludes, "people cannot make up their minds whether I am a hero or a fool I vote for the second. But then they cannot understand what the salvation of even one soul means to a priest. So I just laugh and go my way, happy in the thought that I was in time." This diversity of judgement is just as applicable to Fr. Doyle's life as a whole. Was he a hero or a fool? That is because we forget the possibility of his being both. [10]

"My second adventure, if I may so style it, (says Fr. Doyle) was of a different kind. Preparations had been made for the blowing up of a gigantic mine sunk under the German trenches, while at the same time our men were to make a raid or night attack on the enemy. The hour fixed was eleven o'clock, so shortly after ten I made my way up to the firing line, where the attacking party, were waiting. They were grouped in two bodies, one on either side of the mine, waiting for the explosion to rush over the parapet and seize the newly formed mine-crater.

"As I came along the trench I could hear the men whisper, 'Here's the priest,' while the faces which a moment before had been marked with the awful strain of the waiting lit up with pleasure. As I gave the absolution and the blessing of God on their work, I could not help thinking how many a poor fellow would soon be stretched lifeless a few paces from where he stood; and though I ought to be hardened by this time, I found it difficult to choke down the sadness which filled my heart. 'God bless you, Father, we're ready now,' was reward enough for facing the danger, since every man realized that each moment was full of dreadful possibilities.

"It was well known that the Germans were countermining, and if they got wind of our intention would certainly try and explode their mine before ours. It was uncanny walking along, knowing that at any moment you might find yourself sailing skywards, wafted by the gentle breath of four or five tons of explosive. Fortunately nothing happened, but the moments were running out, so I hurried down the communication trench to the dressing station in a dug-out about a hundred yards away, where I intended waiting for the wounded to be brought in.

"On the stroke of eleven I climbed up the parapet out of the trench, and as I did there was a mighty roar in the bowels of the earth, the ground trembled and rocked and quivered, and then a huge column of clay and stones was shot hundreds of feet in the air. As the earth opened dense clouds of smoke and flames burst out, an awful and never to be forgotten sight. God help the poor fellows, even though they be our enemies, who were caught in that inferno and buried alive or blown to bits.

"For a second there was a lull, and then it seemed as if hell were let loose. Our artillery in the rear were standing ready, waiting for the signal; the moment the roar of the explosion was heard every gun opened fire with a deafening crash. Already our men were over the parapet with a yell which must have terrified the enemy, up the side of the crater, and were digging themselves in for their lives. Under cover of our guns the raiding party had raced for the enemy's trench, fought their way in and out again, as our object was not to gain ground."

At this stage, the German guns having come into action, Fr. Doyle retired to the dug-out and was soon busy with the wounded and dying. One of these was a slightly wounded German prisoner; he was only a young lad and his teeth chattered with fear. With great difficulty Fr. Doyle, who knew no German, calmed the poor fellow who turned out to be a Bavarian Catholic. It was by no means the only occasion on which this true minister of Christ practised that brotherhood and love of which war seems to be the cruel negation. More than once too he preached (in rather strong terms) to his men on their obligation to respect the lives of prisoners.

Still another adventure. "August 15th has always been a day of many graces for me," writes Fr. Doyle. "It is the anniversary of my consecration to Mary and of my vows in the Society; it was very nearly making me surpass our Lady herself by sending me higher up than she ever got in her life." The men were out of the trenches, staying in the village of Mazingarbe. On the afternoon of 15th August, 1916, most of the men were engaged in athletic sports in a field outside when the Germans began shelling the town. Needless to say, Fr. Doyle at once started for the scene of danger.

"Knowing there were a good number of my boys about (he writes) I hurried back as quickly as I could, and made my way up the long, narrow street. The shells were all coming in one direction, across the road, not down it, so that by keeping close to the houses on the shady side there was little danger, though occasional thrills of excitement enough to satisfy Don Quixote himself. I reached the village cross-roads in time to lift up the poor sentry who had been badly hit, and with the help of a couple of men carried him to the side of the road. He was unconscious, but I gave him absolution and was half way through the anointing when with a scream and a roar which made our hearts jump a shell whizzed over our heads and crashed into the wall directly opposite on the other side of the street, covering us with brick dust and dirt. Bits of shrapnel came thud, thud, on the ground and wall around us, but neither I nor the men were touched.

"'Begorra, Father, that was a near one, anyhow,' said one of them, as he brushed the dust off his tunic, and started to fill his pipe. 'It was well we had your Reverence with us when Jerry (a nickname for German) sent that one across.' 'You must not thank me, boys,' I said, 'don't you know it is our Lady's feast, and Mary had her mantle spread over us to save us from all harm?' 'True for you, Father', came the answer. But I could see by their faces that they were by no means convinced that I had not worked the miracle.

"Though it was the 15th of August I was taking no risks, especially with this reputation to maintain! So, the poor boy being dead, I bundled the rest of them down a cellar out of harm's way, and started off again. Heavy as the shelling was, little damage was done thanks to the fact that the sports had emptied the town. One man was beyond my aid, a few slightly wounded, and that was all. As I came round the corner of the Church I met four of my boys calmly strolling along in the middle of the street as if they were walking on Kingstown pier. I won't record what I said, but my words helped by the opportune arrival of an unpleasantly near H.E. (high explosive) had the desired effect, and we all took cover in the church. It was only then I realised my mistake, for it soon became evident the Germans were firing at the church itself. One after another the shells came in rapid succession, first on one side then on the other, dropping in front and behind the building, which was a target with its tall, white tower. It was madness to go out, and I do not think the men, some score of them, knew of their danger, nor did I tell them, but 'man of little faith,' as I was, I cast anxious eyes at the roof and wished it were stronger. All's well that ends well, they say. Not a shot hit the church, though the houses and road got it hot. Our fiery ordeal ended at last, safely and happily for all of us. And August 15th, 1916, went down on my list as another day of special grace and favour at Mary's hands."

Quite apart from these special escapes, Fr. Doyle's ordinary days were filled with thrilling dangers and exhausting toil. "I often congratulate myself," he says, "on my good fortune in being appointed to the Irish Brigade, more especially as the last vacancy fell to me. The vast majority of the chaplains at the Front seldom see anything more dangerous than the shell of an egg of doubtful age. They are doing splendid work along the lines of communication, in the hospitals, or at the base. Even those who are attached to non-Catholic Divisions have little time to get to the trenches, their men are so scattered; but we with the Irish Regiments live in the thick of it. We share the hardships and dangers with our men, and if we have less polish on our boots and belts than other spruce padres, let us hope we have something more to our bank account in a better world."

Almost before daybreak Fr. Doyle was up and had the happiness of offering the Holy Sacrifice. In August, 1916, he was able to fit up a room in a deserted house and here from time to time he was able to celebrate Mass for the men, "a privilege which the poor fellows appreciate." In one corner were the cellar steps down which, when occasion required, priest and congregation vanished with marvellous celerity. Once a shell came through the wall and fell on the floor without bursting, covering the little altar with bricks and plaster. But when in the trenches he celebrated in his dug-out. The morning was spent in visits to five dressing stations in various parts of the trenches, saying some of his Office, Confessions or chats with the men. "Quite often," he says, "an officer will drop in for a friendly controversial talk, resulting, thank God, in much good. There is no doubt that the faith and sincere piety of our men have made an immense impression on non-Catholics, and have made them anxious to know more about the true Church." "In the afternoon," he continues, "I make a tour of the front line trenches. To be candid, it is part of my work which I do *not* like. We chaplains are not bound to go into the firing line; in fact are not supposed to do so, but the officers welcome us warmly, as a chat and a cheery word bucks the men up so much. It is not that the danger is very great; in fact, I think it is much less than in other parts of the trenches, because the track being built in a zigzag, you are perfectly safe in a 'bay' owing to the walls of clay on either side, unless a shell falls on the very spot where you are standing. But it is the uncanny feeling, which comes over one, knowing that the enemy in some parts are only thirty yards away, which makes the trip unpleasant. I have often come to a 'bay' blown in shortly before by a shell from a mortar, a little gentleman weighing 200lbs.; you can see him coming in the air, and when you do, well you slip into the next 'bay' and try to feel as small as you can. I have had to crawl past a gap in the trench, but I can honestly say I have never had anything approaching a near shave. The Lord does not forget His goats when He is minding His sheep!"

Night did not mean rest for Fr. Doyle, for it was then that he usually conducted burials. Moreover as most of the ordinary fighting was done at night it was then that he was most liable to 'sick calls.' He might perhaps have just turned in at 2 a.m., when word would come that one of his men in a distant part of the trench had his leg shot off. His 'home' itself was a hole dug in the side of the trench, his 'bed' was a couple of planks raised off the ground. "We have rats and fleas by the million," he writes, "innumerable flies which eat the jam off your bread before you can get it into your mouth, smells wondrous and varied, not to speak of other unmentionable things."

Amid all these hardships he was consoled by the thought of how much his presence and ministrations meant to the poor fellows around him. "Though the life at times is rough and hard enough (at least the floor feels so at night) there are many consolations for a priest, not the least of which is the number of converts, both officers and men coming into the Church. Many of them have never been in contact with Catholics before, knew nothing about the grandeur and beauty of our religion, and above all have been immensely impressed by what the Catholic priests, alone of all the chaplains at the Front, are able to do for their men, both living and dying. It is an admitted fact, that the Irish Catholic soldier is the bravest and best man in a fight, but few know that he draws that courage from the strong Faith with which he is filled and the help which comes from the exercise of his religion."

He was naturally solicitous for his men, especially as the months dragged on with no intermission save a few brief days spent in reserve amid the ruins of a shattered village behind the lines. It was customary for a division which had been in the line for three months to get back to the base for a month's rest. The other divisions round the Sixteenth went back and returned, but the Irishmen were now six months without relief. "I suppose," writes Fr. Doyle, "it is a compliment to the fighting qualities of the i6th Division, for we are holding the most critical sector of the line; but it is a compliment all of us would willingly forego." "As a matter of fact," he adds, "the very night we handed over a certain portion of the Front to another regiment, the Germans how did they know of the change? came over and captured the trenches. So we had to go back again." Still the unfortunate Irishmen could not be kept in the trenches for ever. And on 25th August came the welcome order to move to the rear. Sudden and secret as the order was, the Germans knew all about it and put up a board with the message, "Good-bye, 16th Division, we shall give it hot to the English when they come." The Irish did their work well in Loos; in the six months they did not lose a trench or a yard of ground; and out of the Division of 20,000 over 15,000 men (including, of course, many sick and slightly wounded) had passed through the doctor's hands.

Back through Amiens to the rear away from the sounds and sights of war. These long marches, made more trying by official incompetence, were very exhausting. As usual Fr. Doyle was where his Master would have been, following the Ignatian ideal of *mecum laborare* in the *Kingdom of Christ.* "The officers, from captain up," he writes, "have horses; but I prefer to shoulder my pack and foot it with my boys, for I know they like it, and besides I don't see why I should not share a little of their hardship." Incidentally we learn that he had been carrying a young lad's equipment in addition to his own, all day too without dinner or supper. It is clear that the saints are incorrigibly 'imprudent.'

(7.) THE SOMME.

The men of the 16th Division were under the impression that, after having done so much more than their share, they were making their way steadily towards the place appointed for their well-deserved rest. But as a matter of fact many of these brave fellows were never to enjoy that promised time of quiet on this earth, for their road was leading them to the battle field of the Somme. By way of rest they were to be asked to achieve what English regiments had failed to do. They did it; Guillemont and Ginchy were taken; and many an Irish hearth is the poorer and lonelier "But 'twas a famous victory."

The opening sentences of Fr. Doyle's next letter to his lather (11th September, 1916) sufficiently indicate the terrible nature of the ordeal which we are about to recount.

"I have been through the most terrible experience of my whole life, in comparison with which all that I have witnessed or suffered since my arrival in France seems of little consequence; a time of such awful horror that I believe if the good God had not helped me powerfully by His grace I could never have endured it. To sum up all in one word, for the past week I have been living literally in hell, amid sights and scenes and dangers enough to test the courage of the bravest; but through it all my confidence and trust in our Blessed Lord's protection never wavered, for I felt that somehow, even if it needed a miracle, He would bring me safe through the furnace of tribulation. I was hit three times, on the last occasion by a piece of shell big enough to have taken off half my leg, but wonderful to relate I did not receive a wound or scratch there is some advantage, you see, in having a good thick skin! As you can imagine, I am pretty well worn out and exhausted, rather shaken by the terrific strain of those days and nights without any real sleep or repose, with nerves tingling, ever on the jump, like the rest of us; but it is all over now; we are well behind the firing line on our way at last for a good long rest, which report says will be enjoyed close to the sea."

His previous letter had been written from Bray, (see map) near Albert, on the river Somme, where there was a huge concentration of French and British forces. Each morning Fr. Doyle said Mass in the open and gave Holy Communion to hundreds of the men. "I wish you could have seen them," he writes, "kneeling there before the whole camp, recollected and prayerful a grand profession surely of the faith that is in them. More than one non-Catholic was touched by it; and it made many a one, I am sure, turn to God in the hour of need." On the evening of Sunday, 3rd September, just as they were sitting down to dinner, spread on a pile of empty shell boxes, urgent orders reached the 16th Division to march in ten minuses. "There was only time," says Fr. Doyle, "to grab a slice of bread and hack off a piece of meat before rushing to get one's kit." "As luck would have it," he adds, "I had had nothing to eat since the morning and was famished, but there was nothing for it but to tighten one's belt and look happy." There are occasions when even the world can appreciate Jesuit obedience! After a couple of hours' tramp a halt was called and an order came to stock all impedimenta kits, packs, blankets, etc., - by the side of the road. Fr. Doyle,, it is almost needless to say, held on to his Mass things, though to his great sorrow for five days he was unable to offer the Holy Sacrifice - "the biggest privation of the whole campaign."

The night was spent without covering or blankets, sitting on the ground. Next morning there was a short march over the brow of a hill and down into a valley still nearer to the front line. It was a great change from the trench life of the past six months, since at Loos for days one never saw a soul overground and all guns were carefully hidden But here there were scores and hundreds of cannon of all shapes and sizes, standing out boldly in the fields and "roaring as if they had swallowed a dish of uncooked shells."' Amid this infernal din and never-ending roar and crash of bursting shells, men and horses moved about as if there were no war. In this valley of death Fr. Doyle's men had their first casualties and he himself had a very narrow escape which is best described in his own words.

"I was standing about 100 yards away watching a party of my men crossing the valley, when I saw the earth under their feet open and the twenty men disappear in a cloud of smoke, while a column of stones and clay was shot a couple of hundred feet into the air. A big German shell by the merest chance had landed in the middle of the party. I rushed down the slope, getting a most unmerciful 'whack' between the shoulders, probably from a falling stone, as it did not wound me, but it was no time to think of one's safety. I gave them all a General Absolution, scraped the clay from the faces of a couple of buried men who were not wounded, and then anointed as many of the poor lads as I could reach. Two of them had no faces to anoint and others were ten feet under the clay, but a few were living still. By this time half a dozen volunteers had run up and were digging the buried men out. War may be horrible, but it certainly brings out the best side of a man's character; over and over again I have seen men risking their lives to help or save a comrade, and these brave fellows knew the risk they were taking, for when a German shell falls in a certain place, you clear as quickly as you can since several more are pretty certain to land close. It was a case of duty for me, but real courage for them. We dug like demons for our lads' lives and our own, to tell the truth, for every few minutes another 'iron pill' from a Krupp gun would come tearing down the valley, making our very hearts leap into our mouths. More than once we were well sprinkled with clay and stones, but the cup of cold water promise was well kept, and not one of the party received a scratch. We got three buried men out alive, not much the worse for their trying experience, but so thoroughly had the shell done its work that there was not a single wounded man in the rest of the party; all had gone to a better land. As I walked back I nearly shared the fate of my boys, but somehow escaped again, and pulled out two more lads who were only buried up to the waist and uninjured. Meanwhile the regiment had been ordered back to a safer position on the hill, and we were able to breathe once more."

The men's resting place that night consisted of some open shell holes. "To make matters worse," writes Fr. Doyle "we were posted fifteen yards in front of two batteries of field guns, while on our right a little further off were half a dozen huge sixty-pounders; not once during the whole night did these guns cease firing." This proximity not only contributed an ear-splitting din but added considerably to the men's risk owing to the occasional premature bursting of the shells. In spite of these discomforts and the torrential downpour of rain, the men slept out of sheer weariness. "I could not help thinking," says Fr. Doyle, "of Him who often had not where to lay His head, and it helped me to resemble Him a little."

At last came the expected order to advance at once and hold the front line, the part assigned being Leuze Wood, the scene of much desperate fighting. Fr. Doyle may be left to describe the journey and the scene.

"The first part of our journey lay through a narrow trench, the floor of which consisted of deep thick mud, and the bodies of dead men trodden under foot. It was horrible beyond description, but there was no help for it, and on the half-rotten corpses of our own brave men we marched in silence, everyone busy with his own thoughts. I shall spare you gruesome details, but you can picture one's sensations as one felt the ground yield under one's foot, and one sank down through the body of some poor fellow.

"Half an hour of this brought us out on the open into the middle of the battlefield of some days previous. The wounded, at least I hope so, had all been removed, but the dead lay there stiff and stark, with open staring eyes, just as they had fallen. Good God, such a sight! I had tried to prepare myself for this, but all I had read or pictured gave me little idea of the reality. Some lay as if they were sleeping quietly, others had died in agony, or had had the life crushed out of them by mortal fear, while the whole ground, every foot of it, was littered with heads or limbs, or pieces of torn human bodies. In the bottom of one hole lay a British and a German soldier, locked in a deadly embrace, neither had any weapon, but they had fought on to the bitter end. Another couple seemed to have realised that the horrible struggle was none of their making, and that they were both children of the same God; they had died hand-in-hand praying for and forgiving one another. A third face caught my eye, a tall, strikingly handsome young German, not more, I should say, than eighteen. He lay there calm and peaceful, with a smile of happiness on his face, as if he had had a glimpse of Heaven before he died. Ah, if only his poor mother could have seen her boy it would have soothed the pain of her broken heart.

"We pushed on rapidly through that charnel house, for the stench was fearful, till we stumbled across a sunken road. Here the retreating Germans had evidently made a last desperate stand, but had been caught by our artillery fire. The dead lay in piles, the blue grey uniforms broken by many a khaki-clad body. I saw the ruins of what was evidently the dressing station, judging by the number of bandaged men about; but a shell had found them out even here and swept them all into the net of death.

"A halt for a few minutes gave me the opportunity I was waiting for. I hurried along from group to group, and as I did the men fell on their knees to receive absolution. A few words to give them courage, for no man knew if he would return alive. A 'God bless and protect you, boys,' and I passed on to the next company. As I did, a soldier stepped out of the ranks, caught me by the hand, and said: 'I am not a Catholic, sir, but I want to thank you for that beautiful prayer.' The regiments moved on to the wood, while the doctor and I took up our positions in the dressing station to wait for the wounded. This was a dug-out on the hill facing Leuze Wood, and had been in German occupation the previous afternoon.

"To give you an idea of my position. From where I stood the ground sloped down steeply into a narrow valley, while on the opposite hill lay the wood, half of which the Fusiliers were holding, the Germans occupying the rest; the distance across being so short I could easily follow the movements of our men without a glass.

"Fighting was going on all round, so that I was kept busy, but all the time my thoughts and my heart were with my poor boys in the wood opposite. They had reached it safely, but the Germans somehow had worked round the sides and temporarily cut them off. No food or water could be sent up, while ten slightly wounded men who tried to come back were shot down, one after another. To make matters worse, our own artillery began to shell them, inflicting heavy losses, and though repeated messages were sent back, continued doing so for a long time. It appears the guns had fired so much that they were becoming worn out, making the shells fall 300 yards short.

"Under these circumstances it would be madness to try and reach the wood, but my heart bled for the wounded and dying lying there alone. When dusk came I made up my mind to try and creep through the valley, more especially as the fire had slackened very much, but once again the Providence of God watched over me. As I was setting out I met a sergeant who argued the point with me. 'You can do little good, Father,' he said, 'down there in the wood, and will only run a great risk. Wait till night comes and then we shall be able to bring all the wounded up here. Don't forget that, though we have plenty of officers and to spare, we have only one priest to look after us.' The poor fellow was so much in earnest I decided to wait a little at least. It was well I did so, for shortly afterwards the Germans opened a terrific bombardment and launched a counterattack on the wood. Some of the Cornwalls, who were holding a corner of the wood, broke and ran, jumping right on top of the Fusiliers. Brave Paddy from the Green Isle stood his ground...and drove the Germans back with cold steel.

"Meanwhile we on the opposite hill were having a most unpleasant time. A wounded man had reported that the enemy had captured the wood. Communication was broken and Headquarters had no information of what was going on. At that moment an orderly dashed in with the startling news that the Germans were in the valley, and actually climbing our hill. Jerusalem! We non-combatants might easily escape to the rear, but who would protect the wounded? They could not be abandoned. If it were daylight the Red Cross would give us protection, but in the darkness of the night the enemy would not think twice about flinging a dozen bombs down the steps of the dug-out. I looked round at the bloodstained walls and shivered. A nice coward, am I not? Thank God, the situation was not quite so bad as reported; our men got the upper hand, and drove back the attack, but that half-hour of suspense will live long in my memory."

Unfortunately, Fr. Doyle gives no further details of his experiences except a brief account of Saturday, 9th September. In a subsequent letter (11th October) he described a Mass for the Dead which he celebrated at the Somme, apparently on this Saturday morning. "By cutting a piece out of the side of the trench," he says, "I was just able to stand in front of my tiny altar, a biscuit box supported on two German bayonets. God's angels, no doubt, were hovering overhead, but so were the shells, hundreds of them, and I was a little afraid that when the earth shook with the crash of the guns, the chalice might be overturned. Round about me on every side was the biggest congregation I ever had: behind the altar, on either side, and in front, row after row, sometimes crowding one upon the other, but all quiet and silent, as if they were straining their ears to catch every syllable of that tremendous act of Sacrifice but every man was dead! Some had lain there for a week and were foul and horrible to look at, with faces black and green. Others had only just fallen, and seemed rather sleeping than dead, but there they lay, for none had time to bury them, brave fellows, every one, friend and foe alike, while I held in my unworthy hands the God of Battles, their Creator and their Judge, and prayed Him to give rest to their souls. Surely that Mass for the Dead, in the midst of, and surrounded by the dead, was an experience not easily to be forgotten."

It was arranged that on the 9th September the 16th Division should storm Ginchy, a strong village against which previous English attacks had failed. The 8th Fusiliers, having lost so many officers, were held in reserve. From seven in the morning till five in the evening the guns played on Ginchy. "Shortly before five," writes Fr. Doyle, "I went up to the hill in front of the town, and was just in time to see our men leap from their trenches and dart up the slope, only to be met by a storm of bullets from concealed machine guns. It was my first real view of a battle at close quarters, an experience not easily forgotten. Almost simultaneously all our guns, big and little, opened a terrific barrage behind the village, to prevent the enemy bringing up reinforcements, and in half a minute the scene was hidden by the smoke of thousands of bursting shells, British and German. The wild rush of our Irish lads swept the Germans away like chaff. The first line went clean through the village and out the other side, and were it not for the officers, acting under orders, would certainly be in Berlin by this time! Meanwhile the supports had cleared the cellars and dugouts of their defenders; the town was ours and all was well. At the same time a feeling of uneasiness was about. Rumour said some other part of the line had failed to advance, the Germans were breaking through, etc. One thing was certain, the guns had not ceased. Something was not going well."

About nine o'clock the Fusiliers were getting ready to be relieved by another regiment. But one further experience was to be theirs. There came an urgent order to hurry up to the Front. "To my dying day," says Fr. Doyle, "I shall never forget that half-hour, as we pushed across the open, our only light the flash of bursting shells, tripping over barbed wire, stumbling and walking on the dead, expecting every moment to be blown into Eternity. We were halted in a trench at the rear of the village, and there till four in the morning we lay on the ground listening to the roar of the guns and the scream of the shells flying overhead, not knowing if the next moment might not be our last. Fortunately, we were not called upon to attack, and our casualties were very slight. But probably because the terrible strain of the past week was beginning to tell, or the Lord wished to give me a little merit by suffering more, the agony and fear and suspense of those six hours seemed to surpass the whole of the seven days.

"We were relieved on Sunday morning, 20th, at four o'clock, and crawled back (I can use no other word) to the camp in the rear. My feet, perhaps, are the most painful of all, as we were not allowed to remove our boots even at night. But otherwise I am really well, thank God, and a few days' good rest will make me better than ever. At present we march one day and rest the next, but I do not know where."

On 23rd September Fr. Doyle writes to say that, by rail and motor lorries and especially by "shank's mare," they had travelled into Normandy - but not for their month's rest so long overdue. Within a week they were over the frontier again into Belgium, thankful at least to have a quieter section of the line than that at Loos, a place where in fact there seemed to be a sort of mutual understanding to keep quiet. Here Fr. Doyle went through the ordinary chaplain's work until early in November when he was able to come home on a week's leave of absence.

(8.) CHRISTMAS AT THE FRONT.

All through this terrible time Fr. Doyle's inner life was the same continuous persevering effort at self-conquest, immolation and union. Some of his thoughts and resolutions he, luckily for us, scribbled down in his little notebook. On loth August he records that he is constantly irritated by the ceaseless annoyances and inconveniences of his life. So he resolved thus carrying out the advice he had often given to others:- "(1) to take every single detail of my life as done by Him; (2) lovingly to accept it all in the spirit of immolation that my will and wishes may be annihilated; (3) never to complain or grumble even to myself; (4) to try and let everyone do with me as he pleases, looking on myself as a slave to be trampled on." "If I kept these rules," he added, "I should never be annoyed or upset about anything and should never lose my peace of soul." Less than a week after his fearful experience at the Somme surely sufficient to justify a long respite from strain and suffering we find

Fr. William Doyle, S.J., as Military Chaplain.

this entry (15th September): "Again I felt most strongly urged to make the 50,000 aspirations the penance of my life, and to force myself, no matter at what cost, to get through them daily." A month later he made another effort to add to the inevitable hardships of his life by renewing his resolution to bear 'little sufferings' without relief. And on his return from his short much-needed visit home, he reproached himself thus: "While away on leave I deliberately resisted the urging of the Holy Spirit to do many hard things, *e.g.* to rise early and get all the Masses I could, make the Holy Hour, etc. I did none of these things and in consequence was very unhappy. I never have peace unless I am going against myself. I notice a continual interior urging to resume the marking of 'hard things,' because when I give up doing so the acts almost cease." On 13th December he reverts to this thought in the following record: "Since I became chaplain I have grown very lazy and unmortified, the cause of much unhappiness and remorse to me. My excuse is that my present life is so hard and repugnant that I need these little indulgences. Then I think of Blessed Charles Spinola, for example, amid the horrors of his prison, practising great austerities, fasting, etc., which make me ashamed of my cowardice. The Holy Spirit is constantly urging me not to let this precious time slip by, when even a small sacrifice is worth many a big one at other times. I see the only chance is to mark down the special acts I do, for though I hate doing so, I know it is an immense help, and otherwise nothing is done. I have begun the 'Book of Little Sacrifices' again to-day."

Another entry, made ten days later, may be quoted to show how difficult he really found that affability and calmness which others remarked in him: "I was very much annoyed because someone burnt the floor of my dug-out and also on finding my candles had been taken. On arriving at Locre I found a second bed in my room and heard that X was coming. This upset and worried me terribly till I realized that all these things were God's doing and that He wished to annihilate my will, so that I should never feel even the smallest interior disturbance no matter what might happen. I have secretly given permission to everyone to treat me as he wishes and to trample on me; why then should I not try and live up to this life?" [11]

Some quotations from letters written at this time to a few intimate friends and relatives will help to give us a further glimpse of that inner life which was naturally not revealed in the letters which he wrote home and destined for private circulation among a circle of acquaintances.

"I am getting to feel that God does not want the sacrifice of my life, and that I shall return safely to do His work. Some time ago I was feeling very depressed because that sacrifice was greater than even you know, when my eyes I fell on these words: 'The essence of the act of sacrifice did not consist in the slaying of the victim but in its offering.' That seemed to make me realize that God was satisfied with my willingness to die and that He had granted me my heart's desire to be a martyr, because the mere act of dying would add little to the crown of suffering I have gone through. At the same time I feel, oh! with what joy since it is for Him, that I have still very much to face and that I shall have the happiness of being wounded and shedding my blood for Jesus. I try to crush down the longing and to wish only what He wishes. One word more about self. You have guessed my little secret concerning decorations. I have asked God that I may not receive any. For my dear Father's sake and the pleasure it would give my loved ones at home it would be great happiness to hear I had been honoured. But I have made the sacrifice of this to God, and so though my name has again gone to Head Quarters, nothing has come of it."

As a matter of fact, however, early in January Fr. Doyle was awarded the Military Cross for his bravery at the Somme. For various reasons he disliked this distinction but was glad inasmuch as it gave pleasure to his Father, to whom he thus wrote on 4th January: "I am sorry these rewards are given to chaplains, for surely he would be a poor specimen of the Lord's Anointed who would do his work for such a thing. But seeing that they are going I must say I am really glad because I know it will give pleasure to an 'old soldier' at home, who ought long ago to have had all the medals and distinctions ever conferred." [12]

Fr. Doyle's interests and happiness lay elsewhere. "They have given me the M.C.," he said, "but His crosses are far more welcome." "I wonder," he wrote on 7th November, "I wonder is there a happier man in France than I am. Just now Jesus is giving me great joy in tribulation, though conditions of living are about as uncomfortable as even S. Teresa could wish perpetual rain, oceans of mud, damp, cold and a plague of rats. Yet I feel that all this is a preparation for the future and that God is labouring in my soul for ends I do not clearly see as yet. Sometimes I kneel down with outstretched arms and pray God, if it is a part of His divine plan, to rain down fresh privations and sufferings." "But," he adds with a characteristic touch of whimsical humour, "I stopped when the mud wall of my little hut fell in upon me that was too much of a good joke!"

The idea that his hard experience was preparatory to some great consummation reappears in the following interesting letter which he addressed to his sister on 19th December, "I want to have a little chat with you," he begins. "But you must promise to keep to yourself what I write to you. Did I ever tell you that my present life was just the one I dreaded most, being from a natural point of view repugnant to me in every way? So when our Blessed Lord sent me to the Front I felt 'angry' with Him for taking me away from a sphere of work where the possibilities, at least, of doing good were so enormous, and giving me a task others could perform much better. It was only after a time that I began to understand that 'God's ways are not our ways, nor His thoughts our thoughts,' and the meaning of it all began to dawn on me. In the first place my life, especially here in the trenches, has become a real hermit's one, cave and all, a mixture of solitude with a touch of the hardships of a foreign mission. The result has been that God has come into my life in a way He never did before. He has put strange thoughts into my head and given me many lights which I feel have changed my whole outlook upon life.

Then I feel, oh, so strongly, that I am going through a kind of noviceship, a sort of spiritual training, for some big work He wants me to do in the future. I feel every day as if spiritual strength and power were growing in my soul. This thought of being trained or fitted for God's work (if I may use the comparison with all reverence) like St. John the Baptist, has filled me with extraordinary joy and made me delight in a life which could not well be much harder.

"Here I am in a bit of a hole in the side of a ditch, so low that I cannot stand upright and have to bend my head and shoulders during Mass - I can tell you my back aches at the end. My only window is the door (without a door) through which the wind blows day and night; and a cold wind it is just now. I was offered a little stove but my 'Novice Master' did not want that luxury, for it never came. My home would be fairly dry if I could keep out the damp mists and persuade the drops of water not to trickle from the roof. As a rule I sleep well, though one is often roused to attend some poor fellow who has been hit. Still it is rather reversing the order of things to be glad to get up in the morning to try and get warm; and it is certainly not pleasant to be wakened from sweet dreams by a huge rat burrowing under your pillow or scampering over your face! This has actually happened to me. There is no great luxury in the matter of food, as you may well guess. Recently, owing to someone's carelessness, or possibly because the bag was made to pay toll on the way up to the trenches, my day's rations consisted of half a pot of jam and a piece of cheese!

"Through all this, and much in addition, the one thought ever in my mind is the goodness and love of God in choosing me to lead this life, and thus preparing me without a chance of refusal for the work He wants doing. No amount of reading or meditating could have proved to me so convincingly that a life of privation, suffering and sacrifice, accepted lovingly for the love of Jesus, is a life of great joy, and surely of great graces You see, therefore, that I have reasons in abundance for being happy, and I am truly so. Hence you ought to be glad that I have been counted worthy to suffer something for our dear Lord, the better to be prepared to do His work. Ask Him, won't you, that I may not lose this golden opportunity, but may profit to the full by the graces He is giving me. Every loving wish from my heart for a holy and happy Xmas. Let our gift to the divine Babe be the absolute sacrifice of even our desires, so that His Will alone may be done."

One final quotation will be given from an intimate Christmas letter, so that while we are following Fr. Doyle's outward career, so heroic and, at a safe distance, so picturesque, we may not misread the real man within, so hidden and unsuspected and, to most men, so unintelligible.

"I certainly did not think this time twelve months (he writes) that my next Christmas greetings to you would be from a military camp. I cannot help wondering where my good wishes will reach you from when another year has passed. God has given me one grace at least since I came here. I feel absolutely in His Hands and joyous in the thought that no matter what may happen it will be all for His greater glory. Though Christmas Day was miserably wet, the Divine Babe filled my heart with joy at the thought that my life now was a little bit at least more like to His. I am learning here better every day that there is no life of happiness like one full of 'hard things' borne for love of God. For some time past I have felt, I know not why, an intense longing for holiness at any price. I wonder what the price is? Do you ever ask God to make me a saint? No use asking for miracles, I suppose! Well, I shall take my revenge by begging holiness for you.

"In some ways I have found life out here much easier than I expected and in other respects a good deal more trying. Still if I get only a little bit of holiness out of it all, will it not be well worth it all? Jesus knows I have only one wish in this world to love Him and Him alone for the rest He has *carte blanche* to do as He pleases in my regard. I just leave myself in His loving Hands and so have no anxiety or care, but great peace of soul. I am off now for a fortnight's spell in the trenches, and if it is not to.be Saint Teresa's *mori* it will at least be *pati*."

This is not an inappropriate place for inserting an excerpt from a similar letter though it was written some months later (March, 1917): "Two great lights or graces seem to have come to me as a result of my present life. The first is that God's will is everything to me now... True, nature rebels at times, for He has filled me with such a longing to labour for Him, to live and suffer for His dear sake, that the thought of death is very bitter. I can only call it a living martyrdom. But I conquer the feeling by saying this little prayer: 'Take, O Lord, and receive my liberty, my health and strength, my limbs, my flesh, my blood, my very life. Do with me just as You wish; I embrace all lovingly suffering, wounds, death if only it will glorify You one tiny bit.' That always brings back peace, even when a bullet grazing my head drives home the reality of the offering. The second grace is the realisation of the immense power of prayer I had almost said it is everything. This urging to a constant life of prayer has been going on for years, but I had a kind of scruple about 'wasting time' in this way. God has set these, doubts at rest. ... I have a little system of my own for counting my prayers; to represent it by figures, the 10,000 before the war has grown to 100,000 daily now, with the result that He has entered into my life as He had never done before."

These citations will suffice to demonstrate the perfect continuity of Fr Doyle's inner life and to preclude the possibility of imagining any discrepancy between the later and the earlier stages of his ministry, however different be the setting.

We must now indicate some of the events and conditions which intervened before his next home-coming (19th February, 1917). Early in December, 1916, Fr. Doyle was changed from the Irish Fusiliers to the 8th Dublins; accordingly he was henceforth attached to the 48th Brigade which was also part of the 16th Division. He was naturally sorry to part with his men, some of whom cried when told that he was leaving. But he was once more among Irishmen and quite close to his old Battalion in the line. Fr. Doyle was not far from the convent of Locre where he had a comfortable week's billet when his six days' spell in the trenches was done. His dug-out merits a passing notice. Fr. Doyle gives a humorous description: "Picture a good respectable deep Irish ditch with plenty of water and mud in the bottom; scrape a fair-sized hole in the bank, cover the top with some sheets of iron, pile sandbags on top; and you have my dwelling. The door serves also as window and lets in not only light and air, but stray cats, rats galore and many creepy crawly beasties, not to mention rain, snow, and at times a breeze which must have been hatched at the North Pole." It was in this dug-out that Fr. F. M. Browne, S.J., met Fr. Doyle on the evening of 23rd December, 1916, when he came up with the 2nd and 9th Dublins who were relieving the 8th Dublins and R. I. Rifles. "During our whole time there," writes Fr. Browne, "we relieved each other in this way every eight days I remember how decent Fr. Willie used to be, coming up early on the relief days, before his Battalion came up, in order that I might get away. He knew how I hated it - and I did not hate it *half* as much as he did. We used generally to confess each other before leaving. We were very exact about waiting for each other, so that I do not think the (48th) Brigade was ever without a priest in the line." A curious thing about this chaplains' dug-out was that it was No. 13 on the side of the hill where Strong Point 13 was situated. [13] Moreover the two chaplains always violated the three candle superstition. Yet, in spite of the fact that it was one of the least protected there were no sandbags on portion of the roof and only two rows on the sides it was the only dug-out, existing in Dec. 1916, which was still untouched when the position was evacuated on 7th June, 1917. The men used to say, "Little Fr. Doyle's dug-out can't be hit!" [14] Whenever there was heavy firing, cooks and other non-combatants used to crowd into it. Once when Fr. Doyle hurriedly returned to get something he had forgotten, he found twelve men squeezed into the little dug-out which was hardly big enough to contain four!

Though this interval at the Front was comparatively quiet, it was not altogether devoid of incidents. For example, one day in December Fr. Doyle had just finished breakfast principally smoky tea tasting of petrol when he heard a shell come singing overhead with that peculiar note which to the experienced betokens proximity. He ran to the door the running consisted of one step and saw the explosion about two hundred yards away at the foot of the hill. Two more shells came, each fifty yards shorter in range than its predecessor, the direct line of fire passing through the dug-out, into which Fr. Doyle retired and anxiously awaited the unwelcome visitor. Fortunately the dug-out escaped with a shower of stones and clay on the roof. "It is a curious thing," he observes, "that I have never had a moment's hesitation nor ever felt fear in going into the greatest danger when duty called and some poor chap needed help. But to sit in cold blood, so to speak, and to wait to be blown to pieces or buried by a crump is an experience which tests one's nerves to the limit. Thank God, I have been able to conceal my feelings and so to help others to despise the danger, when I was just longing to take to my heels. An officer said to me at the Somme, 'I have often envied you your coolness and cheerfulness in hot corners.' I rather surprised him by saying that my real feeling was abject fear and I often shook like a leaf." That same afternoon another big shell came plump down close to where he was sitting at his lunch. "Three of my lads," he recounts, "came tearing in to my dug-out; they had nearly been sent to glory and felt they were safe with the priest. The poor priest cracks a joke or two, makes them forget their terror, and goes on with his lunch while every morsel sticks in his throat from fear and dread of the next shell. A moment passes, one, two, here it comes; dead silence and anxious faces for a second, and then we all laugh, for it is one of our own shells going over. Five minutes more and we know all danger has passed. It has been a memorable day for me, though only one of many such in the past."

The approach of Christmas meant the arrival of many presents to Fr. Doyle, which, needless to say, soon found their way to the Dublins. "L. and W.'s gift of 'smokes,'" he writes, "was a God-send. The parcel arrived in the midst of pelting rain which had been going on all day. I put on my big boots and coat, and trotted or I should rather say, waded up to the front line and gave each man a handful. You would not believe how it bucked them up or how welcome that smoke was to the brave fellows, as they stood there in mud and water, soaked through and through, hungry and sleepless. 'Sure, Father, it's little enough to bear for our sins,' is the way the rough lads look at their hardships. Almighty God would be a queer God if He did not forgive and forget whatever they may have done, with such a spirit as this."

Christmas itself Fr. Doyle had the good luck of spending in billets. He got permission from General Hickie to have Midnight Mass for his men in the Convent. The chapel was a fine large one, as in pre-war times over three hundred boarders and orphans were resident in the Convent; and by opening folding-doors the refectory was added to the chapel and thus doubled the available room. An hour before Mass every inch of space was filled, even inside the altar rails and in the corridor, while numbers had to remain in the open. Word had in fact gone round about the Mass, and men from other battalions came to hear it, some having walked several miles from another village. Before the Mass there was strenuous Confession-work. "We were kept hard at work hearing confessions all the evening till nine o'clock," writes Fr. Doyle, "the sort of Confessions you would like, the real serious business, no nonsense and no trimmings. As I was leaving the village church, a big soldier stopped' me to know, like our Gardiner Street friend, 'if the Fathers would be *sittin'* any more that night.' He was soon polished off, poor chap, and then insisted on escorting me home. He was one of my old boys, and having had a couple of glasses of beer 'It wouldn't scratch the back of your throat, Father, that French stuff' was in the mood to be complimentary. 'We miss you sorely, Father, in the battalion,' he said, 'we do be always talking about you.' Then in a tone of great confidence: 'Look, Father, there isn't a man who wouldn't give the whole of the world, if he had it, for your little toe! That's the truth.' The poor fellow meant well, but 'the stuff that would not scratch his throat' certainly helped his imagination and eloquence. I reached the Convent a bit tired, intending to have a rest before Mass, but found a string of the boys awaiting my arrival, determined that they at least would not be left out in the cold. I was kept hard at it hearing Confessions till the stroke of twelve and seldom had a more fruitful or consoling couple of hours' work, the love of the little Babe of Bethlehem softening hearts which all the terrors of war had failed to touch."

The Mass itself was a great success and brought consolation and spiritual peace to many a war-weary exile. This is what Fr. Doyle says:

"I sang the Mass, the girls' choir doing the needful. One of the Tommies, from Dolphin's Barn, sang the Adeste beautifully with just a touch of the sweet Dublin accent to remind us of 'home, sweet home,' the whole congregation joining in the chorus. It was a curious contrast: the chapel packed with men and officers, almost strangely quiet and reverent (the nuns were particularly struck by this), praying and singing most devoutly, while the big tears ran down many a rough cheek: outside the cannon boomed and the machine-guns spat out a hail of lead: peace and good will hatred and bloodshed!

"It was a Midnight Mass none of us will ever forget. A good 500 men came to Holy Communion, so that I was more than rewarded for my work."

On Christmas Day itself all was quiet up at the front line. The Germans hung white flags all along their barbed wire and did not fire a shot all day, neither did the English. For at least one day homage was paid to the Prince of Peace. Slaughter began next day with renewed energy. Two little incidents which Fr. Doyle chronicles as having occurred on 26th December may be here given in his own words.

"On St. Stephen's Day the men were engaged in a football match, when the Germans saw them, sent over a lovely shot at long range, which carried away the goal post the umpire gave a 'foul' and bursting in the middle of the men, killed three and wounded seven. The wounded were bandaged up and hurried off to hospital, the dead carried away for burial; and then the ball was kicked off once more, and the game went on as if nothing had happened. The Germans must have admired the cool pluck of the players, for they did not fire any more. This is just one little incident of the war, showing how little is thought of human life out here; it sounds callous but there is no room for sentiment in warfare, and I suppose it is better so."

The other incident is of more personal interest.

"I was riding on my bicycle past a waggon when the machine slipped, throwing me between the front and back wheels of the limber. Fortunately the horses were going very slowly and I was able, how I cannot tell, to roll out before the wheel went over my legs. I have no luck, you see, else I should be home now with a couple of broken legs, not to speak of a crushed head. The only commiseration I received was the remark of some passing officers that 'the Christmas champagne must have been very strong.'"

From a few more of his letters despatched at this time we can fill in some details and conditions of his life during the first two months of 1917. The

cold was intense. Fr. Doyle's references thereto are suggestive and eloquent:
"Jan. 27th. Cold!
Jan. 28th. Colder!!
Jan. 29th. More colder!!!
Jan. 30th.!!!!!!."

Once he apologises for not writing by saying that he could not hold a pencil in his fingers. "Before I have finished dressing in the mornings, not a very long process," he says, "the water in which I had washed is frozen again. [15] One has to be very careful, too, of one's feet, keeping them well rubbed with whale oil, otherwise you would soon find yourself unable to walk, with half a dozen frozen toes. A dug-out is not the warmest of spots just at present; but even if I felt inclined to growl, I should be ashamed to do so, seeing what the poor men are suffering in the trenches." One would fancy that living mostly in an open hole in the side of a ditch while the thermometer registered several degrees below zero, would cool even a saint's ardour for suffering. But here is the inexorable entry in his diary (1st Feb.): "Constant urging of Jesus to do 'hard things' for Him, things which cost. I shrink from sacrifice, but I know well He wants it and I can never be happy or at peace otherwise. I find I am falling off in the 100,000 aspirations. Have bound myself for a week by vow to make the full number."

Before starting a spell in the trenches Fr. Doyle used to endeavour to get as many men as possible to Confession on the previous evening and then to Mass and Holy Communion in the morning. As one battalion was some miles from the other, this meant an early start and ride or walk, through rain, slush and snow or, later, over hard-frozen ground "I have celebrated Mass in some strange places and under extraordinary conditions," he writes from the trenches on 28th December, "but somehow I was more than usually impressed this morning. The men had gathered in what was once a small convent. For with all their faults, their devil-may-care recklessness, they love the Mass and regret when they cannot come. It was a poor miserable place, cold and wet, the only light being two small candles. Yet they knelt there and prayed as only our own Irish poor can pray, with a fervour and faith which would touch the heart of any unbeliever. They are as shy as children, and men of few words; but I know they are grateful when one tries to be kind to them and warmly appreciate all that is done for their soul's interest." While in the trenches Fr. Doyle was not allowed to have Mass for his men, owing to the danger of having many gathered together near the firing line. So each morning he went back to where the reserve company was stationed, about twenty minutes' walk; which gave those who were free a chance of coming often to Holy Communion. On February 2nd, however, he was able to offer the Holy Sacrifice in the trenches, his chapel being a dug-out capable of holding ten or a dozen "But as my congregation numbered forty-six," he says, "the vacant space was small. How they all managed to squeeze in I cannot say. There was no question of kneeling down; the men simply stood silently and reverently round the little improvised altar of ammunition boxes, 'glad,' as one of them quaintly expressed it, 'to have a say in it.' Surely our Lord must have been glad also, for every one of the forty-six received Holy Communion, and went back to his post happy at heart and strengthened to face the hardships of these days and nights of cold." What a difference the Real Presence made in the ministrations and influence of a Catholic chaplain!

These Irish lads had a simple strong faith and reverence for the priest. That same afternoon (2nd Feb.) as Fr. Doyle was coming back from his round of the front line trench, he found it necessary to get under cover as shelling began. So he crawled into a hole in which six men were already crouching. No one could have been more welcome. "Come in, Father," cried one, "we're safe now, anyhow." On another similar occasion the remark was made, "Isn't the priest of God with us, what more do you want?" The poor fellows fancied that Fr. Doyle was invulnerable; no wonder when they saw him sauntering coolly around amid shells and splinters. He was always near to cheer them up when depressed and nervous and to minister to them when wounded. If a raid was to be made into the enemy trenches, he was sure to come round the line in the early hours of the morning to relieve the men's tense strain by a cheery word and to give each man Absolution before 'going over the top.' Often he had but one hour's sleep. Often too as he was fast asleep, tucked up in his blankets, dreaming pleasantly of something 'hot' - the favourite dream on these, cold nights would come the call, say, "Two men badly wounded in the firing line, Sir." In a few seconds he had pulled on his big boots and jumped into his waterproof and was darting down the trench, floundering along the dark ditch with an occasional star shell to intensify the gloom, perhaps being misdirected along these tortuous passages, more than once having to run the gauntlet of a machine gun. And all the while there was before the chaplain's mind the picture of "the wounded soldier, with his torn and bleeding body, lying out there in this awful biting cold, praying for the help that seems so slow in coming." Here is a description of one such 'sick-call' in the early hours of 13th January, 1917.

"I found the dying lad - he was not much more - so tightly jammed into a corner of the trench that it was almost impossible to get him out. Both legs were smashed, one in two or three places, so his chances of life were small, and there were other injuries as well. What a harrowing picture that scene would have made. A splendid young soldier, married only a month they told me, lying there pale and motionless in the mud and water, with the life crushed out of him by a cruel shell. The stretcher bearers hard at work binding up, as well as they may, his broken limbs; round about a group of silent Tommies looking on and wondering when will their turn come. Peace for a moment seems to have taken possession of the battle field, not a sound save the deep boom of some far-off gun and the stifled moans of the dying boy, while as if anxious to hide the scene, nature drops her soft mantle of snow on the living and dead alike.

"Then, while every head is bared, come the solemn words of absolution, 'Ego te absolvo, I absolve thee from thy sins. Depart Christian soul, and may the Lord Jesus Christ receive thee with a smiling and benign countenance. Amen.' Oh 1 surely the gentle Saviour did receive with open arms the brave lad, who had laid down his life for Him, and as I turned away I felt happy in the thought that his soul was already safe in that land where 'God will wipe away all sorrow from our eyes, for weeping and mourning shall be no more.'"

This was the message which the Catholic priest brought with him into this arena of brutal strife and cruel bloodshed, the vision of a world of peace. "God shall wipe away all tears from their eyes; and death shall be no more, nor mourning nor crying nor sorrow shall be any more, for the former things are passed away. And He that sat on the throne said, Behold I make all things new." (*Apoc.* 21. 4.) A new heaven and a new earth, let us hope, after the slaughter of so many guiltless and brave men and the agony of countless widows and orphans. "The cry of them hath entered into the ears of the Lord of sabaoth." (*Jas.* 5. 4.)

[1] The most advanced Red Cross position, where the wounded are first brought in by the battalion stretcher-bearers and where they are cleared by R.A.M.C. men to the Advanced Dressing Station. The chaplains of Irish regiments, where Catholics were so numerous, usually stationed themselves in the Regimental Aid Post.

[2] As a result of this experience Fr. Doyle at once learnt the burial service off by heart.

[3] The first night he arrived in the trenches he found two officers in the dug-out intended for him. "But," he adds characteristically, "as they were leaving next day I did not care to evict them." So he slept on a trench-board in "an unoccupied glorified rabbit-hole."

[4] A few weeks later this convent was utterly destroyed.

[5] On the anniversary of this escape he once more asserted: "Some invisible, almost physical, force turned me back to get my helmet.'"

[6] His Colonel recommended him for the Military Cross but was told that Fr. Doyle had not been long enough at the Front. So he was presented with the Parchment of Merit of the 49th Brigade.

[7] P. Goepfert, *Life of the Ven F. M. P. Liberman,* Dublin, 1880.

[8] He is alluding to the Blessed Sacrament which he was carrying. It was only two days after his superhuman work and miraculous recovery that he wrote in his diary: "Jesus said to me, You must make your life a martyrdom of prayer."

[9] In the first edition I quoted this extract from Fr. Doyle's letter of 28th June: "All last week there was fearful slaughter in our trenches. In fact I am quite worn out with carrying off the dead and burying them. To save time and trouble I made a big grave behind my dug-out and just pitched in the dead bodies; one gets very callous, I fear, during war." I am afraid I took too literally this elaborate joke so typical of Fr. Doyle. The next sentence, overlooked by me, gives the key. "I was much helped in this by a lady whom you know well, as it was her tins of deadly explosives which laid the enemy low; I have only to say *Keating's* once to make the foe flee."

[10] "We are fools for Christ's sake," says S. Paul (*I. Cor.* 4. 10), "but you are wise in Christ." Surely there is room for both types of goodness.

[11] A few months previously he had come across an account of Luisa de Carvajal who, as Fr. Doyle remarked in a letter, 'made herself the slave of her two maids.' (Cf. the C.T.S. pamphlet, *A Spanish Heroine in England.*) So he wrote in a let-

ter dated 26th October: "I am slowly learning the lesson Jesus brought me out here to teach me. The first and greatest is that I must have no will of my own, only His, and this in all things. It is hard to let everyone walk on you, even your own servant; but Jeus asks this and I try to let Him arrange all as He pleases. Result: yesterday I got no dinner, though I foresaw this would be the consequence of this planning." "My genius of an orderly," he wrote on 22nd December, "fried meat and pudding together and, with a smile of triumph on his face, brought both on the same plate to my dug-out. He is a good poor chap, but I would not recommend him as a cook."

[12] The M.C. was subsequently to Fr. Doyle's death presented to his Father.

[13] On the reverse slope of the ridge running along the valley between Wytschaete and Kemmel Hill. See map.

[14] The men used to say "Little Fr. Doyle," the adjective denoting endearment rather than stature Fr. Doyle was 5 ft. 10 ins. high.

[15] As a matter of fact the temperature was for over a fortnight many degrees below zero. During this time it took five or six hours of hard labour to dig a grave. "I think the limit was reached," writes Fr. Doyle, "when the wine froze in the chalice at Mass, and a lamp had to be procured to melt it before going on with the Consecration. I am thinking it will take fifty lamps to thaw out the poor chaplain!"

Chapter Ten - Military Chaplain

(1.) EASTER IN THE PAS DE CALAIS

FR. Doyle was only a week back in the trenches after his short trip home, when the 48th Brigade received welcome orders to move to the rear for a rest. The rest, however, seems to have consisted chiefly of extra drill, apparently in preparation for the coming offensive. "We left Belgium," he writes, "on the Saturday before Palm Sunday (*i.e.* 31st March) a glorious morning, dry under foot, with brilliant sunshine. The Brigade of four regiments made a gallant show, each headed by its band of pipers, and followed by the transport, etc. We were the first to move off, and so came in for an extra share of greetings from the villagers who turned out to see us pass, as fine a lot of sturdy lads as you could wish to gaze on, not to mention the gallant chaplain.

"Our march for the first day was not a very long one, something about 20 miles, but as every pace took us further and further from the trenches, the march was a labour of love. At mid-day a halt was called for dinner, which had been cooking slowly in the travelling kitchens which accompanied us, and in a few minutes every man was sitting by the road-side negotiating a big supply of hot meat and potatoes with a substantial chunk of bread. We, poor officers, were left to hunt for ourselves, a hunt which did not promise well at first, as the people in the estaminets were anything but friendly and said they had nothing to give us to eat. The reason, I discovered later, was that some British officers had gone away without paying their bill, a not uncommon thing I am sorry to say Eventually, with the help of a little palaver and my bad French, our party secured some excellent bread and butter, coffee, and a basket of fresh eggs. On again after an hour's rest; "Marching with a heavy rifle and full kit is no joke, hence our pace is slow. I often wonder how the poor men stick it, and stick it they do, most of them at least, till I have seen them drop senseless by the road from sheer exhaustion. As a rule they are left there to follow the column as best they can, for if they knew that falling out meant a lift, not many of the regiment would reach their destination on foot. To make matters worse we had to tramp along over the rough paved roads, which must be an invention of the Old Boy to torture people. At first the road feels like this **mmmmm** then after ten miles ΛΛΛΛΛΛ till at last you are positive that they have paved the way with spikes instead of stones, something in this fashion **AAAAAAAA** – my poor feet!

"At last the town we were bound for came in sight, and hopes of a good rest were high, when word came along that we were not to stay in that haven of peace and plenty but trudge on another three miles. The camel is supposed to be a patient animal, but Tommy can give him points any day. Our lodging was a mutilated country farmhouse, dirty and uncomfortable, the less said about it the better, but everyone was too tired to care much even though we officers, snoring on the floor, felt inclined to envy the sardines in their comfortable box.

"It was impossible to have Mass for the men in the morning, even though it was Palm Sunday, as there was much work to be done and we had to be off early I got away to the little village and offered up the Holy Sacrifice for them, emptied a coffee pot, and fell into my place as the regiment marched off. That was a hard day We were all stiff and sore for want of previous exercise, and in addition were well scourged by sleet, and rain, and snow, though at times the sun did its best to brighten things up a bit. Our luck turned when we reached our night's halting place, a good-sized town with comfortable billets. A big party of my men were quartered in the public ball-room, which contained an automatic organ. The last I saw of them was a score of 'couples' waltzing round quite gaily, without a sign of having the best part of a forty mile march to their credit.

"Monday saw us early afoot. Nothing of great interest, except that the country was becoming more hilly, and prettier, the stones harder, our feet and shoulders sorer, quite a longing for the repose of the trenches was springing up in many a heart. That evening ended our tramp, and here we have been ever since, and are to remain for some time longer, much to our joy. Probably we shall return to the same place we came from, but no one really knows our future movements."

"Here" was a little village in the Pas de Calais called Nordausques, on the right (east) of the main Saint-Omer-Calais road, about sixteen kilometres from each of these places. During this fortnight away from the sound of the guns, Fr. Doyle had a very busy time. So indeed had the men. "The morning," he says, "is given up to various exercises, one of which is the storming of a dummy German trench to the accompaniment of fearful, blood-curdling yells, enough to terrify the bravest enemy. The afternoon is spent at football and athletic sports, so that the men are having a good, if a strenuous, time. So is the poor Padre. My two regiments are quartered in two villages some miles apart. The four companies of each regiment in different hamlets, and to make things more inconvenient still, the two platoons of each company, thirty-two in all, are distributed in as many farmhouses. You can imagine I have no easy task to get round to see all my men, which I am anxious to do, so as to make sure that every man, if possible, gets to his Easter Duty. I have Mass every morning for them with many Communions daily, seventy to-day in one church; and then in the evening, having finished Devotions in one village and heard the men's Confessions, I ride over to the other for Rosary and Benediction, with more Confessions. In addition to this, there are many stray units scattered about in various places, machine-gunners, trench mortar battery men, etc., who, with the instruction of converts, prevent me from feeling time hanging on my hands."

This brief sojourn in the Pas de Calais enabled Fr. Doyle to celebrate Holy Week and Easter fittingly and thus to bring into these poor fellows' rest-interval emotions higher than those involved in rehearsals for future bloodshed. "On Spy Wednesday evening," he recounts, "after Benediction, I told the men I wanted nine volunteers to watch an hour during the following night before the Altar of Repose. I had barely finished speaking when the whole church made a rush up to the altar rails, and were keenly disappointed when I told them I could only take the first nine, though I could have had thirty an hour if I wanted them. I was touched by the poor fellows' generosity, for they had just finished a long, hard day's work with more before them. I got the nine men to bring their blankets into the little sacristy, and while one watched, the others slept. Surely our Lord must have been pleased with His Guard of Honour, and will bless them as only He can."

"Easter Sunday," he continues, "was quite a red letter day in the annals of the town. The regiment turned out in full strength, headed by the pipers, and crowded the sanctuary, every inch of the church, and out beyond. I had eight stalwart sergeants standing guard with fixed bayonets round the altar. At the Consecration and also at the Communion of the Mass the buglers sounded the Royal Salute which is only given to Monarchs. The guard at the word of command presented arms, and in our poor humble way we tried to do honour to the Almighty King of Kings on the day of His glorious triumph. I must not forget to add that the lassies and maidens did us the honour of coming to sing during Mass, casting many an envious glance (so rumour says) down on the handsome Irish lads praying so devoutly below."

No wonder that Fr. Doyle wrote a little later: "The faith and fervour of our Irish lads have made a great impression everywhere. I was once quite delighted to hear the cure rubbing it into his congregation, drawing a contrast between them and the Irish soldiers much to the disadvantage of the former." On Easter Sunday the good cure received a very tangible proof of Irish faith, for his collection bag contained a very unprecedented number of silver coins and five franc notes. When referring to his host in Nordausques, Fr. Doyle was led to make some general observations which may be worth recording:

"The village was blest by the presence of a holy, zealous cure, who seemed more anxious even than I, that the men should profit spiritually by their stay in his parish, and not only gave me every facility for my work, but himself helped as far as he could. I am convinced the French clergy will benefit very much by this war. All over the country, as you know, there are a multitude of tiny parishes, numbering often less than 200 souls including children. Even if all therein were practical Catholics, that would never give work for a priest with two wooden legs, the result being that a man with little to do often does less than he has to do, for abundance of work creates a spirit of zeal. Now that the ranks of the clergy have been sorely decimated, some three thousand French priests have been killed already, the survivors will have to multiply their efforts, and take charge of perhaps two or three parishes, much to their own personal advantage, I think."

The quiet if strenuous interlude amid the hills and pinewoods of the Pas de Calais came to an end all too soon. Low Sunday saw the men once more on their trenchward march, to the tune of cold pelting rain. That night a halt was made close to Saint-Omer, which gave Fr. Doyle an opportunity of visiting the twelfth century Cathedral and the old Jesuit College from which Stonyhurst was founded. The final stage of the journey was very trying, the men "had to face the cobble stones at six in the morning with a hurricane of rain and sleet which slashed like a whip," and arrived near Locre after tramping for over eight hours without a morsel of food. Once more life in and out of the trenches began.

(2.) MAY DEVOTIONS.

During the first fortnight of May the whole 48th Brigade consisting of 2nd, 8th, and 9th R. Dublin Fusiliers and 67th R. Irish Rifles was out of the trenches. The 2nd and 8th Dublins were in Locre and the 9th were at Clare Camp less than two miles west of Locre; the Rifles were at Kemmel, three miles east of Locre. (see map) The two chaplains, Fr. Browne and Fr. Doyle, availed themselves of this interval to organize Month of May devotions for the men. Every evening they had rosary, hymns, short sermon, and Benediction, followed by more hymns the 'boys' liked to hear their own voices. "One result of the devotions," writes Fr. Doyle, "has been the conversion of the only really black sheep in the regiment, a man very many years away from his duty, a hard morose character, upon whom I had many times failed to make any impression. I saw it was useless to argue with him, so at the beginning of the month I handed him over to the Blessed Virgin as a hopeless case with which she alone could deal. Last evening I met him and thought I would try once more to make him see the awful danger he was running of losing his soul. It was all no use, the devil had his prey too tightly held to shake him off like that. Then a thought struck me, 'Look,' I said, 'this is the month of May; you surely won't refuse our Blessed Lady.' The poor fellow fell on his knees, and there and then made his confession. I gave him Holy Communion and now he is a changed man, as happv as a lark."

In Fr. Doyle's notebook there are some hastily written outlines of talks to his men. Though they refer to an earlier period of the year during this May he preached chiefly on the Litany of our Lady [1] these rough notes will give us an idea of his practical homely style. Hence a few extracts will be given here.

"TWO SOLEMN MOMENTS."

"The end of that life which God gave to be spent in His service.

"A solemn moment when we lie down for the last time and look back upon our life which is gone for ever a precious talent entrusted to us, not to misuse, or bury in ground, like slothful servant, but to spend to good use till the Master comes.

"What is true of end of life equally true of end of a year. Another milestone of our journey to eternity. Just 365 days of a life already so short passed away. All of us have taken a big stride towards the hour of our death, and let us not forget it, the happiness and reward of Heaven.

"For a moment let us pause in this journey of life and look back. What strikes us? (1) God's goodness. How many began last year well and strong, full of plans, now dead. How many a young life quenched on the battle field. A million a week died. Ah 1 that time God's Providence has watched over us and protected us from danger. His love surrounded us.

"(2) Our opportunities. Life means more than the mere enjoyment of living, the time of sowing the seed of good works whose harvest we shall reap in Heaven; as long as we live we can merit. Pile up treasures in Heaven and increase our happiness for all eternity. Holy Mass, Sacraments, and prayers, every act we do for God means greater joy and glory.

"(3) Our return. Walk back the road our angel has kept the watch of every act. Tablets to mark spots where our acts were done, (*a*) Piles of curses, bad language. (*b*) Rows of empty beer bottles with all the sins they bring, (*c*) In a word little good but much evil.

"A sad picture, but we must not lose heart. Last mile of march, tighten knapsack on back, pull ourselves together and step out more hardy for the last mile. For many the last mile of life. We shall make it worthy of Him so good to us: more prayers, duty better done; greater watchfulness over our tongues and our evil inclinations, so that we may exclaim: I have fought a good fight, done my duty to my country and my God: a crown of glory."

"CONFESSION."

"A serious word: matter of life and death, eternal life, the salvation or damnation of many depend upon it. Going to the Front in a couple of weeks, in middle of shot and shell, in danger at any moment of instant death Are you ready to face God? None of us are afraid, it has to come sometime, but, 'know ye not there is a judgement?' 'O Lord preserve thou my soul,' So much depends on it.' What shall I do...to judge God won't be very angry about our sins He knows our weakness. He is a patient and merciful God but furious that we should appear before His holy Face covered with sin and every abomination when we could have got rid of all.

"The Wedding Garment. You know where you can find the white 'wedding garment,' find the pond of the Sacred Blood where to wash stains away. Don't delay. Hell is full of men who said 'later on,' God help the man who when he had the chance did not make his peace with God.

"I am pleading for your immortal souls; it matters little in the end whether we have been rich or poor, lives of hardship or pleasure, but to save one's soul or lose it matters much.

"It may be hard for some to square up accounts (not half so hard as you think) but a million times harder to burn in Hell, cursing your folly.

Confessions 4 to 6 in C. Hut."

"THIRD SUNDAY AFTER EPIPHANY."

"Saddened and disappointed not better response (Confession). Man who said he would go after Boer War. All intend to go; miserable. 'Later on,' Hell full of men who said 'later on,' Public house.

"To-day's Gospel (*S. Matthew* 8. 1-13.): Leper, awful sight, image of sin. 'Lord, Thou canst make me clean,'. Go show yourself to the priest,' Christ says same now. He is longing to forgive the past; to wash away every iniquity: to make sins red as scarlet, whiter than snow. For the sake of your immortal souls. Far harder to hear the awful words 'Depart ye cursed, I know ye not.'"

"FOURTH SUNDAY AFTER EPIPHANY."

"'Lord save us we perish' Gospel (*S. Matthew* 8. 23-27). Man's life a warfare; not for country, body, but immortal souls.

"Our Lord wishes to remind us of this incident hinted in gospel. We often find fierce storms springing up in our souls. We call them temptation, storms of anger impurity, craving for drink, stirred up by the devil who hopes' to lead us to destruction. We need not fear temptation.

(1) Not sin: Christ's temptation.

(2) A good sign Blessed Curé d'Ars. 'Became pleasing to God.' 'Prepare thy soul for temptation.'

(3) Merit.

"*Remedies,* (a) Avoid devil (women), (b) Pray. Christ knew danger of disciples. 'Came a great calm,' the reward of victory; remorse after sin; each victory means strength. 'Count it all joy.'"

(3.) THE PADRE IN THE TRENCHES.

Long before the titles of our Lady's Litany were exhausted it was time to return to the trenches. At the conclusion of such a respite the chaplain used to give General Absolution. In a letter written to his father about this time Fr. Doyle thus describes and comments on the touching scene:

"We reap a good harvest with confessions every day, at any time the men care to come, but there are many who for one reason or another cannot get away, hence before going into the trenches, which nearly always means death for some poor fellows, we give them a General Absolution. I do not think there can be a more touching or soul inspiring sight than to see a whole regiment go down upon their knees, to hear that wave of prayer go up to Heaven, as hundreds of voices repeat the Act of Contrition in unison, 'My God, I am heartily sorry that I have ever offended You.' There is an earnestness and a depth of feeling in their voices, which tells of real sorrow, even if one did not see the tears gather in the eyes of more than one brave man. And then the deep, reverent silence as the priest raises his hand over the bowed heads and pronounces the words of forgiveness. Human nature is ever human nature, and even Irish soldiers commit sins; you can picture then the feelings of any priest standing before that kneeling throng, knowing that by the power of God his words have washed every soul pure and white. I love to picture the foul garment of sin falling from every man there at the words of Absolution, and to watch the look of peace and happiness on the men's faces as they lift their rifles and fall into rank, ready for anything, even 'to meet the divil himself,' as my friend of long ago shouted out as he marched by me. Don't you agree with me that the consolations and real joys of my life far outweigh the hard things and privations, even if there were no 'little nest-egg' being laid up in a better and happier world?"

It is when we read such an extract that we most clearly realise the inner motive-power which sustained Fr. Doyle amid 'the hard things and privations,' far more irksome and painful to him than to one mentally less, idealistic or physically less highly strung and sensitive. He was brave and untiring, not because he found life congenial, but because he found it so hard. His interests were concentrated on his mission to be 'another Christ'; this was the ideal in whose consuming fire all other ideas were fused. "I can say with all truth," he wrote, "I have never spent a happier year. For though I have occasionally felt as if the limit of endurance were reached, I have never lost my good spirits, which have helped me over many a rough road." He needed all his courage. What a life it was! From extremes of heat to unimagined depths of cold; for days water above, below, everywhere, and then from this aquatic misery to burning sun and parching thirst. There were long tramps by day, with pack and equipment growing heavier each hour, till one became a mass of sweat and mud; nights without sleep, burying the dead or stumbling along trenches to minister to the dying; nights, too, made hideous by bursting shells or the still more terrible warning of approaching poison-gas. Our thoughts go back to Paul of Tarsus, whose life was spent "in journeying often, in perils of waters, in perils of robbers, ... in labour and painfulness, in much watchings, in hunger and thirst, in fastings often, in cold and nakedness." (*II. Cor.* II. 26.) [2] Yet, as. Fr. Doyle pointed out, these physical sufferings were light in comparison with that constant sense of insecurity and suspense, the strain of being *never* really out of danger for miles behind the front, the oppressive feeling of waiting for the stroke of an uplifted sword. "Pain and privation," he writes, "are only momentary, they quickly pass and become even delightfully sweet, if only borne in the spirit with which many of my grand boys take these things: 'Shure, Father, it's not worth talking about; after all, is it not well to have some little thing to suffer for God and His Blessed Mother?' But the craven fear which at times clutches the heart, the involuntary shrinking and dread of human nature at danger and even death, are things which cannot be expressed in words. An officer, who had gone through a good deal himself, said to me recently: 'I never realized before what our Lord must have suffered in the Garden of Gethsemane when He began to fear and grow sorrowful.' Yet His grace is always there to help one when most needed, and though the life is hard and trying at times, I have never ceased to thank Him for the privilege (I can call it nothing else) of sharing in this glorious work."

In a letter written to his father on 25th July, he invited him to come in spirit with him on a visit to the trenches. He is thus led to describe a typical incident of his 'glorious work,' which must have been as consoling to the father as it was to the son. "There is a party coming towards us. down the trench," he writes; "and as they have the right of way, we must squeeze into a corner to let them pass. A poor wounded fellow lies on a stretcher with death already stamped on his face. The bearers lay their burden gently down these rough men have the tender heart of a woman for the wounded reverently uncover their heads and withdraw a little as the priest kneels behind the dying man's head. A glance at the identity-disc on his wrist, stamped with his name, regiment, and religion, shows that he is a Catholic for there are few men, no matter what their belief, who do not carry a rosary or a Catholic medal round their necks. I wonder what the non-Catholic Padres think of this fearful increase of Idolatry! 'Ah, Father, is that you? Thanks be to God for His goodness in sending you; my heart was sore to die without the priest. Father the voice was weak and came in gasps Father, oh, I am glad now, I always tried to live a good life, it makes death so easy.' The Rites of the Church were quickly administered though it was hard to find a sound spot on that poor smashed face for the Holy Oils, and my hands were covered with his blood. The moaning stopped; I have noticed that a score of times, as if the very touch of the anointing brought relief. I pressed the crucifix to his lips as he murmured after me: 'My Jesus mercy,' and then as I gave him the Last Blessing his head fell back, and the loving arms of Jesus were pressing to His Sacred Heart the soul of another of His friends, who I trust will not forget, amid the joys of Heaven, him who was sent across his path to help him in his last moments.

"It is little things like this which help one over the hard days and sweeten a life which has little in it naturally attractive. If you had come up the trench with me twelve months ago on the morning of the gas attack and watched that same scene repeated hour after hour, I think you would have thanked God for the big share you have in the salvation of so many souls."

We are able to narrate one or two incidents of 'this glorious work' which occurred at this period. "The enemy for once did me a good turn," he writes on 22nd May. "I had arranged to hear the men's confessions shortly before he opened fire, and a couple of well-directed shells helped my work immensely by putting the fear of God into the hearts of a few careless boys who might not have troubled about coining near me otherwise. I wonder were the Sacraments ever administered under stranger circumstances? Picture my little dug-out (none too big at any time) packed with men who had dashed in for shelter from the splinters and shrapnel coming down like hail. In one corner is kneeling a poor fellow recently joined who has not 'knelt to the priest,' as the men quaintly say, for many a day trying to make his Confession. I make short work of that, for a shower of clay and stones falling at the door, is a gentle hint that the 'crumps' are getting uncomfortably near, and I want to give him Absolution in case an unwelcome visitor should walk in. Then, while the ground outside rocks and seems to split with the crash of the shells, I give them all Holy Communion, say a short prayer, and perform the wonderful feat of packing a few more men into our sardine tin of a house.

"As soon as I got the chance, I slipped round to see how many casualties there were, for I thought not a mouse could survive the bombardment. Thank God, no one was killed or even badly hit, and the firing having ceased, we could breathe again. I was walking up the trench from the dressing station when I suddenly heard the scream of another shell...It was then I realized my good fortune. There are two ways to my dug-out, and naturally I choose the shorter. This time, without any special reason, I went by the longer way; and it was well I did, for the shell pitched in the other trench, and probably would have caught me nicely as I went by. But instead of that it wreaked its vengeance on my unfortunate orderly, who was close by in his dug-out, sending him spinning on his head but otherwise not injuring him I found another string of men awaiting my return in order to get Confession and Holy Communion. In fact I had quite a busy evening, thanks once more to Fritz's High Explosive, which has a wonderful persuasive effect of its own. I am wondering how many pounds of H.E. I shall require when giving my next retreat."

In his letter of 29th May he records an exploit of his in which, he thinks, "there was really little danger." "A few nights ago," he writes, "I had been along the front line as usual to give the men a General Absolution which they are almost as anxious to receive for the comfort it will be for their friends at home, should they fall, as for themselves. I was coming down to the advanced dressing station, when I learned that a small party had 'gone over the top' on our right, though I had been told the raid was only from the left. When I got to the spot I found they had all gone and were lying well out in No Man's Land. It was a case of Mahomet and the mountain once more. The poor 'mountain' could not come back, though they were just longing to, but the prophet could go out, could he not? So Mahomet rolled over the top of the sandbags into a friendly shell hole, and started to crawl on his hands and knees and stomach towards the German trenches. Mahomet, being only a prophet, was allowed to use bad language, of which privilege he availed himself, so report goes, to the full, for the ground was covered with bits of broken barbed wire, shell splinters, nettles, etc., etc., and the poor prophet on his penitential pilgrimage left behind him much honest sweat and not a few drops of blood.

"That was a strange scene! A group of men lying on their faces, waiting for certain death to come to some of them, whispering a fervent act of contrition, and God's priest, feeling mighty uncomfortable and wishing he were safely in bed a thousand miles away, raising his hand in Absolution over the prostrate figures. One boy, some little distance off, thinking the Absolution had not reached him, knelt bolt upright, and made an act of contrition you could have heard in Berlin, nearly giving the whole show away and drawing the enemy's fire.

"There was really little danger, as shell holes were plentiful, but not a little consolation when I buried the dead next day to think that none of them had died without Absolution. I was more afraid getting back into our own trenches; for sentries, seeing a man coming from the direction of No Man's Land, do not bother much about asking questions and object to nocturnal visitors."

The next night (24th May) another raid was made and Fr -Doyle recounts how he was able to help a poor prisoner. "One German prisoner, badly wounded in the leg, was brought in," he writes. "He knew only a few words of English, but spoke French fluently. I try to do all I can for the unfortunate prisoners, as sometimes not much sympathy is shown them, and they have evidently been drilled into believing that we promptly roast and eat them alive. I gave him a drink, made him as comfortable as possible, and then seeing a rosary in his pocket, asked him was he a Catholic. 'I am a Catholic priest,' I said, 'and you need not have any fear.' 'Ah, monsieur.' he replied, 'vous etes un vrai pretre' (you are a true priest). He gave me his home address in Germany, and asked me to write to his parents. 'Poor father and mother will be uneasy,' he said, as his eyes filled with tears. 'O mon Dieu, how I am suffering, but I offer it all up to You.' I hope to get a letter through by means of the Swiss Red Cross, which will be a comfort to his anxious parents, who seem good pious souls."

What a consoling little picture of Christian charity rising above human strife and passion! What an insight into the noble peace-mission of "a true priest"!

One other quotation will give a further little illustration of Fr. Doyle's ministry while his men were in reserve. Early on the morning of Sunday, 3rd June, they were relieved, after a rather strenuous time of sixteen days in the front line, more than usually trying for want of sleep. As Mass for the men was not till mid-day, Fr. Doyle had "planned a glorious *soak* in the convent, an unblushing gluttonous feast of blankets, for the poor old tired 'oss." But through some misunderstanding his orderly did not turn up with his horse, so he had to trudge back with his heavy pack. On reaching his billet at 2 a.m., he found the door of his room locked. "I had not the heart to wake up the poor nuns," he says; "and after all when one is fast asleep, is not a hard plank just as soft as a feather bed? You see I am becoming a bit of a philosopher!" "The next morning," he continues, "I had Mass in a field close to the camp. I wish you could have seen the men as they knelt in a hollow square round the improvised altar, brilliant sunshine overhead, and the soft green of spring about them.

They looked so happy, poor lads, as I went down one line and up the other, giving them the Bread of the Strong, and I could not help thinking of another scene long ago when our Lord made the multitude sit down on the grass, and fed them miraculously with the seven loaves. Before I got to the end of my 700 Communions I felt wondrous pity for the twelve Apostles, for they must have been jolly tired also.

"At present I am living in the camp which is further back even than the convent, out in the green fields of the country, most peaceful and restful. I have a little tent to myself, but have Rosary, Mass, Confessions, etc., out in the open. The men have absolutely no human respect, and kneel in rows waiting for their turn 'to scrape,' [3] as if they were in the church at home, paying no heed to the endless stream of traffic. I am sure non-Catholics must wonder what on earth we are at."

While solicitous for his flock when under his charge, he was not unmindful of them when dead. The following letter, which appeared in the *Irish Catholic* for 26th May, 1917, was written by Fr. Doyle.

"Dear Sir - One is often struck, on glancing over the papers, at the numerous appeals made to provide 'comforts for our troops,' but no one ever seems to think that the souls of those who have fallen in battle may possibly be in need of much greater comfort than the bodies of their comrades who survive

"With all the spiritual help now at their disposal, even in the very firing line, we may be fairly confident that few, if any, of our Catholic men are unprepared to meet Almighty God. That does not mean they are fit for Heaven. God's justice must be fully satisfied, and the debt of forgiven sin fully atoned for in Purgatory. Hence I venture to appeal to the great charity of your readers to provide 'comforts for our dead soldiers' by 'having Masses offered for their souls. Remembrance of our dead and gratitude are virtues dear to every

Irish heart. Our brave lads have suffered and fought and died for us. They have nobly given their lives for God and country. It is now our turn to make some slight sacrifice, so that they may soon enter into the joy of eternal rest. Very faithfully yours, NEMO."

(4.) WYTSCHAETE RIDGE.

(see map)

"To save you unnecessary anxiety," Fr. Doyle wrote to his father on nth June, "I told you in my last note (that of 5th June already quoted) that we were again on the march, which was quite true, but the march was not backwards but towards the enemy. When I wrote we were on the eve of one of the biggest battles of the war, details of which you will have read in the morning papers." In another confidential letter of the same date (5th June), however, he was more communicative. "I have not told them at home," he wrote, "and do not want them to know but we have had a terrible time for the last three weeks, constant and increasing shelling, with many wonderful escapes. We are on the eve of a tremendous battle and the danger will be very great. Sometimes I think God wishes the actual sacrifice of my life the offering of it was made long ago. But if so, that almost useless life will be given most joyfully. I feel wonderful peace and confidence in leaving myself absolutely in God's Hands. Only I know it would not be right, I would like never to take shelter from bursting shells; and up to a few days ago, till ordered by the Colonel, I never wore a steel helmet. I want to give myself absolutely to Him to do with me just as He pleases, to strike or kill me, as He wishes, trying to go along bravely and truthfully, looking up into His loving Face, for surely He knows best. On the other hand I have the conviction, growing stronger every day, that nothing serious will befall me; a wound would be joy, 'to shed one's blood for Jesus,' when I would gladly empty my veins for Him. Otherwise why would He impress so strongly on my mind that this 'novitiate' out here is only the preparation for my real life's work? Why does He put so many schemes and plans into my mind? Why has He mapped out several little books, one of which will do great good, I believe, because every word will be His? Then the possibilities of the Holy Childhood have gripped me, and His little perishing souls, 10,000 a day, seem ever to be pleading for a sight of Jesus! Yet I have laid even the desire to do these things at His Feet, and I strive might and main to have no will but His, for this pleases Him most. I am very calm and trustful in face of the awful storm so soon to burst. But could it be otherwise, when He is ever with me and when I know that should I fall, it will only be into His Arms of love?"

Fr. Doyle atoned for his previous reticence by sending his father, immediately after the battle, a rather long account of his own experiences during the few weeks prior to the attack of 7th June, as well as during the actual engagement.

"For months past preparations on a gigantic scale were being made for the coming attack, every detail of which the Germans knew. For some reason or other they left us in comparative peace for a long time, and then suddenly started to shell us day and night.

"We had just gone into the line for our eight days, and a lively week it was. How we escaped uninjured from the rain of shells which fell round about us, I do not know. The men had practically no shelter, as their dug-outs would scarcely keep out a respectable fat bullet, not to speak of a nine or twelve-inch shell (this is the diameter of the shell-base, not its length), and used to run to me for protection like so many big children with a confidence I was far from feeling, that the 'priest' was a far better protection than yards of reinforced concrete.

"I have come back to my little home more than once in the early hours of the morning to find it packed with two-legged smoking 'sardines,' quite happy and content in spite of Fritz's crumps, to be greeted with the remark: 'We were just saying, Father, that this is a lucky dug-out, and it is well for us that we have your Reverence with us.' God bless them for their simple faith and trust in Him, for I feel I owe it to my brave boys that we were not blown sky-high twenty times. In fact the 'Padre's Dug-out' was quite a standing joke among the officers, who used to come after a *strafe* to see how much of it was left.

"Our next eight days in support were even worse, as the Germans had brought up more guns, and used them freely. Our Head-Quarters was a good sized house, which had never been touched since the war began, being well screened by a wood behind. We were in the middle of dinner the first evening, when in quick succession half a dozen shells burst close around. It was only later on we learned the reason of this unexpected attack. One of the officers, in spite of strict orders to the contrary, had gone on a raid with a map in his pocket on which he had marked various positions, our H.Q. among others. He was captured, and 'the fat was in the fire.' Owing to someone's carelessness no provision had been made for protection against bombardment, and we had to stand in the open with our backs against a brick wall, watching the shells pitching right and left and in front, wondering when would our turn come.

"Three or four times each night at a couple of hours' interval the torture began afresh, just as one was dozing off to sleep, sending men and officers flying for safety to the 'shady side' of the house. Shelling in the open or in a trench is not so pleasant, but this was horrible, for we knew the guns were searching for the spot so obligingly marked on our map. One morning about 2 a.m. I had gone down the road to look after some men, when two shells smashed in the roof of the house I had left, killing five of our staff, and nearly knocking out the Colonel and two other officers. We got shelter in another Mess only to find that this was a marked spot too, though the aim was not so accurate.

"All during this time our guns were keeping up the bombardment of the Wytschaete Village and Ridge, which the 16th Irish Division were to storm. I think I am accurate in saying that not for ten minutes at any time during these sixteen days did the roar of our guns cease. At times one or two batteries would keep the ball rolling, and then with a majestic crash every gun, from the rasping field piece up to the giant fifteen-inch howitzer, would answer to the call of battle, till not only the walls of the ruined houses shook and swayed but the very ground quivered. You may fancy the amount of rest and sleep we got during that period, seeing that we lived in front of the cannon, many of them only a few yards away, while the Germans with clockwork regularity pelted us with shells from behind. If you want to know what a real headache is like, or to experience the pleasure of every nerve in your body jumping about like so many mad cats, take the shilling, and spend a week or two near the next position we hope to capture.

"All things come to an end, and at last we finished our sixteen days Limbo (Purgatory is not near enough to Hell!) and marched back to the rest camp with tongues, to vary the metaphor, hanging out for sleep. That night a villainous enemy airman dropped bombs close to our tents, and the following day the guns shelled us, far back as we were. We must be a bad lot, for 'there is no rest for the wicked,' they say. For once my heart stood still with fear, not so much for myself as for the poor men. There we were on the side of a hill, four regiments crowded together, our only protection the canvas walls of the tents, with big shells creeping nearer and nearer.

"Orders had been given to scatter, but it takes time to disperse some 4,000 men, and one well-aimed shell would play havoc in such a crowd. Forgive me for mentioning this little incident. I want to do so in gratitude and to bring out the wonderful love and tenderness of our Divine Lord for His own Irish soldiers, not to claim the smallest credit for myself. I had brought the Ciborium to my tent after Mass, as the men were coming to Confession and Holy Communion all the day. Human beings could not help us then, but He, Who stilled the tempest, could do so easily. There was only time for one earnest 'Lord save my poor, boys,' for at any moment the camp might be shambles full of dead and dying, before I rushed out into the open. As I did a shell landed a few feet behind an officer, sending him spinning, but he jumped up unhurt. A moment more down came a second right into the middle of a group of men, and, miracle of miracles, failed to explode. A third burst so close to another party I was sure half were killed, though I must confess I never saw dead men run so fast before. And so it went on, first on one side, then on another, but at the end of the half hour's bombardment not a single man of the four regiments had been hit, even slightly.

"The chances of a good night's rest were at an end, for we had to turn out to sleep, as best we could, under the hedges and trees of the surrounding country. It was a big loss to the men, as once the attack (which was due in three days) began, there was little chance of closing an eye. We priests say a prayer at the end of our Office asking the Lord to grant *noctem quietam* (a peaceful night). I never fully appreciated this prayer till now, and have said it more than once lately with heart-felt earnestness.

"These few days were busy ones for us, Fr. Browne and myself. The men knew they were preparing for death, and availed themselves fully of the opportunities we were able to give them. Fortunately the weather was gloriously fine, so there was no difficulty about Mass in the open. There was a general cleaning up and polishing of souls, some of them not too shiny, a General Communion on two days for all the men and officers, with the usual rosary and prayers each evening, consoling for us, because we felt the men had done their best, and the future might be safely left in the hands of the great and merciful Judge.

"I fancy the feelings of most of us were the same: awe, not a little fear, and a big longing to have it all over. We knew the seriousness of the task before us, for Wytschaete Hill, the key of the whole position, was regarded even by the General Staff, as almost impregnable, and the German boast was that it would never be taken. Without detracting one bit from the dash and bravery of our Irish lads, which won unstinted praise from everyone - 'The best show I have seen since I came to France,' said Sir D. Haig - full credit must be given to the artillery for pounding the defences to dust, without which our troops would still be on this side of the 300 ft. hill, instead of a couple of miles on the other side. Everyone felt the losses would be severe, if not colossal, and, as we sat on our hill and gazed down into the valley beyond, crammed with roaring guns, and watched the shells bursting in hundreds, knowing the moment was near for us to march down into that hell of fire and smoke, it was small wonder if many a stout heart quaked, and thoughts flew to the dear ones at home, whom one hardly hoped to see again.

"There were many little touching incidents during these days; one especially I shall not easily forget. When the men had left the field after the evening devotions, I noticed a group of three young boys, brothers I think, still kneeling saying another rosary. They knew it was probably their last meeting on earth and they seemed to cling to one another for mutual comfort and strength, and instinctively turned to the Blessed Mother to help them in their hour of need. There they knelt as if they were alone and unobserved, their hands clasped and faces turned towards heaven, with such a look of beseeching earnestness that the Mother of Mercy surely must have heard their prayer: 'Holy Mary pray for us now at the hour of our death. Amen.'"

In a subsequent letter (25th July) Fr. Doyle refers to some of the talks which he gave to his men during, these days. So the passage may be inserted here "Before the last big battle," he writes, "I gave the men a few talks about Heaven, where I hope many of them are now. I have the satisfaction of knowing that what I said helped the poor fellows a good deal, and made them face the coming dangers with a stouter heart. The man of whom I told you last year, who said he 'did not care a d--- for all the b--- German shells, (please excuse language), because he was with the priest that morning,' expressed in a forcible manner what many another felt, that when all is said and done, a man's religion is his biggest (and only true) consolation, and the source of real courage. I reminded them of the saying of the Blessed Cure d' Ars: 'When we get to Heaven and see all the happiness which is to be ours for ever, we shall wonder why we wanted to remain even one day on earth.' God hides these things from our eyes, for if we saw now 'the things God has prepared for those that love Him,' life on earth would be absolutely unlivable, and so, I said, the man who falls in the charge is not the loser but immensely the gainer, is not the unlucky one but the fortunate and blessed. You should have seen how the poor chaps drank in every word, for rough and ignorant as they are, they are full of Faith; though I fear their conception of an ideal Heaven, for some at least, would be a place of unlimited drinks and no closing time There was a broad smile when I told them so!"

"On Wednesday night, June 6th," continues Fr. Doyle, "we moved off, so as to be in position for the attack at 3.10 a.m. on Thursday morning, the Feast of Corpus Christi, I got to the little temporary chapel at the rear of our trenches soon after twelve, and tried to get a few moments' sleep before beginning Mass at one, a hopeless task, you may imagine, as the guns had gone raging mad. I could not help thinking would this be my last Mass, though I really never had any doubt the good God would continue to protect me in the future as He had done in the past, and I was quite content to leave myself in His hands, since He knows what is best for us all."

It was 11.50 when Fr. Browne and Fr. Doyle reached the little sandbag chapel which they had used when holding the line. There they lay down for an hour's rest on two stretchers borrowed from the huge pile waiting nearby for the morrow's bloody work. Leaving their servant lying fast asleep through sheer exhaustion, the two chaplains got up at 1 a.m. and prepared the altar. Fr. Doyle said Mass first and was served by Fr Browne, who, not having yet made his Last Vows, renewed his Vows at the Mass, as he always did at home on Corpus Christi. It was surely a weird and solemn Renovation. While Fr. Browne unvested after his own Mass and packed up the things, Fr. Doyle and his servant (now awake) prepared breakfast. At 2.30 the two chaplains put on their battle kit and made for their respective aid posts. Up near the front line, along the hedgerows, the battalions of the 48th Brigade were massed in support position. Their task was not to attack, but to follow up and consolidate and, should need arise, to help the leading brigades. "As I walked up to my post at the advanced dressing station," says Fr. Doyle, "I prayed for that peace of a perfect trust which seems to be so pleasing to our Lord." And he repeated to himself the verses of a little leaflet which a friend had sent to him when he first became chaplain:

> Oh! for the peace of a perfect trust,
>   My loving" God, in Thee;
> Unwavering faith that never doubts
>   Thou choosest best for me.

In this spirit, in which he had so often schooled himself during his years of spiritual struggle, he waited for the coming crash of battle.

"It wanted half an hour," he continues, "to zero time the phrase used for the moment of attack. The guns had ceased firing, to give their crews a breathing space before the storm of battle broke; for a moment at least there was peace on earth and a calm which was almost more trying than the previous roar to us who knew what was coming. A prisoner told us that the enemy knew we were about to attack, but did not expect it for another couple of days. I pictured to myself our men, row upon row waiting in the darkness for the word to charge, and on the other side the Germans in their trenches and dug-outs, little thinking that seven huge mines were laid under their feet, needing only a spark to blow them into eternity. The tension of waiting was terrific, the strain almost unbearable. One felt inclined to scream out and send them warning. But all I could do was to stand on top of the trench and give them Absolution, trusting to God's mercy to speed it so far.

"Even now I can scarcely think of the scene which followed without trembling with horror. Punctually to the second at 3.10 a.m. there was a deep muffled roar; the ground in front of where I stood rose up, as if some giant had wakened from his sleep and was bursting his way through the earth's crust, and then I saw seven huge columns of smoke and flames shoot hundreds of feet into the air, while masses of clay and stones, tons in weight, were hurled about like pebbles. I never before realized what an earthquake was like, for not only did the ground quiver and shake, but actually rocked backwards and forwards, so that I kept on my feet with difficulty.

"Later on I examined one of the mine craters, an appalling sight, for I knew that many a brave man, torn and burnt by the explosion, lay buried there. If you expand very considerably the old Dalkey quarry near the railway and dig it twice as deep, you will have some idea of the size of one of our mine craters, twenty of which were blown along the front of our attack.

"Before the débris of the mines had begun to fall to earth, the 'wild Irish' were over the top of the trenches and on the enemy, though it seemed certain they must be killed to a man by the falling avalanche of clay. Even a stolid English Colonel standing near was moved to enthusiasm 'My God!' he said, 'what soldiers! They fear neither man nor devil!' Why should they? They had made their peace with God. He had given them His own Sacred Body to eat that morning, and they were going out now to face death, as only Irish Catholic lads can do, confident of victory and cheered by the thought that the reward of Heaven was theirs. Nothing could stop such a rush, and so fast was the advance that the leading files actually ran into the barrage of our own guns, and had to retire.

"Meanwhile hell itself seemed to have been let loose. With the roar of the mines came the deafening crash of our guns, hundreds of them. This much I can say: never before, even in this war, have so many batteries especially of heavy pieces been concentrated on one objective, and how the Germans were able to put up the resistance they did was a marvel to everybody, for our shells fell like hailstones. In a few moments they took up the challenge, and soon things on our side became warm and lively.

"In a short time the wounded began to come in, and a number of German prisoners, many of them wounded, also. I must confess my heart goes out to these unfortunate soldiers, whose sufferings have been terrific. I can't share the general sentiment that 'they deserve what they get and one better.' For after all are they not children of the same loving Saviour Who said: 'Whatever you do to one of these My least ones you do it to Me.' I try to show them any little kindness I can, getting them a drink, taking off the boots from smashed and bleeding feet, or helping to dress their wounds, and more than once I have seen the eyes of these rough men fill with tears as I bent over them, or felt my hand squeezed in gratitude.

"My men did not go over in the first wave; they were held in reserve to move up as soon as the first objective was taken, hold the position and resist any counter attack. Most of them were waiting behind a thick sand-bag wall not far from the advanced dressing station where I was, which enabled me to keep an eye upon them.

"The shells were coming over thick and fast now, and at last, what I expected and feared happened. A big 'crump' (shrapnel) hit the wall fair and square, blew three men into the field 50 yards away, and buried five others who were in a small dug-out. For a moment I hesitated, for the horrible sight fairly knocked the 'starch' out of me and a couple more 'crumps' did not help to restore my courage.

"I climbed over the trench and ran across the open, as abject a coward as ever walked on two legs, till I reached the three dying men, and then the 'perfect trust' came back to me and I felt no fear. A few seconds sufficed to absolve and anoint my poor boys, and I jumped to my feet, only to go down on my face faster than I got up, as an express train from Berlin roared by.

"The five buried men were calling for help, but the others standing around seemed paralysed with fear, all save one sergeant, whose language was worthy of the occasion and rose to a noble height of sublimity. He was working like a Trojan, tearing the sand-bags aside, and welcomed my help with a mingled blessing and curse. The others joined in with pick and shovel, digging and pulling, till the sweat streamed from our faces, and the blood from our hands, but we got three of the buried men out alive, the other two had been killed by the explosion. [4]

"Once again I had evidence of the immense confidence our men have in the priest. It was quite evident they were rapidly becoming demoralized, as the best of troops will who have to remain inactive under heavy shell fire. Little groups were running from place to place for greater shelter, and the .officers seemed to have lost control. I walked along the line of men, crouching behind the sand-bag wall, and was amused to see the ripple of smiles light up the terrified lads' faces, (so many are mere boys) as I went by. By the time I got back again the men were laughing and chatting as if all danger was miles away, for quite unintentionally, I had given them courage by walking along without my gas mask or steel helmet, both of which I had; forgotten in my hurry.

"When the regiment moved forward, the Doctor and I went with it. By this time the 'impregnable' ridge was in our hands and the enemy retreating down the far side. I spent the rest of that memorable day wandering over the battlefield looking for the wounded, and had the happiness, of helping many a poor chap, for shells were flying about, on all sides."

"As I knew there was no chance of saying Mass next morning, I had taken the precaution of bringing several Consecrated Particles with me, so that I should not be deprived of Holy Communion. It was the Feast of Corpus Christi and I thought of the many processions of the Blessed Sacrament which were being held at that moment all over the world. Surely there never was a stranger one than mine that day, as I carried the God of Consolation in my unworthy arms over the blood-stained battle field. There was no music to welcome His coming save the scream of a passing shell; the flowers that strewed His path were the broken, bleeding bodies of those for whom He had once died; and the only Altar of Repose He could find was the heart of one who was working for Him alone, striving in a feeble way to make Him some return for all His love and goodness

"I shall make no attempt to describe the battle field. Thank God, our casualties were extraordinarily light, but there was not a yard of ground on which a shell had not pitched, which made getting about very laborious, sliding down one crater and climbing up the next, and also increased the difficulty of finding the wounded. [5]

"Providence certainly directed my steps on two occasions at least. I came across one young soldier horribly mutilated, all his intestines hanging out, but quite conscious and able to speak to me. He lived long enough to receive the Last Sacraments, and died in peace. Later on in the evening I was going in a certain direction when something made me turn back when I saw in the distance a man being carried on a stretcher. He belonged to the artillery, and had no chance of seeing a priest for a long time, but he must have been a good lad, for Mary did not forget him 'at the hour of his death.'

"The things I remember best of that day of twenty-four hours' work are: the sweltering heat, a devouring thirst which comes from the excitement of battle, physical weakness from want of food, and a weariness and footsoreness which I trust will pay a little at least of St. Peter's heavy score against me."

The next two days, Friday and Saturday, were a repetition of Thursday. Fighting was practically over, but guns were being brought up and positions consolidated. Fr. Doyle had little rest and plenty to do, and on at least one occasion had a very narrow escape from an eight-inch shell. Early on Sunday morning the exhausted Battalions were relieved. After the battle the men marched back by easy stages to the rear, and in a few days were settled down 'in quite a nice part of France,' billeted in comfortable farmhouses for a few weeks of rest and training the only rest which was allowed to the 16th Division in the two years and three months that it was in the field.

(5.) HIS LAST SERMON.

The 48th Brigade was at rest or rather down for a rifle shooting course near St. Omer. The 2nd and 8th Dublins were in and around the little village of St. Martin au Laert about a mile and a half from St. Omer, the 9th Dublins about a mile distant in a country camp, and the R. I. Rifles a little further away. The new Bishop of Arras, Boulogne and St. Omer, Mgr. Julien, was to make his formal entry into Arras on Saturday, 20th July, and to be present next day at the conclusion of the No vena to our Lady of Miracles. Through the instrumentality of Fr. Browne, with the ready compliance of General Hickie, it was arranged that there should be a church parade in honour of the Bishop on Sunday, 21st. About 2,500 men came down. Fr. Browne said Mass and Fr. Doyle preached. The ceremony, which was most impressive and successful, has fortunately been described in a letter of Fr. Browne's, which we are allowed to reproduce: "I arrived at the Cathedral about n o'clock (says Fr. Browne), and was in despair to find that the Pontifical High Mass was not yet finished. Our people are so punctual and the French so regardless of timetables that I was sure there would be confusion and delay when our 2,000 Catholics would begin to arrive. But it was not to be. Quietly and wonderfully quickly the Mass ended, and the people went out to watch the Bishop go back in procession to his house close by. I was relieved to see that neither he nor any of the priests unvested. Then Fr. Doyle and I had to try to clear away the hundred or so people who remained and the other hundred or so people who came wandering in for the last Mass which for the day was to be ours. 'Donnez place, s'il vous plait, aux soldats qui vont arriver,' [6] I went round saying to everyone. They moved from the great aisle and got into the side-chapels, leaving the transepts and aisles free. Many refused to do this when with pious exaggeration I said, 'Presque 3,000 soldats Irlandais vont arriver tout à l'heure.' [7] And lo! they were coming. Through all the various doors they came, the gth Dubs. marching in by the great western door, the 8th Dubs, through the beautiful southern door, through which St. Louis was the first to pass just 700 years ago, the 2nd Dubs, coming into the northern aisle and making their way up to the northern transept. Rank after rank the men poured in until the vast nave was one solid mass of khaki with the red caps of General Hickie and his staff and the Brigadiers in front.

Then up the long nave at a quick clanking march came the Guard of Honour. Every button of its men, every badge, shone and shone again; their belts were scrubbed till not even the strictest inspection could reveal the slightest stain, and their fixed bayonets only wanted the sun to show how they could flash. Up they came, and with magnificent precision took their places on either side of the altar. I was just leaving the sacristy to begin Mass when I saw the Bishop's procession arriving. He had promised to come only after the sermon, but here he was at the beginning of the ceremony, making everything complete. Of course, I saw nothing, being engaged in saying Mass, but those who did said it was a wonderful sight. The beautiful altar, standing at the crossing of the transepts and backed by the long arches of the apse and choir, was for the feast surrounded by a lofty throne bearing the statue of our Lady of Miracles. The sides were banked up high with palms; then the Guard of Honour standing rigidly in two lines on either side; lastly the Bishop in his beautiful purple robes on his throne. From the pulpit Fr. Doyle directed the singing of the hymns, and then, after the Gospel, he preached. I knew he *could* preach, but I had hardly expected that anyone could speak as he spoke then. First of all he referred to the Bishop's coming, and very, very tactfully spoke of the terrible circumstances of the time. Next he went on to speak of our Lady and the Shrine to which we had come. Gradually the story was unfolded; he spoke wonderfully of the coming of the Old Irish Brigade in their wanderings over the Low Countries. It was here that he touched daringly, but ever so cleverly, on Ireland's part in the war. Fighting for Ireland and not fighting for Ireland, or rather fighting for Ireland through another. Then he passed on to Daniel O'Connell's time as a schoolboy at St. Omer and his visit to the Shrine. It certainly was very eloquent. Everyone spoke most highly of it afterwards, the men particularly, *they* were delighted. [8]

"After the sermon Mass went on. At the Sanctus I heard the subdued order, 'Guard of Honour, 'shun!' There was a click as rifles and feet came to position together. Then as the Bishop came from his throne to kneel before the altar, twelve little boys in scarlet soutanes, with scarlet sashes over their lace surplices, appeared with lighted torches and knelt behind his Lordship. At the second bell came the command, 'Guard of Honour, slope rifles'!' And then as I bent over the Host, I heard, 'Present arms!' There was the quick click, click, click, and silence, till, as I genuflected, from the organ-gallery rang out the loud clear notes of the buglers sounding the General's Salute."

At the end of the Mass the Bishop in a neat little speech thanked the men for the great honour they had paid him. He was especially struck, he said, by the fact that most of them had marched a long way (some nearly ten kilometres) to attend, and he asked those of his flock who were present to learn a lesson from the grand spirit and deep faith of the Irish soldiers. The ceremony concluded by a march past, with bands playing, in front of the Episcopal Palace. The Bishop stood on the steps of his house, beaming as he replied to the 'eyes right' of each company as it passed him.

This last sermon of Fr. Doyle will serve as a final proof - if such be needed - that the man, whose inner life has been portrayed in previous chapters, was no awkward recluse or unpractical pietist. He was full of lovable human qualities; especially conspicuous was his unselfish thoughtfulness which always seemed so natural, so intertwined with playful spontaneity, that one came to take it for granted. He had a wonderful influence over others and knew how to win the human heart because he had learnt the Master's secret of drawing all to himself. He could, as we have just seen, preach persuasively when occasion demanded; but his real sermon was his own life. And from this pulpit he spoke alike to Protestants and Catholics. "For fifteen months," writes Dr. C. Buchanan (9th Sept., 1917), "Fr. Doyle and I worked together out here, generally sharing the same dug-outs and billets, so we became fast friends, I acting as medical officer to his first Battalion. Often I envied him his coolness and courage in the face of danger: for this alone his men would have loved him, but he had other sterling qualities, which we all recognised only too well. He was beloved and respected, not only by those of his own Faith, but equally by Protestants, to which denomination I belong. To illustrate this - Poor Captain Eaton, before going into action last September, asked Fr. Doyle to do what was needful for him if anything happened to him, as he should feel happier if he had a friend to bury him. Capt. Eaton was one of many whom Fr. Doyle and I placed in their last resting place with a few simple prayers. For his broadmindedness we loved him. He seldom if ever preached, but he set us a shining example of a Christian life." [9]

A similar testimony is eloquently conveyed in a little incident recorded by Fr. Doyle in a letter which he wrote to his father on 25th July, 1917. He wroteit seated on a comfortable roadside bank under a leafy hedge, listening, during this intermezzo from the dreadful drama of war, to the nightingales singing in the Bois de Rossignol nearby. "While I was writing," he says, "one of my men, belonging to the Irish Rifles, of which I have charge also, passed by. We chatted for a few minutes and then he went on, but came back shortly with a steaming bowl of coffee which he had bought for me. 'I am not one of your flock, Father,' he said, 'but we have all a great liking for you.' And then he added: 'If all the officers treated us as you do, our lives would be different.' I was greatly touched by the poor lad's thoughtfulness, and impressed by what he said: a kind word often goes further than one thinks, and one loses nothing by remembering that even soldiers are human beings and have feelings like anyone else."

There lies the secret of Fr. Doyle's popularity his Christlike *democracy.* With him there was neither Jew nor Gentile, neither officer nor private; all were men, human beings, souls for whom Christ died. Every man was equally precious to him; beneath every mud-begrimed unkempt figure he discerned a human personality. [10] He would risk ten lives, if he had them, to bring help and comfort to a dying soldier no matter who he was. Once he rushed up to a wounded Ulsterman and knelt beside him. "Ah, Father," said the man, "I don't belong to your Church." "No," replied Fr Doyle, "but you belong to my God." To Fr. Doyle all were brothers to be ministered unto. "He that will be first among you shall be your servant, even as the Son of Man is not come to be ministered unto but to minister, and to give His life a redemption for many." (*S. Matthew* 20. 27.)

(6.) THE BATTLE OF YPRES.

(see map)

"We shall have desperate fighting soon," wrote Fr, Doyle in a private letter dated 25th July, "but I have not the least fear, on the contrary a great joy in the thought that I shall be able to make a real offering of my life to God, even if He does not think that poor life worth taking." To avoid causing anxiety he said nothing to his father about the impending battle until the first phase was over. On 12th August he sent home his last letter, a long budget or diary which will enable us to describe, chiefly in his own words, the events which occurred up to that date.

By way of preface we shall first transcribe from the letter a little story which, in spite of its humorous setting, has a serious application to his own hard life. "Help comes to one in strange ways," he writes, "and the remembrance of a quaint old story has lightened for me the weight of a heavy pair of boots over many a mile of muddy road. The story may interest you:

"In the good old days of yore a holy hermit built him a cell in a spot a few miles from the well, so that he might have a little act of penance to offer to Almighty God each day by tramping across the hot sand and back again with his pitcher. All went gaily for a while, and if the holy man did lose many a drop of honest sweat he knew he was piling up sacks of treasure in Heaven, and his heart was light. But oh! that little 'but' which spoils so many things but though the spirit was willing, the sun was very warm, the sand most provokingly hot, the pitcher the devil and all of a weight, and the road seemingly longer each day. 'It is a bit too much of a good joke,' thought the man of God, 'to tramp these miles day in and day out, with my old bones clanking like a traction engine. Why not move the cell to the edge of the water, save time (and much bad language probably) and have cool water in abundance, and a dry hair shirt on my back?'

"Away home he faced for the last time with his brimming water jar, kicking the sand about in sheer delight, for the morrow would see him on the trek, and an end to his weary trudging, when suddenly he heard a voice, an angel's voice he knew it to be. counting slowly 'One, two, three, four.' The hermit stopped in wonder and so did the voice, but at the next steps he took the counting began again, 'Five, six, seven.5 Falling on his knees the old man prayed that he might know the meaning of this wonder. 'I am the angel of God,' came the answer, 'counting up each step which long ago you offered up to my Lord and Master, so that not a single one may lose its reward. Don't be so foolish as to throw away the immense merit you are gaining, by moving your cell to the water's edge, for know that in the eyes of the heavenly court nothing is small which is done or borne for the love of God.'

"That very night down came the hermit's hut, and before morning broke he had built it again five miles *further* from the well. For all I know he is merrily tramping still backwards and forwards across the burning sand, very hot and tired no doubt, but happy in the thought that the recording angel is busy counting each step.

"I do not think I need point the moral. But I hope and pray that my own good angel is strong at arithmetic, and won't get mixed when he starts his long tot!"

To understand this little parable is to understand much of Fr. Doyle's life, his desire to emulate his angel guardian's arithmetic as well as his inveterate habit of adding to, instead of subtracting from, the 'hard things' of life.

We can now begin his record of these last terrible experiences.

30th July.

"For the past week we have been moving steadily up to the Front once more to face the hardships and horrors of another big push, which report says is to be the biggest effort since the War began. The blood-stained Ypres battlefield is to be the centre of the fight, with our left wing running down to the Belgian coast from which it is hoped to drive the enemy and, perhaps, force him by a turning movement to fall back very far.

"The preparations are on a colossal scale, the mass of men and guns enormous. 'Success is certain' our Generals tell us, but I cannot help wondering what are the plans of the Great Leader, and what the result will be when He has issued His orders. This much is certain: the fight will be a desperate one, for our foe is not only brave, but clever and cunning, as we have learned to our cost.

"Mass in the open this morning under a drizzling rain was a trying if edifying experience. Colonel, officers and men knelt on the wet grass with the water trickling off them, while a happy if somewhat damp chaplain moved from rank to rank giving every man Holy Communion. Poor fellows: with all their faults God must love them dearly for their simple faith and love of their religion, and for the confident way in which they turn to Him for help in the hour of trial.

"One of my converts, received into the Church last night, made his First Holy Communion this morning under circumstances he will not easily forget. I see in the paper that 13,000 soldiers and officers have become Catholics since the War began, but I should say this number is much below the mark. Ireland's missionaries, the light-hearted lads who shoulder a rifle and swing along the muddy roads, have taught many a man more religion, by their silent example, than he ever dreamed of before. [11]

"Many a time one's heart grows sick to think how few will ever see home and country again, for their pluck and daring have marked them down for the positions which only the Celtic dash can take: a post of honour, no doubt, but it means slaughter as well. [12]

"We moved off at 10 p.m., a welcome hour in one way, as it means marching in the cool of the night instead of sweating under a blazing sun. Still when one has put in a long day of hard work, and legs and body are pretty well tired out already, the prospect of a stiff march is not too pleasant."

31st July.

"It was 1.30 a.m. when our first halting place was reached, and as we march again at three, little time was wasted getting to sleep. It was the morning of July 31st, the Feast of St. Ignatius, a day dear to every Jesuit, but doubly so to the soldier sons of the soldier saint. Was it to be Mass or sleep? Nature said sleep, but grace won the day, and while the weary soldiers slumbered the Adorable Sacrifice was offered for them, that God would bless them in the coming fight and, if it were His Holy Will, bring them safely through it. Mass and thanksgiving over, a few precious moments of rest on the floor of the hut, and we have fallen into line once more.

"As we do, the dark clouds are lit up with red and golden flashes of light, the earth quivers with the simultaneous crash of thousands of guns and in imagination we can picture the miles of our trenches spring to life as the living stream of men pours over the top the Fourth Battle of Ypres has begun.

"Men's hearts beat faster, and nerves seem to stretch and vibrate like harp strings as we march steadily on ever nearer and nearer towards the raging fight, on past battery after battery of huge guns and howitzers belching forth shells which ten men could scarcely lift, on past the growing streams of motor ambulances, each with its sad burden of broken bodies, the first drops of that torrent of wounded which will pour along the road. I fancy not a few were wondering how long would it be till they were carried past in the same way, or was this' the last march they would ever make till the final Roll Call on the Great Review Day.

"We were to be held in reserve for the opening stages of the battle, so we lay all that day (the 31st) in the open fields ready to march at a moment's notice should things go badly at the Front. Bit by bit news of the fight came trickling in. The Jocks (15th Scottish Division) in front of us, had taken the first and second objective with little opposition, and were pushing on to their final goal. All was going well, and the steady stream of prisoners showed that for once Dame Rumour was not playing false. Our spirits rose rapidly in spite of the falling rain, for word reached us that we were to return to the camp for the night as our services would 'not be required. Then the sun of good news began to set, and ugly rumours to float about.

"Whether it was the impetuous Celtic dash that won the ground, or part of German strategy, the enemy centre gave way while the wings held firm. This trick has been played so often and so successfully one would imagine we should not have been caught napping again, but the temptation for victorious troops to rush into an opening is almost too strong to be resisted, and probably the real state of affairs on the wings was not known. The Scotties reached their objective, only to find they were the centre of a murderous fire from three sides, and having beaten off repeated counter-attacks of the 'demoralized enemy' were obliged to retire some distance. So far the Germans had not done too badly.

"It was nearly eight o'clock, and our dinner was simmering in the pot with a tempting odour, when the fatal telegram came: 'the battalion will move forward in support at once.' I was quite prepared for this little change of plans having experienced such surprises before, and had taken the precaution of laying in a solid lunch early in the day. I did not hear a single growl from anyone, though it meant we had to set out for another march hungry and dinnerless, with the prospect of passing a second night without sleep. When I give my next nuns' retreat I think I shall try the experiment of a few supperless and bedless nights on them, just to see what they would say, and compare notes with the soldiers. The only disadvantage would be that I should be inundated with applications to give similar retreats in other convents, everyone being so delighted with the experiment, especially the good Mother Bursar who would simply coin money!

"On the road once more in strict fighting kit, the clothes we stood in, a rain coat, and a stout heart. A miserable night with a cold wind driving the drizzling rain into our faces and the ground underfoot being rapidly churned into a quagmire of slush and mud. I hope the Recording Angel will not be afraid of the weather and will not get as tired of counting the steps as I did: 'Ten thousand and one, ten thousand and two,' - a bit monotonous even with the memory of the old hermit to help one.

"The road was a sight never to be forgotten. On one side marched our column in close formation, on the other galloped by an endless line of ammunition waggons, extra guns hurrying up to the Front, and motor lorries packed with stores of all kinds, while between the two flowed back the stream of empties and ambulance after ambulance filled with wounded and dying.

"In silence, save for the never ceasing roar of the guns and the rumble of cart wheels, we marched on through the city of the dead, Ypres, not a little anxious, for a shower of shells might come at any minute. Ruin and desolation, desolation and ruin, is the only description I can give of a spot once the pride and glory of Belgium. The hand of war has fallen heavy on the city of Ypres; scarce a stone remains of the glorious Cathedral and equally famous Cloth Hall; the churches, a dozen of them, are piles of rubbish, gone are the convents, the hospitals and public buildings, and though many of the inhabitants are still there, their bodies lie buried in the ruins of their homes, and the smell of rotting corpses poisons the air. I have seen strange sights in the last two years, but this was the worst of all. Out again by the opposite gate of this stricken spot, which people say was not undeserving of God's chastisement, across the moat and along the road pitted all over with half-filled in shell-holes. Broken carts and dead horses, with human bodies too if one looked, lie on all sides, but one is too weary to think of anything except how many more miles must be covered.

"A welcome halt at last with, perhaps, an hour or more delay. The men were already stretched by the side of the road, and I was not slow to follow their example. I often used to wonder how anyone could sleep lying in mud or water, but at that moment the place for sleep, as far as I was concerned, did not matter two straws, a thorn bush, the bed of a stream, anywhere would do to satisfy the longing for even a few moments' slumber after nearly two days and nights of marching without sleep. I picked out a soft spot on the ruins of a home, lay down with a sigh of relief, and then, for all I cared, all the King's guns and the Kaiser's combined might roar till they were hoarse, and all the rain in the heavens might fall, as it was falling then, I was too tired and happy to bother.

"I was chuckling over the disappearance of the officer in front of me into a friendly trench from which he emerged if possible a little more muddy than he was, when I felt my two legs shoot from under me, and I vanished down the sides of a shell-hole which I had not noticed. As I am not making a confession of my whole life, I shall not tell you what I said, but it was something different from the exclamation of the pious old gentleman who used to mutter 'Tut, tut' every time he missed the golf ball.

"The Head Quarters Staff found shelter in an old mineshaft, dark, foul-smelling, and dripping water which promised soon to flood us out. Still it was some protection from the down-pour outside, and I slept like a top for some hours in a dry corner sitting on a coil of wire."

1st August.

"Morning brought a leaden sky, more rain, and no breakfast! Our cook with the rations had got lost during the night, so there was nothing for it but to tighten one's belt and bless the man (backwards) who invented eating. But He Who feeds the birds of the air did not forget us, and by mid-day we were sitting down before a steaming tin of tea, bully beef and biscuits, a banquet fit to set before an emperor after nearly twenty-four hours' fast. Not for a moment during the whole of the day did the merciless rain cease. The men, soaked to the skin and beyond it, were standing up to their knees in a river of mud and water, and like ourselves were unable to get any hot food till the afternoon. Our only consolation was that our trenches were not shelled and we had no casualties. Someone must have had compassion on our plight, for when night fell a new Brigade came in to relieve us, much to our surprise and joy. Back to the camp we had left the previous night, one of the hardest marches I ever put in, but cheered at the thought of a rest. Once again we got through Ypres without a shell, though they fell before and after our passing; good luck was on our side for once."

Here they remained for a couple of days, and it was during this interval that Fr Doyle wrote the above little chronicle. He resumed it on the morning of Sunday, 12th August. "Dearest Father," he began, "when I finished writing the last line I could not help asking myself should I ever continue this little narrative of my adventures and experiences, for we were under marching orders to make our way that night to the Front Line, a series of shell holes in the ground won from the enemy. To hold this we knew would be no easy task, but I little thought of what lay before me, of the thousand and one dangers I was to pass through unscathed, or of the hardship and suffering which were to be crowded into the next few days.

"It is Sunday morning, August 12th. We have just got back to camp after (for me at least) six days and seven continuous nights on the battle-field. There was no chance last night of a moment's rest, and you may imagine there was little sleep the previous nights either, sitting on a box with one's feet in 12 inches of water. For the past forty-eight hours we have lived, eaten and slept in a flooded dug-out, which you left at the peril of your life, so you may fancy what relief it was to change one's sodden muddy clothes.

"Tired as I am, I cannot rest till I try to give you some account of what has happened, for I know you must be on the look-out for news of your boy, and also because my heart is bursting to tell you of God's love and protection, never so manifest as during this week.

"He has shielded me from almost countless dangers with more than the tender care of an earthly mother what I have to say sounds in parts almost like a fairy tale and if He has tried my endurance, once at least almost to breaking point, it was only to fill me with joy at the thought that I 'was deemed worthy to suffer (a little) for Him.'

"I shall give you as simply as I can the principal events of these exciting days as I jotted them down in my note-book."

Before resuming the diary it is necessary to remark that after the death of Fr Knapp (31st July), Fr. Browne was appointed chaplain to the 2nd Irish Guards. Hence from 2nd August till his death Fr. Doyle had the four Battalions to look after, as no other priest had come to the 48th Brigade. A certain priest had indeed been appointed as Fr. Browne's successor by Fr. Rawlinson. But by some error the order was brought to a namesake, who, on arriving at Poperinghe and discovering the mistake, absolutely refused to have anything to do with the battle. This will explain why Fr. Doyle had such hard work and why he would not allow himself any rest or relief. On 15th August, the day before Fr. Doyle's death, Fr. Browne wrote to his brother (Rev. W. F Browne, C.C.):

"Fr. Doyle is a marvel. You may talk of heroes and saints, they are hardly in it! I went back the other day to see the old Dubs, as I heard they were having, we'll say, a taste of the War.

"No one has been yet appointed to my place, and Fr. Doyle has done double work. So unpleasant were the conditions that the men had to be relieved frequently. 'Fr. Doyle had no one to relieve him and so he stuck to the mud and the shells, the gas and the terror. Day after day he stuck it out.

"I met the Adjutant of one of my two Battalions, who previously had only known Fr. Doyle by sight. His first greeting to me was:- 'Little Fr. Doyle' they all call him that, more in affection than anything else 'deserves the V.C. more than any man that ever wore it. We cannot get him away from the line while the men are there, he is with his own and he is with us. The men couldn't stick it half so well if he weren't there. If we give him an orderly, he sends the man back, he wears no tin hat, and he is always so cheery.' Another officer, also a Protestant, said: 'Fr. Doyle never rests. Night and day he is with us. He finds a dying or dead man, does all, comes back smiling, makes a little cross, and goes out to bury him, and then begins all over again.'

"I needn't say, that through all this, the conditions of ground, and air and discomfort, surpass anything that I ever dreamt of in the worst days of the Somme."

We can now give the last fragment of Fr. Doyle's diary.

5th August.

"All day I have been busy hearing the men's confessions, and giving batch after batch Holy Communion. A consolation surely to see them crowding to the Sacraments, but a sad one too, because I know for many of them it is the last Absolution they will ever receive, and the next time they meet our Blessed Lord will be when they see Him face to face in Heaven."

And here - he was writing a week later - Fr. Doyle interrupts his narrative by a spontaneous outburst of grief for the loss of those whom he loved as 'his own children.' "My poor brave boys!" he exclaims. "They are lying now out on the battle-field; some in a little grave dug and blessed by their chaplain, who loves them all as if they were his own children; others stiff and stark with staring eyes, hidden in a shell-hole where they had crept to die; while perhaps in some far-off thatched cabin an anxious mother sits listening for the well-known step and voice which will never gladden her ear again. Do you wonder in spite of the joy that fills my heart that many a time the tears gather in my eyes, as I think of those who are gone?"

"As the men stand lined up on Parade, I go from company to company giving a General Absolution which I know is a big comfort to them, and then I shoulder my pack and make for the train which this time is to carry us part of our journey. 'Top end for Blighty, boys, bottom end Berlin,' I tell them as they clamber in, for they like a cheery word. 'If you're for Jerryland, Father, we're with you too,' shouts one big giant, which is greeted with a roar of approval and Berlin wins the day hands down.

"Though we are in fighting kit, there is no small load to carry: a haversack containing little necessary things, and three days' rations which consist of tinned corn beef, hard biscuits, tea and sugar, with usually some solidified methylated spirit for boiling water when a fire cannot be lighted; two full water-bottles; a couple of gas-helmets the new one weighing nine pounds, but guaranteed to keep out the smell of the Old Boy himself; then a waterproof trench coat; and in addition my Mass kit strapped on my back on the off chance that some days at least I may be able to offer the Holy Sacrifice on the spot where so many men have fallen. My orderly should carry this, but I prefer to leave him behind when we go into action, to which he does not object. On a roasting hot day, tramping along a dusty road or scrambling up and down shell-holes, the extra weight tells. But then I think of my friend the hermit, and the pack grows light and easy!

"As I marched through Ypres at the head of the column, an officer ran across the road and stopped me: 'Are you a Catholic priest?' he asked, 'I should like to go to Confession.' There and then, by the side of the road, while the men marched by, he made his peace with God, and went away, let us hope, as happy as I felt at that moment It was a trivial incident, but it brought home vividly to me what a priest was and the wondrous power given him by God. All the time we were pushing on steadily towards our goal across the battle-field of the previous week. Five days almost continuous rain had made the torn ground worse than any ploughed field, but none seemed to care as so far not a shot had fallen near.

"We were congratulating ourselves on our good luck, when suddenly the storm burst. Away along the front trenches, we saw the S.O.S. signal shoot into the air, two red and two green rockets, telling the artillery behind of an attack and calling for support. There was little need to send any signal as the enemy's guns had opened fire with a crash, and in a moment pandemonium, in fact fifty of them were set loose. I can but describe the din by asking you to start together fifty first class thunder storms, though even then the swish and scream, the deafening crash of the shells, would be wanting.

"On we hurried in the hope of reaching cover which was close at hand, when right before us the enemy started to put down a heavy barrage, literally a curtain of shells, to prevent re-inf or cements coming up. There was no getting through that alive and, to make matters worse, the barrage was creeping nearer and nearer, only fifty yards away, while shell fragments hummed uncomfortably close. Old shell holes there were in abundance, but every one of them was brim full of water, and one would only float on top. Here was a fix! Yet somehow I felt that though the boat seemed in a bad way, the Master was watching even while He seemed to sleep, and help would surely come. In the darkness I stumbled across a huge shell-hole crater, recently made, with no water. Into it we rolled and lay on our faces, while the tempest howled around and angry shells hissed overhead and burst on every side. For a few moments I shivered with fear, for we were now right in the middle of the barrage and the danger was very great, but my courage came back when I remembered how easily He Who had raised the tempest saved His Apostles from it, and I never doubted He would do the same for us. Not a man was touched, though one had his rifle smashed to bits.

"We reached Head Quarters, a strong block house made of concrete and iron rails, a master-piece of German cleverness. From time to time all during the night the enemy gunners kept firing at our shelter, having the range to a nicety. Scores exploded within a few feet of it, shaking us till our bones rattled; a few went smash against the walls and roof, and one burst at the entrance nearly blowing us over, but doing no harm thanks to the scientific construction of the passage. I tried to get a few winks of sleep on a stool, there was no room to lie down with sixteen men in a small hut. And I came to the conclusion that so far we had not done badly and there was every promise of an exciting time."

6th August.

"The following morning, though the Colonel and other officers pressed me very much to remain with them on the ground that I would be more comfortable, I felt I could do better work at the advanced dressing-station, or rather aid-post, and went and joined the doctor. It was a providential step and saved me from being the victim of an extraordinary accident. The following night a shell again rushed into the dug-out severely burning some and almost suffocating all the officers and men, fifteen in number, with poisonous fumes before they made their escape. Had I been there, I should have shared the same fate, so you can imagine what I felt as I saw all my friends carried off to hospital, possibly to suffer ill effects for life, while I by the merest chance was left behind well and strong to carry on God's work. I am afraid you will think me ungrateful, but more than once I almost regretted my escape, so great had been the strain of these past days now happily over.

"For once getting out of bed (save the mark) was an easy, in fact, delightful task, for I was stiff and sore from my night's rest. My first task was to look round and see what were the possibilities for Mass. As all the dug-outs were occupied if not destroyed or flooded, I was delighted to discover a tiny ammunition store which I speedily converted into a chapel, building an altar with the boxes. The fact that it barely held myself did not signify as I had no server and had to be both priest and acolyte, and in a way I was not sorry I could not stand up, as I was able for once to offer the Holy Sacrifice on my knees.

"It is strange that out here a desire I have long cherished should be gratified, viz.: to be able to celebrate alone, taking as much time as I wished without inconveniencing anyone. I read long ago in the Acts of the Martyrs of a captive priest, chained to the floor of the Coliseum, offering up the Mass on the altar of his own bare breast, but apart from that, Mass that morning must have been a strange one in the eyes of God's angels, and I trust not unacceptable to Him. Returning to the dressing-station, I refreshed the inner man in preparation for a hard day's work. You may be curious to know what an aid-post is like. Get out of your mind all ideas of a clean hospital ward, for our first aid dressing-station is any place, as near as possible to the fighting line, which will afford a little shelter - a cellar, a coal hole, sometimes even a shell-hole. Here the wounded who have been roughly bandaged on the field are brought by the stretcher bearers to be dressed by the doctor. Our aid-post was a rough tin shed built beside a concrete dug-out which we christened the Pig Sty. You could just crawl in on hands and knees to the solitary chamber which served as a dressing room, recreation hall, sleeping apartment and anything else you cared to use it for. One could not very well sit up much less stand in our chateau, but you could stretch your legs and get a snooze if the German shells and the wounded men let you. On the floor were some wood-shavings, kept well moistened in damp weather by a steady drip from the ceiling, and which gave covert to a host of curious little creatures, all most friendly and affectionate. There was room for three but as a rule we slept six or seven officers side by side. I had the post of honour next the wall, which had the double advantage of keeping me cool and damp, and of offering a stout resistance if anyone wanted to pinch more space, not an easy task, you may well conclude.

"I spent a good part of the day, when not occupied with the wounded, wandering round the battle-field with a spade to bury stray dead. Though there was not very much infantry fighting owing to the state of the ground, not for a moment during the week did the artillery duel cease, reaching at times a pitch of unimaginable intensity. I have been through some hot stuff at Loos, and the Somme was warm enough for most of us, but neither of them could compare to the fierceness of the German fire here. For example, we once counted fifty shells, big chaps too, whizzing over our little nest in sixty seconds, not counting those that burst close by. In fact you became so accustomed to it all that you ceased to bother about them, unless some battery started 'strafing' your particular position when you began to feel a keen personal interest in every new comer. I have walked about for hours at a time getting through my work, with 'crumps' of all sizes bursting in dozens on every side. More than once my heart has nearly jumped out of my mouth from sudden terror, but not once during all these days have I had what I could call a narrow escape, but always a strange confident feeling of trust and security in the all-powerful protection of our Blessed Lord. You will see before the end that my trust was not misplaced. All the same I am not foolhardy nor do I expose myself to danger unnecessarily, the coward is too strong in me for that; but when duty calls I know I can count on the help of One Who has never failed me yet."

7th August.

"No Mass this morning, thanks, I suppose, to the kindly attention of the evil one. I reached my chapel of the previous morning only to find that a big 9.5 inch shell had landed on the top of it during the day; went away feeling very grateful I had not been inside at the time, but had to abandon all thought of Mass as no shelter could be found from the heavy rain.

"The Battalion went out to-day for three days' rest, but I remained behind. Fr. Browne has gone back to the Irish Guards. He is a tremendous loss, not only to myself personally, but to the whole Brigade where he did magnificent work and made a host of friends. And so I was left alone. Another chaplain was appointed, but for reasons best known to himself he did not take over his battalion and let them go into the fight alone. There was nothing for it but to remain on and do his work, and glad I was I did so, for many a man went down that night, the majority of whom I was able to anoint.

"Word reached me about mid-night that a party of men had been caught by shell fire nearly a mile away. I dashed off in the darkness, this time hugging my helmet as the enemy was firing gas shells. A moment's pause to absolve a couple of dying men, and then I reached the group of smashed and bleeding bodies, most of them still breathing. The first thing I saw almost unnerved me; a young soldier lying on his back, his hands and face a mass of blue phosphorus flame, smoking horribly in the darkness. He was the first victim I had seen of the new gas the Germans are using, a fresh horror in this awful war. The poor lad recognized me, I anointed him on a little spot of unburnt flesh, not a little nervously, as the place was reeking with gas, gave him a drink which he begged for so earnestly, and then hastened to the others.

"Back again to the aid-post for stretchers and help to carry in the wounded, while all the time the shells are coming down like hail. Good God! how can any human thing live in this? As I hurry back I hear that two men have been hit twenty yards away. I am with them in a moment, splashing through mud and water. A quick absolution and the last rites of the Church. A flash from a gun shows me that the poor boy in my arms is my own servant, or rather one who took the place of my orderly while he was away, a wonderfully good and pious lad.

"By the time we reached the first party, all were dead, most of them with charred hands and faces. One man with a pulverized leg was still living. I saw him off to hospital made as comfortable as could be, but I could not help thinking of his torture as the stretcher jolted over the rough ground and up and down the shell holes.

"Little rest that night, for the Germans simply pelted us with gas shells of every description, which, however thanks to our new helmets, did no harm."

8th August.

There is little to record during the next couple of days except the discovery of a new cathedral and the happiness of daily Mass. This time I was not quite so well off, as I i could not kneel upright and my feet were in the water which helped to keep the fires of devotion from growing too warm. Having carefully removed an ancient German leg, I managed to vest by sitting on the ground, a new rubric I had to introduce also at the Communion, as otherwise I could not have emptied the Chalice. I feel that when I get home again I shall be absolutely miserable because everything will be so clean and dry and comfortable. Perhaps some kind friend will pour a bucket or two of water over my bed occasionally to keep me in good spirits.

"When night fell, I made my way up to a part of the Line which could not be approached in daylight, to bury an officer and some men. A couple of grimy, unwashed figures emerged from the bowels of the earth to help me, but first knelt down and asked for Absolution. They then leisurely set to work to fill in the grave. 'Hurry up, boys,' I said, 'I don't want to have to bury you as well,' for the spot was a hot one. They both stopped working much to my disgust, for I was just longing to get away. 'Be gobs, Father,' replied one, 'I haven't the divil a bit of fear in me now after the holy Absolution.' 'Nor I,' chimed in the other, 'I am as happy as a king.' The poor Padre who had been keeping his eye on a row of 'crumps' which were coming unpleasantly near felt anything but happy; however there was nothing for it but to stick it out as the men were in a pious mood; and he escaped at last, grateful that he was not asked to say the rosary."

10th August.

"A sad morning as casualties were heavy and many men came in dreadfully wounded. One man was the bravest I ever met. He was in dreadful agony, for both legs had been blown off at the knee But never a complaint fell from his lips, even while they dressed his wounds, and he tried to make light of his injuries. 'Thank God, Father,' he said, 'I am able to stick it out to the end. Is it not ail for little Belgium?' The Extreme Unction, as I have noticed time and again, eased his bodily pain. 'I am much better now and easier, God bless you,' he said, as I left him to attend a dying man. He opened his eyes as I knelt beside him: 'Ah! Fr. Doyle, Fr. Doyle,' he whispered faintly, and then motioned me to bend lower as if he had some message to give. As I did so, he put his two arms round my neck and kissed me. It was all the poor fellow could do to show his gratitude that he had not been left to die alone and that he would have the consolation of receiving the Last Sacraments before he went to God. Sitting a little way off I saw a hideous bleeding object, a man with his face smashed by a shell, with one if not both eyes torn out. He raised his head as I spoke. 'Is that the priest? Thank God, I am all right now.' I took his blood-covered hands in mine as I searched his face for some whole spot on which to anoint him. I think I know better now why Pilate said 'Behold the Man' when he showed our Lord to the people.

"In the afternoon, while going my rounds, I was forced to take shelter in the dug-out of a young officer belonging to another regiment. For nearly two hours I was a prisoner and found out he was a Catholic from Dublin, and had been married just a month. Was this a chance visit, or did God send me there to prepare him for death, for I had not long left the spot when a shell burst and killed him? I carried his body out the next day and buried him in a shell hole, and once again I blessed that protecting Hand which had shielded me from his fate.

"That night we moved head quarters and aid-post to a more advanced position, a strong concrete emplacement, but a splendid target for the German gunners. For the forty-eight hours we were there they hammered us almost constantly day and night till I thought our last hour had come. There we lived with a foot, sometimes more, of water on the floor, pretty well soaked through, for it was raining hard at times. Sleep was almost impossible fifty shells a minute made some noise and to venture out without necessity was foolishness. We were well provided with tinned food, and a spirit lamp for making hot tea, so that we were not too badly off, and rather enjoyed hearing the German shells hopping off the roof or bursting on the walls of their own strong fort."

11th August.

"Close beside us I had found the remains of a dug-out which had been blown in the previous day and three men killed. I made up my mind to offer up Mass there for the repose of their souls. In any case 'I did not know a better 'ole to go to,' and to this little act of charity I attribute the saving of my life later on in the day. I had barely fitted up my altar when a couple of shells burst overhead, sending the clay tumbling down. For a moment I felt very tempted not to continue as the place was far from safe. But later I was glad I went on for the Holy Souls certainly came to my aid as I did to theirs.

"I had finished breakfast and had ventured a bit down the trench to find a spot to bury some bodies left lying there. I had reached a sheltered corner, when I heard the scream of a shell coming towards me rapidly, and judging by the sound, straight for the spot where I stood. Instinctively I crouched down, and well I did so, for the shell whizzed past my head - I felt my hair blown about by the hot air and burst in front of me with a deafening crash. It seemed to me as if a heavy wooden hammer had hit me on the top of the head, and I reeled like a drunken man, my ears ringing with the explosion. For a moment I stood wondering how many pieces of shrapnel had hit me, or how many legs and arms I had left, and then dashed through the thick smoke to save myself from being buried alive by the shower of falling clay which was rapidly covering me. I hardly know how I reached the dug-out for I was speechless and so badly shaken that it was only by a tremendous effort I was able to prevent myself from collapsing utterly as I had seen so many do from shell shock. Then a strange thing happened: something seemed to whisper in my ear, one of those sudden thoughts which flash through the mind: 'Did not that shell come from the hand of God? He willed it should be so. Is it not a proof that He can protect you no matter what the danger?'

"The thought that it was all God's doing acted like a tonic; my nerves calmed down, and shortly after I was out again to see could I meet another iron friend. As a matter of fact I wanted to see exactly what had happened, for the report of a high explosive shell is so terrific that one is apt to exaggerate distances. An officer recently assured me he was only one foot from a bursting shell, when in reality he was a good 40 yards away. You may perhaps find it hard to believe, as I do myself, what I saw. I had been standing by a trellis work of thin sticks. By stretching out my hand I could touch the screen, and the *shell fell smashing the woodwork*. "My escape" last year at Loos was wonderful, but then I was some yards away, and partly protected by a bend in the trench. Here the shell fell, I might say, at my very feet; there was no bank, no protection except the wall of your good prayers and the protecting arm of God.

"That night we were relieved, or rather it was early morning, 4.30 a.m., when the last company marched out. I went with them so that I might leave no casualties behind. We hurried over the open as fast as we could, floundering in the thick mud, tripping over wires in the darkness, and, I hope, some of the lay members cursing the German gunners for disturbing us by an odd shot. We had nearly reached the road, not knowing it was a marked spot when like a hurricane a shower of shells came smashing down upon us. We were fairly caught and for once I almost lost hope of getting through in safety. For five minutes or more we pushed on in desperation; we could not stop to take shelter, for dawn was breaking and we should have been seen by the enemy. Right and left in front and behind, some far away, many very close, the shells kept falling Crash! One has pitched in the middle of the line, wounding five men, none of them seriously. Surely God is good to us, for it seems impossible a single man will escape unhurt, and then when the end seemed at hand, our batteries opened fire with a roar to support an attack that was beginning The German guns ceased like magic, or turned their attention elsewhere, and we scrambled on to the road and reached home without further loss."

(7.) THE END.

This was the end of Fr. Doyle's diary. There followed just this last message to his Father, so pathetic in the light of his death two days later: "I have told you all my escapes, dearest Father, because I think what I have written will give you the same confidence which I feel, that my old armchair up in Heaven is not ready yet, and I do not want you to be uneasy about me. I am alt the better for these couple of days' rest, and am quite on my fighting legs again. Leave will be possible very shortly, I think, so I shall only say au revoir in view of an early meeting. Heaps of love to every dear one. As ever, dearest Father, your loving son, Willie. 14/8/17." Before this letter had reached home, the great Leave Day had come for Willie Doyle. He was called Home. "Blessed are the dead who die in the Lord. From henceforth now, saith the spirit, that they may rest from their labours, for their works follow them." (*Apoc.* 14. 13.)

The recital, which has just been given, of Fr. Doyle's superhuman exertions and hairbreadth escapes, has made it abundantly clear that only by some continuous miracle could he hope to survive another such advance. It came next day, the 15th, when once more the Irish troops were moved up through and beyond Ypres. Here on the dawn of Thursday, 16th August, the front line from St. Julien to the Roulers railway south of Frezenberg was held by Irishmen waiting for the order to advance. Every insignificant rise in the undulating Flemish farmlands in front of them was crowned by a German post; there were several strong 'pill-boxes' (concrete blockhouses) and in the middle of the line of attack a spur (Hill 35) dominated every approach. It was these redoubts especially Borry Farm Redoubt with its sixty expert gunners and five machineguns which frustrated all attempts of the Irish, infantry. Moreover, no supporting waves came up for no living beings could get through the transverse fire of the German machineguns. And so when the German counterattack was launched in the afternoon, the Rifles, the Dublins, and the Inniskillings had to retire, taking with them what wounded they could. Many groups were surrounded and cut off or had to fight their way back in the night. [13]

Fr. Doyle was speeding ail day hither and thither over the battlefield like an angel of mercy; his words of Absolution were the last words heard on earth by many an Irish lad that day, and the stooping figure of priest and father, seen through blinding blood, filled the glance of many in their agony. Perhaps once more some speechless youth ebbing out his life's blood, kissed his beloved padre, or by a silent handshake bade farewell to the father of his soul. "Ah, Father Doyle, Father Doyle." "Is that the priest? Thank God, I am all right now." "Ah, Father is that you? Thanks be to God for His goodness in sending yon; my heart was sore to die without the priest." ...All the little stories come back to us as we try to reconstruct that last great day of priestly ministry and sacrifice. We shall never know here below, for towards the evening of that heroic day Fr. Doyle died a martyr of charity. The great dream which had haunted him for a lifetime had come true; he shed his blood while working for Christ. "Greater love than this no man hath, that a man lay down his life for his friends." (*S. John* 15. 13.) "The good shepherd giveth his life for his sheep." (*S. John* 10. 11.)

Few authentic details can be gathered concerning that day of carnage and confusion, especially as the troops were retiring from ground which was not finally occupied until about six weeks later after severe fighting. What little is known may be recounted from letters and newspaper reports. [14] Here are a few tributes from war correspondents:

"All through the worst hours an Irish padre went about among the dead and dying giving Absolution to his boys. Once he came back to head quarters, but he would not take a bite of food or stay, though his friends urged him. He went back to the field to minister to those who were glad to see him bending over them in their last agony. Four men were killed by shell fire as he knelt beside them, and he was not touched not touched until his own turn came. A shell burst close by, and the padre fell dead."

(Sir Philip Gibbs in the *Daily Chronicle* and the *Daily Telegraph;* also in his book *From Bapaume to Passchendaele,* 1917, p. 254.)

"The Orangemen will not forget a certain Roman Catholic chaplain who lies in a soldier's grave in that sinister plain beyond Ypres. He went forward and back over the battlefield with bullets whining about him, seeking out the dying and kneeling in the mud beside them to give them Absolution, walking with death with a smile on his face, watched by his men with reverence and a kind of awe until a shell burst near him and he was killed. His familiar figure was seen and welcomed by hundreds of Irishmen who lay in that bloody place. Each time he came back across the field he was begged to remain in comparative safety. Smilingly he shook his head and went again into the storm. He had been with his boys at Ginchy and through other times of stress, and he would not desert them in their agony. [15] They remember him as a saint they speak his name with tears."

(Percival Phillips in the *Daily Express* and also the *Morning Post,* 22nd August, 1917.)

"Many tales of individual gallantry are told; two instances especially which should be recorded; one being that of an officer of the Royal Army Medical Corps attached to the Leinsters, who spent five hours in circumstances of the greatest danger tending the wounded, and behaving in all ways with consummate heroism; and the other that of a Roman Catholic chaplain who went up with the men, sustained and cheered them to the last, till he was killed."

(*The Times,* 22nd August, 1917.)

The following passage is from a letter of General Hickie written to a friend on 18th Nov., 1917.

"Fr. Doyle was one of the best priests I have ever met, and one of the bravest men who have fought or worked out here. He did his duty, and more than his duty, most nobly, and has left a memory and a name behind him that will never be forgotten. On the day of his death, 16th August, he had worked in the front line, and even in front of that line, and appeared to know no fatigue he never knew fear. He was killed by a shell towards the close of the day, and was buried on the Frezenberg Ridge... He was recommended for the Victoria Cross by his Commanding Officer, by his Brigadier, and by myself. Superior Authority, however, has not granted it, and as no other posthumous reward is given, his name will, I believe, be mentioned in the Commander-in-Chief's Despatch... I can say without boasting that this is a Division of brave men; and even among these, Fr. Doyle stood out."

Though Fr Doyle cared nothing for human decoration? it was another Commander-in-Chief under Whom he served it seems right to chronicle this judgement of others and to record the fact that he was recommended for the D.S.O. at Wytschaete and the V.C. at Frezenberg. However the triple disqualification of being an Irishman, a Catholic and a Jesuit proved insuperable. [16]

On 15th December, 1917, General Hickie, having discovered Mr. Doyle's address, paid another tribute: "I could not say too much about your son," he wrote. "He was loved and reverenced by us all; his gallantry, self-sacrifice, and devotion to duty were all so well known and recognized. I think that his was the most wonderful character that I have ever known."

"Strong Point 13 and the little dug-out of the brave padre rise before me as I write," says an Irish officer in the *Catholic News* (15th September, 1917.) "I recall the early Mass when our battalion was in reserve. Often have I knelt at the impromptu altar serving that Mass for the padre in the upper barn, hail, rain, and snow blowing in gusts through the shell-torn roof. He knew no fear. As company officers, how many times have we accompanied him through the front line system to speak a word to the men. Well do we remember when at long last we went back for rest and training, how our beloved padre did the long three days' march at the head of the battalion.

"Which of the men do not recall with a tear and a smile how he went 'over the top' at Wytschaete? He lived with us in our newly-won position, and endured our hardships with unfailing cheerfulness. In billets he was an ever welcome visitor to the companies, and our only trouble was that he could not always live with whatever company he might be visiting.

"Ypres sounded the knell. Recommended for the D.S.O. for Wytschaete, he did wonderful work at Ypres, and was recommended for the V.C. Many a dying soldier on that bloody field has flashed a last look of loving recognition as our brave padre rushed to his aid, braving the fearful barrage and whistling machine-gun bullets, to give his boy a last few words of hope."

"He was one of the finest fellows I ever met," wrote Lt. Col. H. R. Stirke (commanding the 8th Dublins) on 13th September, 1917, "utterly fearless, always with a cheery word on his lips, and ever ready to go out and attend the wounded and dying under the heaviest fire. He was genuinely loved by everyone, and thoroughly deserved the unstinted praise he got from all ranks for his rare pluck and devotion to duty."

In its own way the following generous appreciation by a Belfast Orangeman is rather unique. It was published in the *Glasgow Weekly News* of 1st September, 1917: "Fr. Doyle was a good deal among us. We couldn't possibly agree with his religious opinion, but we simply worshipped him for other things. He didn't know the meaning of fear, and he didn't know what bigotry was. He was as ready to risk his life to take a drop of water to a wounded Ulsterman as to assist men of his own faith and regiment. If he risked his life in looking after Ulster Protestant soldiers once, he did it a hundred times in the last few days... The Ulstermen felt his loss more keenly than anybody, and none were readier to show their marks of respect to the dead hero priest than were our Ulster Presbyterians. Fr. Doyle was a true Christian in every sense of the word, and a credit to any religious faith. He never tried to get things easy. He was always sharing the risks of the men, and had to be kept in restraint by the staff for his own protection. Many a time have I seen him walk beside a stretcher trying to console a wounded man with bullets flying around him and shells bursting every few yards."

"He never tried to get things easy" words conveying a truth deeper than this Ulster soldier could realise! May we not reverently recall S. Paul's sentence: "Having joy set before Him, He endured the cross"? (*Hebr.* 12. 2.)

A similar tribute was paid by Sergeant T. Flynn, Dublin Fusiliers, in a letter written home and published in the *Irish News,* 29th August, 1917:

"We had the misfortune to lose our chaplain, Fr. Doyle, the other day. He was a real saint and would never leave his men, and it was really marvellous to see him burying dead soldiers under terrible shell fire. He did not know what fear was, and everybody in the battalion, Catholic and Protestant alike, idolised him. I went to Confession to him and received Holy Communion from him a day or two before he was killed, and I feel terribly sorry after him.

"He loved the men and spent every hour of his time looking after them, and when we were having a fairly hot time in the trenches he would bring us up boxes of cigarettes and cheer us up. The men would do anything he asked them, and I am sure we will never get another padre like him. Everybody says that he has earned the V.C. many times over, and I can vouch for it myself from what I have seen him do many a time. He was asked not to go into action with the battalion, but he would not stop behind, and I am confident that no braver or holier man ever fell in battle than he."

An even more convincing testimony was borne by a Fusilier who happened to be home in Dublin on leave at the time of Fr. Doyle's death. Meeting a friend who told him the news, he kept repeating incredulously: "He's not dead. He couldn't be killed!" When at last he was shown a paper describing the padre's death, the poor fellow knelt down on the pavement and began to pray. Then to the crowd which gathered round him he recounted how, when he was lying wounded in an exposed position and expecting every moment to be killed by a shell, Fr. Doyle had crept out to him and carried him to a place of safety. [17]

The good sisters of St. Anthony's Institute, Locre, who had always been so kind to Fr. Doyle, were anxious to have his remains, not realising the circumstances of his death. The Superioress wrote to Fr. Browne a touching little note on 21st August:

"What very sad news I have received! Our good brave holy Fr. Doyle has been killed! Compassionate Lord Jesus give him eternal rest! Rev. Fr Browne will accept my condolence, my feelings of sympathy in the great loss of our good Fr. Doyle, your confrere. Notre petit saint, he has now received his recompense for his holy life, his great love for God and neighbour. Oh! he was so much loved by everybody and we shall never forget him. We are all very glad to have had him with us in the convent and to have made his life as comfortable as possible. Were it not possible Rev. Fr. to bring his holy body to the convent? It were a great honour to us to have it."

Fr. Browne himself, who had been with Fr Doyle in Clongowes and Belvedere, who had, above all, been so intimately associated with him in their joint mission to the 48th Brigade, expressed his grief and his esteem in a letter, written on 20th August, from which a passage may be quoted:

"All during these last months he was my greatest help, and to his saintly advice, and still more to his saintly example, I owe everything I felt and did. With him, as with others of us, his bravery was no mere physical show-off. He was afraid and felt fear deeply, how deeply few can realise. And yet the last word said of him to me by the Adjutant of the Royal Irish Rifles in answer to my question, 'I hope you are taking care of Fr. Doyle?', was, 'He is as fond of the shells as ever.' His one idea was to do God's work with the men, to make them saints. How he worked and how he prayed for this! Fine weather and foul he was always thinking of them and what he could do for them. In the cold winter he would not use the stove I bought for our dug-out. He scoffed at the idea as making it 'stuffy' and that when the thermometer was fifteen to twenty degrees below zero, the coldest ever known in living memory here. And how he loathed it all, the life and everything it implied! And yet nobody suspected it. God's Will was his law. And to all who remonstrated, 'Must I not be about the Lord's business?' was his laughing answer in act and deed and not merely in word. May he rest in peace it seems superfluous to pray for him."

There once more we have Fr. Doyle's unmistakable portrait, those characteristic traits familiar now to us who in these pages have read his inner life: the jest-concealed cross, the unsuspected loathing, the fear so pleasantly disguised, the selfless work and incessant prayer, the loving trustfulness in God's Will. And as we come to the close of this life-story, all its incidents are gathered up in memory to blend into a final cadence: the novice's blood-sealed covenant, the consuming love and zeal, the hidden reparation, the vigils and scourgings, the pond at Rathfarnham, the nettles at Delgany, the mud and blood of West Flanders and the Pas de Calais. Nothing befitted such a life like the end of it.

'Did you not know that I must be about my Father's business?' he would have gently asked us had we, prudent ones, expostulated with him that day for being foolhardy. His Father's business: not bloodshed and hate and strife, but mercy and brotherhood and reconciliation. He might, of course, have stayed behind in Ypres or St. Jean; he could, had he wished, have kept out of danger. Perchance there were some who said, 'He saved others, himself he cannot save.' They were right. 'For whoever wishes to save his life will lose it, and whoever for My sake, loses his life, will save it. What does it avail a man if, after gaining the whole world, he has lost or forfeited himself?' 'For My sake' 'I tell you, as often as you did it for one of these My brothers, however lowly, you did it for Me.' Beyond and besides the great legion of faithful ordinary workers, there is need of a handful of heroes, men who save others because they cannot save themselves. Nicely calculated prudence could not survive without some of the foolishness of the Cross. The death of a hero or a martyr is a higher achievement than mere continuance of physical life.

'Lord, if it be Thou,' cried impetuous Peter, 'bid me come to Thee upon the waters.' And Christ said 'Come' to foolish Peter, while the prudent apostles remained in the boat. Surely, as Fr. Doyle on that August morning looked out upon those undulating Flemish fields where shell-barrage and bullet-blasts laid low the advancing waves of brave men, surely he heard the Master's voice bidding him come to Him upon the waters. And he came; with his greathearted faith he never doubted. "I am not foolhardy nor do I expose myself to danger unnecessarily, the coward is too strong in me for that; but when duty calls I know I can count on the help of One who has never failed me yet." How could he resist? Out yonder, in Verlorenhoek and Frezenberg and along the Hannebeek stream, the smashed and bleeding bodies of his poor fellows were lying... "My poor brave boys! They are lying now out on the battle-field: some in a little grave dug and blessed by their chaplain who loves them all as if they were his own children; others stiff and stark with staring eyes, hidden in a shell hole where they had crept to die; while perhaps in some far-off thatched cabin an anxious mother sits listening for the well-known step and voice which will never gladden her ear again." Having loved his 'poor brave boys' in this world and eased their passage to the next, he loved them to the end. He did not desert them in their day of defeat without dishonour. And so, somewhere near the Cross Roads of Frezenberg, where he lies buried with them, the chaplain and men of the 48th Brigade are waiting together for the great Reveille.

[1] "I remember well," writes Fr. F. Browne, "Fr. Doyle's wonderful fervour and eloquence on 'Virgin most faithful' and also on 'Help of Christians.'"

[2] Life at the Front was after all not so different from that of the foreign mission which had been Fr. Doyle's ambition. "You have to be an Indian," wrote the martyr John de Brébeaf in 1635. "Bend

your shoulders to the same burdens as they bear...Remember that Jesus Christ is the true greatness of the missionary. Him alone and His cross are you to seek, in running after these people. With Him you will find roses on thorns, sweets in bitterness, everything in nothingness You will sleep on a skin, and many a night you will never close an eye on account of the vermin that swarm over you...Blasphemy and obscenity are commonly on their lips. You are often without Mass; and when you succeed in saying it, your cabin is full of smoke or snow. The Indians never leave you alone and are continually yelling and shouting at the top of their voice...The food will be insipid, but the gall and vinegar of our Blessed Saviour will make it like honey on your lips... You have only the necessaries of life, and that makes it easy to be united with God...You are obliged to pray, for you are facing death at every moment." - T. J. Campbell, S.J-, *Pioneer Priests of North America: Among the Hurons,* 1910, pp. 104-107.

[3] "Scraping one's kettle" was expressive slang for cleaning one's soul by Confession.

[4] Fr. Doyle did not forget his helper. A little later he was able to write: "You may be interested to hear that the Sergeant of whom I spoke in my long letter 'him of the ruddy language,' has been awarded the D.C.M. (Distinguished Conduct Medal), the private's equivalent of the M.C. I told the Colonel of his coolness and fine work in digging out the rive buried men, and recommended him for a decoration, which I am glad to say was accepted at Head-Quarters. The poor chap is very proud of his medal, which I told him he won by his eloquent language."

[5] As a result of having to wear his boots so continuously, Fr. Doyle was suffering from very severe 'blood blisters' on his feet. This must have made his climbing up and down shell-holes an excruciating torture.

[6] Make room, please, for the soldiers who are coming.

[7] About 3,000 Irish soldiers are just coming.

[8] [The Sermon appealed to the men by its more or less historical reference to the Irish Brigade that had come there three hundred years before. The men of the 8th Dublins declared that Fr. Doyle "ought to get into Jim Larkin's shoes!" It appealed to others for a different reason. General Ramsay (a Protestant) stated afterwards that it was one of the most tactful and impressive sermons he had ever heard, and General Hickie said that he was intensely pleased with the way in which 'dangerous' topics had been handled without offending anyone. It certainly required some diplomatic skill to appeal to Irish regiments in the British Army by evoking memories of the Irish Brigade which fought against England. Nor was it easy, without hurting English susceptibilities, to convey the (act that the Irish soldiers who were listening were fighting for what they believed was Ireland's cause as well as Belgium's. Fr. Doyle succeeded.]

[9] Once when Dr. Buchanan was unwell and there were no blankets to lie upon in the damp dug-out, Fr. Doyle lay flat, face downwards, on the ground, and made the doctor lie upon him.

[10] Hence too he often reverently gathered up in a handkerchief and buried the remains of what had once enshrined a human soul.

[11] As I transcribe these words of Fr. Doyle, there lies before me a letter from another chaplain: "The men are *wonderful* - I ought to write it in capitals so cheerful and so patient amidst their *very* real sufferings. I refer to the Irish element in the battalion, for there is a *most* marked difference in the demeanour and conduct of the various groups. Now I need hardly ask the origin of a particular group or individual; the attitude of mind, body and lips is sufficient for me."

[12] Fr. Doyle met his death in the next 'post of honour' assigned to his Irish flock in spite of what they had suffered during the previous day. On 16th August the 16th Division made an advance along the Frezenberg ridge behind Ypres, where English Divisions had already failed several times.

[13] In the fourth battle of Ypres, from 31st July to 16th August, the 16th Division lost 230 officers and 4,370 other ranks.

[14] The best substantiated account is this. Fr. Doyle had been engaged from early morning in the front line, cheering and consoling his men, and attending to the many wounded. Soon after 3 p.m. he made his way back to the Regimental Aid Post which was in charge of a Corporal Raitt, the doctor having gone back to the rear some hours before. Whilst here word came in that an officer of the Dublins had been badly hit, and was lying out in an exposed position. Fr. Doyle at once decided to go out to him, and left the Aid Post with his runner, Private McInespie, and a Lieutenant Grant. Some twenty minutes' later, at about a quarter to four, McInespie staggered into the Aid Post and fell down in a state of collapse from shell shock. Corporal Raitt went to his assistance and after considerable difficulty managed to revive him. His first words on coming back to consciousness were: "Fr. Doyle has been killed!" Then bit by bit the whole story was told. Fr. Doyle had found the wounded officer lying far out in a shell crater. He crawled out to him, absolved and anointed him, and then, half dragging, half carrying the dying man, managed to get him within the line. Three officers came up at this moment, and McInespie was sent for some water. This he got and was handing it to Fr. Doyle when a shell burst in the midst of the group, killing Fr. Doyle and the three officers instantaneously, and hurling McInespie violently to the ground. Later in the day some of the Dublins when retiring came across the bodies of all four. Recognising Fr. Doyle, they placed him and a Private Meehan, whom they were carrying back dead, behind a portion of the Frezenberg Redoubt and covered the bodies with sods and stones.

[15] Compare what Dom Bede Camm says of Fr. B. Kavanagh, C.S.S R.: "He was warned not to go where he did, for the danger was too great, but he said, 'If my boys can go there, so can I.'" - *Dublin Review*, vol. 165, 1919, p. 62.

[16] A soldier, knowing what Father Knapp and Father Gwynn had done, once asked his chaplain: "Aren't our priests, Father, forbidden to take the V.C.?!" Even before the Frezenberg action Fr. Doyle was reputed by the officers to have earned the V.C. Thus Lieut. Galvin, writing home on 14th August, 1917, says: "If ever a man earned the V.C. in this war, it is Father Doyle. He is simply splendid. He comes up every night under heavy shellfire, burying the dead and binding the wounded and cheering the men. I wish to heavens we had a few doctors like him."

[17] After Fr. Doyle's death some of the men of the 8th Dublins expressed their appreciation in verses whose untutored genuineness will excuse all literary shortcomings. The first stanza runs thus:

He is gone from amongst us, may his soul rest above,
The pride of our regiment whom every man loved,
His life's work is o'er, he has finished his toil,
So may God rest the soul of our brave Father Doyle.

Appendix - Some Further Letters of Father Doyle

SINCE the issue of the first edition of this book some further personal letters of Fr. Doyle have come to light. They are published here because they have a valuable biographical interest. The intimate records which have been utilised in the previous pages present us with one side of his character, a side which was unknown even to those who lived with him. This rather unexpected revelation must not be allowed to obscure his intense humanness and natural gaiety of disposition. These few letters which survive will show us that even as a novice he had a fund of humour and an almost irresistible twitching to play pranks; his letters from the Front have already demonstrated that he retained this jocose buoyancy to the very end. The man who wrestled with aspirations and plunged into austerities could always crack a joke and enjoy a hearty laugh. If the Diary of his Long Retreat conjures up the vision of a sour-visaged, prudish, would-be saint, the error will be quickly dispelled by reading the contemporaneous letters here printed. To which may be added this testimony of one who lived long with Fr. Doyle: "I found the Life very interesting and very wonderful. Certainly I have come across no record of austerities practised on such a scale in recent times. In his early life, until Ordination, I knew Fr. Doyle very well indeed. We were together for two years at Stonyhurst, and I was thrown very much in his company. He was always a very reserved man; it was impossible to know him; he never let you into his secrets, hardly ever, I think, consulted you about anything. It was impossible to be really intimate with him, as one always felt that he would not take you into his confidence. This explains, I think, the fact that people had no conception of the life he led, which would never have been known had not his notes been discovered. In his early life he gave no indication of the sanctity he afterwards attained. He was always, of course, very good; but he was better known for his jokes and freaks than for piety. He was always, however, very determined; and if he set his mind on anything, nothing would deter him from carrying it through. When then, later on, he set himself to become a saint, it is not surprising that he overcame his own inclinations as he had overcome all other obstacles." For those who lived in close association with Fr. Doyle this estimate, being obvious, need not be reproduced. But for such as have come to know Fr. Doyle only through the medium of these printed pages, it is both helpful and consoling to emphasise the human elements of his character. It is also desirable in the interests of biographical accuracy. Hence the publication of these few letters which in themselves may seem unimportant and ordinary.

I. LETTER TO HIS SISTER FROM THE NOVICESHIP.
Tullabeg, Christmas, 1891.

I am sure you must have come to the conclusion that your wild scamp of a brother had gone the way of all flesh, seeing that not so much as a postage stamp has come from him for ages! Perhaps you will forgive my long neglect when I tell you that since I left Ratcliffe I hardly know whether I have been on my head or my heels half the time. It is only now I am beginning to realise all that has happened since then.

It may interest you to know what I have been doing since I left my Alma Mater. I came home about the middle of July with the intention of entering Clonliffe; and what is the strange part of the whole business is that just before I left Ratcliffe, I told Fr. Davis, our Spiritual Director, that I would as soon shoot myself as enter a religious order! But man proposes and God disposes; so it was in my case.

I came down here to see Charlie about the middle of August twelve months, and spent a few days with him. But I uttered a fervent *Deo Gratias* when I found myself on my way home, thanking my stars that I had not the honour of putting N.S.J. after my name. Then came a spell of four months' idleness at home during which someone was praying hard for a brother of his, and not in vain, for on Christmas Day, just a year next Friday, grace had done its work and the ranks of the black-robed Fathers were swelled by a saintly aspirant to perfection! Soon after making up my mind to enter the Society, I applied to the Provincial for admission, which he readily granted and no wonder, seeing the fine fish he had hooked!

I arrived off the coast of Tullabeg on March 31st, and was immediately seized upon by Charlie and initiated into the mysteries and black magic of Jesuit life.

Perhaps you would like to know how things are going with me here. Well, I am as happy as the day is long, though at times, I confess, I find it hard to keep from turning somersaults, jumping out of the window, coming downstairs head first, or from some other mad freak of the kind. I often think that if there was any madness running in the family, it found a resting-place in me! I suppose you heard that I have been through the Long Retreat, as it is called, the retreat of thirty days, which every Jesuit novice has to make. It was a wonderful time. I do not think that I ever spent such a happy time in all my life.

II. LETTER TO HIS MOTHER FROM THE NOVICESHIP.
Tullabeg, Christmas, 1891.

The time down here is most extraordinary! They have only twenty minutes to the hour and about six or seven of these are called a day at least that is the conclusion I have come to. Well, having discovered that Christmas is at hand, I also discovered (and I am very sorry I did) that countless letters have to be written. The very first is going to be to your own loved self to wish you the old wish that is ever new: A merry Christmas and a happy New Year.

At this point an animated discussion took place between the writer and the builders of the Crib as to which of the two animals found among the Crib figures was the donkey and which the ox. "O(a)x them," said I; while some one suggested that if they walked away, the ass would follow, as birds of a feather flock together. Eventually the unfortunate ass was ordered to do duty as one of the kings, and by splitting the ox in two, a capital cow was made out of one half, while the other half served as the donkey. Such are the advantages of holy poverty!

As you see we contrive to get a great deal of fun out of simple things, and since there are thirty young scamps like myself down here, life manages to be fairly lively. Up to this the weather has been very mild, but a touch of frost has come at last and I expect we shall have skating soon.

And now my time (a precious thing here) is up, and I must stop if I am to get this off to you for to-morrow. I am very well and very happy and that is what you want to know most. Is it not, dearest Mother?

III. LETTER TO HIS SISTER FROM CLONGOWES.
8th April, 1902.

I really intended to send you my Easter greetings in good time. But with one thing or another I found myself in Holy Week almost before I well realised that Lent had begun. And with Holy Week came a multiplicity of duties which left little spare time; and then the Easter vacation, vacation at least for the boys, but not vacation for us poor prefects, for we had to be on duty all day. Now however that I am a bit free, I wish you every happiness and blessing, with abundance of grace to make you all that our dear Lord wishes you to be. May you always be faithful to His call.

I was ever so glad to learn that you are keeping well and strong. I have seldom felt better, thank God; and the best proof of this is that I am able to get through my day's work and it is not always a light one as well as any man. I cannot tell you how grateful I am to you for your prayers for myself and my boys, and also for your promise to continue the same. Believe me, you are doing a real apostolic work in praying for these dear little children. I could tell you things that have happened which would show you that your good prayers and those of others have not been thrown away. I have many an anxious hour to go through and many difficulties to face; but the thought that good souls are interceding on my behalf makes the burden light.

Now for a bit of good news. We are to go down south this summer for our vacation... About two months more and you may expect to see me. Till then pray hard for your wild scamp of a brother who is just as anxious as yourself to make some little progress in the spiritual life.

IV. LETTER TO HIS SISTER FROM MILLTOWN PARK.
Morning of his Ordination, 28th July, 1907.

I know that you will be glad to receive a few lines from the hands which a few hours ago have been consecrated with the holy oil. Thank God a thousand thousand times, I can say at long last, I am a priest, even though I be so unworthy of all that holy name implies. How can I tell you all that my heart feels at this moment? It is full to overflowing with joy and peace and gratitude to the good God for all that He has done for me, and with heartfelt thankfulness to the dear old Missionary for all her prayers....I say my first Mass to-morrow at nine at Hampton for the dear Parents, the second (also at nine) at Terenure will be for you... Thank you for all you have done for me; but above all thank the dear Sacred Heart for this crowning grace imparted to your little brother who loves you so dearly.

V. LETTER TO HIS FATHER FROM THE TERTIANSHIP.
Tronchiennes, 14th November, 1907.

Lazarus is risen! But by mistake they left him in the tomb thirty-three instead of the scriptural three days; and poor Lazarus is jolly glad to get out and breathe again! We came out of retreat yesterday, having commenced on the afternoon of Oct. 9th. After each eighth day we were given a walk in the afternoon for some hours, but with the retreat order of time in the morning and evening. These three days, however, did not count as part of the thirty days' retreat. I have nearly forgotten how to talk or write to you so you must excuse all mistakes. As I wrote to Fr. Charles, I have been simply amazed at the good form I have been in all during this trying time, and now at the end I am wonderfully fresh and fit. Many of the fathers were not able to go through all the exercises; but I missed nothing, not even the hour's meditation at midnight. That is perhaps the worst thing in the whole retreat. You go to bed as usual at nine, and then just as you are in the middle of your best dream, a wretch, a perfect villain you think him, puts his head into your room just as all the clocks of Ghent are booming twelve and says: *Benedicamus Domino* (Let us bless the Lord). By all means, you say, but would it not do to bless Him between the blankets? The Psalmist says, Let them rejoice in their beds! You feel it is rather too much of a good joke, but you remark this pleasure only comes once in a lifetime; and so you tumble out on the cold floor (my carpet must have gone off for spring cleaning) and jump into your togs as quickly as you can, for the midnight air of Belgium has a sting in it. However the hour passes quickly, and then one dive for the blanket, though I felt much more inclined for breakfast. Four o'clock came round very quickly - I really think there is something amiss with the clocks here. But in spite of it all and the undoubted strain of the continued retreat, I do not feel one bit the worse and I feel a good deal better in the spiritual life.

The truth is, Tronchiennes agrees with me and the food I find excellent. I was a bit afraid of this, as one fortnight in Enghien long ago knocked me out of tune completely. It is rather hard work getting accustomed to a second dinner at seven, having dined at twelve; but 'I does my endeavours,' and I think I succeed. I now weigh - no, I won't put it on paper, it looks too terrible when worked out in kilos. It is nice to say 'I am nine stone,' but if you say you weigh two or three hundred kilos, people get a bit alarmed.

As you may imagine, life here is not very exciting. My chief amusement is listening to the bells of this house or I should rather say houses, for it is a second Maynooth, huge in size. There is a special bell for the Lay Brothers and one for the Lay Brother Novices; another for the Noviceship, and a fourth for the Juniors. We have our own bell and there is a large bell for the whole house; a bell to call Fathers who are wanted in the parlour, a brazen-tongued beast of a bell at the hall door, and to crown all, the church steeple which was formerly a part of this old abbey of Premonstratensian monks has a chime all of its own. May the Lord be good and send a thunder storm somewhere near that chime that we might have a little peace! ...

I have been very fortunate in getting a room facing south, so that I have the sun all day. My window looks down on the river which flows past the house; and I am able to study Belgian country life and inhale Belgian country smells from a couple of farms just opposite. The grounds around are very large, with pretty walks; one especially along the bank of the river is a great favourite of mine.

VI. LETTER TO HIS FATHER FROM ABERDEEN.
Lent, 1908.

As I know you will be anxious to hear of my doings in Aberdeen during the past three weeks, I will try and jot down as well as I can all that will be of interest to you. I know you will not think me egoistical if I talk chiefly about myself or if I am too self-laudatory; you will understand the motive which inspires the blowing of my own trumpet.

I was rather uneasy on my way to Scotland, as it was the first mission ever given by Jesuits in the "granite city," and naturally we hoped it would be successful. Then, though I was very glad to work under such a great man as Fr. Matthew Power, who is nearly as famous in Scotland as Fr. Tom Burke was in Ireland, I could not help feeling that I should play only a very humble second fiddle beside him. Fr. Power is a tiny creature of only 6 ft. 6 ins. and 18 stone weight, but his heart is as big as himself and from the start he gave me every encouragement and we soon became great friends. I have been most fortunate to begin my missionary career under such a master; for Fr. Power has had a vast and varied experience and I learnt very much from him, and I hope to profit by his advice and hints. My three weeks' training will stand to me in the future and will be simply invaluable in time to come. Fr. Power's personality and name were bound to draw the people, and I was happy also at the thought that so many good prayers were being offered for the success of the mission. As I wrote to you, it has been, thank God, an unqualified success. We were told by the priests that it was impossible to make an impression on the Aberdonian Catholics, they were cold, unemotional, with a great deal of apathy. They are all well-to-do people in the Cathedral parish, many with plenty of money, no poor and no Irish. The congregation numbers 1,300; the Sunday offering (there is no charge at the door) averages 13/-, made up chiefly of coppers: I saw one rich lady in the front bench put a halfpenny in the plate with a look of regret on her face that she had not got a farthing. As a proof that we had touched somewhat even the hard Scottish heart, they contributed £25 on the last Sunday when a collection was made for the expenses of the Mission! The priests declared such a thing was unheard of in Aberdeen; and I fancy will not be again for some time.

We also succeeded in getting the people to take up daily Communion, over a hundred go every morning now, though there were practically none when we came. In many other ways much and lasting good has been done and the people have got a lift which they wanted badly, for though very good at heart, there is far too much coldness and indifference amongst them.

Even the old Bishop a typical Scot caught the general enthusiasm; and after a very complimentary speech on Sunday invited us to come back next year (probably Advent) and give a renewal of the mission. As you may imagine, the work has been hard. We found it necessary to change the original programme and add to the services. This meant I had to speak on a large number of subjects for which I was quite unprepared and often I had to preach after a few moments hasty thought, but certainly the grace of God was in abundance. I was not the least bit nervous and never at a loss for plenty to say. Though the Church is very large and lofty I was easily able to make myself heard in every part of it.

Sunday was a busy day. This was the programme. 1 said Mass at 8 and gave Holy Communion which nearly filled the time till 9. Then Children's Mass which I heard with them explaining the various parts of the Mass as we went along. A rush for breakfast followed by a sermon at n, the Cathedral being as well filled as at night, the Scotch love sermons I am told. At 3 o'clock instructions for children. At 3.30 Fr. Power began a controversial lecture for non-Catholics, which proved a great success and is to be continued by the Bishop. At 6 I gave a double instruction, a quarter of an hour on the Creed, another quarter on one of the Commandments, Fr. Power following with the sermon. Four talks in one day I found quite enough to satisfy my zeal. I got a slight cold and quite lost my voice on the fifth day,' but was able to resume on the day following. Besides the Children's Mass and evening instruction we had every day a sermon in the morning, a double instruction and sermon in the evening, dividing the honours of the pulpit between us. I was rather tired at the end, but feel fit and keen to open at Great Yarmouth, St. Mary's Church, on Sunday.

I have had a *moving* week. Monday I remained in Aberdeen very busy with confessions. Tuesday to Glasgow. Wednesday: came to the Mount. Spent Thursday with L and F, and to-day I start for Yarmouth. I suppose I may take my invitation there as a proof that they were satisfied at Aberdeen, as Fr. Power told me he had written to give me a "good character."

There are many things, funny and consoling, which I could tell you about the mission. One lady, who wanted me to sanction a very shady proceeding, bluntly expressed her great annoyance: "Really, Father, this is very disappointing, I was looking forward to this Mission for I thought that Jesuits were *men of the world!*" What she intended to say was she thought they had no consciences. On the last evening another lady came and said, "Father I want to thank you for the great happiness you have brought to one home in Aberdeen. My daughter has been in great trouble for a long time and for years has longed for someone to whom she could open her heart. You cannot imagine the joy in that house to-night, and I promise you a grateful mother's prayers as long as I live."

I got to like the people very much, they are not effusive, but genuine and sincere, and I felt really sorry at leaving them. At the close of the mission quite a large number came to wish us good-bye and to thank us for the mission. The "holy missioners" have been photographed in various positions, to be sold for the benefit of the church. I shall send you copies when they come. I have never met anywhere such kindness as from the Administrator, Fr. Meany, and his curates. They made us quite at home from the start and did everything to help us and make the mission a success. I have written this in great haste so I know you will excuse it. When I see you next I shall be a "bloatered aristocrat" after my stay in Yarmouth. Just off for the train. A little prayer for my work next week. [1]

VII. LETTER TO HIS FATHER FROM YARMOUTH.
20th April, 1908.

The mission closed last night with a grand flourish of trumpets, renewal of vows, and general scorching of the Old Boy's tail, not to speak of one lady's hat, who, when I told all to raise their lighted candles, calmly thrust hers into the middle of a flower garden which she carried on her head. She was gallantly rescued from the destruction by a young officer behind her; perhaps that encounter may have a happy ending. Naturally speaking I am very glad the week is over. The physical effort of speaking every night for well over an hour is a big one, and then there was the responsibility and strain of having everything on my own shoulders. Supernaturally I am sorry not to have another week, for now that I have "got" the people much good might be done. However I have no reason to complain for God's grace and the effect of all your good prayers have been evident during the course of the mission. Though I cannot say I am quite satisfied - perhaps I expected too much - the Fathers here are more than pleased, thank God, and the people tell me the Yarmouth Catholics surpassed themselves.

I certainly started under great disadvantages... The mission was only announced the preceding Sunday for the first time, no posters put up and no hand bills sent round. In Ireland, people come to a mission without the asking, over here they must be dragged; hence the preparation by the local clergy visiting and inviting the people is looked upon as more important than the sermons of the mission. All this work was neglected, and even at the end of the week I came across families who did not even know a mission was going on. In spite of that, the church was well filled, especially towards the end, for I made the people go round and hunt up their friends, each lady having to bring "six men in tow each night."

I was told the Yarmouth people had very little faith, were very cold and must be taken very quietly; a thing I was quite determined not to do, and with the happiest results, for a bit of Celtic fire and dash was quite refreshing to them after the solemn sermons they are accustomed to in England generally. More than one told me that was just what they wanted, and they proved themselves only too willing to respond. One little thing was gratifying. On the first morning only three people came to Mass; this morning the church was well filled though the mission is over and there were several rails for Holy Communion, which they have promised to keep up.

I have got so hardened about blowing my own trumpet that I make no excuse for doing so again. I was greeted on Friday evening by two ladies from London staying here, with "Father, we have heard Fr. Bernard Vaughan preaching twice on the Passion, but we both prefer your sermon tonight." Do you live near the Blarney Stone? said I to myself. I was told that another Protestant dame, who had been attending the mission, refused to come at the end because she said "I do not want to become a Catholic." When I was offered this work in Aberdeen I was very much inclined to refuse it. I was rather afraid of facing the music alone, and besides tired after my three weeks' work. I cannot say how glad I feel now that I came; it has been a splendid experience for me, and simply invaluable. I was certainly much more at home and preached better than in Scotland.

I had a strange experience which seemed providential. In my wanderings through the slums I came across by accident an old woman over ninety who had not entered a church for long, long years. "I have led a wicked life," she said, "but every day I asked God to send me a good friend before I died and I feel now my prayer is heard." The next day I came back and heard her Confession, and brought her Holy Communion on Easter Sunday. As the tears streamed down her old withered face she said, "Oh, Father this is the first happy day of my life, for I have never known what happiness is since I was a child." I could not help feeling that the opening of heaven to that poor sinner was a reward more than enough for all the long years of preparation now passed.

I remain here till the end of the week, go to London on Saturday, and cross over to Tronchiennes on Monday. I am really very well and not as tired as I expected. Yarmouth is a pretty place, fine sea and magnificent air. All England and his wife here to-day.

VIII. LETTER TO HIS MOTHER FROM THE TERTIANSHIP
Tronchiennes, 21st July.

[2]

Here I am back again safe and sound in Tronchiennes, the Beloved, after my fortnight's tramp round Belgium: legs no doubt a bit tired for they have covered some 200 miles, but feeling as fit as a fiddle and in magnificent form after spending so many days in the fresh air and sun. I intended to send you a long account of my adventures and experiences, comical and otherwise; but as the retreat begins to-morrow and I have much to do, I must content myself with a rapid sketch and fill in details when we meet.

Our pilgrimage was a novel and on the whole enjoyable experience; but at times owing to the great heat and our heavy black soutanes buttoned down to the feet, walking was anything but a pleasure. Everywhere we met with wonderful kindness, though here again, there were, at times, rebuffs which gave one an opportunity of exercising his patience and humility, if he had any.

We started from here on the 7th, our luggage consisting of a night-shirt, a pair of socks, a razor, an extra trouser's button, and the grace of God. I was fortunate in my companion, a Fr. Roberts from the English Province; we got on capitally together though the Belgians we met seemed much amused at two "deadly enemies" tramping along side by side. Our destination was the shrine of our Lady of Chèvremont, near Liège, a famous place for pilgrimages in Belgium, which we reached in five days, walking on an average over 20 miles a day. As we had no money, we had to depend on our sturdy legs to find us a bed for the night, and on our eloquent tongues for food and drink. In the French-speaking parts this was not so difficult, but in the Flemish districts our vocabulary was sorely taxed. However we found this phrase very useful and expressive: "Waar is het grubben"? which sounds very much like, "Where is the grub?" That, with a little pantomime, saved us at least from starvation.

Our first day's walk brought us to Alost, famous for the fact that this is the only one out of 840 colleges which the Society possessed in 1773, the time of the Suppression, which was restored to us on the Restoration of the Society in 1814. It is a magnificent building; every boy, and they number some hundreds, has his own room.

Wednesday. Early afoot for Brussels. On the way made a detour to Jette to visit the famous convent of the Sacred Heart nuns, over 200 in the Community, where the incorrupt body of their foundress B. Madame Barat now rests, having been brought a short time ago from France. Great kindness and warm welcome. Had privilege of seeing the Saint's shrine; prayed for you all. A long trudge over the pavement of Brussels, from end to end of the city, brought us to the new Jesuit College of St. Michael. The old college with 500 boys being too small, our Fathers have just opened a second and expect to have 1,000 boys next summer. A refreshing swim in the bath, food for body and soul, and then to bed to dream of future doings.

Thursday. A delightful walk this morning through the Bois de Soignes, the most beautiful bit of scenery I have seen in Belgium. Four hours' march brought us to the other side of the forest very hungry. A convent loomed in the distance. "The Black Sisters" the people called them, and black they were in name and heart! "No pilgrim fathers wanted to-day, thanks," was all the welcome we got; so we retired as gracefully as we could. When we last saw that convent, it was still standing; but I am sure by this it is a heap of ruins, covering the remains of the wretched Black Sisters. Our next attempt was amusing.

We saw a fine building on a hill and were told the Brothers lived there. Hunger lends wings to the feet and soon that hill was scaled. We rang; a dream of a maid, gorgeous in all the splendour of her noble calling, opened the door: rather a surprise in a holy religious house. "Were the Brothers at home?" A smile. "They are never at home away at Brussels enjoying themselves," was the answer. Rather mystifying; but everything was explained when we learned later in the day that the occupants of that magnificent pile were three old bachelors, brothers!

The poor pilgrim took in several reefs in his belt and plunged down the hill in search of the Cure's house. The good Fathers held up their hands in horror when they heard what we proposed to do. "Ah! les Anglais!" that explains all; the English are all a bit mad, you know. With the inner man well fortified we faced the road for Louvain; afternoon coffee in a friendly convent where the ubiquitous Irish nuns and Irish girls, whom we found in every religious house, came in to see us.

Friday. So far we had managed to lodge in our own houses, but now for a plunge into the great unknown. We left Louvain at 8, and 8 the same evening found us tramping into Landen, ever famous for the death of the great Sarsfield. As I walked across the battlefield his dying words came back to me: "Would that this were for Ireland!" Sarsfield left Ms blood to moisten the plain of Landen, while the big drops of perspiration which rolled from our faces will certainly raise a record crop of wheat. To our dismay the Cure was away from home. At the convent we were told we would find rooms. Alas! they were all in the hands of the painter, so the good Mother said; but it was evident the nuns were afraid of us. We had a hearty meal, however, of bread and cheese washed down with cooling water. I could have eaten a haystack, for we were both famished. On the road again. Here was a fix. Nearly nine, no bed and almost all our Office to say. However the Lord was good and we found an old priest who gave us two rooms for the night.

Saturday. Up with the lark for we had our 26 miles to cover in order to reach Liege in the evening. Old Sol was up before us sharpening his teeth for a blazing day. I shall never forget the heat of that Saturday. Eighty degrees in the shade. You may imagine what we felt on the long dusty road with not a tree to shelter us, quite the exception in Belgium. Only for our umbrellas I am certain we should have got sunstroke, as it was we reached Liege quite worn out and exhausted.

On the road we passed a sign post with the inscription: "Half a mile to Booz." The invitation was too tempting to resist. We turned down the road, found a jovial priest; and an hour afterwards two dusty pilgrims emerged from his house singing "Vive Monsieur le Cure" only the heat, nothing more!

Sunday. On Sunday we rested in Liege. My companion was rather done up, but I felt quite rested and in spite of the intense heat went out to see the city - very beautiful it is, built in two valleys. I have many things to tell you about Liege which I must reserve for another time.

Monday. We started on Monday morning at 4.30 to say Mass at Chevrèmont. Two hours' walk and a climb up the side of a mountain to the shrine I do not recommend before breakfast. We got through our devotions, returned in time for dinner, and then faced the trifle of 12 miles to Tongres. On the way we passed a magnificent chateau, the residence, we learned, of Baron Wautters. The lady of the house received us most graciously, invited us to tea with her sons and daughters, and on leaving told us she was most happy and honoured to entertain two Jesuit Fathers in her house. It is a small world after all, for she told us she was a distant cousin of Fr. Daly, S.J. Tongres is the noviceship of the French Fathers expelled from Toulouse. They have rented a huge house, with a large park for £100 a year. As they make, or save, more than that in fruit, vegetables, and fish which fill the lake, the house is really a gift. Great kindness from all; the good Rector insisted on our resting a day and then sent us off by train to visit Maastricht in Holland. It was a novel sight for me to see the Rector come to meet us with a cigar in his mouth, and after dinner to take recreation while the whole community sat with long clay pipes in their mouths. Maastricht most interesting, especially the church dating from the fourth century.

Our return journey, through another part of the country, was somewhat similar to what I have described. We said Mass in the old home of St. John Berchmans, slept wherever night found us and sampled the good things in many a house. As time was running short when we reached Louvain again, we came back here by train; and thus ended a memorable experience. We had walked nearly 200 miles, seen most of Belgium and its interesting sights, and our expenses at the end were exactly nil. It is the cheapest trip I know, I recommend it strongly!

Retreat ends on July 31st. I then return to Ireland to give retreats in Newry and Wexford. Love to all. My last letter from exile. Till we meet.

IX. LETTER TO HIS SISTER FROM BELVEDERE COLLEGE.
June, 1909.

I have had a very pleasant year at Belvedere, it was my first year in the Ministry as a Priest, hence the work though hard was consoling. I often thank

God for sending me to Dublin, for there one has so many opportunities of doing good and helping poor souls. Indeed if I could have accepted all the work offered to me, I am afraid little would have been done at Belvedere, but all the same I managed to get in a fair share of retreats and sermons, not to speak of some thousands of confessions. In spite of it all I really have never felt better, so you need not be afraid of my "doing too much" as you call it. I am almost certain there will be no change in my present status, and that I shall remain in Belvedere. However, I cannot say yet where I shall be next year.

I hope to send you shortly my little booklet on "Retreats for Workingmen," which is being printed at present. As you know I am very anxious to see these retreats started in Ireland, for I believe they would do a world of good and be the means of checking the dreadful irreligious spirit which is beginning to creep in even here in holy Ireland, especially among our uneducated men. I am hoping this little pamphlet may be the means of starting the good work; at least it will help to do so by giving people an idea of what has been done in other countries. I am very grateful to you all for your good prayers; you must ask St. Joseph to find a suitable house now, for I feel if a start were once made all would be well.

X. LETTER TO HIS SISTER FROM BELVEDERE COLLEGE.
July, 1909.

This little book has a history. For some time back I have been studying the question of retreats for workmen. But last year when I saw in Belgium the wonderful good brought about by them and had an opportunity of seeing some of the houses where these retreats are given, I made up my mind to try to do something here in Ireland... My next discovery was that few people over here knew anything about these retreats and less of the immense good they had already done. I set to work to get all the prayers I could, and really they have been heard, for very many difficulties with regard to this little book have been overcome. I am hopeful it will do much towards bringing about the starting in Ireland of workingmen's retreats. In case you should not know it, I would point out to you that the most important page is the top of the back cover. [3]

XI. LETTER TO HIS SISTER FROM BELVEDERE COLLEGE.
27th October, 1909.

At long last I am a little less busy I wonder am I? for the good Father Rector has just been in to ask me to look after the Plays for Xmas, which is a job as you know. However you have been good to me so I must find time for a little chat. I hope you will not mind a typed letter as I am such a slow writer with the pen and I want to say a lot of things to my little sister.

I would have answered your letter before only for the past two weeks I have been just run off my legs. I had left the preparation of my sermon over till this month and was counting on a nice quiet fortnight when a Father got sick and I was asked to give the retreat for him at the X Convent to the Children of Mary. By the way I am becoming quite a specialist in this line I have had so many retreats lately. In fact I know almost all the good girls in town by this, and a few of the queer ones too! It is consoling work and I find a great deal of good can be done among them, though, at the same time, it is hard work to give a talk in the morning, rush back to class all day and then preach for an hour in the evening again, to say nothing of the confessions. I find it hard to refuse to give these retreats I have had such strange experiences at all of them, in fact sometimes I imagine the guardian angels come in to the box first and whisper questions to be asked. Another consoling thing is that many of the girls induce their young men to come up here to confession, if they have been long away, so I am able to catch two kinds of birds. One poor fellow said to me recently: "Father, I want to straighten things out for I have peace neither with God nor woman. Since your retreat she has given me a time of it and says she will not let me alone till I come up and see you." This was a little hint I gave the girls. You can see, therefore, that I am kept busy. I often have to laugh when I settle down to a quiet bit of work, for my whistle at the speaking tube never seems to stop. The strangest collection of queer characters seem to come here and I as the Minister have to see them. Imposters, beggars and sad cases of all kinds. I am glad of it, for here again much good can be done, and somehow God keeps sending me a few shillings now and again, and this wins their hearts. I think I told you before how grateful I feel to the good God for putting me in Dublin. There are so many openings for a priest which he would not get say down at Clongowes. I know you have told me before that I ought not to do too much and so get knocked up, but how can one keep quiet when one sees so much to be done, sin of all kinds to be prevented and souls to be saved? Is it not better even to shorten one's life a little if needs be in doing good than to become "blue mouldy" through idleness? But the strange thing of all is that in spite of my hard work or is it because of it? I have never felt better or stronger or in finer form than now. Give me credit for a little bit of common sense and ask God to send me more work for Him.

You ask me in your letter about the Retreats for Workmen. I have nothing but good news to give you. The blessing of God is certainly on the work. You remember what led me to write the little book, my bargain with our Lord that if this project was pleasing to Him (for I had been thinking of it for years) He would station me in Dublin when I returned from the Tertianship, for naturally the start would have to be made there. At the time I was positive that there was no chance whatever of this happening, for many reasons; what was my amazement to hear that I was to come to Belvedere. I kept my promise of trying to start these retreats by bringing out the pamphlet. I told you the effort it cost me; I see now that the Old Boy had a hand in that, for the little book has set people talking and thinking, and it is only a question of a short time till the first retreat will be given.

I said the blessing of God was on the work. First of all He has raised up ardent supporters amid the S.J's... Then the workingmen themselves are showing a keen interest in the proposal. A short time ago a deputation from Guinness's Brewery came to see me, saying they had seen the "Retreats for Workingmen," and wanted to know when a start would be made. They promised to send 50 for the first retreat from their department alone, and assured me that hundreds more would follow. They expressed their willingness to pay anything for the privilege of making a retreat such as described and said, if the Archbishop would give permission, they would beg from door to door for money to build a house of retreats: "We would work our fingers down to the bone to get money for this."

Best of all, only yesterday a gentleman of this city promised a donation of £2,000 to start the work. He had just read the book and was so delighted with the idea he resolved to make this generous donation. (At present this is private: you may speak of it in general terms but do not go into details). Is not this encouraging? and is not God good? No doubt this seems a large sum, but it only means an income of about £40 a year, so you must pray on for more benefactors. The rent of a suitable house would come to £150 or £200 a year, for we would require bed rooms for about 25 men, a chapel, dining room, etc., and good grounds. I have my eye on just what is needed. An old Dublin mansion, just outside the city and on the tram line; fully 25 bed rooms or rooms which could be divided, a splendid room for a chapel, a dining hall, sitting room for wet days and eight acres of garden well laid out. It is nearly ideal in size and situation, is actually in the market, only the owner wants too high a rent. You must simply storm Heaven to soften his heart, and get the little ones to do the same. You may perhaps think I exaggerate when I say that if once these retreats are established they will do an amount of good which will surpass all expectations. It would seem to be the divinely appointed new remedy for a new evil, the falling away of the working classes from all religion and the spread of Socialism.

I suppose you have seen my sermon in the *Freeman.* If not let me know and I will send you a copy. I was amazed when I opened it to find that they had given me a verbatim report, for as a rule they devote half a column of small print to such things, and only the "big guns" are well treated. All this must seem like pride on my part, but really it is only another instance of God's great generosity to me. Candidly I have not much ability or talents. Superiors know that, and it was a hard struggle enough to get through my studies, but perhaps for that very reason and because God knows I have no cause for getting proud or attributing any success to myself or my efforts, He seems to take a delight in blessing all I do. I scarcely ever preach a sermon without feeling that it has been a failure, and I come down from the pulpit sometimes in real blues; then I am told everyone liked it immensely, the money comes flowing in, and invitations for charity sermons (I have just refused three) and retreats come pouring in also. I simply cannot thank God for all He is doing for me, and I ask myself over and over again "What does it all mean?" I really feel like a spoiled, petted child and it frightens me sometimes not a little. Well, I suppose the good God knows what He is about, but I do not.

I have spoken very freely to you, for I have no secrets from you, but of course this letter is intended for your eye only - this you must promise me. I know you pray for me constantly, as I do for you every morning at Mass, but you must do more now, for I feel the want of prayer more than ever. I feel too that not much real work will be done for God without holiness, and that if one were only a saint then the mills of the Lord would hum. You will do a grand work for God by trying to sanctify our brother. God help you for you have a hard nut to crack!

[1] The Bishop was Dr. Chisholm who died in 1918. Father M. Power, S.J., to whom reference is made in the above letter, wrote thus to Mr. Hugh Doyle on 3ist August, 1917: "My very dear brother and colleague on the Aberdeen Mission, Father Wm. Doyle, S.J., is gone...Young and inexperienced at the start of our great mission some years ago, he proved conclusively to me, his senior, and to all the local clergy and people, that he was a Jesuit Missioner 'to the manner born,' and this from the very first sermon he preached. Every day he grew in the affection of the Aberdonians until we parted to his great grief and mine...A little panegyric on him has been preached in the Cathedral, Aberdeen."

[2] Besides giving a Mission during 1 Lent, the Tertian Fathers are supposed, in any country in which it is possible, to make a Pilgrimage, begging 1 their way.

[3] On this we read: "What can I do? (1) Pray that God may provide the means to establish retreats for workingmen. (2) Distribute copies of this pamphlet among the men of your district."

Afterword - An Apology for Saints

IN the preceding pages Fr. Doyle has, as far as possible, been allowed to speak in his own words. This was accomplished by quoting not only from letters kindly lent by correspondents, but also from private journals found after his death. There is no new-fangled principle involved in the use of such documents. We have such instances as S. Ignatius Loyola, S. John Berchmans, Ven. Luis de la Puente, Ven. Claude de la Colombière, Fr. Paul Segneri, and many other members of the Society of Jesus; not to speak of seculars such as Eugénie de Guerin, Lady Georgiana Fullerton, Elizabeth Leseur, Giosuè Borsi; in all which cases private journals, sometimes exceedingly intimate, were published after the author's death. [1] Moreover there are other instances in which saints have actually written such records with the deliberate intention of securing at least posthumous publication; [2] and, of course, there are numerous examples of intimate spiritual autobiographies written by the order of a superior or confessor and subsequently made public. [3] The legitimacy, even for a confessor, of revealing the graces and virtues of a deceased penitent is admitted by all theologians. [4] But one occasionally hears a half-uttered protest from those amateur theologians who desire to make Catholicism easy and fashionable by making Cana compete with Calvary. That the saints of long ago were horribly austere and painfully uncompromising must apparently be accepted as an unfortunate fact. What is intolerable is that anyone should violate conventional religious respectability by exhibiting a contemporary specimen of a species supposed to be extinct; it is against all the canons of evolution. [5] Thus there was an outcry when the great preacher of Notre Dame was revealed to the world as one addicted to the medieval habit of scourging himself and insisting on a strict observance of rule. "We have long asked ourselves," writes his friend and biographer, [6] "how we should make known all that we know on this subject. Should we let the truth be rather guessed than plainly told in detail? Should we veil our narrative under a transparent cloud of terms and images in order not to shock timid and fastidious minds? Or ought we not rather simply and frankly to tell the truth at all risks? This last course appeared to us preferable; it seemed worthier of the man whose victories we are relating and of the holy actions with which his life is filled. Why should not we have the courage to tell and the public to hear of those things which he had the courage to do? ...I well know how jealous he was in keeping a veil over these secret practices; and I ask myself if his severe eye from the height of heaven will not blame me for what I have dared to do... And yet how can one speak of this life without saying what was the soul of it? without revealing what was the hidden and powerful spring which gave motion to all its virtues, to its tenderness, its eloquence and its piety?"

Surely, unless the inner life of Catholicism be something of which we must be ashamed, it is not only allowable but desirable to hold up for our help and inspiration the struggles and strivings, the graces and achievements of one who once lived beside us but is now beyond the bourne of temptation and pride, that so we may say as the Church says of others, *Ecce sacerdos magnus qui in diebus suis placuit Deo.* Without indicating the sources and methods of his spirituality, what would there be to chronicle in the life of Fr. Doyle? Unless perchance, as has been actually suggested, we were to reduce him to the level of a war journalist! The reception already accorded to his biography is ample vindication of the decision to reveal the story of his soul. The letter of the wish which Fr. Doyle expressed when on earth has been deliberately overruled in view of the greater good he must now surely desire: the continuation of his apostolate after his death. [7]

But how, it may be asked, can the publication of singularities, however heroic, help ordinary readers? To which it may in the first place be replied that a life without some such distinguishing characteristics, without something of the abnormal or supernormal in it, could hardly be written at all. Even in the case of our Lord the evangelist sums up His hidden life in the words "He was subject to them." And if we wanted to write the life of an obedient religious, we should perforce be equally laconic, unless, of course, we could give instances of abnormal punctiliousness such as S. John Berchmans practised or recount the miraculous flowering of an obediently watered stick. No one expects to read the life of a man who ate and slept and talked just as a few million others do. What we look for in the life of a saint or religious is to find that he did what we do but much better and much more. Such a man always excites prejudices in certain minds; he is inexplicable and the inexplicable is always irritating; he disturbs our complacency and upsets our conclusions. And it is usually moderate religious people who most resent the intrusion of an extremist; the good is the greatest enemy of the better. [8] How familiar sounds the temptation which so long assailed B. Henry Suso: [9] "It may be all right that you should amend your life, but do not set about it so impetuously. Begin with such moderation that you may be able to bring it to completion. You should eat and drink heartily and treat yourself well, and at the same time be on your guard against sins. Be as good as you please within yourself, and yet with such moderation that the world without may not take-'fright at you, as the saying is. Is the heart good, all is good. Surely you may be merry with people and still be a good man. Others too wish to go to heaven, and yet do not lead a life of exercises such as yours." Which sounds eminently sane and modern advice, and was doubtless accepted by most of Suso's contemporaries.

But this, cult of mediocrity is wrong and unnecessary. Mediocrity propagates itself without any special advocacy; it is only heroism or extremism which it requires effort and care to keep alive in the world. Even when appealing to ordinary folk the mistake is often made of not asking enough. There is latent heroism in most men; the ability to inspire men is simply the power of evoking this heroism. [10] The tendency to wet-blanket and discourage all efforts after the heroic and extraordinary is extremely dangerous to spiritual idealism. No doubt, as has already been many times pointed out in this book, [11] every human life, even that of a canonised saint, is a tissue of trivial incidents and commonplace actions But even here, right at the heart of our ordinary lives, there is the perennial struggle of the spiritual man against his impulses, of grace against nature. What may be called ordinary virtue, marital fidelity, for instance, or business honesty or social justice, is not in the least natural; it is already an extraordinary conquest of nature. To attempt, as Protestantism has done, to segregate these virtues from the religious counsels of perfection or 'the impetuous heroism of the saints, is bad psychology as well as bad spirituality. "It is an indisputable fact," writes a distinguished Protestant professor, [12] "that Protestantism, with its objection on principle to the ascetic ideal of life, occupies an entirely isolated position amidst all the great religions, including those of the Ancient World. This should indeed give us pause. And the matter is not by any means settled by drawing attention to the unnatural character of asceticism or by reference to the abuses and exaggerations which naturally accompany such a great and difficult attempt to elevate man above himself. Protestantism should rather ask itself if as a result of this position it does not lend assistance to a species of naturalism which may some day prove disastrous to itself." In principle the very same objection applies to that tendency which sometimes makes even Catholics look askance at the heroism of the saints; it is simply an infiltration of the current naturalism.

We have largely got into the habit of judging the saints from a purely analytic standpoint; we are inclined to seize upon certain details, to examine them in isolation and to express them in terms of our own psychology; we, as it were, remove the facts from their proper molten medium and reduce them to our own temperature. Whereas the true significance of those spiritual heroes whom we call saints lies not in this or that mode of expression, but in their lives as a whole. They are a concrete proof of the spiritual greatness of man in his age-long struggle with what is of the brute, they represent so many conquests of grace-aided humanity over mere nature. And in every generation such testimonies are needed, for there are always those to whisper in our willing ears that our impulses are unconquerable, that certain virtues are unnatural, and that suffering is the primary evil of life. The soul of a saint is a sacred laboratory wherein once more man's spirituality is tested and his destiny demonstrated. How often was the Parish Priest of Ars seen to display the joy of victory over a vanquished enemy after some especially severe test of endurance! Sometimes he was utterly prostrate, unable even to stand, after a long spell of fasting and work. "On these occasions," says his companion and biographer, [13] "he would laugh merrily and seem as much delighted with himself as a schoolboy who has succeeded in some mischievous frolic." Or rather, let us say, like a man of science who has succeeded in some new experiment. There is a good deal of truth in an American psychologist's admission, that "Fr. Vianney's asceticism taken in its totality was simply the result of a permanent flood of high spiritual enthusiasm longing to make proof of itself." [14]

But in the lives of the saints there is something deeper than mere asceticism. Pain has profounder and more mysterious functions than simply to serve as spiritual athletics. [15] The problem of suffering is one whose theoretic solution well-nigh baffles the human intellect; yet in real life and practice it is solved and overcome by the followers of the Crucified. The saint is one who voluntarily plunges into the great stream of suffering and so, in ways ineffable but experienced, joins in a spiritual process whereby humanity is purified, energized and reconciled. Even William James, [16] alluding to men's instinctive appreciation of heroism and self-sacrifice, confesses: "The metaphysical mystery thus recognised by common sense that he who feeds on death that feeds on men possesses life supereminently and excellently and meets best the demands of the universe is the truth of which asceticism has been the faithful champion. The folly of the cross, so inexplicable by the intellect, has yet its indestructible and vital meaning."

It is more important, however, to realise that a good deal of what is called asceticism or mortification is not really such at all. Apart from the personal love of Christ it would be immeasurable folly. "As valiant knights of our imperial Lord, let 'us not lose heart," writes B. Henry Suso. [17] "As noble followers of our venerable Leader, let us be of good cheer and rejoice to suffer. For if there were no other profit and good in suffering, than that we became more like the fair bright mirror Christ the more closety that we copied Him in this, our sufferings would be well laid out. It seems to me in truth that even if God meant to give the same reward hereafter to those who suffer and to those who do not suffer, we ought still to choose suffering for our lot, were it only to be like Him. For love produces likeness arid devotion to the beloved, so far as it can and may." Likeness to Christ is thus the dominant note; the pain-aspect is quite subsidiary. This becomes still more apparent when we examine some of the 'holy follies' of the saints. When they are not regular acts of rigorous methodic asceticism, they will be found to be impetuous and perhaps clumsy efforts to externate intense love. They are mystic and dramatic episodes, and not mere freaks of self-infliction. Thus we are told of Pere Lacordaire [18] that "one Good Friday he made himself a large cross, caused it to be set up in a subterranean chapel, had himself fastened to it with ropes, and remained suspended to it for the space of three hours." A passion-play one might say, a dramatic re-enactment of Calvary, certainly not a fakir-like seeking of pain. It would be more correct to say that it was done to lessen pain, the pain of love. "Once," says Fr. Doyle, "*to ease the pain of love* I tried with a penknife to cut the sweet name of Jesus on my breast." B. Henry Suso did the same, and he has described the incident with such beautiful simplicity and clearness that his words will be quoted in full. While he was one day "suffering exceedingly from the torments of divine love," it occurred to him to "devise some love-token."

"In this fervour of devotion,, he threw back his scapular, and baring his breast, took in his hand a style. Then,, looking at his heart, he said: Ah, mighty God, give me to-day strength and power to accomplish my desire, for Thou must be burnt to-day into my very inmost heart. Thereupon he set to work and thrust the style into the flesh above his heart, drawing it backwards and forwards, up and down, until he had inscribed the Name of Jesus upon his heart. The blood flowed plenteously out of his flesh from the sharp stabs, and ran down over his body into his bosom; but this was so ravishing a sight to him through the ardour of his love, that he cared little for the pain.

"When he had finished, he went thus torn and bleeding from his ceil to the pulpit under the crucifix, and kneeling down said: Ah, Lord! my heart and soul's only love! look now upon my heart's intense desire. Lord, I cannot imprint Thee any deeper in myself; but do Thou, O Lord,. I beseech Thee, complete the work and imprint Thyself deep down into my very inmost heart, and so inscribe Thy Holy Name in me that Thou mayest nevermore depart from my heart.

"Thus he bore upon him for a long time love's wound,, until at length it healed up. But ... he bore the Name upon his heart until his death, and at every beat of his heart the Name moved with it... Thenceforth when any trouble befell him, he used to look at the love-token and his trouble became lighter. It was his wont also at times to say within himself fond words like these: See, Lord, earthly lovers write their beloved's name upon their garments; but I have written Thee upon the fresh blood of my heart." [19]

This account of a deed, so full of heroic love and poetry, will enable us to see that many similar incidents in the lives of the saints are not ascetic and penitential, but mystical and joyous. Their object is not to seek pain but to find an outlet for pent-up love; and like all expressions of love, they are liable to be misinterpreted and even ridiculed by an outsider. "When these impetuosities (of love) are not very violent," says S. Teresa, [20] "they seem to admit of a little mitigation at least the soul seeks some relief because it knows not what to do through certain penances; the painfulness of which, and even the shedding of its blood, are no more felt than if the body were dead. The soul seeks for ways and means to do something that may be felt, for the love of God; but the first pain is so great that no bodily torture I know of can take it away." From the very terms used it is clear that such an outburst has nothing whatever to do with penance in the ordinary sense. A similar remark applies to that intense desire to shed one's blood for Christ which characterised so many saints and is particularly prominent in the life of Fr. Doyle. This "blood-letting is not a form of mortification at all; it is a sacrificial act, a mystic rite of self-immolation to Him whose Blood was shed for many unto the remission of sins. [21]

Yet since we must perforce view the saints from the outside, untouched by their almost incomprehensible love, our natural tendency is to be struck, and even horror-struck, at the purely physical aspect. For every ten who read the account of Fr. Doyle's nettle-bath, scarcely one will see that the only really important sentence is this (p. 165): "That day the love of Jesus Crucified was burning in my heart with the old longing to suffer much for Him and even give Him my life by martyrdom." It is as the expression of love, and not as a mere freak of penance, that we must view such an act. "By ancient right," says B. Henry Suso, "love and suffering go together. There is no wooer but he is a sufferer; no lover but he is a martyr." [22] There can be no question of any literal imitation of such acts by those who are merely striving for self-mastery. To introduce the idea of mechanical manipulation and self-conscious method into such deeds would be sheer sacrilege and presumptuous perversion. When Christ's love reaches a certain intensity in a man, it will then spontaneously seek such outlets; and these must be judged by special criteria. [23]

Even when we have eliminated from the lives of the saints all these outpourings of love and reparation, there remains, of course, especially in their earlier years, a constant striving after self-conquest expressed in a succession of mortifications. Here too, in the lower region of asceticism, [24] the unthinking transference of practices from the lives of others into our own would be reprehensible. Fr. Doyle had a great devotion to S. Benedict Joseph Labre, but it never occurred to him to imitate his heroic dirt. [25] When the Church made S. Rose of Lima the patroness of America, it was clearly not intended to encourage American Catholic women to cut off their hair and to disfigure themselves, to wear spiked crowns and chains and to sleep on broken glass. All such actions are in themselves morally indifferent; in any concrete case they may be right if they are means proportionate to attaining a noble end, or they may be wrong inasmuch as they are self-willed freaks, morbid self-delusions, or zeal without knowledge. "In the spiritual life," says S. Thomas Aquinas, [26] "the love of God is the end in view. Fasting, watching and suchlike bodily exercises are not sought as an end, they are employed as necessary for the end, i.e. to restrain the passions... Hence they must be used with due discretion, that passion may be overcome but nature not extinguished. ... If anyone weakens his natural strength by fasting, watching and suchlike, so that he cannot do his work, ...without any doubt such a one sins." When once these practices are relegated to the level of means or mechanism or contrivance and it often requires an effort so to regard them, for like a miser or any slave to habit, we are prone to forget the end and worship the means it is easy to see that while the end is the same the means must vary infinitely with time and place and person. B. Henry Suso is an outstanding example of extraordinary penances; yet there came a time when they ceased to be a means to the end and were abandoned. "At length after the Servitor had led, from his eighteenth to his fortieth year, a life of exercises according to the outer man, ... he left them off. And God showed him that all this austerity and all these practices were nothing more than a good beginning and a breaking through his uncrushed natural man. And he saw that he must press on still further in quite another way if he wished to reach perfection." "Look inwards, friend," he said to himself, "and you will find yourself still really there, and will perceive that, notwithstanding all your outward practices in which you did of your own choice exercise yourself, you are still undetached from self in what relates to contradictions at the hands of others... When you should let yourself be humiliated, you take to flight; when you should expose yourself to the blow, you hide; when you are praised, you laugh; when you are blamed, you mourn. It may be true that you need a higher school." [27] It is indeed characteristic of true spirituality that interior mortification is always paramount to, and often dispenses with, exterior penances. S. Philip Neri used to touch his forehead and say, "A man's sanctity lies within the compass of three fingers." "Another advice which he gave was to take care not to become so attached to the means as to forget the end; and that it is not well to be so taken up with mortifying the flesh as to omit to mortify the brain, which after all is the principal matter." [28]

While not neglecting the mortification of the will and those safe chastisements which come to us from God's hands, it may very well be that many of the saints indulged in excessive austerities. The Church is not responsible for the aberrations of even the holiest of her children. [29] Yet we must not be too ready to condemn as exaggerated in others what might be too much for *us.* B. Henry Suso, for example, who seems a clear case of exaggeration, had a mind of childlike simplicity and logical directness; he knew exactly why he adopted his terrible austerities and why he gave them up. [30] "He was in his youth of a temperament full of fire and life. And when this began to make itself felt and he perceived what a heavy burden he had in himself, it was very bitter and grievous to him. And he sought, by many devices and great penances, how he might bring his body into subjection to his spirit... He continued this tormenting exercise for about sixteen years. At the end of this time, when his blood was now chilled and the fire of his temperament destroyed, there appeared to him in a vision on Whit Sunday a messenger from heaven, who told him that God required this of him no longer. Whereupon he discontinued it and threw all these things away into a running stream." Not a trace of morbidity or self-will, not the slightest evidence of mental distortion, not even any proof of ill effect on his health, for he lived to be sixty-five. Moreover, like S. Catherine of Siena, S. Rose of Lima and other saints, he was at times privileged to receive a spiritual mystic drink which served in lieu of bodily nourishment. But apart from any such miraculous intervention, there is abundant evidence to show that the austere practice of the saints is often actually more conducive to health than would be for them a normal life of ease. And modern experiments on bodily fatigue have shown the enormous influence and power of mental ideals. S. Teresa [31] enunciated a very helpful truth when she said: "Being myself so sickly, I was always under constraint and good for nothing, till I resolved to make no account of my body nor of my health... My health has been much better since I have ceased to look after my ease and comforts."

Whatever about their practice, the saints' advice to others is clear and unanimous. The case of B. Henry Suso is so striking that his advice to a spiritual daughter, a Dominican nun, is worth reproducing:

"Dear daughter, if your purpose is to order your spiritual life according to my teaching, as was your request to me, cease from all such austerities, for they suit not the weakness of your sex and your well-ordered frame. The dear Jesus did not say, Take My cross upon you. But He said to each, Take up your cross. You should not seek to imitate the austerity of the ancient fathers nor the severe exercises of your spiritual father. You should only take for yourself a portion of them such as you can practise easily with your infirm body, to the end that sin may die in you and yet your bodily life may not be shortened... Our natures are not all alike and what is suitable for one suits not another. Therefore it must not be thought that, if perchance a man has not practised such great austerities, he will be thereby hindered from arriving at perfection. At the same time, those who are soft and delicate should not despise austerities in others or judge them harshly. Let each look to himself and see what God wants of him, and attend to this, leaving all else." [32] To this counsel of a saint we shall add the sound and solid advice of a well-known writer on the spiritual life: [33]

"In aiming at sanctity each individual should consult the peculiar call of grace, and take into consideration the especial duties which God has allotted to him according to his condition in life. The astonishing penance and austerities practised by some saints under the inspiration of divine grace should never be condemned; yet it is essential to attend to the following recommendations:

"(1) To limit our admiration of these holy excesses within certain bounds, lest they produce too strong an impression on the imagination, and neither to propose to imitate them nor to look on them as an indispensable requisite to sanctity.

"(2) Whether we embrace the practice of great corporal mortification or not, to attach ourselves principally to interior virtues, these being the essence of sanctity, and all the rest a mere appendage which can be separated from the spirit without detriment to either.

"(3) As far as the choice depends on ourselves, to prefer a common life, in order the more perfectly to imitate Jesus Christ, to preserve humility, to guard against pride which loves singularity, and to render virtue attractive to our neighbour instead of prejudicing him against it by presenting it to his view encumbered with almost endless exterior practices."

Such eminently moderate and prudent advice fails, however, to meet the more fundamental objection that all these ascetic practices are absurdly out of date. "Even in the Mother Church herself," roundly asserts W. James, "where ascetic discipline has such a fixed traditional prestige as a factor of merit, it has largely come into desuetude if not discredit. A believer who flagellates or macerates himself to-day arouses more wonder and fear than emulation. Many Catholic writers' who admit that the times have changed in this respect do so resignedly." To do James justice it must be said that he is referring not to asceticism in general but only to the ways in which it finds expression. "I believe," he says, "that a more useful consideration of the whole matter, distinguishing between the general good intention of asceticism and the uselessness of some of the particular acts of which it may be guilty, ought to rehabilitate it in our esteem. For in its spiritual meaning asceticism stands for nothing less than for the essence of the twice-born philosophy It symbolises, lamely enough no doubt but sincerely, the belief that there is an element of real wrongness in this world, which is neither to be ignored nor evaded, but which must be squarely met and overcome by an appeal to the soul's heroic resources and neutralized and cleansed away by suffering." [34] But if we eliminate all or most of the practices approved by the experience of centuries, how can asceticism itself survive? Apart from acts, it is merely an abstract idea. If, as James himself advises, we must "be systematically ascetic or heroic in little unnecessary points" and strive after "self-denial in unnecessary things," we shall soon be perilously near to a return to the old-fashioned fasting, abstention, self-restraint and physical pain. "But to our generation," complains Francis Thompson, [35] "uncompromising fasts and severities of conduct are found to be piteously alien; not because, as rash censors say, we are too luxurious, but because we are too nervous, intricate, devitalised. We find our austerities ready-made. The east wind has replaced the discipline, dyspepsia the hair-shirt. It grows a vain thing for us to mortify the appetite would we had the appetite to mortify!" And so on, in a similar slightly flippant vein. Yet within ten years the men for whom this pleading was made were ready for the horrors and hardships of a terrible war. Fr. Doyle despaired of ever equalling "the worldly generosity of these men". It is only when the invitation is from Christ that we begin all at once to make excuse. The ridiculous unmanly plea that "we" are too nervous, intricate, devitalised and dyspeptic to face a fast or a discipline, may be applicable to a decadent industrial civilisation; there are other spots on the globe. But for such by all means let the east wind and dyspepsia suffice; [36] the saints would have no quarrel with such advice, as is apparent from all that has already been quoted. And let the abstinence be gentle. "The Vigil of S. Peter, you mean, Watkins," said Mr. Vincent. [37] "I thought so. Then let us have a plain beefsteak and a saddle of mutton; no Portugal onions, Watkins, or currant jelly; and some simple pudding, Charlotte pudding, Watkins, that will do."

But what is intolerable is that lovers of Christ who can still dare and do what their spiritual forbears did, should be pooh-poohed as disagreeable anachronisms or, still worse, pitied as half insane. It is not by such compromise that men will be won to Christ. The truth alone will set men free. Let us not be ashamed of the gospel; let us openly utter those hard sayings which are to the Jews a stumbling block and to the Gentiles foolishness. Once principles are admitted, the decadent and the dyspeptic shall have every consideration except that of being allowed to set a standard for the virile and the healthy. How curiously nervous are certain apologists lest Protestants should suspect that contemporary Catholics used fast and scourge! The lives of the saints are published of course, but apparently they are to be regarded as ancient history. And how scrupulous we are lest, owing to imprudent example, there be one discipline too much or one meal too little! And all this in a world teeming with luxury, callousness and self-indulgence. Catholics, at least, who confess Jesus and Him Crucified, can strive after the tolerance of the saints when it is a question merely of the means suited to each individual. All that is claimed in this book is the right of a man to follow unflinchingly, if God calls him, in that royal road of the Cross which has been trod by so many lovers and heroic followers of Christ. If any of us are otherwise called or find elsewhere our cross, we can close this book with Christ's words echoing in our ears, *Quid ad te? Tu Me sequere.* What is it to thee? Do thou follow Me.

[1] Cf. foreword to *A Soldiers Confidences with God,* New York, 1918, pp. viii., xiii.: "These meditations...were not written for publication, they were the intimate talks of a soul with God...While he lived they could never be printed. But these records of a soldier's soul were far too precious to be lost...G. Borsi's death alone made these Colloquies the property of the world." With Fr. Doyle's loving outbursts (printed on pp. 102 ff) may be compared this prayer of the young Italian lieutenant: "My Jesus...Thou knowest and seest how madly I love Thee, how I adore Thee, how the very thought of Thee inebriates me, exalts me, and makes me happy, Jesus, my God, my Father, my Light, my Joy, my Love! Thou knowest that nothing in the world pleases me so well as to behold Thee, to think of Thee, to gaze upon and kiss the sacred wounds that on the Cross saved and redeemed me and paid all for me."

[2] S. Augustine's *Confessions* and S. Teresa's *Life* are the most famous examples. S. Gertrude represents our Lord as saying to her: "I desire your writings to be an indisputable evidence of My divine goodness in these latter times in which I purpose to do good to many." - *Life and Revelations of S. Gertrude,* Eng. trans, by a Religious of the Order of Poor Clares, London, 1865, p. 93. B. Henry Suso tells us that he did not burn his Autobiography because "he was stopped by a heavenly message from God forbidding it." *The Life of B. Henry Suso by Himself,* c. i; Eng. trans, by T. Knox,. reissue [1914], p. 6.

[3] For example, Ven. Marie-Térèse, Foundress of the Congregation of the Adoration of Reparation, "The Little Flower," and Sister Gertrude-Marie.

[4] Nemo dubitat post mortem sancti viri extraordinarias gratias illi factas revelare. - Ballerini-Palmieri, *Opus theologicum morale* (de sacramento poenitentiae 953), 1893, v. 518. Cf. Bartoli, *S. Ignatius de Loyola* (New York, 1855) ii. 205: Fr. Eguia "was even overheard to express a hope that he might survive the saint were it but for a few hours, so that, freed from the obedience which he owed him, he might reveal certain secret things which would fill all those who heard them with admiration."

[5] If Fr. Doyle "had lived in Italy in the thirteenth or fourteenth century, his life would certainly have been the subject of enthusiastic study in many quarters today." - *Messenger of the Sacred Heart,* June, 1920, p. 86.

[6] D. Chocarne, O.P., *The Inner Life of the V. Rev. Pere Lacordaire,* Eng. trans. Dublin [1867], pp. 331, 344. It would be comically irrelevant to cite against such procedure what Fr. Gerard Hopkins, S.J., said to Coventry Patmore about the latter's immolated book: "That's tellings." Patmore's *Sponsa Dei* "was not more nor less than an interpretation of the love be-

tween the soul and God by an analogy of the love between a woman and a man." Fr. Hopkins "placed before Patmore the dilemma of having either to burn the book or to show it to his director - and the latter alternative was offensive to the poet's pride." E. Gosse, *Coventry Patmore*, 1905, pp. 169f.

[7] As a matter of fact, some of the most intimate revelations related in the foregoing' pages (*e.g.*, those concerning "holy follies") were contained in letters and papers on the destiny of which Fr. Doyle expressed no wish.

[8] Thus the Curé of Ars was preached against and denounced to his bishop. "Those who did so were not bad priests; they thought they were giving glory to God by combating superstition and defending the faith against dangerous novelties and wild enthusiasm." - Monnin, *Life of the B. Curé d'Ars*, p. 136.

[9] *Life* ch. 2, p. 7 (tr. Knox).

[10] For example, Fr. Doyle's advocacy of the Holy Hour will seem a little outlandish to many good people. Yet see the enthusiastic response he got from his Irish soldiers (pp. 277f). At Isleworth (London) more than ten years ago the devotion of the Holy Hour (on the night before each First Friday) was started in connection with the local Men's Confraternity of the Blessed Sacrament. It has been a continued success owing to the fervour of the men -nearly all of them workers who have to start early on the Friday.

[11] It is worth while emphasising once again that, in spite of his secret heroism, Fr. Doyle was by no means exteriorly singular or abnormal. "There was nothing much to distinguish him from other young Jesuits," writes one who lived with him in Stonyhurst (*Messenger of the Sacred Heart*, June, 1920, p. 86), "except perhaps that he was more lively and fond of what, for want of a better word, we must call harmless mischief."

[12] F. Foerster, - *Marriage and the Sex-Problem*, ch. 9, Eng. trans. (1912), pp. 154f. Also p. 153: "The Protestant manse itself, like the whole family of Christians, is still unconsciously nourished by the spiritual greatness of the institution of celibacy, of the mighty advance against the dominion of the senses which it represents." It is significant that the Church which upholds celibacy is also the only guardian of family life.

[13] Monnin, *Life of the Blessed Curé d'Ars*, Eng. trans. (Burns & Gates, n.d.), pp. 118. Rather like Fr. Doyle; compare pp. 132, 167, above.

[14] W. James, *Varieties of Religious Experience*, 1906, p. 304. The term Asceticism is not comprehensive enough.

[15] "A young man," Père Lacordaire used to say (*Inner Life*, p. 397), "must feel the sting of pain if he would not feel the sting of pleasure."

[16] *Ibid.*, p. 364.

[17] *Life*, c. 33, pp. 118, trans. Knox.

[18] Chocarne, *Inner Life*, Eng. trans. [1867], p. 335.

[19] *Life*, c. 5, pp. 17 f. The Ven. Anne Madeleine Remuzat did the same, the wound on her breast being miraculously healed. - *Life* (By the Sisters of the Visitation of Harrow), Dublin, 1920, pp. 85f.

[20] *Life* 29. 15. Alluding to the wound of love, she says "this pain is so sweet that there is no joy in the world which gives greater delight."

[21] We read in Bacci, *Life of S. Philip Neri*, Eng. tr., 1868, p. 126: "When blood issued from his nose or from his mouth, he prayed the Lord that so much might flow as would correspond in some manner to the Blood shed for love of him...Thus we read of S. Lutgarde that when she longed for martyrdom and God did not see fit to grant her request, He contented her by allowing a large quantity of blood to flow from her mouth." Here there is no question of pain-seeking. Of course it does not follow that the saints always analysed and distinguished the entirely different phenomena which are loosely called penance; that is the busi-

ness of the theologian and the psychologist. In Fr. Doyle's life there are numerous indications of this longing for sacrificial bloodshed and martyrdom. On the occasion of his two miles' walk barefooted to a country chapel, while making the Holy Hour, he made a gash on his breast in order to offer up some of his blood.

[22] *Life,* c. 4, p. 13, tr. Knox. Fr. Doyle's question can easily be answered: "Had not the saints suffered in this way for Him with joy and gladness of heart?" If any Catholic does not 'feel that the fact that such thing's occur in the lives of the saints entirely justifies' the publication of such a passage, he ought to be able to produce some reason. Those who resent the acts of a contemporary like Fr. Doyle are singularly reticent concerning the saints. What do they think of S. Peter of Alcantara who scourged himself with iron chains and nettles and often threw himself into a frozen pond and remained three or four hours in it (Life, London, 1856, ii. 95 f.)? or of B. Paul of the Cross who rolled himself naked in a thorn bush? (Mgr. Strambi, *B. Paul of the Cross,* London, 1853, iii. 343), or of the Jesuit Father Segneri?

[23] "The three best and most assured marks of lawful inspirations are perseverance against inconstancy and levity, peace and gentleness of heart against disquiet and solicitude, humble obedience against obstinacy and extravagance." - S. Francis de Sales, *Treatise on the Lave of God,* viii. 13.

[24] Compare what the great Dominican theologian D. Banes wrote to S. Teresa in 1572: "It is said of S. Francis that men took him for a fool; that he stripped himself and put on clothes fit only for the poorest of men. I respect that because it was the work of the Holy Ghost. S. Francis at this time wore no religious habit, belonged to no Order and had taken no vows; his conduct was prudent in the state he was in." - D. Lewis, *Life of S. John of the Cross,* 1897 pp. 67f. That is, an asceticism which would be right in one state or religious order, would be wrong in another. So S. Teresa said of the mortifications of the nuns m a certain monastery: "I fear for their health and would rather they kept the rule, for that gives them enough to do; and anything extra should be done in moderation." - *Foundations,* 18. 7.

[25] "Cleanliness, which helps both to health and edification, should be observed by all concerning their persons and everything else." - *Regulae Communes S.J.,* 19. "He was a lover of cleanliness and held dirt in the greatest abhorrence, particularly dirty clothes." - Bacci, *Life of S. Philip Neri,* p. 223. Which need not prevent us from seeing the spiritual heroism of him who for seven years wandered as a scantily-clad, ulcerous, verminous beggar: a useful much-needed protest against the modern superstition that soap-and-water is synonymous with the grace of God.

[26] *Quodlibeta* 5, a. 18.

[27] *Life,* chapters 21, 22; pp. 64, 67, tr. Knox. Suso was delighted to be freed from his life of penance, "he used to weep for joy whenever he called to mind his penitential bonds." "Henceforth, dear Lord," he said, "I will lead a quiet life and enjoy myself. I will quench my thirst fully with wine and water, and I will sleep unbound on my straw bed." - c. 22, p. 68. He did not realize that harder combats awaited him: loss of good name, suspicion and ingratitude, interior desolation.

[28] Bacci, *Life of S. Philip Neri,* 1868, pp. 268, 285. Similarly S. John of the Cross (*Dark Night of the Soul,* i. 6) speaks of "discretion, submission and obedience, which is the penance of the reason and therefore a sacrifice more sweet and acceptable to God than all the other acts of bodily penance."

[29] S. Bernard admitted that his excessive penance had ruined his health. - *Life* by William of S. Thierry, iv. 21. See also T. Campbell, S. J., "Asceticism" in *Cath. En-*

cycl., i. 770 and A. Hamon in *Dict. Apologétique* i. (1913) 313. Fr. C. Martindale, S.J., speaks of the "ill-judged and perhaps obstinate and perverse behaviour" of S. Aloysius. - *In God's Army: Christ's Cadets*, 1917, pp. 18f.

[30] *Life*, c. 17, pp. 46, 48 f. W. James (*Varieties of Rel. Exp.*, p. 360) calls him a "tragic mountebank" - a judgement which reveals James's blindness to the finer and more personal elements of Christian perfection, on a par with his contempt for S. Gertrude, S. Teresa, S. Aloysius, and S. Margaret Mary. Even Dean Inge says of Suso: "The story of the terrible penances which he inflicted on himself for part of his life is painful and almost repulsive to read; but they have nothing in common with the ostentatious self-torture of the fakir." Christian Mysticism, 1912, p. 172. To say of Fr. Doyle that 'he was nearer the Salvationist freelance than the *modern* conception of the Jesuit' is a trifle too reminiscent of James's flippant obtusity to be worthy of a Catholic.

[31] *Life*, 13. 9-10. Fr. Doyle, who was naturally delicate, seems actually to have improved in health owing to his hard life. Compare also p. 95: "The result was a most marvellous increase of bodily vigour." Also p. 162f: "I am convinced that my health will not suffer, as past experience has shown me that I am always better when giving Him all." Care of health is particularly incumbent on a Jesuit. "With a healthy body you can do much," says St. Ignatius, "but what can you do with an ailing one?" - *Monumenta Ignatiana*, i. 108. Another saying attributed to him is this: "An ounce of holiness with excellent health is worth more in work for souls than excellent holiness with an ounce of health." - *Epistolae S. Ignatii*, p. 566 (Liber Sententiarum No. 69), Bononiae, 1837.

[32] *Life*, c. 37, pp. I38f. This, as being applicable to lay people, may be also cited from the Cur of Ars (*Life* by A. Monnin, p. 102): "Suppose, for example, a man who has to earn his bread by his daily labour. It comes into that man's head to do great penances, to pass the half of his night in prayer. If he is well instructed, he will say: 'No, I must not do that, because I shall not be able to do my duty tomorrow if I do; I shall be sleepy and the least thing will make me impatient; I shall not do half as much work as if I had a night's rest; I must not do this.'"

[33] Père J. N. Grou, S.J., *The Interior of Jesus and Mary*, i. 29; Eng. trans, by S. Frisbee, S.J., 1891, i. 217.

[34] *Varieties of Religious Experience*, pp. 297f, 362.

[35] *Health and Holiness*, pp. 20f. It is curious to find S. Teresa (*Life*, 27. 17) saying half-sarcastically: "The world cannot bear such perfection now; it is said that men's health is grown feebler and that we are not now in those former times."

[36] As a matter of fact a little of the Church's mortifications might be quite hygienic for such people. Cf. Père J. Tissot, *The Interior Life*, Eng. tr. 1913, pp. 126, 263.

[37] Newman, *Loss and Gain*, ch. 10, p. 80.

www.ingramcontent.com/pod-product-compliance
Lightning Source LLC
LaVergne TN
LVHW011415080426
835512LV00005B/76